Adva

"This book provides an excellent and insightful set of chapters on how to build and manage brands by some of the best-known experts on the topic. A must read for brand builders!"

Amitava Chattopadhyay
INSEAD Chair Professor,
Marketing and Innovation

"*The Definitive Book of Branding* lives up its name with an absolutely all-star set of contributors who offer key branding insights and guidelines from their unique vantage points. You won't find a more valuable compendium on branding out there—this is definitely a book to buy and study!"

Kevin Lane Keller
E.B. Osborn Professor of Marketing,
Tuck School of Business

"*The Definitive Book of Branding* brings together the field's experts to provide a comprehensive, intelligent overview of the most important strategic and tactical elements of brand management. This book deconstructs the branding process to uncover the different ways in which brands drive the company's strategy, bring meaning to employees, instil passion in consumers, and maintain their appeal over time and across countries.

For marketing and brand managers, *The Definitive Book of Branding* offers state-of-the-art frameworks and best-practice examples to hone their ability to build, understand, and develop brands. For managers in other functions, it illustrates how brands contribute to the company's profitability through the creation of value, both internally and externally.

A definitive read!"

Simona Botti
London Business School Term Associate Professor,
Marketing

"Everything is branded whether a nation or a process and everything has a brand dimension to it whether it's retail policy toward return of merchandise or the look and feel of the brand website.

The Definitive Book of Branding covers many extremely important aspects of branding. The authors are all experts on their respective topics and express their opinions with candor. The diversity of thoughts and opinions makes the book do what a collection should—provoke deep thinking on the subject. This book is a valuable resource for professionals and students."

John A. Quelch
Charles Edward Wilson Professor of Business Administration,
Harvard Business School

"There has been rapid growth over the past two decades in the literature exploring the concept of branding. *The Definitive Book of Branding* is a great primer on the many different perspectives, approaches, and specialty areas that make up this vibrant field. It's rare to find this diversity of thought from top branding experts all in one place. This is a book that will be of value to both experienced professionals and scholars, as well as students or anyone who is curious about growing and protecting intangible assets like brands."

Matt Ragas, PhD
Assistant Professor, College of Communication,
DePaul University, USA, and
co-author, *The Power of Cult Branding*

"In *The Definitive Book of Branding*, Kartikeya Kompella has succeeded in an impossible task: editing the 'ultimate' book on branding with great authors, be they professors or practitioners.

I read it, loved it, and recommend it to all students, marketers, or advertisers interested in building, expanding, and developing brands."

Maurice Levy
Chairman Publicis Groupe

"This book is a compilation of contributions from 18 different authors. As such it is inevitably something of a *pot pourri*. There are some famous and familiar names among the cast list of authors; some more venerable, others perhaps less known.

The content is strong and engaging. The compilation structure allows the reader to 'dip in', and one is rewarded for doing so.

So in truth this book is akin to a patchwork quilt: richly patterned, varied, and stimulating: in reading it you will be better informed and enlightened."

Leslie Butterfield
Group Chief Strategy Officer,
Interbrand

"Kompella has marshaled an outstanding body of brand thought, both contemporary and timeless, paying into my own beliefs and prejudices. The thesis is that brands must be at and in the hearts of our organizations. Brands that keep winning are built to make the world a little better every day, built with clarity of purpose and authenticity behind causes which resonate. They create compelling connections and new perspectives which celebrate their unique brand distinctiveness through everything that they do, every day. This is in the face of two enormous challenges: firstly, most shopper decisions are unconscious and implicit, when forced to articulation they are often misleading, misconstrued, or misinterpreted. Secondly, in the age of real-time global social digital connection, the days of controlled brand ownership and confidentiality are over. It is only what we stand for, communicate, and deliver that counts. We had better do it better, faster, and more tenaciously than others. This book is a great starting point to understanding branding success today."

Phil Chapman
Vice President Equity and Communication, Global Chocolate,
Mondelēz International

"Look at the book and its scope and authors are impressive. You will benefit from the amazing scope of content, perspectives, and authors in *The Definitive Book of Branding*. There are original and useful ideas in every chapter."

David Aaker
Author of *Brand Relevance: Making Competitors Irrelevant*

"This is an important collection of thinking on branding. Kartik has assembled some of the best thinkers from around the world and the content speaks for itself. Highly recommended!"

Dan Foreman
President ESOMAR

"Read this book. But first, read the Preface.

Books about brands and the process of branding number in the 1000s. (At this writing 3,345 titles were available on amazon.com.) Kompella didn't just 'pull together' a set of authors of books about brands. The Preface reveals the reasoning behind his careful selection of authors and neatly presents the organizational scheme for the book, making it even easier for readers to decide which chapters to read when.

The beauty of the book is that the authors each condense their point of view into one chapter, presenting the essence of their books but often going well beyond the original, introducing even newer ways of thinking about brands.

If you are new to branding, this book covers the basics, but also reveals many of the nuances that are often overlooked as part of branding. If you're an old hand at branding, you'll appreciate the particular nuances Kompella chose to include."

Marian Chapman Moore
Professor,
Darden Graduate School of Business,
University of Virginia

"For those of you who have managed, over the past five years, to read all of the leading authors, articles, and books on modern day marketing and communications, this book might pass simply as a refresher. For the rest of us mere mortals, this book is a superb collection of the world's best and brightest marketing specialists and one that I highly recommend.

It successfully covers all elements of modern marketing and would be an invaluable read for all those working in the field of communications and branding. By keeping the unique original style and tone of the contributing authors within a concise chapter format, Kartik is able to deliver an engaging, accessible, and enjoyable journey through the best thinking of today's industry leaders and so avoid the turgidity of what is otherwise often found."

Charles Cadell
President, Asia Pacific,
McCann Worldgroup

The Definitive Book of Branding

The Definitive Book of Branding

Edited by
Kartikeya Kompella

SAGE | Response Business Books
www.sagepublications.com
Los Angeles • London • New Delhi • Singapore • Washington DC

First published in 2014 by

SAGE Response
B1/I-1 Mohan Cooperative Industrial Area
Mathura Road, New Delhi 110 044, India

SAGE Publications Inc
2455 Teller Road
Thousand Oaks, California 91320, USA

SAGE Publications Ltd
1 Oliver's Yard, 55 City Road
London EC1Y 1SP, United Kingdom

SAGE Publications Asia-Pacific Pte Ltd
3 Church Street
#10-04 Samsung Hub
Singapore 049483

Published by Vivek Mehra for SAGE Publications India Pvt Ltd, typeset in 11/13 Baskerville by RECTO Graphics, Delhi, and printed at Chaman Enterprises, New Delhi.

Library of Congress Cataloging-in-Publication Data

The definitive book of branding / edited by Kartikeya Kompella.
pages cm
Includes bibliographical references and index.
1. Branding (Marketing) 2. Globalization—Economic aspects. I. Kompella, Kartikeya, editor of compilation.
HF5415.1255.D44 658.8'27—dc23 2014 2014012534

ISBN: 978-81-321-1773-5 (PB)

The SAGE Team: Sachin Sharma, Vandana Gupta, Rajib Chatterjee, and Rajinder Kaur

For my daughter Mithya

Contents

Section 3: Branding beyond Marketing

Section 4: Together We Stand

Section 5: Building Brands on Belief

List of Tables and Figures

TABLES

FIGURES

Foreword

This book is for anyone with an interest in branding and its role in today's culture, both in society as a whole and inside organizations, and its future as a powerful agent for positive change.

Kartik has done an admirable job in assembling a panel of experts who, in their respective chapters, explore this multifaceted discipline.

They each provide some incisive comments on how they see brands, the way they behave, and, more importantly, how they impact the behavior of the consumers they seek to serve.

Successful brands have always made an important contribution to the way we think and the way we live. They always will. Our challenge now is to understand the dynamics of branding in an increasingly complex and connected world.

I am privileged to work for a company which is credited with developing one of the world's first "brands." Up to that moment, products were named after the entrepreneur—Henry Ford; William Hoover; Thomas Lipton.

In 1886, William Lever launched a new bar soap in response to the Victorian Health Act. He called it Sunlight. Its purpose was, and still is, to "make hygiene commonplace."

Today, we still talk of brands with "purpose." In that sense nothing has changed.

And yet the reality is that everything has changed.

In a world of more consumers—a predicted 9 billion by 2050—and less to consume as the pressure on natural resources intensifies, brands have a major part to play in reassuring consumers that they are buying products they can trust from companies they can trust.

At Unilever, we are acutely aware of the social significance of our portfolio of brands and the Unilever brand itself. Our ambition is to double the size of our business while reducing our environmental footprint and increasing our positive social impact.

Our Unilever Sustainable Living Plan, with its stretching targets for improving the health and well-being of more than 1 billion people, sourcing 100 percent of agricultural raw materials sustainably by 2020 and halving the environmental impact of our products, is at the heart of our business model.

My vision for the Unilever brand is that it will become the "trustmark" for Sustainable Living and earn its place in history, as it has always done, as a brand that is not afraid to address some of the more difficult challenges that we face in order to protect the well-being and the livelihoods of ours and future generations.

Against this backdrop, the role of branding in the modern world has never been so important, nor have brands ever been so influential.

Much of the innovation in branding is driven by new technologies. The ubiquity of mobile telephony is transforming consumer behavior. Brands now have the opportunity to engage with consumers and build a completely new and intimate relationship with them through a hand-held device which transcends geographical and cultural norms.

Brands that underestimate the power of this technology will simply become outclassed by others that innovate in this space and craft brands that provide real consumer benefit through new forms of openness, transparency, and engagement.

These trends are not confined to the developed world. I recently visited a village in India, outside Bhopal, to experience the work of the Unilever Foundation in bringing safe drinking water, through our Pureit water-filter brand, to people who live in water-stressed areas.

I visited a home where eight people live on a combined income of a dollar a day. My visit to the living area, a windowless room at the rear of the two-room house with a fire but no chimney, was illuminated by the light from their mobile phone.

In a place where electricity is only sporadic and entertainment and information is limited, the mobile phone, not the TV, lights the way and provides the means of connection to the wider world.

This connectivity to all things has a profound impact on how brands engage with people and how people engage with brands: a new balance of data and creativity or, if you like, logic and magic. We are only just beginning to understand the implications of this for the way we market our brands and, more broadly, the way we manage our businesses.

The call for greater transparency, integrity, and responsibility on a scale never before imagined will present challenges. But these challenges are opportunities. Brands have the power to provide some of the answers, to shed some light on the challenges we face.

In this book, you have an opportunity to explore how brands can shape popular culture generally, and also the culture within a particular company or organization. Cultures develop over time; they are subject to constant change but, just like successful brands, they remain loyal to the values that have shaped them.

I hope this book serves as a provocation for us to think about the part brands can play in illuminating our lives, providing light in areas where there is darkness, and, to paraphrase William Lever, helping to make Sustainable Living commonplace.

Keith Weed
Chief Marketing and Communications Officer,
Unilever plc

Preface

If you are reading these words, it's likely that a large part of what I set out to do has been achieved. My ambition, simply put, was to create a unique book of branding that gives great value to millions of readers.

In March 2012, this book was but a distant dream, and its existence today is testimony to the generosity of spirit of a set of individuals from across the world whom I'd heard of, whose books I'd read but never imagined that I'd ever collaborate with.

From the beginning of my career I've been fascinated by branding. I've been involved with brands as a marketer, advertising professional, CRM consultant, and brand consultant for over 22 years. During this time, I've seen the concept of branding gain importance and achieve near ubiquity. New interpretations of branding, new approaches to branding, and the discovery of new nuances to branding have made this topic more interesting, complex, and deep.

The growing body of knowledge of this subject has meant that there are now more facets of branding that brand custodians need to know than ever before. While the proliferation of branding literature has ensured that there are many great books on branding available, the number of must-read books on branding in existence is far more than is practical for anyone to seriously consider reading. However, in today's rapidly changing environment, it is important to have a contemporary perspective of branding.

I hit upon the idea of developing a book of branding that covers many important themes with each topic being written by an expert who has already written at least one book on that topic. The authors having written books on these topics were in a great position to pack a lot of knowledge into each chapter. They also were able to share their latest discovery of nuances, understanding, examples, and cases based on their ongoing work in their respective specializations within branding. The reader, therefore, gets to read a wide variety of rich, substantial, and well-researched contemporary topics at the same time that it would normally take to read a single book of branding.

The selection of themes was based on the audience that I had in mind for this book. While marketers are an obvious audience for this book, branding is today more than just a marketing tool but has several facets that impact an organization be they in the areas of human resources, leadership, or finance. Anyone who wants to move to the top position in a company needs to understand both the "organizational" and the "marketing" aspects of branding.

I would like students to read this book, as I believe that this book will give them a fairly holistic exposure to branding and inspire them to create and run inspirational brands in the future.

The selection of topics and authors directly impacts the quality and success of an edited volume, and I believe that it's important for me to briefly explain my selection.

A firm foundation is required to build anything of stature, so Section 1 looks at important concepts in branding. The term "positioning" has become so much a part of marketing vocabulary that it is easy to forget how profound this concept is and the integral role it plays in branding. As markets get more and more saturated, the relevance of this concept can only become more pronounced. No one understands this subject better than Al Ries, and his selection was automatic.

Brands exist because they have a special meaning for consumers. Much of brand building is an effort to imbue meaning into a brand, but there isn't much literature that explains what brand meaning is, how it develops, and how it should be managed. As marketers increasingly try to make their brands more "meaningful," an understanding of this concept would be more than necessary and Mark Batey has done some very fine work in this area—not least his seminal book *Brand Meaning*.

As branding as a subject has grown, a lot of niche topics have now gained a lot of importance. These topics play an important role in understanding branding, building brands, and managing brands. They are niche because they either don't apply to all brands or these topics despite some very good literature have not yet become mainstream. Section 2 is a collection of topics that I believe are currently not as well known or understood as they deserve to be. I'm sure that the world will be studying, understanding, and applying them vigorously in the years to come. Most of the authors in this section are "pioneers" in their respective areas.

Language defines brands as it does people. Stories have engaged people for centuries, but unfortunately most brands still aren't using this powerful tool. As brands seek to express themselves more and better, I believe they will need to harness the power of words and stories. John Simmons is an expert in the area of verbal identity and has a rare understanding of this topic.

Brand communities like the HOGs existed well before the advent of the Internet and were the envy of many. With the Internet enabling quick, easy, and relatively inexpensive creation of communities, this is an area that will grow tremendously. I wanted an author who understood communities to write this chapter and Douglas Atkin with his understanding of both offline brand cults and online communities was perfectly suited to this task.

Challenger brand strategy is an exciting and challenging area. As more and more brands understand the principles of building and running challenger brands, I expect this topic will gain even more widespread interest and importance. It was only fitting that Adam Morgan, the guru of Challenger Brand understanding, should be invited to contribute this chapter.

The phenomenon of brand authenticity may not apply to all brands, but it explains the success of some brands that have overcome far more moneyed professional competitors. Professor Michael B. Beverland's concept of brand authenticity is unique and lends itself to a better more nuanced understanding of branding.

There is increasing research evidence to show that our feelings play a larger role than rationality-led marketers would like to believe. As this body of research increases, marketers are likely to *have* to appreciate how consumers "think" about brands with their feelings. Daryl Travis recognized the importance of "emotional branding" well before this area started attracting any attention.

Brands need to innovate to keep ahead; however, the nature and importance of innovation varies from brand to brand. While there is a lot of literature on innovation, these days there is very little literature on the role of innovation for brands and the various aspects of branding of innovations. Fortunately this important area has been studied by Professor Jean-Noël Kapferer who has written an excellent book on this topic.

I've always believed that brands should have a sense of social responsibility and that their social responsibility initiatives should be aligned to their brand in a manner that helps society as well as the brand. It's a very powerful topic and something that I believe I understand well hence the choice of subject and author.

Section 3 looks at the aspects of branding that impact brands but have their roots outside the marketing department. These need to be understood by professionals who want to lead a company and harness the power of branding across the organization.

I've always believed that employees should be aligned with the brand, and while researching the subject, I came across the book *Living the Brand* by Nicholas Ind. I realized that his concept of employees developing a brand that employees willingly engage with was truly special.

Brands depend on employees to deliver great brand experiences. Across the world there is an ever increasing battle for talent, and HR departments are employing branding techniques to acquire and retain talent. Richard Mosley is a pioneer in this field and the co-author of one of the pioneering books in this field.

Changes in the global economic scenario and consumers have forced brands to change their approach. Understanding the factors that will help a global brand succeed in these conditions is of importance to CEOs and marketers. Sicco van Gelder, the author of a book on global brand strategy, has an exceptionally fine understanding of this extremely specialized area.

The most important asset for many companies is their brand. However, brands lie in an intangible form and are not easy to value. Brands have financial value and are bought and sold; however, the specialized knowledge on how brand valuation is done is not widely known. Brand valuation has emerged to be an important topic for marketers, CEOs, and CFOs. Jan Lindemann is an expert with immense understanding of this area as can be seen from his two books on the subject.

Success in today's world lies in collaboration, and I was keen to add a short segment in this book on how brands need to collaborate resulting in Section 4.

Collaboration through co-branding is seen almost everywhere and may soon become ubiquitous. Tom Blackett, former group deputy chairman of Interbrand, was probably the first person to recognize the importance of this subject through his book on the subject written many years ago.

As I was trying to get a better understanding of brand collaboration, I came across the concept of co-creation in the context of branding and found it to be compelling. Clare Fuller, co-author of *Brand Together*, and Arunima Kapoor are pioneers in this space and have an excellent understanding of the subject.

Belief has emerged to be a very powerful but not well-understood means of building brands. There are different aspects of belief that impact a brand. Section 5 looks at explaining the different nuances of belief in building brands.

Many successful brands can be viewed from the lens of belief systems. Patrick Hanlon deconstructed brands into seven distinct elements that create a belief system in his book *Primal Branding*. I was very impressed with Patrick's approach which I thought was both interesting and practical.

What one believes in identifies and differentiates people, and it's the same with brands. Building brands using the brand's belief is a very interesting and powerful theme which no one knows better than Dr Helen Edwards and Derek Day, the authors of the highly recommended book *Creating Passion Brands*.

Every marketer wants his/her brand to inspire more than loyalty, but most brands struggle to even inspire loyalty. I thought that in today's fast-moving, rapidly changing world characterized by fickleness, Kevin Roberts' concept of "Lovemarks" explained how brands can go beyond loyalty to love was of utmost importance.

This book celebrates diversity of approach and expression in branding and will hopefully expose the reader to a lot of varied but valuable lessons on branding. All the authors have been encouraged to follow their beliefs and natural style of expression and you will encounter different viewpoints and expression. I believe that this diversity of topic and expression will provoke greater thinking on the subject. Diversity of viewpoints is a good ground for fostering debate; it's also great ground for making unusual connections between topics to help see the subject differently.

I'd like to put on record my appreciation to all those involved with this book. My thanks first and foremost to all the authors but for whose contributions this book would not have been possible. I'd like to also thank the people who took the time to read and endorse this book and for their suggestions. Special thanks to Keith Weed for writing the foreword of this book.

I would like to thank Chandra, Associate Vice President Commissioning, SAGE, and Sachin, Commissioning Editor, SAGE, for their help in guiding me through this book. There are many more people to be thanked for their help—Subbu for his recommendations, Satish Chandra for his guidance on writing books and all-round advice on life, and Bhavneet and Ashish for their constant support.

I'd like to thank Sundar, Karuna, and Manisha of Crest Law Partners for patiently explaining to me the different nuances of my book contract. I would recommend them to anyone who wants top notch legal advice.

Thanks to my family. My parents' role in building in me love for books, especially my mother's constant support to my attempts at writing played an invaluable role in making me want to create this book. My brothers, Kireeti and Vach for always inspiring me to be better than I am.

Nothing would have been possible without my wife Vinitha but for whose constant support and encouragement this book would never have happened. A special word of thanks to my daughter Mithya who tolerated with good humor my moody silences and numerous hours at the computer.

I hope you enjoy reading this book and find it useful.

Do send me your comments at kartik@purposefulbrands.in.

Section 1
Building Blocks

Chapter 1
The Essence of Positioning

Al Ries

In 1972, *Advertising Age*, our leading marketing magazine, published a series of articles by Jack Trout and me entitled "The Positioning Era Cometh."

Nine years later, McGraw-Hill published our book *Positioning: The Battle for Your Mind*. In the years that followed, "positioning" became one of the most talked-about concepts in the marketing community. (In 2001, McGraw-Hill released a 20th-anniversary edition of the book.)

To date, more than a million copies of *Positioning* have been sold, plus another 400,000 copies in China alone.

Forty years is a long time for any idea to remain relevant, especially in the fast-changing world of marketing. By now, positioning is probably obsolete.

Or is it?

Many companies still write "positioning" statements for their brands. Many marketing programs call for establishing "positions" in consumers' minds.

As recently as 2009, readers of *Advertising Age* selected *Positioning: The Battle for Your Mind* as the best book they've ever read on marketing.

(That same year, the Harvard Business School Press published a book entitled *The 100 Best Business Books of All Time*. *Positioning* was one of them.)

Other authors are still writing books on the subject. In the last few years, *Positioning the Brand*, *Competitive Positioning*, and *Positioning for Professionals* were published.

Positioning seems to be still important in spite of the many revolutionary changes that have taken place in marketing in the last four decades. The Internet, social media, mobile marketing, and the rise of PR. Then there're Google, Facebook, Twitter, Groupon, LinkedIn, and dozens of other digital ways to influence consumers.

As important and as revolutionary as these developments are, they are still tactics. And to be successful, a brand needs more than the latest tactic. A brand also needs a strategy, and that's why "positioning" continues to attract attention.

WHAT IS POSITIONING?

Here is a quote from the original articles written more than 40 years ago:

> Today's marketplace is no longer responsive to the kind of advertising that worked in the past. There are just too many products, too many companies, too much marketing "noise." To succeed in our overcommunicated society, a company must create a "position" in the prospect's mind. A position that takes into consideration not only its own strength and weaknesses, but those of its competitors as well.

You could write the same thing today and it would still be true. "Today's marketplace is no longer responsive to the kind of advertising that worked in the past." Why should this be true if marketing people have accepted positioning as a vital part of their marketing programs?

What many marketing people have apparently forgotten is that a position needs to take into consideration the "strengths and weaknesses of your competitors." Companies today tend to ignore the competition as if it does not exist. (That only works if you're a leader like Coca-Cola and McDonald's.)

In a marketing battle, you win or lose not just because of the strength or weakness of your own brand. Consumers always consider your product or service in relation to other brands. You need a position that is clearly different than your major competitors.

Positioning is the process of looking inside consumers' minds and trying to find an "open" hole. You don't start with your brand;

you start with the minds of your prospects. Then if you can't find an open hole, you try to change your brand in order to facilitate the positioning process.

WHAT IS A POSITION?

A "position," on the other hand, is the verbalization of the empty hole your brand will be trying to fill. Consumers think in words. To launch a successful brand, you must try to preempt a word or concept and then associate that word with your brand.

Simple, but not easy.

When you can preempt a word, you can own that word for decades to come. A simple position can be the basis for building a world-class brand that can live almost forever.

Volvo owns "safety." BMW owns "driving." Mercedes-Benz owns "prestige." Three words built three powerful global brands.

There are hundreds of automobile brands on the global market. Yet only a handful own positions in the mind. Why is that? Because most brands don't want to limit their sales to a single conceptual idea. They want to appeal to a broader audience.

Take Chevrolet, the largest selling American automobile brand on the global market. What's a Chevrolet? It's a large, small, cheap, and expensive car or truck. In other words, it's everything . . . and nothing. No wonder General Motors, the owners of Chevrolet, went bankrupt in 2009 and had to be rescued by the U.S. government.

Currently, what is Chevrolet using as its advertising slogan? "Chevrolet runs deep," a conceptual idea alluding to the fact that Chevrolet was one of the first automobile brands on the U.S. market.

But consumers take these things literally. What consumer would think, I want a car that runs deep? Furthermore, where in the mind does a consumer file an idea like "runs deep." Let's see, you might suppose a consumer would think. There are cars that run shallow, and there are cars that run deep.

Does this make any sense to you? Of course, not! And it doesn't make any sense to the average automobile prospect.

On the other hand, there's BMW. First imported into the American market from Germany in 1962, BMW went sideways for years. Like many automobile brands, BMW tried to appeal to a wide range of consumers.

> Typical headline: "Our new BMW is a unique combination of luxury, performance and handling. And it's amazingly easy on fuel."

In 1974, for example, BMW sold just 15,007 automobiles in the American market, which made the brand the 11th largest selling European vehicle.

The following year, BMW launched an advertising campaign that would make the brand world famous: "The ultimate driving machine."

Ultimately, BMW became the largest selling luxury vehicle in the American market and then the global market. In 2012, BMW sold 1,222,800 vehicles, Mercedes sold 1,167,700 vehicles, and Audi sold 1,092,400 vehicles on the global market, the three leading luxury-vehicle brands.

That's the power of owning a single word in the mind. "Driving."

THE HALO EFFECT

But don't automobile buyers want a lot more in a vehicle than just "driving"? They sure do. Watch a prospect walk into a dealership and look over a vehicle he or she might want to buy.

They walk around the vehicle to see how it looks. From the front. From the side. From the rear.

Then they look at the sticker to see how much the vehicle costs. And what the estimated gas consumption is.

Then they sit down in the front seat to see how the interior looks and if the seating is comfortable.

Then they put the kids in the back seat to see if there's enough leg room.

And often they ask if they can take a test drive. They want to know how the vehicle handles on the road.

In other words, besides "driving," almost every buyer wants a vehicle that *looks good,* is relatively *inexpensive,* gets good *gas mileage,* has *nice interiors,* and has plenty of *room* for the family.

So what happens when an automobile manufacturer runs an advertisement that says his or her vehicle looks good, is inexpensive, gets good gas mileage, has nice interiors plus plenty of room for the family, and also handles well on the road?

Nothing. Prospects ignore such messages. There is no place in the mind for a vehicle that has everything. An automobile manufacturer is lucky if he or she can attach a single attribute to the vehicle, like BMW did with "driving."

But here's the twist. If you can own one attribute in the mind, the prospect is likely to associate other favorable attributes to your brand. If you ask BMW owners if their vehicles are "well-built," they might say, "Sure, any vehicle that drives well is likely to be well-built and durable."

In psychology, this is known as the "halo effect." It's the psychological principle underlying the entire theory of positioning.

Own one word in the mind and consumers are likely to give you many other words.

THE LEADERSHIP POSITION

What word do leaders own? What word does McDonald's own? What word does IBM own? What word does Starbucks own? What word does Nike own?

Leaders own the "category." word. In other words, when a consumer thinks "fast food," the first brand to come to mind is McDonald's, the leader in the category.

But here's the more important point. Not only do consumers associate "fast food" with McDonald's, but they also assume that McDonald's must be the best brand in the category.

Why is this so? Because of the widely held belief that the best brand wins in the marketplace. If Burger King, for example, were a better choice than McDonald's, then Burger King would be the leader.

In the mind of the consumer, the leader owns the category which puts also-rans in a difficult position.

Furthermore, once a brand owns the leadership position, it can often hold that position for decades if not centuries.

A research firm once measured the leading brands in 25 different categories in the American market in the year 1923. Of those 25 brands, 18 are still the leaders in their categories today.

Perhaps you will recognize some of these brands: Swift, Nabisco, Gold Medal, Coca-Cola, Life Savers, Campbell's, Del Monte, Sherwin-Williams, Crisco, Carnation, Lipton, Goodyear, Wrigley's, Gillette, Palmolive, Hershey's, Singer, and Colgate.

How do you get to be the leader? The best and easiest way is to be the first brand in the category.

The leading auction house for high-end artwork is Sotheby's. The No. 2 auction house is Christie's. Not too surprising is the fact that Sotheby's was the first high-end auction house and Christie's was second. Together the two houses handle 80 percent of all high-value artwork.

What is surprising is the fact that Sotheby's was founded in 1744. And Christie's was founded in 1766.

Sotheby's has been the leader in the category for more than 268 years. That's the power of a leadership position.

Many of the world's best brands were first in their categories. Lipton in tea. Nescafé in instant coffee. Starbucks in high-end coffee shops. Red Bull in energy drinks. Gatorade in sports drinks. Coca-Cola in cola. Colgate in toothpaste. Tide in detergent. General Electric in light bulbs. Hewlett-Packard in desktop laser printers. Intel in microprocessors. Microsoft in personal computer (PC) operating systems.

THE ADVANTAGE OF BEING FIRST

This principle is widely discussed in management publications such as *The Wall Street Journal* and *Harvard Business Review.*

But they get it wrong.

In management circles, it's called the "first mover" advantage and it's usually considered not an advantage at all. Sperry Rand is a typical example.

Sperry Rand was the first company to introduce a mainframe computer. TheUNIVAC, an acronym for "Universal Automatic Computer."

But thanks to a massive marketing program, IBM was the first mainframe computer brand in the mind.

The positioning articles should have called the concept the "first minder" advantage, and there are a lot of examples to demonstrate the principle.

- The MITS Altair 8800 was the first PC on the market, but Apple was the first brand in the mind.
- Powells.com was the first Internet bookstore, but not in the mind. The first Internet bookstore in the mind was Amazon.com.
- The Creative Nomad Jukebox was the first high-capacity MP3 player on the market, but the iPod was the first brand in the mind.

This happens in many categories. Early on, there may be dozens of brands in a new category. The winner is not necessarily the best brand or the first brand on the market. The winner is almost always the first brand that establishes a leadership position in the mind.

THE ISSUE OF FOCUS

It's always possible to become the first brand in a new category by narrowing your focus.

Take Dell, which became the world's No. 1 brand of PCs. Dell wasn't the first PC in the mind. (Apple, IBM, and a host of other brands got into the mind long before Dell did.)

Dell Computer narrowed its focus to direct sales only, the first brand to do so. This was the key decision that made the Dell brand a worldwide success.

Dell didn't get started until 1984, nine years after the first PC hit the market. By 1984, the market was saturated with computer manufacturers. As *BusinessWeek* reported in its August 8, 1983, issue: "Pounding on corporate doors are more than 150 makers of personal computers."

Suppose you had said to one of these 150 makers of PCs: "Let's narrow the focus to direct sales only."

That's probably the opposite of what they wanted to do. "We need more distribution, not less," might have been the likely response.

It went worse. In that same issue, *BusinessWeek* reported:

> Computer and office automation companies are beginning to pitch comprehensive office systems that offer everything from personal computers to large central computers as well as the communications to connect all the equipment. This list of companies includes Burroughs, Data General, Digital Equipment, International Business Machines, Sperry, and Wang.

None of these PC brands are currently being marketed.

Narrow the focus? Everybody was doing exactly the opposite. Expansion, not contraction was the order of the day.

It's also the order of today. You've probably noticed that Dell has joined the expansion crowd with predictable results.

In the 1990s, Dell had the best stock-market performance of the 500 companies in the Standard & Poor's index, a compilation of the 500 most important companies in America.

In January 2001, Dell stock was selling for $59.69 a share. Today, it's less than $12 a share.

What mystifies many marketing mavens is how two companies (Dell and Hewlett-Packard) can use the same strategy with diametrically different results. One is successful; the other is not. A mystery that can be solved by assuming that the successful company has superior products.

And we're left with the same old canard: "The better product wins in the marketplace."

Hewlett-Packard is expanding its product line at the same rate as Dell. By 2006, the two companies had virtually identical worldwide PC market shares: Dell 17.1 percent and Hewlett-Packard 17.0 percent.

Today, Hewlett-Packard's market share is 17.2 percent, and Dell's market share is 12.1 percent.

Even more ominous is Dell's drop in net profit margins. In the decade ending in 2006, Dell had a net profit margin of 6.2 percent. In 2012, it was 4.1 percent versus Hewlett-Packard's 7.0 percent.

What differentiates Hewlett-Packard from Dell? Hewlett-Packard is perceived as the leader in PCs. And "leadership" is the most important aspect of a marketing program. You lose your leadership (as Dell has done) and you lose your marketing power.

Dell used to mean "direct." What does Dell mean today? A company with problems.

THE "OPPOSITE" POSITION

What can you do if you didn't get there first? What should Pepsi-Cola do? What should Burger King do? What should every No. 2 brand do?

Be the opposite of the leader.

That's exactly the way Pepsi-Cola got to be a strong No. 2 brand to Coca-Cola. Years ago, Coca-Cola was sold in small 6-oz. "contour" bottles. These iconic bottles were powerful symbols for the brand.

So what did Pepsi-Cola do? They launched the brand in 12-oz. bottles and then ran a massive marketing program dramatizing the difference.

Pepsi-Cola hits the spot. Twelve full ounces, that's a lot.
Twice as much for a nickel, too. Pepsi-Cola is the drink for you.

That was back in the 1930s. Even today, Pepsi-Cola is a strong No. 2 brand to Coca-Cola. As a category matures, odds are that two brands will wind up dominating the category, putting the also-rans in a difficult position.

If you can't be the leader, then you need to try to be the No. 2 brand, and the best way to do that is to be the opposite of the leader.

Red Bull was the first energy drink and rapidly became a global brand with sales of $5.6 billion. One factor that helped establish the Red Bull brand was its small 8.3-oz. cans that symbolized "energy," much like a stick of dynamite.

Small cans were such an obvious concept for an energy drink that virtually all the early competitors of Red Bull were introduced in 8.3-oz. cans.

Except Monster.

Monster was one of the first energy drinks introduced in 16-oz. cans. Today in many countries of the world, Monster is the No. 2 brand of energy drink. In the American market, for example, Monster has a market share of 35 percent versus 43 percent for

Red Bull. Rockstar, the No. 3 brand, has a market share of just 12 percent.

And on the stock market, Monster Beverage Corp. has a market cap of $11.4 billion. Not bad for a company whose major brand wasn't launched until 2002.

Why don't more Brands use an "opposite" approach? Because they assume the leader was successful because its strategy was right. So they try to emulate the strategy of the leader, only executing it better. Introduce an energy drink in 8.3-oz. cans, for example, but making the drink taste better.

That seldom works. "Better" is a very difficult concept to communicate to consumers. Does Coca-Cola taste better than Pepsi-Cola? Or does Pepsi taste better than Coke? The truth is, they taste about the same, which is usually the case for any No. 1 and No. 2 brands.

Therefore, to create a difference consumers will recognize, you normally have to exaggerate that difference. In other words, be the opposite.

Listerine, a bad-tasting mouthwash, has been the long-time leader in the category. The assumption was that mouthwashes had to taste bad (to kill the germs in your mouth). That's why many other bad-tasting mouthwashes such as Colgate 100, C paco, and Micrin were introduced, but none of them were successful.

Procter & Gamble had another idea. They introduced Scope, the first good-tasting mouthwash, which became a strong No. 2 brand to Listerine.

Years ago, most of the engagement rings and wedding bands sold in America were made with gold. Then Scott Kay introduced a line of platinum rings and built an enormously successful jewelry brand.

The leading high-end pen brand used to be Cross, a thin and elegant instrument. Not today. Montblanc introduced a "thick" pen and became the leading global brand with a 28 percent market share.

Mercedes-Benz made big, comfortable vehicles, so BMW focused on smaller, more nimble machines using "the ultimate driving machine" as its strategy. And currently, BMW outsells Mercedes on the global market.

The first advertisement in BMW's "driving" campaign had the headline: "The ultimate sitting machine vs. the ultimate driving machine."

Now that's advertisement that makes the "opposite" strategy crystal clear.

THE ROLE OF THE BRAND NAME

In the normal course of events, a company selects a brand name that sounds good, is easy to spell and pronounce, and is different than existing brand names.

That's the wrong approach.

The first step in creating a new brand name is to define the strategy for the brand. Take Monster energy drink. To be the opposite, the company (Hansen Beverage Corp. at the time) decided to launch the new brand in 16-oz. cans, rather than 8.3-oz. cans. Was that an improvement? Not really, but it was different.

So Hansen gave its new brand the name "Monster" to communicate the concept that the brand was giant size. And later, after the brand was successful, the company changed its corporate name to Monster Beverage Corp.

Most furniture retailers in America sell individual items of furniture: chairs, tables, sofas, beds, etc. So a new furniture retailer decided to be the opposite. Instead of promoting individual items, the company promoted entire "rooms of furniture."

Then they selected a name for the chain: "Rooms to Go."

So successful was the concept that Rooms to Go became the largest furniture chain in America. The chain uses the slogan: "Buy the piece, save a little. Buy the room, save a lot."

Years ago, Eveready was the largest selling appliance battery in America. Then the company introduced an alkaline battery, with the brand name "Eveready Alkaline," that could last twice as long as the zinc–carbon batteries they were already selling.

That name created an opportunity for a company called P.R. Mallory. Six years after the launch of Eveready Alkaline batteries, P.R. Mallory introduced its own alkaline battery.

But it didn't call its new battery the "Mallory" battery, the obvious choice. Mallory was a recognized name, but unfortunately didn't stand for anything.

Instead, P.R. Mallory first decided the strategy it wanted to use. Because Eveready had used a line-extension name on its alkaline battery, there was an opportunity to preempt the category with a specific brand name.

The choice was obvious. Use a brand name that would communicate the benefit of alkaline batteries. They last longer.

Duracell, the name P.R. Mallory chose, went on to dominate the category for decades to come. Finally, Eveready responded by introducing a new name for its alkaline battery, the Energizer. But it was too late and Eveready never regained the leadership it once enjoyed.

Names are important. In the positioning era, the most important decision you can make is what to name the product. And the best approach is to first determine the strategy of the brand and then pick a name that communicates that strategy.

THE LINE-EXTENSION TRAP

Eveready's loss of its appliance-battery leadership is typical of what can happen when you line-extend a brand.

Yet, line extension is the preferred approach used by most companies. Why is that so? Because it makes sense.

We have this terrific brand, goes the thinking, so why can't we use it on a second product? Or on a third product? That's the way it is in many corporations today.

No wonder line extension is so popular. It's logical. And it supports the No. 1 goal of most management executives, which is to "expand the business."

"And what is the better way to expand the business," thinks the typical executive, "then by using our great brand on a number of new products and new markets."

Not only is line extension logical, you can always find examples where line extensions have worked. Bud Light. Diet Coke. General Electric. Kraft. Dove. Tide. McDonald's. Chevrolet. And many others.

Would you like to smoke? Forget the warnings you have read in the paper. You can always find people who smoked all their lives and never got lung cancer. Therefore, it's safe to smoke.

The case against line extension doesn't depend on case histories. If everyone in an industry line extends his/her brands (as happened in the beer business), then it's not an issue at all. The winner will be the leading brand and its line extension (e.g., Budweiser and Bud Light) regardless of what the competition does or doesn't do. (And in the cola business, Coke and Diet Coke.)

The case against line extension is a philosophical case. For a brand to exist, it needs to be filed away in the mind. And where does a consumer put your brand in the mind?

If you say, "Xerox this document," the consumer thinks "make a copy." The Xerox brand is apparently filed in a mental category called "copier."

So what happened when Xerox, the copier company, introduced Xerox computers? Nothing. And Xerox went on to lose billions of dollars.

Once a brand like Xerox gets filed in a category called "copiers," it's very difficult to use that brand name for a new category.

Then there's Sony. In a recent survey of 3,600 Asian consumers, the No. 1 brand was Sony. In a recent survey of 1,500 American consumers, the No. 1 brand was Sony.

Like most Japanese electronics companies, Sony is heavily line-extended. Sony puts its brand name on television sets, videocassette recorders, digital cameras, PCs, cellphones, semiconductors, camcorders, DVD players, MP3 players, stereos, broadcast video equipment, batteries, and a host of other products.

In which categories is Sony the leader?

I don't know and I'm pretty sure that most consumers don't know either. Sony is a well-known brand name which accounts for its success in market surveys, but most consumers don't associate the brand as a leader in any single category. That's the ultimate fate of any well-known brand that falls into the line-extension trap.

Sony's lack of a leadership perception in any individual category, in my opinion, is the reason for Sony's recent lackluster financial performance.

In the past four years, for example, Sony has had revenues of $324.5 billion and managed to lose $10.3 billion.

Yahoo followed a similar path. Initially, Yahoo became the world's most valuable Internet brand by focusing on "search." At one point in time, Yahoo had a market capitalization of $114 billion.

So what did Yahoo do next? They tried to expand the brand.

A decade ago, Yahoo's CEO said: "In online commerce and shopping you can expect to see us extend aggressively by broadening and deepening the range of consumer buying, transaction, and fulfillment services we provide across all major categories."

Which is exactly what it did.

In addition to search, Yahoo added a raft of features: auctions, calendars, chat rooms, classifieds, email, games, maps, news, pager services, people searches, personals, radio, shopping, sports, stock quotes, weather reports, and yellow pages.

As a result, Yahoo lost its leadership in search to Google. Today, Yahoo is worth $19.4 billion on the stock market and Google is worth $189.1 billion, almost 10 times as much. Furthermore, Yahoo revenues continue to fall. From $7.2 billion in 2008 to $5.0 billion in 2012.

Next to line extension, the most common way to expand a brand is market segmentation. You market the brand with a different approach for each segment.

It's like the elephant and the six blind men. One "sees" a wall, another a spear, a snake, a tree, a fan, and a rope.

So instead of marketing "elephants," the company adopts a wall/spear/snake/tree/fan/rope approach. In certain circles, it's called "market segmentation."

There's a logic to this approach. One segment needs a wall. One segment needs a spear. Another segment needs a snake. And so on.

Instead of one position for a brand, you have multiple positions. To the business community, Dell is a direct-to-business computer company. To consumers, Dell is a consumer computer. That was a strategy that was supposed to double sales.

It didn't work.

Everywhere you look, companies are racing to expand their brands when they should be doing exactly the opposite. Launching a second brand.

THE POWER OF SECOND BRANDS

Whenever a fashion or technological change occurs, an existing brand, no matter how dominant, faces a choice.

Should the brand be "stretched" to encompass the new fashion or technology or should the company launch a second brand? If the change is significant enough, the better answer is almost always "launch a second brand."

The rise of casual clothing in the workplace led Levi Strauss to introduce Dockers, which has become a billion dollar worldwide brand.

The success of Mercedes-Benz and BMW led Toyota to introduce Lexus, which has become the largest selling luxury-vehicle brand in America.

The success of Makita, a Japanese professional-tool brand, led Black & Decker to introduce DeWalt, which has become the dominant brand in the professional-tool category.

The success of Costco led Walmart to introduce Sam's Club, which is a strong No. 2 brand to Costco.

When it comes to launching successful second brands, you rapidly run out of case histories. By far the majority of marketers prefer to expand their core brand to cover the new category. With mediocre success. Some examples:

- IBM's failure to extend its mainframe dominance to the PC field.
- Xerox's failure to extend its copier dominance to the computer field.
- Polaroid's failure to move its brand out of instant photography.
- Kodak's failure to duplicate its film photography success in the digital field.

Companies that shy away from second brands usually end up paying a high price for their insularity. The latest victims of second-brand skittishness are Visa U.S.A. and MasterCard International. So far, it has cost the two credit card companies $3 billion with possibly more financial bad news to come.

A number of years ago, the two credit card giants decided to get into debit card business. It would be hard to find two categories that are more competitive. Credit cards are the enemy of debit cards. And vice versa.

So what do Visa and MasterCard do? They put the same names on both cards, Visa on credit cards and Visa on debit cards. And the same for Master Card. To compound the problem, both card companies force their retailers to "honor all cards." In other words, if a retailer accepts a Visa credit card, the retailer must also accept a Visa debit card.

Then they put the debit card charges through the same signature-based system as the credit-card charges, forcing the retailer to pay five to ten times as much in fees as they would if the customer has used one of the alternate debit card networks such as Star, Pulse, or NYCE, which use a personal identification number, or a PIN-based system.

In the biggest antitrust settlement in history, Visa U.S.A. agreed to pay $2 billion and MasterCard International $1 billion to a group of retailers led by Walmart. Their contention "Honor all cards" was an illegal tie-in scheme.

Why not launch a second "debit" brand to complement the Visa or MasterCard "credit" brands? It's the chicken-and-egg problem, explained one Visa executive. Visa would have had to start a new brand from scratch, one not yet issued by any bank or honored by any merchant. "But why would you possibly have done that?"

I can think of three billion reasons. But more important than the short-term financial losses at Visa and MasterCard are the long-term implications of their "honor all cards" strategy. By integrating its debit with its credit card system, Visa (as well as MasterCard) is locked into a slower, less secure, and more expensive way of processing debit card charges.

Here is where the power of conceptual thinking comes in. Categories tend to diverge, not converge. You may not know how, when, or where that divergence will take place, but you can be sure that ultimately it will. Two different categories, credit cards and debit cards, will become more and more different, and there's nothing one company can do about it. Trying to keep them together under the same brand name is an exercise in futility.

Never fight a trend. As time goes on, there's always a room for new brands. If you don't not launch a second brand, you can be sure that one of your competitors will.

THINK LONG-TERM

It took Red Bull 9 years to break $100 million in annual sales.

It took Volkswagen 10 years to break 100,000 vehicles in U.S. annual sales.

It took Microsoft 10 years to break $100 million in annual sales. In 2012, Microsoft booked $69.9 billion in sales.

It took Walmart 14 years to break $100 million in annual sales. In 2012, Walmart was the world's largest retailer with $447.0 in sales.

Then there's Apple. The late Steve Jobs is widely considered one of the most brilliant marketing people who ever lived. In 1985, Steve Jobs was effectively fired from Apple. Twelve years later, in 1997, he returned to Apple, a year the company had revenues of $7.1 billion.

In the seven years that followed (from 1998 to 2004), Apple's revenues averaged just $6.5 billion a year. And Apple's net profit margin was just 4.6 percent.

But those seven years were crucial in preparing the company for the surge to follow. In the next seven years (from 2005 to 2011), Apple literally exploded in sales and profits, averaging $43.7 billion in annual revenues and 19.5 percent in net profit margin.

And today, Apple is the world's most valuable company. You can't turn around a company overnight. It takes time.

THINK GLOBAL

Long term, the world will be filled with global brands. But short term, it's difficult to see much of a trend toward global branding.

Marketing is a long-term discipline. What you do today might not bear fruit for years. Or even decades. Furthermore, what works in the short term doesn't necessarily work in the long term.

Line extension, for example, usually works in the short term, but not in the long term. Initially, the IBM PC was a big success. Three years after its launch, the IBM PC had about 50 percent of the PC market.

Then competition in the form of narrowly focused brands entered the market, Compaq and Dell in particular. And IBM's share began to shrink. By the time IBM sold its PC operations to Lenovo in 2004 for $1.75 billion, it had only 7 percent of the market share.

In the 23 years that IBM tried to build a position in PCs, it reportedly lost $15 billion.

Today, the PC market has become a global one, dominated by two American brands (Hewlett-Packard and Dell), one Chinese brand (Lenovo), two Taiwanese brands (Acer and Asus), and one Japanese brand (Toshiba).

This is a pattern many other markets are likely to follow.

On the other hand, launching a new brand usually doesn't work in the short term, but can work exceptionally well in the long term.

The iPod launched by Apple in 2002 sold only 345,000 units in its first year, losing millions of dollars for the company. But in its fifth year, 2007, the iPod sold 52 million units.

Actually a brand that takes off too quickly is likely to turn into a fad. A brand that starts slowly often turns into a long-term trend.

So how do you build a global brand? Start with the name. A global brand needs a name that "works" in English. It doesn't need to be an English word; it just needs to be a word that an English speaker can pronounce and spell.

English has become the second language of the world and the primary language of the global business community. Brand builders need to pay attention to this fact.

Second, a global brand needs a position. And not just a verbal expression of the brand's singularity. A global brand needs a leadership position on the category ladder in its home country.

Japan is known for high-quality automobiles. So Toyota, the leading automobile brand in Japan, was able to use its position in the local market to go global. That's the pattern. Build a position in your home market and then take your brand global.

But what if your brand is not the leader in its category? What do you do then?

Create a new category by narrowing your focus. In the Japanese market, Subaru is a minor automobile brand. So instead of marketing a full range of models like the three leading Japanese brands (Toyota, Honda, and Nissan), Subaru markets four-wheel drive vehicles only.

Its leadership in four-wheel drive has helped Subaru become a big brand in the American market. In 2013, Subaru sold 424,683 vehicles, ahead of such well-known brands as Volkswagen, Mercedes-Benz, BMW, Chrysler, Lexus, Buick, Cadillac, Acura, and Volvo.

POSITIONING IS NOT A FORMULA

It is not a set of rules you can apply to your brand. Positioning is a way of thinking about the discipline of marketing.

You look inside the mind of your prospect and you try to find an "open" hole you can fill with your brand.

It is as simple and as difficult as that.

Chapter 2

Creating Meaningful Brands: How Brands Evolve from Labels on Products to Icons of Meaning

Mark Batey

Brands allow marketers to add meanings to products and services, but it is consumers who ultimately determine what a brand means. Simply put, while companies create brand identities, people create brand meaning. Brand meaning refers to the semantic and symbolic properties of a brand. Symbolism connects us to other things—thoughts and values—by stimulating the imagination through suggestions and associations. Think of the associative and symbolic power of the Marlboro cowboy, Ferrari's prancing horse, or a diamond as a symbol of eternal love (De Beers).

The components referred to in these examples are brand properties. They provide varying degrees of brand recognition, differentiation, and meaning. The strongest brand properties become the brand's signature cues—the Striding Man of Johnnie Walker and the blatting of a Harley engine. The more meaningful the components, the more meaningful the brand. Over time, consumers' exposure to these components and their experiences with the brand form what is technically called a brand associative network. In other words, consumers carry the brand around in their minds as a cluster of meanings. The manager's role, as will be discussed later, is to reinforce, revitalize, and at times rotate the meanings associated with the brand. Like a mosaic or kaleidoscope, the individual and particular way that these meanings line up with each other is what gives the brand its uniqueness.

HOW BRAND MEANING FORMS IN THE CONSUMER'S MIND

Meaning is at the heart of consumer behavior, because meaning is at the heart of human behavior. The millennia may have passed, but we are still hunters and gatherers—of meaning. Yet meaning is not some manufactured, concrete entity. Meaning is up for negotiation and interpretation, and the role of the individual in the creation of meaning is a very active one. Structuralist semioticians such as Roland Barthes have pointed out that individuals are not passive receivers of meaning created by some external agent or authority. Rather, they are actively involved in the process of *signification*, in the production of meaning. Further, they are very creative in their meaning making, deriving meaning not just from words and images, but from sounds, shapes, textures, colors, and aromas.

The objects with which we surround ourselves, whether branded consumer goods or common household items, are rich and diverse in meaning. It is important to understand the underlying product and category meanings that brands can successfully tap into. Consider fabrics, for example, and related categories such as laundry detergents. Fabrics hold meaning for women because, from jeans to sheets, they are filled with emotions, stories, feelings, and memories. Fabrics also allow them to express their personalities and assert their identities. These are significant considerations for brands operating in the category.

In a similar vein, from a maternal perspective, whiter-than-white whites have traditionally been the benchmark when it comes to cleaning kids' clothes. Smiling children in bright white t-shirts at the end of a TV commercial betoken the care and attention of a dutiful mother. But there is another side to the story. Kids' clothes don't just display evidence of a doting mom—they carry the signs of a child's development. The stains and blemishes that come from playing soccer, painting, climbing a tree, and frolicking in the sand or mud are the corollary of a child's mental and physical growth. Getting dirty is part of the process. Declaring that "there's no learning without stains," Unilever encouraged mothers to let their kids go ahead and get dirty while playing, discovering, and learning. Seemingly challenging conventional category wisdom, the global "Dirt is good"

Persil
dirt is good

SOURCE: Unilever.

campaign from Omo[1] effectively told moms: "You take care of your child's development, we'll take care of the laundry."

In the 1990s, the Smith Kline Beecham Company (as it was then known) faced a challenging and unforeseen situation in the U.K. soft drink market. Their Lucozade brand had been marketed since its launch as an energy-providing carbonated drink. It had extended this product platform to address the opportunity in sports drinks, using well-known athletes in its advertising. In 1993, the company decided it wanted to more specifically target teenagers as it was not commanding much share among this market. Though teenagers were aware of Lucozade's sports drink profile, the product's energy properties had in the meantime been reinterpreted in the rave scene and in the country's young black community. It had thus been endowed with a kind of underground street credibility by certain

[1] Also sold as Persil, Skip, Breeze, Ala, Surf, and Rinso.

sections of the teenage population. Although the identification of young black people with the brand was possibly due in part to the fact that most of the athletes used in the advertising were black (e.g., Linford Christie), there was certainly nothing in the marketing of the brand to link it with the rave culture, nor was there a specific marketing intention to target black teenagers. This was an example of a particular group investing a certain meaning in a brand—a meaning appropriated from their own cultural milieu. It also exemplifies the fact that, quite often, it is not so much brands that confer meaning and values on consumers but consumers who confer meaning and values on brands. Smith Kline Beecham eventually introduced a sub-brand, Lucozade NRG, to take advantage of the teenage opportunity.

Material goods are consumed not only for their functional benefits, but also as symbolic signifiers of taste, lifestyle, and identity—both personal identity (self-expressiveness, personal values, and history) and social identity (group affiliation and social standing). People construct identities for themselves employing a variety of means, including brands and the meanings that they come to hold for them.

In a kind of self-symbolizing process, a person may buy and use a certain brand to affirm his or her actual self-concept or buy and use a brand to "lay claim" to a desired or idealized identity image. The latter is a form of symbolic self-completion:

Actual self + Brand = Ideal self

From the customer perspective, brands and their meaning operate at different levels, reflecting the three dimensions involved in consumer behavior:

- Conscious rationality
- Semiconscious emotions
- Unconscious biological drives and "hardwired" instincts

These three areas do not operate independently of each other but are intertwined, as has been recently demonstrated by findings in the field of neuroscience. Meaningful brands connect with their consumers across this spectrum, with particularly forceful connections at the emotional and instinctual levels. It has been well documented since the mid-1980s that strong brands form emotional connections with their consumers. In 1985, David Ogilvy wrote, in *Ogilvy on Advertising*, "... customers also need a *rational excuse* to justify their emotional decisions" (emphasis in original). In the 1980s, marketers gradually became aware of the enormous value of the brand as distinct from the product or service. At the same time, advances in manufacturing capabilities meant it became increasingly difficult to gain competitive advantage through functional product performance attributes. So marketers sought differentiation along more emotional lines. They began to build brands, endowing them with personalities and symbolic qualities.

As an example, Volvo pioneered automotive safety long before it was fashionable. The company spent a lot of money in crash testing and invested heavily in cutting-edge R&D in automotive technology. Features such as ABS (antilock brakes) and SIPS (side impact protection system), together with early advertising imagery, which conditioned consumers to think of the car as a protective cage, helped establish Volvo's safety credentials. A dramatic press ad from the late 1980s shows a menacing great white shark dangerously close to a diver, protected only by the cage which surrounds him. "Cages save lives" is the slogan, appealing directly to our primal instinct for survival. Emotional brand connections were forged through advertising that focused less on functional safety features and more on the beneficiaries of those features: family and loved ones. "Is your family worth the extra protection?" asks one ad, while another shows a father standing next to his Volvo on a foggy night and smiling down at his young son and daughter. "Home sweet home," reads the headline. The company's website even has a "Volvo Saved My Life Club" section, with emotionally gripping stories of real people who were protected by their Volvos in car accidents. One of them is signed off with the line "My S40 gave its life for mine."

Brands, then, are dimensional. Accordingly, in considering the full depth of meaning of a brand, it is imperative to consider two distinct but related dimensions of brand meaning: Primary Brand Meaning® and Implicit Brand Meaning®.

SOURCE: Volvo Car UK Ltd.

DIMENSIONS OF BRAND MEANING

Primary Brand Meaning®

Primary Brand Meaning® is the meaning of the brand that would be played back by consumers in research without too much reflection or probing. Rolex means luxury watches. eBay means online auctions. Starbucks means coffee in different varieties, and a nice place to drink it. Primary Brand Meaning® is a summation of the consumer's primary associations and dominant perceptions about a brand, the snapshot that immediately comes to the mind's eye upon hearing the brand name. Simply stated, it is how consumers spontaneously define a brand.

Researching Primary Brand Meaning® among consumers is important in that it clarifies and confirms the extent to which the consumers' definition of a brand's essential meaning coincides with the marketer's intentions. An article published in *The Journal of Advertising Research* in late 2000, for example, describes how a team from Miami University, Ohio, working with researchers from Pennzoil conducted research into the meaning of the Pennzoil brand. Interestingly, although Pennzoil managers had deemed "protection" to be a fundamental component of the brand's meaning (the word featured in the brand slogan: "We're driving protection"), research results and other company findings indicated that while *protection* may have been a *property* of Pennzoil, it did not *define* the brand in the public eye. The brand slogan has since changed.

Such research regarding Primary Brand Meaning® is important in the context of brand extension. What is the "fit" between the Primary Brand Meaning® and the proposed brand extension? Looking at it another way, what will be the effect of an extension on the Primary Brand Meaning®? Of course, brand extension may seek to deliberately modify Primary Brand Meaning®, as in the case of Xerox extending away from its outdated association with paper copying only.

Besides the more rational and functional associations, which contribute to Primary Brand Meaning®, a brand's composite meaning may encompass a greater or lesser number of associations of a more symbolic and socio-cultural nature. While concepts such as the brand associative network help illuminate Primary Brand Meaning®, brands are more than just fixed cognitive associations of meanings. The actual or potential symbolic and socio-cultural meanings of a brand need to be understood because such meanings provide two important elements for the brand: differentiation and depth. We are here dealing with a second dimension of brand meaning, one which is less manifest, more subtle, and in the long run more motivating: Implicit Brand Meaning®.

Implicit Brand Meaning®

Implicit Brand Meaning® refers to the ultimate emotional and psychological implications and significance of a brand, to the psychic resonance that the brand has for its consumers. It is highly symbolic, psycho-social meaning, influenced in great measure by cultural norms and values. It may tap into archetypal patterns and is at the heart of brand mythology (more on this later). It may find expression and reinforcement though ritual. Implicit Brand Meaning®

evolves from the central truth that bonds the consumer to the product or brand, and underpins that bond in a visceral, deep-seated, and enduring way. As an example, while on the surface Hallmark is a brand of greeting cards, it is the emotional satisfaction of giving and receiving love, which is inherent in the implicit meaning of the brand. Disney is about fun and family entertainment, but its Implicit Brand Meaning® resides more in keeping alive the magic and wonder of childhood. The laundry category is one of the most fiercely competitive arenas in which a brand could choose to compete. Product performance and innovation are and always have been critical to the category. Unilever's long-standing Persil brand, mentioned earlier, has been no exception to this rule. Yet, the brand really evolved through its instinctive understanding of a mother's pride, and the caring and nurturing values behind it.

Despite Implicit Brand Meaning® being where brands and consumers really connect, marketers often fail to understand the actual or potential symbolic meanings of their brands to consumers. A cursory appraisal of brand perceptions is inadequate if truly fertile territory is to be identified. Probing Implicit Brand Meaning® is a complex process. Precisely because of its more derivative, symbolic nature, this dimension of brand meaning is unlikely to be that at which a brand readily and predominantly defines itself in a consumer's mind. A brand's more immediate, manifest meaning is perceived at a less abstract level. Nobody goes into a supermarket and asks: "Where do you keep your maternal solicitude products?" or tells a car dealer: "I was looking for something in the way of symbolic self-completion."

The Brand Meaning Model

It is worth highlighting that Primary Brand Meaning® and Implicit Brand Meaning® are two distinct concepts, two separate dimensions of total brand meaning, with a greater or lesser degree of interrelationship. They are like two different lenses for looking at a brand. Each will bring the brand into focus in a somewhat different manner. The differences between the two types of brand meaning are illustrated in Figure 2.1.

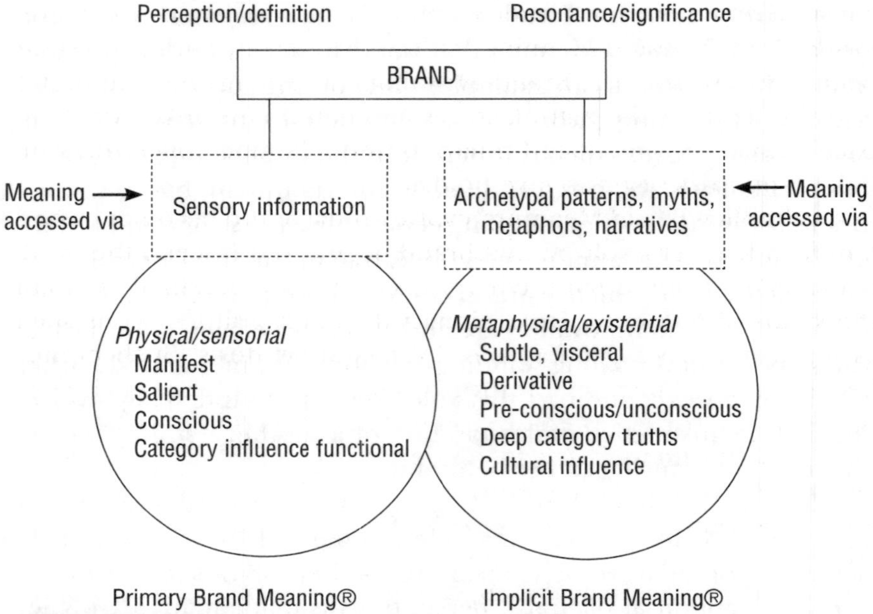

Figure 2.1 Brand Meaning Model

SOURCE: Mark Batey, *Brand Meaning* (New York: Routledge/Taylor and Francis Group, 2008).

EVOLUTION OF BRAND MEANING

When a company launches a product, that product will have a number of distinguishing features. It will have a name, a logo, a physical format, distinctive packaging, a certain taste, maybe special design features, and so forth. Yet, at the beginning these elements lack meaning for consumers. Though they are elements that will contribute to the brand meaning, at the outset they, and by extension the brand, have no real meaning. From a meaning perspective, the brand still does not exist. As consumers become acquainted with and gain experience of the product—purchasing it, using it, discussing it with friends, and seeing advertising for it—the Primary Brand Meaning® begins to form. More gradually, and with the further passage of time, the abstract and symbolic properties of the brand begin to percolate through—qualities which are often assigned by consumers themselves. Implicit Brand Meaning® begins to evolve. While Primary Brand Meaning® is likely to remain fairly consistent once it forms, Implicit Brand Meaning®, assuming that the brand is given depth by the manufacturer and consumers alike, will "outpace" the development of Primary Brand Meaning® once the symbolic properties begin to take hold.

As Implicit Brand Meaning® evolves and a brand becomes important for what it symbolizes, that brand begins to transcend the product category from which it emerges, and has the potential to attain the status of a cultural icon, along with other cultural icons such as magazines, rock groups, and TV talk show hosts. Such brands become compelling symbols for a set of values or ideals which resonate within a society or culture. The meaning and importance they hold for consumers come to reside less in their category context and more in their socio-cultural context. As brands evolve in this way, their center of gravity gradually shifts from manufacturer to consumer. By the time the brand has evolved from category to culture, from a name on a label to an icon of meaning, its passage into consumer ownership is complete. These dynamics are illustrated in the brand evolution model shown in Figure 2.2. We will return to the theme of iconic brands later.

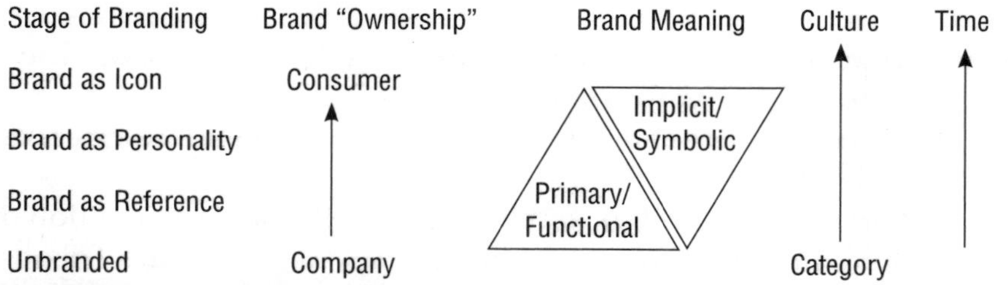

Figure 2.2 Brand Evolution Model

SOURCE: Mark Batey, *Brand Meaning* (New York: Routledge/Taylor and Francis Group, 2008).

MANAGEMENT OF MEANINGFUL BRANDS

Disney has been so phenomenally successful not because it branded a product but because it branded a meaning. Indeed, marketing and brand managers should see themselves as brand meaning managers. We have evolved from a mere understanding of features and benefits of brands, to the extent that the way meaning is managed has become the determining factor in a brand's success—or otherwise. Failing to understand the full meaning of the brand can be a costly mistake, as countless ill-conceived brand extensions and erratic advertising campaigns have proved.

Brand meaning management is no easy task. Given that brands exist in a permanently evolving socio-cultural context, and that their meaning for consumers is mediated by constant direct personal experience, it is not unusual for divergence to occur between company-intended and consumer-perceived brand meaning. Moreover, today's fragmented and diversified media landscape exacerbates the situation. The explosive proliferation of new media and the Internet in particular has presented consumers with a very public and accessible forum to directly exchange experiences and opinions of brands completely independently of the brand owner. Yet, despite the self-seeking and misguided claims of "social media experts" and the frequent faddish attempts of practitioners to rebrand branding itself, brands today are built the same way as they always have been and always will be: through brand expression, brand experience, and brand advocacy.

- *Brand expression*: the way in which the brand expresses itself, from packaging to communications.
- *Brand experience*: how the consumer encounters, experiences, and lives the brand.
- *Brand advocacy*: refers to the (hopefully) positive promotion of the brand at a person-to-person level via family and friends' recommendations and endorsements, and via editorial and opinion leaders.

The management process of branding is that of transforming a product or service into something meaningful and differentiated for the consumer. There are two elements to branding, which can be thought of as "brand-ing." On the one hand, there is the brand and its meaning, and on the other, there is the signaling and activation of that meaning. The branding goal is to create meaningful connections between brands and people. With this in mind, it should be possible to distill the intended brand meaning in a strategic brand concept, or brand idea.

Brand Idea

The brand idea can best be described as shorthand for the meaning the marketer would like the brand to have in the mind of the consumer. Meaningful brands always enact a distinct brand idea: *moments of connection* in the case of Oreo; *personal progress* in the case of Johnnie Walker. A well-defined and deftly articulated brand idea makes immediately clear, either directly or by implication, that which meaningfully differentiates the brand. The brand idea is not intended for literal consumer exposure. Neither is the brand idea the advertising idea, nor the slogan, nor a re-statement of the brand benefits. Rather, it ideally conveys the brand's ultimate purpose in addressing the hopes and desires of its users. So, to return to the Omo case mentioned earlier, the brand idea that *learning brings stains; Omo takes care of them* is based on the fact that as kids are learning and developing they sometimes get dirty and moms may worry about this. Omo encourages mothers to embrace the fact that their kids will get dirty as they play, discover and learn, and frees them from the anxiety by taking care of the dirt. Note that this is a particularly meaningful brand idea given a cultural backdrop of kids leading increasingly sedentary lives, often sat for hours glued to the TV or the web.

It is also worth emphasizing that the best brand ideas are rooted in a product truth—otherwise they tend to rely on "borrowed interest." So in the case of Oreo, the *moments of connection* are enabled by the playful consumption ritual (the "twist, lick, and dunk" of the sandwich cookie) that brings family members and friends together. Omo has ingredients that make it very effective at removing stains. Yet neither the (Oreo) ritual nor the (Omo) ingredients are the brand idea. They merely help anchor the respective idea in the brand.

Given that brands exist in the consumer's mind, it follows that the more parts of the consumer's mind the brand is present in, the stronger the brand will be. Different parts of the brain are responsible for different things—emotions, sensorial information, memories, and thinking. The more senses the brand engages, the more vivid and tangible it is to the consumer. If a brand offers engaging experiences, has a strong sensorial profile and a distinctive visual identity, and conveys a compelling set of values and ideals that resonate with people, then all these qualities will help make it a strong, differentiated, and meaningful brand. From a management perspective, these areas all provide scope for bringing to life the brand idea. The most successful brands express and share their ideas, heritage, and ideals in the form of a narrative—an evocative, meaningful, and memorable story: a brand story.

Brand Story: Myth, Meaning, and Mystique

Most of our experience, memories, knowledge, and thinking are organized in the form of stories. Stories are easy for us to remember, because in many ways stories are how we remember. The importance of this for brands cannot be overstated. In an increasingly cluttered and competitive marketplace, products and services are becoming less important than the stories they convey, and the way in which they are interpreted, shared, and reinvented. Like the parables and myths of old, the task of the story is to convey meaning—brand meaning. Marlboro's brand story embraces nostalgia to exploit the myth of the stoic, solitary American cowboy—a heroic, independent, masculine figure in a place of wide-open spaces, away from urban stress, and a time of simple choices, and an honest day's work.

Myths need their symbols, characters, images, and languages. Those characters are usually allegorical and archetypal, such as the Marlboro cowboy or the Jolly Green Giant. In the United States, imported beer Dos Equis created an elaborate mythology around a legendary figure known as the Most Interesting Man in the World (MIMW), a suave, bearded sixty-something-year-old Connery-meets-Castro-meets-Hemingway character who has spent a life of daring exploits and mysterious expeditions. The campaign began in 2006 and produced impressive sales growth for the Mexican beer brand at a time when the import beer category was declining. In faux-grainy images, cobbled together like home movies, the TV spots depict the MIMW, among other feats, rescuing a fox from a hunt, cliff-diving in Acapulco, splashing down in a space capsule, freeing a grizzly bear from a trap while wearing a suit, and lying in a hospital bed stitching up a wound on his own shoulder while surgeons and nurses stand around, chuckling at his jokes. The voiceovers add humor and hyperbole: "The police often question him just because they find him interesting," or, "His personality is so magnetic, he is unable to carry credit cards."

The images are provided without context, chronology, or explanation. The settings are never revealed, only adding to the mystique, for evocation is the modus operandi of brand story. Like in a fable, the Dos Equis brand conveys a message through its narrative, encouraging its users to seek out interesting experiences and live life to the full, even biting off more than they can chew at times. "Stay thirsty, my friends," exhorts the MIMW at the end of each commercial. And the brand provides plenty of opportunity for its enthusiasts to indulge their thirst for life, with consumer promotional programs and events, on-premise retail programs, and digital and social media activities.

While many brands feature characters within their narratives, these are rarely brand spokespeople as such. Neither is the MIMW a typical brand spokesman, and certainly not a typical beer brand spokesman. In fact, he appears more like a scotch drinker, and readily admits in every spot: "I don't always drink beer, but when I do, I prefer *Dos Equis*." He is a figure of inspiration who embodies a brand ethos and set of values to which people can both connect and aspire. Great brand stories encourage people to discover themselves or some latent aspect of themselves. There is perhaps no better example of this than Nike.

A watch company that has been producing some of the finest timepieces in the world since 1839—pieces that have adorned the wrists of popes, royalty, and other dignitaries—could choose to market its products based on heritage, top quality performance and reliability, and unsurpassed craftsmanship. All the more so if the design, crafting, manufacturing, finishing, and assembly of the pieces have always been completed in-house by master craftsmen. And all those things would certainly appeal to the affluent consumers fortunate enough to acquire such an item. Yet those with such means have higher, more heartfelt concerns, such as taking care of family needs and providing for the next generation, who they hope will also provide continuity. The "Generations" campaign from Patek Philippe encourages its male audience to "Begin your own tradition." Launched in 1996, the campaign typically features black-and-white photography of an unidentified father and son, portraying both the universal emotion of father–son relationships and the particular generational aspect of owning a Patek Philippe. "You never actually own a *Patek Philippe.* You merely take care of it for the next generation," reads the copy.

It is a powerful brand story—one which captures the premium distinction, reliability, and timelessness of the product in a highly emotional narrative form. Through it, a Patek Philippe is seen as both an emotional and a financial investment, offsetting any potential guilt at paying such a high price for a watch. For years now, Patek Philippe watches have been the strongest performers in international auctions. Moreover, the campaign neatly mirrors the company's own succession model. The current president is the fourth generation of his family to take the helm of a company that remains fiercely independent and intensely proud of its family tradition.

Iconic Brands: The Ultimate Meaningful Brands

Brands that, via a compelling narrative, manage to gain traction with a large enough group of people have the potential to become iconic brands. The word *iconic* is bandied about indiscriminately these days, both in a general cultural context and with regard to brands. It is a term claimed for far more brands than is or can ever be the case. Only a limited number of brands are truly iconic; yet by implementing some learnings and best practices from iconic brands, marketing managers can at least set their brands on the path toward becoming icons, even if they never quite get there. So what is an iconic brand, and how do you create one?

Despite the ubiquity of the term, a useful, concise definition of an iconic brand is very hard to come by in the branding literature. One will be given later in this section. Iconic brands combine unique iconography with a compelling narrative dimension. Invariably, those narratives tap into a collective desire or anxiety. They address universal needs and values—sometimes even inspiring a shift in those values, and subverting prevailing cultural myths, as was the case with Dove and its Campaign for Real Beauty, or the countercultural Volkswagen Beetle of the 1960s, which urged people in the United States to "Think small" at a time when the prevalent ideology was: "the bigger the car, the better."

In many cases iconic brands develop identity myths that address cultural tensions. Through its "Marlboro Country" campaign, referenced earlier, the cigarette brand depicted a reactionary working-class myth about American frontier masculinity—a stoical, self-reliant, physical masculinity which answered to nobody in its rugged outdoor setting. This was the very antithesis of the evolving middle-class masculinity of the 1950s and 1960s. The cowboys of "Marlboro Country" were from an idealized, different world to the sedentary, corporate men of the new industrial bureaucratic era, with their concerns for technology, status, and social approval.

Even where only a limited number of people may actually embrace their "tribal" values, brands that, for instance, carry anti-establishment connotations, such as Virgin Airlines or Harley-Davidson, nonetheless convey a clear sense of what they stand for, to users and nonusers alike. Yet iconic brands don't depend exclusively on identity myths for their success or resonance. One of the most iconic and meaningful brands in the world, Disney, does not perform any identity myth as such. Rather, as mentioned previously, the brand connects with the very human and universal desire to keep alive the magic and wonder of childhood.

A key characteristic of iconic brands is that they possess powerful sensory cues that make them instantly recognizable. These physical features—visual signs, words, and design elements—if they are unique to the brand and help differentiate it, form the brand iconography. They become "iconic" components of the brand. However, this raises two crucial points. Possessing iconic elements does not necessarily make for an iconic brand. Consider the brown UPS shield, Shell's famous pecten logo, or the Lacoste alligator. These markers uniquely identify their respective brands—and are brand icons—but they don't make these brands iconic. Similarly, advertising icons like the Geico gecko in the United States or the Pillsbury Doughboy make their brands recognizable without making them iconic.

Iconic brands must not only be easily recognizable, but also need to stand for something that people admire and consider meaningful. This brings us to the second point on brand iconography. In the world of iconic brands, brand symbols need to symbolize something. It is not enough to assume that over time the brand myth comes to be seen in the brand markers. That is too passive an approach and disregards both the power and importance of brand meaning management.

Two examples serve to illustrate how brand iconography can and should be actively leveraged in the creation not just of brand recognition, but of brand iconicity as well. The roots of the Jack Daniel's brand lie in pre-industrial Lynchburg Tennessee, its distillery and workers, and in its founder, Jack Daniel. Its story is a countercultural one of the stubborn tenacity of frontier ideology (cf. Marlboro, above), of standing firm in the face of a changing world, proudly preserving traditional ways of producing an artisanal product. The brand's heritage is all over its iconic square bottle with its equally iconic black-and-white label and old world typography. Yet this is not just about nostalgia. Its iconography is more meaningful. It evokes the brand myth and alludes to a universal spirit of maverick independence and standing for something authentic. A notable advertising poster reads: "56 men signed the Declaration of Independence. One man put it in a bottle." You can almost feel Jack Daniel himself, the ultimate brand icon, gazing resolutely from the label. A TV campaign for the brand, called "Label Story" and begun in 2009, brings the ornate label artwork to life as it takes the viewer on a lyrical, cinematic journey through legendary Jack Daniel's folklore. There are few better instances of iconography contributing to, and serving as an integral part of, an iconic brand than Jack Daniel's.

The second example is that of Johnnie Walker. By the end of the 1990s, the blended scotch whiskey category had seen a significant decline in volume and popularity. Young men were increasingly turning to clear liquors like vodka. Brands like Grey Goose were beginning to attract new users through their contemporary image, premium packaging, and mixability. The tired, clichéd associations of material success that the scotch category had exploited for decades were losing relevance for the younger drinkers essential for the long-term health of any alcohol brand. Predictable imagery of self-satisfied business types in private libraries and country clubs had lost its appeal.

Global research at the time indicated that the nature of masculine success was no longer about material wealth, social status, and recognition. It now had an internal quality, and was about self-improvement, becoming a better man. It was more about the journey than arriving. Recognizing this opportunity, Johnnie Walker would come to stand for personal progress. Instead of a reward at the end of a life, the product would be seen as fuel for the journey. To help anchor this "personal progress" meaning in the brand, Johnnie Walker turned to its iconography—specifically, to its logo and name. The Striding Man logo—an image of a man in midstride decked out in a top hat and boots, and carrying a cane—had made its first appearance on the Johnnie Walker bottle in 1909. As part of the brand restage, the resuscitated Striding Man was updated and laterally inverted. He now strode from left to right, symbolizing continuous personal advancement, and signifying the determination necessary to realize one's dreams and goals. Further, the new brand slogan of "Keep walking" echoed the brand name itself. The new campaign thus perfectly integrated a universal human truth about the desire to progress as a person, and a universally meaningful icon. Needless to say, the "Keep walking" campaign was a huge success.

SOURCE: The JOHNNIE WALKER STRIDING MAN device and KEEP WALKING tagline ("courtesy of Diageo").

Becoming iconic is challenging enough for brands; remaining so is even more so. Brands such as Jack Daniel's, Disney, and Coca-Cola have succeeded in evolving over time, refreshing their myths while staying true to their heritage, keeping contemporary and relevant without straying from their ideals and values. It is with such brands in mind that the following definition of an iconic brand is offered:

Iconic brand: a highly recognizable and meaningful brand with enduring cultural resonance.

Brands that transcend their product categories and become compelling symbols for a set of values and ideals can take their place alongside other cultural icons. Like those cultural icons, they become at once a kind of symbolic shorthand and beacon of meaning within society. Maintaining such a lofty position is the definitive test of meaning management.

CONCLUSION

In today's postmodern marketing world, transactions and interactions between marketers and consumers are, above all else, exchanges of meanings. Brands provide benefits in the form of meanings. Consumers interpret and recycle these meanings, and assign their own, in an ongoing process of brand co-creation. Ultimately, they are the arbiters of brand meaning. The foundations of brand meaning are personal, cultural, tribal, and mythic. Brands help people to satisfy their material, symbolic, and emotional needs and aspirations. The meanings people find, and create, in brands help them make sense of, and give shape to, the world around them. Brands help people to define themselves and their place in that world. From an identity viewpoint, the brand performs as a badge and beacon. From a narrative perspective, the brand is an allegory, an encapsulated myth. The implications of all this for brand meaning managers are clear:

- Don't let the product define the brand; let meanings and ideas define the brand. When the brand idea is the product itself, the brand is limited (that's why Polaroid all but disappeared).
- The brand idea is that which meaningfully differentiates the brand. If there is no brand idea, there is no brand.
- Don't let the advertising define the brand; let the brand define the advertising. In fact, brand meaning managers should think

in terms of brand communication rather than advertising, and brand slogans rather than campaign taglines.

- People are natural born storytellers and self-narrators. They are drawn to brand mythology. An engaging brand narrative, imaginatively brought to life at different points of contact with the consumer, will help people understand what the brand stands for and stimulate them to become co-authors of the ongoing brand story.
- The most meaningful brands of all are those that become icons in their own right. Very few brands will ever attain this status, but by following some of the best practices and learnings from existing iconic brands, marketing managers can set their brands on a path that will lead them to a position of greater strength and resonance.

The complexity of brand management is greater today than at any time. The underlying principles, though, remain the same. By identifying and tapping the sources of brand meaning, by understanding the nuanced meanings that brands come to hold for people, and by deftly managing those meanings, brand owners can continue to create and sustain truly meaningful brands.

Section 2

From Niche to Mainstream

Chapter 3

The Power of Words and Stories

John Simmons

Some years ago a question finally became inevitable—and answerable in only one way. The question was: "How do brands communicate if they don't use words?" When I started asking this question of design and brand agencies, there was some uneasy avoidance of eye contact. The reality was that until then, the eyes had it. Brands were understood almost entirely through their visual expressions: a logotype, typefaces, color, the use of photography, or illustration.

But what about the words? I started exploring the possibility of creating distinctive words as an essential element of a brand's personality. At first this was called *tone of voice* and then *verbal identity*. With *verbal* identity I wanted to position the importance of a brand's words alongside its *visual* identity. It was simply to say both aspects—words and images—matter, and they should be seen as working together and reinforcing each other.

LEADING BY EXAMPLE

Examples of this started to become public. The definition of a brand's verbal identity started from the same models that gave visual clues to branding. Brand models showed definitions of a brand's vision and mission, personality, values, and the *idea* that runs through a brand. It was a natural extension to add *tone of voice values* to this, and to relate them to the way the brand overall was defined.

For example, the brand values *understanding, integrity, and passion* mean that:

- We should avoid using language that creates barriers to understanding by being too technical or jargon-ridden.
- We should not use language that undermines our integrity by being too pushy and hard sell.
- We should beware of language that fails to express passion by being boring and flat. (Air Products brand guidelines)

Tone of voice became a powerful means for many brands to connect more engagingly with different audiences, whether internal or external. In many ways, it was most liberating for companies that had low-key approaches to the visual aspect of branding. For example, Air Products (the example shown earlier) is a multinational gases and chemicals company, thinking of its communications as *business to business.* The company is in the Fortune 500, based in Allentown, Pennsylvania on a vast campus, but with operating businesses located around the world.

The dominant spirit of the company was that of the engineer: practical, rational, technical. But it became clear to me that Air Products' success as a business came from its engineers' ability to listen to its customers and solve problems. In doing so, they formed good working relationships that involved the use of stories on both sides. From those relationships sprang examples of innovation that allowed the company to lead in its areas of technology—through applied rather than pure science. As a result, we defined the brand in a particular way with "Relationships built on understanding" at the heart of the brand. The company, being engineers, decided to test the strength of this positioning through extensive global research. They tested it against two other positionings, but the results of the research were overwhelmingly positive about "Relationships built on understanding." Customers and employees recognized its truth to Air Products.

The next step was to look at the visual and verbal aspects of branding. The company was reluctant to change very much visually, so the main thrust there was to move to a cleaner, more contemporary design approach without changing the logo. But there was much more scope for changing the company's use of language.

WORDS BUILD RELATIONSHIPS

The key to it was the central idea which had come from an insight about the company's way of building relationships with customers. In the course of conversations to establish an understanding of the customer's technical problems, it was easy to imagine the phrase "Tell me more" being used to draw out more information. So this phrase became integral to the brand and the starting point for the use of language. It followed that the tone would be more informal and conversational than it had been previously. A more human style emerged, person to person, rather than the corporate persona implied by *business to business.*

Tone of voice guidelines and workshops followed, to establish the language principles in the company. This was helped by a brand management team inside the business who adopted the approach with some enthusiasm. From their point of view, it enabled the company to communicate more effectively. "Tell me more" became a mantra for them, not so much a corporate strapline, as a way of thinking. It guided their approach, for example, to the receiving and giving of briefs, and established the brand team as an intelligent, helpful part of the business. It also meant that informal meetings could be shifted from corporate meeting rooms to the much friendlier, welcoming environment of the new "Tell me more" café on the Allentown campus.

"Tell me more" was also an invitation to tell more stories. We started gathering and writing these, moving from drily factual case studies to real stories that brought out the personalities of Air Products people. It became clear from this and from working with other brands that such stories were a good way to express a more ownable and personal way of expressing what makes a particular brand different.

AN INNOCENT TONE

Other brands were making similar discoveries. In the United Kingdom, but since then spreading to many other European countries, Innocent Drinks came up with a brand tone of voice and form of storytelling that has been much imitated. Innocent makes smoothies out of fruits and nothing but fruits. A natural product received a natural tone of voice that became a word-of-mouth phenomenon. People (myself included) bought Innocent smoothies because they were delicious *and* because they used the space on the packaging to tell stories that made you smile while drinking a smoothie. They also had an authentic *founding story* that gave a real sense of the brand's personality. This appeared on the company's website (http://www.innocentdrinks.co.uk/us/our-story, accessed on March 11, 2014):

> *In the summer of 1998 when we had developed our first smoothie recipes but were still nervous about giving up our proper jobs, we bought £500 worth of fruit, turned it into smoothies and sold them from a stall at a little music festival in London. We put up a big sign saying 'Do you think we should give up our jobs to make these smoothies?' and put out a bin saying 'YES' and a bin saying 'NO' and asked people to put the empty bottle in the right bin. At the end of the weekend the 'YES' bin was full so we went in the next day and resigned.*

LOOK AT THE FOUNDATIONS

All companies have founding stories. Few companies tell them and, after a while, many companies forget the original sense of purpose that led to the founding. If told as a genuine story, the founding story can create a great connection between a brand and its followers, even if the brand goes back 250 years. For example, working with Guinness, I was asked to find stories about Guinness that would demonstrate the truth of its freshly defined brand idea "Guinness reflects your inner strength." The global brand team had arrived at this definition through meetings and workshops around the world. Guinness was a famous product and brand wherever it was sold, in Europe, Africa, the United States, and Asia, but it was marketed differently everywhere. The new brand definition enabled much greater consistency and efficiency in marketing. But they needed evidence, a glue to bind everything together. We came up with stories of decisive moments in Guinness's history and told these in a book and at gatherings of the Guinness global community. For me, the most important of these was the founding story, telling how Arthur Guinness defended his right to use Dublin's water in his beer-making process back in the 18th century.

> *But it was water that did it. The whole history of Guinness is built on water.*
>
> *Think of that the next time you sink a pint. If Arthur hadn't made his first stand against the bureaucrats and stood up for his commercial rights we wouldn't be here now thinking of new ways to fight the Guinness cause.*
>
> *"I did a deal, dammit, so let's stick to it!"*
>
> *Arthur stuck to it. It took him twelve years to win his fight for the Dublin water rights, but he won. And that was the first crucial turning point in the story of Guinness.*
>
> *It takes strength to do it. Not necessarily the girder-lifting strength of a strong man, but the commitment that comes with an inner certainty.*
>
> *Think about it. Savour it. And lift your glass to Arthur.*
>
> *We owe it to him.* (Internal Guinness book *Believe*, by author, published by Guinness for its worldwide marketing teams)

As a result, the year 1759, when the company began, took on even greater importance in the brand's thinking. It started appearing more prominently on labels and advertising, and for a couple of years *1759 moments* became part of the brand's internal communication program. The number could be seen not just as a date in history but also, 17:59, as that time on a Friday evening that signaled the end of the working week. So every week new stories would go out by emails to the Guinness marketing team around the world. These email stories would reflect on the week just passed and give people food for thought for the week that was to begin on Monday. Here is one of those stories:

> *Sometimes you need to face facts. Actually you need to do that all the time. Fact 1: many people don't like the taste of Guinness. Fact 2: tough!*
>
> *So let's face facts and be true to ourselves. That's the line the South African team took when introducing "New Guinness ES. The less preferred beer." With a*

campaign created by Saatchi & Saatchi, they came out loud and proud and said "you're either with us or you're not." The cheeky, irreverent campaign featured a Complaints Hotline on radio ads and messages like "0.34% of beer drinkers can't be wrong" on billboards. It made people laugh, and it made people talk. And it recognised that Guinness is an acquired taste.

It was just a case of meeting the barriers to drinking Guinness head-on. Which then happened to turn into 22,000 cases of Guinness ES, 40% over target. And everyone found it liberating, as well as a phenomenal success. Because Guinness isn't for everyone, let's be honest. Only for people with taste. As the billboard ad said "Joe Bloggs hated it." Want one? Good for you. And who wants to be Joe Bloggs? (Email written by author for Guinness in 2004)

WHOSE STORY IS IT?

This all gave an extra meaning to Jeff Bezos' (Amazon's founder) saying: "A brand is what people say about you when you're not in the room." The best stories about a brand are those told by customers who tell others about extraordinary examples of customer service and brand behavior. Brands cannot control such stories, but they can encourage them by being very clear about their own narrative. Politicians, for example, are now determined to establish campaign narratives driven by their policies and beliefs—and to avoid media stories that do the opposite. Successive American Presidential elections have made the *narrative* the key element of the candidate's campaign.

Our understanding of brands has developed in recent times from a focus on consumer products to encompass politics, sports, and countries. The 2012 Olympic Games in London was an interesting example. Here is a global event that attracts the world's biggest brands which seek to link their own brand stories to those of the world's greatest sportsmen and sportswomen. So they sponsor the Olympics, tacking themselves to borrowed stories of human achievement, and its power to motivate internal and external adherents to particular brands. It's a small, obvious step for a company like BP to promote British athletes and to make a link to itself through *performance.*

At the same time, no one had grasped the opportunity well in terms of language and storytelling—at least not until the opening ceremony. This was an event of great creativity and imagination that worked by being single-minded in its determination to tell stories that would project the brand of Britain to the world. So the performance in the Olympic Stadium began quietly with a bucolic scene of rural life, with country people and farm animals, before this idyll was swept away by furnaces and clangor of the Industrial Revolution. Isambard Kingdom Brunel watched inventions being forged in fire in a frenzied rush through 19th-century history. At the heart of the 20th-century story were two narrative threads: the creation of the National Health Service (NHS) and the importance of children's stories in the British culture. From Peter Pan through to Harry Potter, the show celebrated Britain's gift of great stories to the world. With the dance of doctors, nurses, and children almost trampolining on hospital beds, the performance proclaimed Britain's pride in its ability to care for the physical and imaginative well-being of young people.

Now this might have been baffling to many viewers who saw it in other countries—and it might seem even more baffling as you now read this if you did not see the show—but this was a brand story of enormous emotional power to its British audience. The creators had taken the brave decision to make that audience the primary one. If parts of the world were baffled, then as Guinness put it in the earlier example: "Tough." The first need was to get as many of the country's own population behind the Olympics as possible: joyful volunteering, crowd enthusiasm, and national engagement would follow and communicate these qualities to the watching world in every event. The way to achieve that was through the performance of stories, because stories have such potential to move hearts and minds. It certainly worked.

This raises another truth about brands: they cannot be loved by everyone. You cannot attempt to please all the people, all the time. If you do, you will create a bland brand that will touch people only at the most superficial level. But brands that create real brand loyalty—Apple, for example—do so by taking risks. The willingness to take risks becomes part of that brand's story. It took a brand from outside the mobile phone world to take the risk, to do the essential rethinking of needs and possibilities, to make the leaps of faith, and to come up with the iPhone. The Apple story continues to develop with each new product and venture, but, like all good stories, it has real people at its heart. For many years, Steve Jobs—a man with a human story of personal struggle against sickness—represented the Apple brand. Who will now carry forward the story by embodying the Apple brand? Time will tell.

STORIES ARE INDIVIDUAL AND UNIVERSAL

The drama inherent in a struggle against life-threatening illness is familiar to us all. Stories make connections between the individual and the universal, and this is the source of their power. This too was a feature of the Olympic opening ceremony, and it linked the two narrative threads I referred to earlier. Since the foundation of the NHS in 1948, individual hospitals have established international reputations. Great Ormond Street Hospital, for example, has become globally famous, a brand in its own right, for the quality of its care for sick children. As a brand, it has benefitted from investment generated by its Tear Fund. This receives enormous support from the public who relate to its heart-warming stories of compassion, but it is significant in the context of this chapter to point out that one storyteller and one famous story provide a significant amount of its historic funding.

Peter Pan

Peter Pan—the boy who would not grow up—has been helping other children to grow up for over 80 years.

"Peter Pan by David Wyatt © 2006 Great Ormond Street Hospital Children's Charity"

Sir J.M. Barrie gave all the rights to play and novel Peter Pan to the hospital in April 1929, and since then the children's classic has continued to benefit its patients.

The Olympic opening ceremony and Great Ormond Street Hospital examples are unusual in terms of conventional branding. With the Olympics, it would be more usual to write about the Olympic rings, the values of the movement based on the achievements gained by international competition, the use of symbols such as the torch, medals and flags, the London logo, and colors splashed everywhere across the city and the world. I have focused on the importance of the story because it seems to me vital to the London Olympic brand's success, and because it is relatively unrecognized, almost invisible, except that the stories generate and are generated by the visual symbols, for example, the Olympic torch and flame. These symbols became more powerful because of their ability to inspire a stream of stories with which people identify. The torch relay drew enormous crowds across Britain every day in the lead-up to the 2012 Olympics. The relay allowed individual stories of human heroism and local pride to be told through the media and word of mouth.

WHAT'S THE DIFFERENCE?

More overtly commercial brands have much to learn from these examples, just as the Olympics has learnt much from the expertise of commercial companies in visual branding. Brands now routinely include *tone of voice* in the essential elements of branding and they are becoming increasingly aware of the potential of storytelling. The branding discipline of tone of voice—a vital part of verbal identity—helps any brand to communicate more effectively and more consistently the messages that matter to it. Yet there is an issue to be faced in relation to the central branding issue of differentiation. After all, differentiation is the reason for branding. You need to show what makes your brand special and different from other competing brands.

With tone of voice, now that most brands are embracing it, there is a danger that too many brands are beginning to sound too much like each other. For example, I mentioned Innocent Drinks earlier as a pioneer in the use of distinctive brand language. The labels on their smoothies' bottles would talk like this:

> You can tell if a pineapple is ready to eat by sniffing its bottom (it should smell all ripe and pineappley). And seeing as sniffing at bottoms in public is a rare treat, it's worth having a go. Sure, you might get a few funny looks in the supermarket. And the manager might ask you to leave the store for interfering with tropical fruit. But then again, you'll be the one going home with a tasty ripe pineapple for your tea. PS: please remember to stick to pineapples.

When Innocent first entered the market, this tone—conversational, natural, gently funny like a friend chatting to you—was a breath of fresh air. I believe it remains so because Innocent have managed, through skilled writing, to keep the brand's language developing. But other brands have tried to adopt the same exterior of language without realizing that the distinctiveness of a brand's words must come from a reality deep inside the brand. There is no point—indeed there is a dishonesty—in so many brands talking to you as if they were your best mate. If the bank, or accountancy firm, or lawyer, were a person you look to them to provide an efficient service. But you probably would not invite them into your kitchen for a bit of banter over a cup of coffee.

The reality is that tone of voice can provide some level of differentiation but much of the times its results are relatively generic. "We want our language to be clear, warm and fresh" generally captures what many brands are doing with their approach to tone of voice. There are certain principles of writing that help to achieve that: active not passive verbs, writing in the first not third person, avoidance of long, convoluted sentences. It's the Plain English Campaign with a sprinkling of extra personality. But let's not forget that that is itself eminently worth doing when surveys show that customers are 84 percent "more likely to trust a brand that uses simple, jargon-free language" (Siegel + Gale survey).

BEYOND THE PLAIN

Story, however, has the ability to do something extra about this. While there is a common ground between tone of voice guidelines for many brands, each brand can find more genuine differentiation, even uniqueness, in its individual stories.

Let's take the example of Three, the mobile phone/broadband company which operates in many markets around the world. This is an extract from a document written for its own brand teams:

> Customers respond well to brands where the dots are all joined up, where the brochure is written in the same language as the direct mail, which fits with the believable script in the call centre, and whose shops tell the same story in 3D. The user experience is complete and whole and marvellous. The brand experiences all add-ups to the same clear, great story. It sounds a bit like the unattainable holy grail, or brand heaven, only found in dreams, but it does happen. But it doesn't happen by accident. ("A celebration of Ten Years of Three," published by WHAM, 2013. It was written by author and distributed only to staff members of Three as a gift to celebrate 10 years in business. Not available to the public.)

The company and brand Three only came into being in 2003, so it's very much a global brand of the 21st century. It grew up with the notion well established of tone of voice as an integral element of the brand. It started with such a commitment to mobile broadband—the 3G technology—that it featured it even in its name. By contrast, Three's competitors developed from the late 20th century mobile phone technology and the business model that went with it. This meant that, even in this new market with relatively new technology everywhere, Three was able to set itself apart as different in its vision, thinking, and language in relation to its brand.

Tone of voice—first summed up for Three in a booklet called *A pocketful of Oomph*—was identified as an important branding issue from the start. We expressed the aspiration for Three's language like this in the booklet:

> *So we went on a journey. We wanted to find the right words. The words that we can all use and say "That's 3."*
>
> *We've come to know the look of the 3 brand pretty well. But what does it sound like? What signals do our words send when people hear them or read them? They must be saying something about 3—but are they saying what we want them to say?*
>
> *Perhaps, we thought, the day will come when we can close our eyes, listen and say "That's 3." Our journey has only just begun. As we get a feel for how 3 sounds, we'll also become more comfortable with 3 words, our language, our style. Our words will begin to feel a strong part of the 3 identity.* (*Three's Tone of Voice Guidelines*, by author)

The initial tone of voice for Three was based on principles that aimed to achieve simplicity, energy, and emotion in language. We used before and after examples in the guidelines and there were regular workshops that trained Three's own staff and agencies in the tone of voice. One important aim, and achievement, was to reduce the generic oversell that is common in this kind of market. We were able to challenge lazy formulaic conventions like "while stocks last"—replacing it with phrases like "there's only 1,157 left (and counting)." Styles that didn't fit with the brand personality were laughed out of use.

> **The parody policeman**—don't be too formal or straight-laced
> **Cheesy cliché**—no naff stock phrases
> **The relentless salesman**—*exciting, amazing, fantastic*... they just don't sound believable
> **The exclamation mark**—it's just too shouty!!! Take it off and you'll find it makes us sound more confident. (*Three's Tone of Voice Guidelines,* by author)

All of this provided, Three with an approach to its language gave distinctiveness to the brand. But, to be honest, I'm not sure if we ever passed that "close your eyes, that's 3" test. This was partly because Three is such a restless, fast-changing brand (even shifting brand naming conventions between 3/Three) that it adapted its tone of voice guidance regularly while keeping to the overall framework. And it was partly because its competitors were adopting similar principles, either in imitation or because they made such sense.

DISTINCTIVENESS FROM STORYTELLING

But, in the end, Three did achieve a distinctiveness through its story. It had been the first mobile company completely committed to broadband (rather than seeing paid calls and texts as the immovable foundation stones of its revenue). As the technology improved, moving reality closer to its vision, the Three story became more credible and more individual. By the end of 2012, nearly 10 years old and ready to celebrate its anniversary, the story of Three could be written with confidence. It could also set out its place in history with a playful sense of wonder at the rapid passing of time. For example:

> In 2003, Dolly, the world's first cloned sheep, died. The Iraq war began. China sent its first man into space, and Concorde scheduled its last flight. Technology was in flux. A new company called Three launched in Australia, Austria, Denmark, Italy, Sweden and the UK.
>
> ...
>
> In 2012 Aung San SuuKyi, recently released from a Burmese prison, accepted the Nobel Peace Prize. The London Olympic and Paralympic Games were watched by record audiences. The internet turned thirty. In Austria, Three bought Orange. (*Three's Tone of Voice Guidelines*, by author)

The use of story in that way (as one of many possible ways) allowed Three to project its own view of the world. The tone is true to the brand (there are no parody policemen or relentless salesmen in the style), but what makes it true to the brand is its easy association of Three with the forward movement of the world and technology. Three defined its outlook as "the natural next step," whereas other brands might have spoken of "our commitment to innovation."

There is, then, a close connection between brand tone of voice and story. Brands will find it more effective to tell their stories by developing their tone of voice, and they will find it easier to create a distinctive tone of voice by telling stories that are close to them. Sometimes that will be the founder's story, sometimes it will be case studies about customers or products, and sometimes it will even be the essential brand story. In the latter case, *story* is almost identical to brand. As the Guinness brand team put it, "all brands are stories."

A COFFEE BREAK

Let me take one final example, one of the world's most ubiquitous brands—Starbucks. In my book *The Starbucks Story* (originally *My Sister's a Barista*), I described Starbucks as the quintessential modern brand. It is actually one of the purest examples of a brand that we have. It starts with a commodity product—coffee beans—and invests them with extraordinary added value by creating an experience that transcends the simple act of drinking an unnecessary beverage.

As with any brand, there is a name; the right name can immediately start to suggest a tone of voice or story, because a name is based on words. Through its choice of name, from the very start, Starbucks suggested that it recognized a link to the adventure and romance of storytelling. The founders of the company took the name from a character in the classic American novel *Moby Dick* by Herman Melville. Starbuck was the first mate who sailed on the ship skippered by the mad Captain Ahab, a man obsessed by the need to hunt down the white whale of the book's title. There is no use of the Melville story in the Starbucks brand yet the reference established, at least in the founders' minds, the idea of a constant quest for something difficult to find and worth hunting for: in their case perfect coffee beans rather than a large sea mammal. They set up their first shop in Pike Place Market in the west coast city of Seattle. Here they faced across the Pacific Ocean, with trading boats sailing in and out of port, carrying fresh goods to and from all parts of the world. Starbucks became the ideal brand name that had the additional advantage of suggesting a visual image. The siren or mermaid figure in Starbucks' logo is now one of the most easily recognized anywhere in the world.

In time, particularly after Howard Schultz's entry into the business 30 years ago, Starbucks also began to develop its own brand language. Schultz had been inspired in the design of his shops by real Italian coffee bars, but he also adopted and subtly adapted the international language of coffee as if it were the brand's native language, with words now used every day that were unknown to most people a couple of decades ago. Starbucks has a core vocabulary of such product words derived from Italian. So mine's a doppio espresso with a tally skinny latte to go and a venti mocha cappuccino with cinnamon on top. The words are spoken in an international tone that keeps a trace of its Seattle provenance: a laid-back, west coast, easygoing feel that makes it natural to treat yourself regularly to a coffee break. But it's a break in the *third place* between work and home, a place where you might meet your friends socially or have an informal business meeting.

THE STORY CYCLE

The rise of Starbucks was inexorable for at least two decades, while the brand's way of life and language became accepted and desirable throughout the world. Yet cycles are inevitable in business: such cycles, the rise and fall and rise again of businesses, are also story structures in themselves. By the mid-2000s, Howard Schultz had withdrawn from day-to-day running of the company. Things started to go badly. Trading performance declined. Schultz watched in exasperation from the sidelines until he decided he could bear no more. He stepped back into the company as CEO at the beginning of 2008.

Howard Schultz returned because he believed that Starbucks had *lost its soul*. He was determined to recover it by returning to the principles that had created the Starbucks brand, as well as bringing in thinking about the future. On February 26, 2008, Howard Schultz closed every Starbucks store in the United States. It was a dramatic and unprecedented move. The one-day store closure was to retrain the baristas, to reassert the Starbucks romance with coffee, and to send out a signal about the brand's continuing story based on the love of its product. This came with a huge risk and cost—actual and potential—but it paid off. Stock that had been trading at $7 subsequently rose to $55 after Schultz's return to brand principles.

What Howard Schultz did was to reassert the importance of the Starbucks story and his own personal story. This story is about a passion for coffee as a drink, but also as an occasion and sometimes a metaphor for relaxed human interaction. As a symbol of his return to first principles, Schultz took to brandishing his key to the original Pike Place store in meetings, emphasizing his personal, emotional attachment. His team also redrafted the mission statement to begin with the following words: "To inspire and nurture the human spirit—one person, one cup and one neighborhood at a time."

Starbucks is a brand that (genuinely, I believe) thinks it can and should be a force for good in the world. In demonstrating that, through work in local communities that neighbor its shops, as well as in the places where its coffee beans are grown, Starbucks is constantly creating stories. It uses these, mainly, for internal consumption, as they might be treated cynically if broadcast constantly to the outside world. But, in a sense, this deepens the power of the stories by removing them from the arena of spin and PR. They are held close to the heart of the brand, as examples to people inside the business of what makes Starbucks different. For example, after the New Orleans devastation, Starbucks partners (their name for *employees*) voluntarily contributed their own efforts to help get the city on its feet again. It's part of Starbucks' mission to do that wherever they operate: one person, one cup, one neighborhood, and perhaps one story at a time.

CONCLUSION

So my main conclusions are, I hope, clear. Verbal identity needs to be seen alongside visual identity as an essential aspect of branding. Verbal identity is made up of all the verbal elements that a brand relies on to communicate its personality and values: its name, tone of voice, straplines, messages, and stories. The aim of all these elements is to build awareness, loyalty, and affection toward the brand—and to show how it is different from any other competitor.

It has become accepted that brands are powerful as central organizing tools of management. Define the brand and it will drive your business's direction; it will give you a constant touchstone against which to assess courses of action. You need words to do that, but also the right words. It's important to remember that brands are, and have always been, creations even if we derive them from reality and insist that they reflect the truth. All this means that branding needs to be a creative discipline in business not just a managerial one. And brands need to be creative with words just as much as with images.

Chapter 4

All Together Now: The New and Vital Strategy of "Community"

Douglas Atkin

"Community is becoming the Marketing Plan." "In the next few years, Community will be one of the top three or four drivers of the Business." "Community is the customer experience."

These statements, and many like them, have been made to me over the past few months by founders of new hypergrowth companies, marketing directors of old and established brands, and C-suite directors of major companies. Yet six years ago, *Community* was unheard of as any kind of business strategy.

What's led to this rapid innovation? Why has it become so central to both the customer's experience of the brand and the company's success as a business? And how do you get one? It certainly doesn't *appear* as easy as, say, in the good old days when I was a brand manager at P&G and could rustle up a new ad campaign or fiendishly clever in-store promotion and significantly affect the business. And, in fact, it's not. There are more moving parts, more intelligent and subtle strategies and tactics required, and frankly, less control than in the glorious days when the brand manager felt like master of all he or she surveyed.

But there are also many more rewards, both for the customer who experiences a well-built brand community and the brand that enables it.

IT IS (MOSTLY) ABOUT LOYALTY

> I think a lot of Mac users feel like almost personally responsible for the well being of like the mother company. I'm much more prone to like buy directly from Apple rather than through a re-seller. It's because you want ... you want Apple to get everything ... you want them to get your money. It's almost like a charity case, it's like take my money. (Sean, an impecunious student who could barely afford his lunch)

> This community, it's literally based around a machine. But actually it's based around a certain way of thinking." (Paul, mid-thirties, describing what unifies the Apple community)

The strongest form of commitment you can hope for is emotionally derived. And community is the most emotional kind of loyalty you are likely get. It's hard won, but it's very. hard to shake. It takes time to build, but will last much longer than any other loyalty strategy you choose. And it is the stickiest strategy because it relies on multiple emotional bonds, not just one.

This chapter is (mostly) about loyalty. There are many more benefits derived from creating Community that are covered in this chapter. But loyalty is the biggie.

We'll look first at two very familiar and old examples of brand communities. Then we'll look in detail at more recent examples that also use the latest crop of community-building tools: Social Technologies.

EMOTIONAL VERSUS TRANSACTIONAL LOYALTY

Rewards, miles, points, goodies, and free travel are all proven ways to wed a customer to a brand. Actually, not so proven. In fact, the jury remains out on the ROI of such schemes. But even if it was indisputable that these schemes yielded results, *transactional loyalty*—loyalty based on rational trade of your or my commitment to a store/airline/publication in exchange for miles, points, access, information, or whatever—is unlikely to ever surpass *emotional loyalty*.

Ideally you should have both. But emotional loyalty trumps the transactional kind every time. Buying a customer's loyalty is never as good as a customer happily committing to a brand because they feel deeply about it and would feel a profound loss if they ever leave it.

How do you get emotional loyalty? There are many ways, but one of the best is to create a shared identity between the individual and the brand. Whether for a brand, religion, sports team, political party, or even country, close identification between it and you, especially at the level of shared values, is an extremely powerful source of commitment. Harley riders may be dentists or management consultants by day, but when they slap on their tattoos and don their leathers at the weekend, they self-identify as rebels and lovers of freedom. To leave that brand would mean leaving a part of themselves.

Imagine, then, an emotional connection that is powerful, but to the power of a million. There are over a million members of HOG, the Harley Owners Group. What makes community-driven loyalty so powerful, and why Harley devotes most of its marketing budget to supporting this huge group, is that they not only identify with the brand, but with each other as well. To leave that brand would not only be saying goodbye to a great product, but it would also mean saying goodbye to the brotherhood with whom you share values, experiences, and memories. Whether the Harley riders I spoke to were on the lam, cops, or CEOs of big companies, what unified them was that deep down they saw themselves as rebels. It may be taboo to admit this, but they were not themselves when amongst the things that society says we all *should* love—a good career, a nice house, even our lovely families. They only felt they became their true selves when drinking beer with their brothers and shooting the breeze around their bikes, or turning disapproving heads as they roared past as a pack. Leaving that community would mean breaking a multitude of bonds forged by the strongest of ties: emotional.

MANY BONDS ARE BETTER THAN ONE

Brands are discovering the benefits of relationships not just *with* their customers, but also enabling relationships *between* their customers.

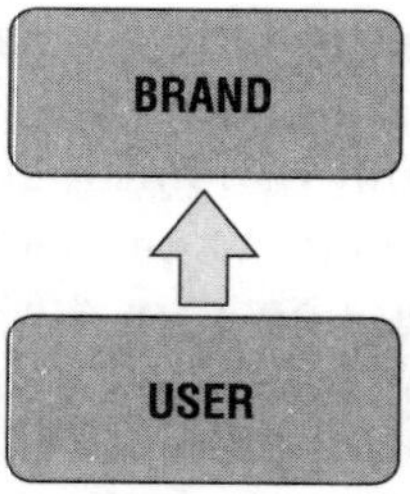

When you build a community around a brand, the bond is not just between the user and the brand, but also between the user and all the other users who, like him or her, buy into the identity and values of the brand. This triangulated relationship is much stronger than the single user-to-brand bond.

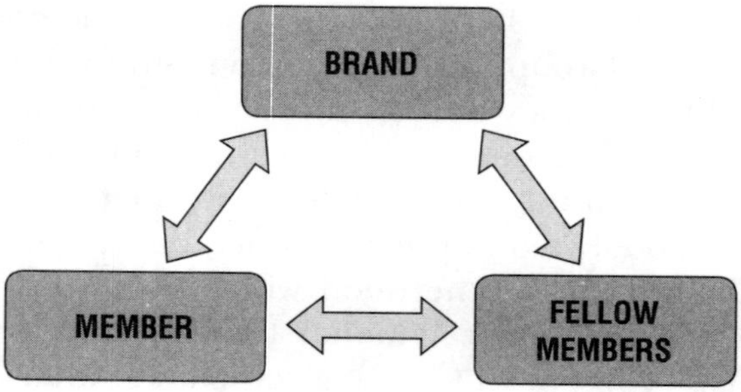

For example, I may have bought into Apple not just because the products are good, but because they've stood for creativity, nonconformity, and passion—qualities I've prided myself (well, perhaps deluded myself) define me. When I wrote my book (*The Culting of Brands*) about this very subject, I would escape the office to write in a Soho café in New York whose regulars were journalists, writers, and university professors. We all knew each other by our first names. And we all used Macs. It was sort of a given we used Macs. We never discussed it. But if someone walked in with a Dell, the temperature palpably dropped. We were perfectly polite to them should they talk to us. But they would never return.

To leave the Apple fraternity would be to sever both conscious and unconscious bonds I've had with people I consider to be *like me.* This triangulated relationship between the brand, me, and the other members of the community who also buy into the same values and share the same identity as I do is much harder to break than the single bond between an individual and a brand they love.

Nowadays there are tools that can scale this: enable more people to find and engage richly with *like-others* rather than serendipitously stumbling upon them in a café. Brands can be the standard-bearers of well-defined and tightly bound communities. But now there are tools that enable them to instigate and nurture these bonds at great scale, to both their customers' and their own advantage.

A NEW GENERATION OF BRANDS IS BUILDING IN COMMUNITY FROM THE GET-GO

This could just have been a story about a new brand that reinvented an old business (guest accommodation) by introducing value and an efficient marketplace. That would have been interesting enough. What makes it especially interesting is that Airbnb put community into the center of the customer experience from Day 1. And four years later, it's pouring investment into Community because the founders believe it's the fuel for the company's meteoric growth.

Mark Andreessen—inventor of the modern web browser, Internet guru, and leading Silicon Valley Venture Capitalist—has called Airbnb one of the very few hypergrowth companies that have ever existed. Instead of booking a hotel room for a business or vacation trip, travelers can now go to Airbnb, key in their destination, and choose from tens of thousands of rooms hosted by private citizens in their houses, apartments, boats, tree houses, and even caves. Hosts and guests rate each other after the stay, and Airbnb takes care of the money exchange—it's as simple as that.

Except that, in four years the number of guests using Airbnb to stay in New York City (NYC) alone has grown from 30 to 10,000 each night. It's bitten 10 percent out of the hotel market in Manhattan. In June 2012, Airbnb celebrated 10 million guest nights booked globally on 200,000 listings in 192 countries. And to think that this came from a couple of guys who, desperate to pay the rent, blew up three air mattresses and charged people to sleep on them during an overbooked conference in San Francisco in 2008.

Even though Airbnb is now the biggest provider of accommodation in Manhattan, London, San Francisco, and many other locations, it doesn't see its core competence as an accommodation provider. Joe Gebbia, one of the three co-founders, told me that he defined his business this way:

> Airbnb is a place where what is inspiring in every person, in every home, in every country on the planet, can be shared.

In other words, he sees Community at the heart of the customer experience. And he is laboring to ensure that that can become even more fundamental as the company grows. The founders realized what business they were in on day three of the company's existence when they hosted their first guests.

> I remember coming down the stairs that first morning and Michael (a 45-year-old designer and family man) was laying on his airbed in the kitchen in his whitey tighties, and we started talking about industrial design. And then the woman from Boston comes down for breakfast and we started talking and she says to me, "Oh I have some ideas for how to improve your website." And then the guy from India comes down and he's a grad student and he starts talking about his project, which is about artificial intelligence. It was just such a cool experience. And for us it transcended so far beyond money it wasn't even funny. And I remember our guests leaving and Brian (co-founder and CEO) and I looked at each other and said: "Oh my God, did that just happen? We have to do more of this and let more people share in this as well." That weekend was a big light bulb.

Airbnb has moved on from air mattresses on the floor to hosts offering a Frank Lloyd Wright house for $1,000 a night to a room in a Manhattan apartment for $95 a night to a Mongolian Yurt in Germany for $42 a night. But the motivation to invite complete strangers into your home is not just the revenue they generate. Michelle, a host in NYC, now earns most of her income from the five rooms she rents through Airbnb in her loft in Brooklyn. But it is not just about the money: "The benefit of Airbnb is that you're not just sharing your space, but your culture."

The founders of the company quickly identified that the essential benefit of the brand to its customers was not just tangible. It was not just cheap accommodation for guests or extra income for hosts.

It was the exchange of ideas, culture, experiences, and the emerging friendships that would often occur. The transactional benefit was income earned (hosts) and money saved (guests). The emotional benefit was the community that emerged between the two.

Having understood that community was at the center of the customer experience, they are now building their own community platform to enable hosts to engage and support each other, guests to congregate and build relationships around shared travel interests, and for hosts and guests to interact beyond their stay. It's a big investment and a significant move for a company that is only four years old and still focusing on developing its core business. But they are making this bet precisely because they see Community as integral to their future.

WHY IS A COMMUNITY STRATEGY SO IMPORTANT TO AIRBNB?

Community is the core benefit delivered by a brand. It's not necessarily apparent either to hosts before they start hosting or the guests before they enjoy their first stay. Just like it was not immediately obvious to the founders that first weekend. But it emerged as the key benefit nonetheless.

However, there are significant additional benefits they are reaping (especially now that they have built their own recently launched Community Platform) that also happen to align closely to those that other brands have discovered.

Brand Advocacy

"The first week, our revenue was $200. By the second week it was $400. After four weeks we were up to $1,600." Joe told me. This exponential growth, albeit with tiny amounts at the very early days, has continued to the present day as the company passes 10 million nights booked. And it is largely the result of word of mouth by passionate brand advocates.

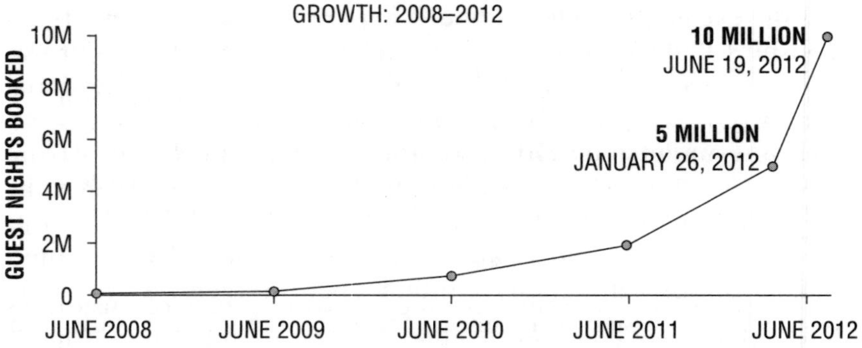

SOURCE: www.Airbnb.com, accessed April 24, 2014.

Customer advocacy (the best marketing that exists) is one of the happy outcomes of Community. Like all good things, it is not that easy to generate. Especially if you're the impecunious founder of a start-up, discovering that starting a start-up is really not that glamorous. Chastised by an early investor to leave San Francisco and "go to where your customers are," Brian Chessky (co-founder and CEO) and Joe Gebbia tramped around New York with a rented Nikon 5 camera and visited each of the first 30 hosts, taking pictures of the properties to improve their presence on the website and thus increase bookings.

> It was on this third trip that we came back to New York and it was February and it was really cold, snowdrifts were everywhere, my socks were soaked, I had 20 lbs. of camera equipment on my back, the sun had set and I was lost in Brooklyn, it was a blizzard, I was at an intersection, my iPhone was dead and I thought "wow is this what it's like to be an Internet entrepreneur?"

The answer was yes, and through it they learnt a valuable lesson. Get out from the office and talk to your customers. As well as taking photographs, Joe and Brian would listen to their customers' needs and phone them back to Nate (the third founder, and programmer) in San Francisco who would code the improvements overnight. By the third week, realizing that as the number of hosts grew and they couldn't visit each one individually, they invited groups of hosts to bars and cafes to hold impromptu focus groups. What emerged was not just a more efficient way to get customer feedback but the germ of the current host-community platform.

> What captivated us was them being able to meet each other. It was very gratifying for them to meet somebody who did the same thing they did. Gives people reassurance. "Ok, I'm not crazy to invite strangers into my home." They could meet people who had the same stories to share with each other. And you could see these bonds and these friendships start to develop between the early hosts. "How do you check-in?" "I got this cleaner who helps out." "I get all these extra requests; can I send people to you?" You could see these friendships develop because of these in-person get-togethers.

The company has relied on the network effects of customers motivated by the community they felt. Hosts told their friends and families about the fun they were having, the money they were making, and how responsive the company was to their needs. Joe told me: "The Hosts became our biggest advocates. They fell in love with us. When they described us they would use the word love in the same sentence." Guests returned home, saw that they too had an extra room in their apartment in Berlin, London, or Tokyo and decided to continue the fun, make some money, and rent it out via Airbnb. "That's when the Network Effects kicked in," said Joe.

Loyalty

"It's better to have a 100 people who love you than a million people who kind of like you. That's a phrase that we throw around the company all the time." Of course, they have more than a 100 people who love them. But as Elizabeth Mueller (Airbnb's Community programs manager) told me, the focus of the company is to create experiences that make the customers love the brand. And most of those are not to do with the ease of use or cleverness of the site, but the community they feel when amongst each other.

She continued: "We know that kind of open, honest connection, not only between the user and the company, but between the users themselves is what makes it a lasting movement."

And hosts regularly redirect guests to Airbnb from other sites where their property may be listed because they prefer Airbnb to get the income. And they can get the feedback from guests and improve their reputation to get more guests on the site they love.

Customer Feedback and Co-creation

The benefits of a rapid and tight feedback loop that Brian and Joe learnt traipsing between host meetups have been operationalized. Twenty-one community managers around the world continue to run get-togethers amongst hosts to generate the benefits of community but also continue the feedback. "An investment in Community is also an investment in a two way conversation. That brings a lot of insights to the table, and helps us build intuition into our product, which creates a better user experience all around," says Elizabeth.

Improved Customer Experience

Swapping practical tips and getting emotional support from others doing the same thing enables hosts to continually improve the experience they deliver to their guests. Says Michelle, the Brooklyn host: "We share stories about our guests and what it's done to our lives. They're also a little bit of a dish session or support group" so they can share not just ideas but also reinforcement and moral support.

Being able to mentor new hosts, share top notch cleaners, refer guests to each other when fully booked, and swap tips on how to introduce guests to the city (some hosts provide subway cards, maps, an insiders list of great locations to visit, etc.) raises the standard of the product, not by the company dictating policy or investing in service programs, but by the *community helping each other be better*.

Elizabeth summed up Airbnb's focus on Community this way:

> An investment in Community helps with creating shared memories, shared identity, trust and a more supportive and integrated network of members. In a nutshell, we are successful when our community is successful. Creating the best user experience possible allows everyone to win.

ESTABLISHED BRANDS ARE RAPIDLY REENGINEERING THEIR BUSINESS MODELS TO INTEGRATE COMMUNITY

WebMD may seem like a new brand to most. It is a child of the Internet after all. But it was born before the advent of social networks as a pure-play content provider of health information. A decade later, it's become the No. 1 source of health information in the United States, gets in excess of 16 million page views a day, and is the most trusted brand in America (according to Millward Brown).

However, it's realizing it has to recalibrate its business model, its customer experience, and its product strategy if it wants to remain relevant, profitable, and a leading brand.

Bill Pence, COO and CTO of WebMD, looks at the next few years and believes: "Community will become one of the top two or three planks of the WebMD experience. In the US, consumers will be forced to take charge of their own healthcare and so community, together with their go-to professionals, will become part of their healthcare team."

This is already happening of course. WebMD has a basic Community platform (mostly just traditional forums) on which people are finding others who share their issues and giving each other the kind of support the medical professionals just can't: such as practical advice on how to live with chronic condition, and perhaps the most important benefit of community-emotional support. Here's why just one of the many users I spoke to couldn't live without this community:

> There isn't a community like it in the U.S.
> I was relieved I didn't have to walk alone.
> I hoped to find understanding … I found it.
> I've made some very good friends … we truly support each other.
> It's not just support … we've moved on from that to true friendship.
> It's all about trust and having a safe place.

The users I interviewed are already looking for ways to connect with each other beyond simple forums. This is inevitable and happens in every community. Once some users join, interact with the other members, and begin to enjoy the rewards of belonging, they will almost always want more. They begin to form deeper relationships, make friends, and will want to engage more richly with them.

WebMD has invested in its community platform to provide a multitude of ways for this to happen. The idea is to move the WebMD brand beyond *Access, Authority and Trust,* and to add *Community Support*: a growing need in the healthcare market, as Bill Pence points out. They'll continue to deliver this by providing a whole range of tools on the Community Commitment Curve (see page 75) to provide rich engagement at scale.

EVEN A UTILITARIAN PRODUCT CAN ENABLE A PASSIONATE AND CREATIVE COMMUNITY

Sharpie is definitely a child of the analog world. What's more, the product is definitely not a sexy motorbike, groovy computer, or rich source of essential information. It's a bit of plastic with some ink, and some of them are sharp.

Yet this utilitarian product has become a center of a community defined by self-expression and creativity. "Uncapping limitless possibilities" is how Ryan Rouse, the CMO, defines it. Go to Sharpie.com and you don't see a predictable catalog of products, a boring mission statement, and the company's latest stock price. Instead, there's a vivid gallery of their customers' creations using this simple product. It's playful, exciting, and all about what happens when their users get together and *uncap what's inside.*

The gallery, which is front and center, has 98,000 active registered members and 18,000 uploads of customer creations which people can comment on, share via their own networks, and fan and follow the contributors. Their 3.7 million active fans on their Facebook page can do the same as do their Instagram and Pinterest followers (30,000 and 20,000, respectively).

The brand recruited 20 of the most passionate and inspiring customers to the *Sharpie Squad* as the community's leaders. They write blog posts and feature in ads that focus on Sharpie users and their creations. I say recruit, but they're not paid. They get early access to new products and plans, and for this help the brand team *inspire, curate, and showcase* the community's output. My only criticism of Sharpie's intelligent attempt to turn a rudimentary product into a vibrant community experience is that they could do more. Like WebMD has learnt, they could provide more ways for their users to self-organize, meet-up, engage richly and form even stronger bonds, and produce even more stunning content. This is something they have planned of course.

HOW DOES COMMUNITY MAKE PEOPLE STICKY?

What Are the Ingredients of Social Glue?

Do not take as your guide the rather limp dictionary definitions of a community: usually along the lines of *a group of people sharing something in common.* Your goal should be to enable a community that people feel both committed to and compelled to recruit others into. The markers of such a community, in fact any strong community, are the following. If you can answer yes to most of these questions, you have a vibrant community on your hands.

- Does it satisfy a real need? Do its members learn more, have more fun, get more done, or get support?
- Does it have a clearly articulated purpose?
- Is it clear about who belongs and who doesn't?
- Do members feel like they're amongst *like-others*?
- Is there interaction between members?
- Are there enduring relationships formed between members that go beyond the original reason for connecting?
- Do they contribute, do they participate, and do they work together to achieve the common purpose? Being an audience is not a community.
- Do they feel responsibility for each other and the community at large?
- Are there roles, responsibilities, and jobs performed by the membership?
- Is it self-policing? Do people censure or eject unruly or unreasonable members?
- Are there guidelines, rules, or norms of behavior?

There's no space here to explain each of these in detail. So I 'll focus on the most important, all of which center around one key insight: it's the Power of the Person.

What makes communities sticky is *the people, and how much, and how richly they interact with each other.*

I first got this insight when I interviewed members of cults and cult-like organizations (including cult brands) about why members joined and stayed. Then I worked at Meetup where millions of people form offline communities about a multitude of topics, and I found the same key ingredients of social glue. Meetup is a social network that does an old thing in a new way: it enables people to meet online around shared interests and causes so they can create thriving offline communities about whatever: pugs, parenting, peak oil, whatever takes their fancy. We measured when and why people became committed to these communities.

Loyalty to the group kicked in after members attended four or five events. We found that they were no longer just showing up just to improve their Spanish, become a better knitter, or meet other parents in the neighborhood. They showed up because they wanted to see Bill, Mustapha, or Sheena again. After four or five visits, relationships began to form, a feeling of mutual responsibility emerged, and mutual support started happening.

> We have such a diversity of members from all backgrounds and professions, from plumbers to dentists, tree surgeons to television directors, car dealers to accountants.
>
> From this, if you're ever in need of advice with something (e.g., a blocked sink, what's the best second hand car to buy, or how do you do a tax return) there is always someone in the group who can help out—usually in exchange for no more than a beer or a smile.
>
> We've got a great community. (Matt—Poker Meetup Group, UK)

Community is a contact sport. The more people rub together, they stickier they become. This is the basic process of loyalty creation within any community:

Interaction ➔ Bonding ➔ Mutual Responsibility ➔ Mutual Support = Strong Social Glue

How to Ramp People Up the Commitment Curve

Your goal should be to get as *many people* as you can to interact with each other as *frequently* as you can. But that's not all. In order to get a highly committed membership, you need to get them engage with each other as *richly* as you can. That means getting your membership to invest time, emotion, and effort into doing stuff together, contributing content, and building relationships and friendships.

The point is that you're unlikely to get that the moment they join. Instead, you need to make a series of *escalating tasks that will ease people into full commitment.*

The Community Commitment Curve will help you to ramp people up the curve. Start by lowering the barrier to entry with small tasks, such as liking someone, completing their profile, or commenting on a post. Then make increasingly bigger tasks, such as contributing to a blog, attending an offline event, or running a subgroup. Making successive tasks of escalating, but appropriate difficulty will ramp people into greater degrees of commitment as they learn that each investment delivers an equivalent reward. Leaving your warm home on a cold night to attend an event doesn't seem such a big deal if you've already met the people in a forum, seen them on a live chat, and are now ready to share a beer with them. Once a small easy action is undertaken, people tend to be predisposed to take a slightly harder one. They're already invested, and the next step doesn't seem such a big deal.

This is a typical Community Commitment Curve with the actions you might expect at each stage.

The Community Commitment Curve

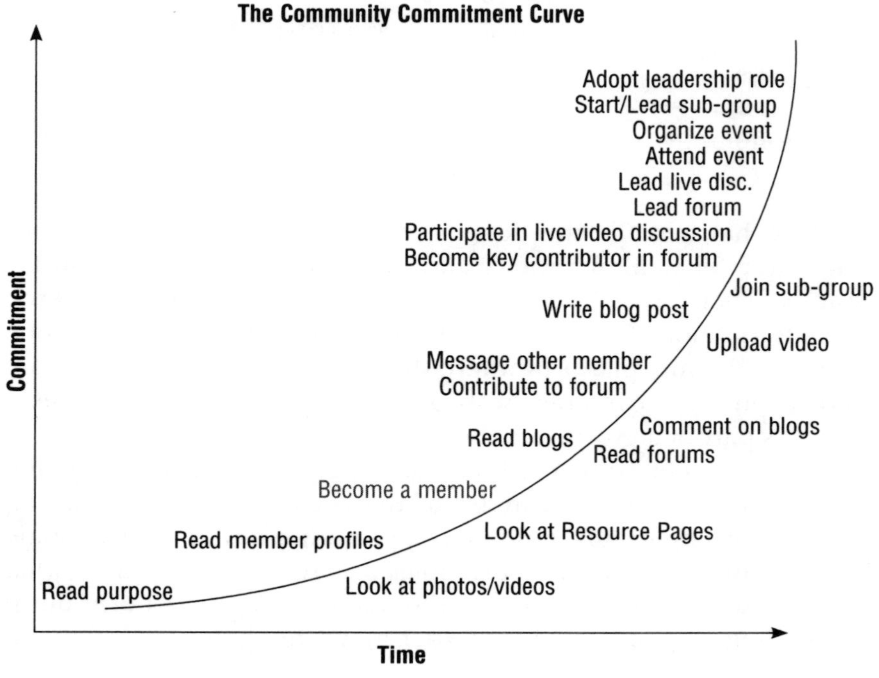

Yelp, a brand that built community into their customer experience from the get-go, absolutely understands the necessity of ramping people up into higher commitment. This is what their curve looks like:

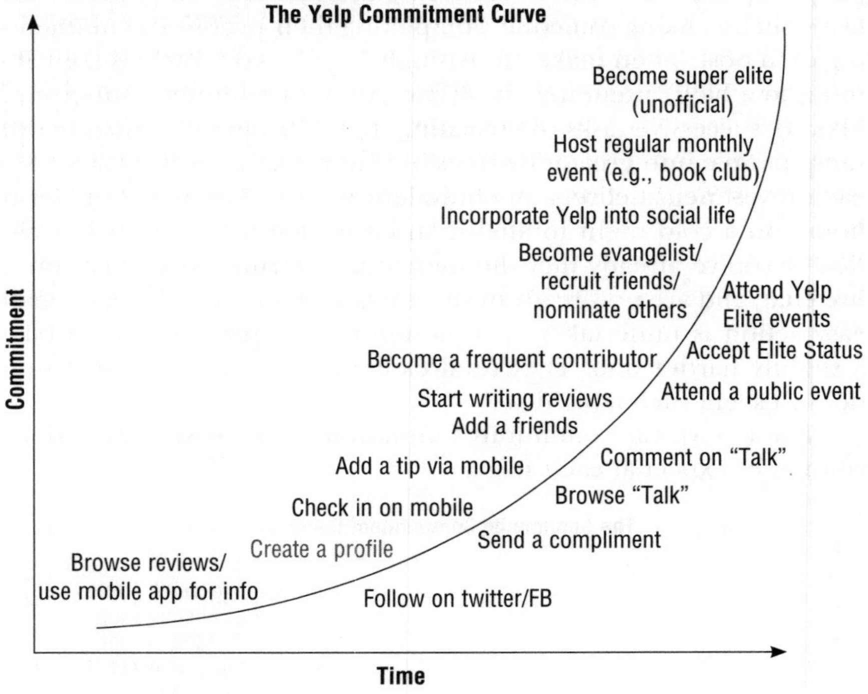

Yelp has become the definer of a customer review site. They have over 30 million reviews and get nearly 80 million monthly visitors. Their goal should also be your goal: get more registered users to do more. The way they do this is to make the site into one huge community platform where there are plenty of opportunities and incentives to interact with others, contribute, identify themselves as part of a group, and become invested.

Yelp has been so successful at ramping people up the curve that you can see plenty of examples of the classic markers of a strong community, especially mutual responsibility and support. Some of the more extraordinary examples are Yelpers (for that is what they call themselves) who have rebuilt a fellow Yelper's burnt down house, helped another fellow Yelper move into a new house after a divorce, and attended a wedding of Yelpers who met on Yelp—all organized via the Event tool on the Yelp site. Of course, these are examples of very significant investments of time, effort, emotion, and money from very committed members. But they all have a history of a multitude of smaller, but increasingly invested actions that led to them being open to these levels of commitment and reward.

Yelp also has an *Elite* group: an inner circle of community members who really operate at the top of the commitment curve. These members not only have written plenty of entertaining and helpful reviews, but also have engaged with others online and offline well, welcomed new members, and begun to take leadership roles in their local neighborhoods by organizing events. They are highly interactive members—makers of social glue, if you like. Their reward is similar to the Sharpie Squad's: status (they get a special online badge), and access (they get invited to cool, elite-only events).

IMPORTANT NOTE: COMMUNITY IS NOT "SOCIAL"

If you're thinking you can get away with slapping up a Facebook Brand Page to build Community, please think again. Many people use the terms *social media* and *community* interchangeably—mistakenly in my view. *Social* tends to foster the kind engagement that adheres to that limp dictionary definition of "people sharing things in common" (like baby pictures and cat videos). What's more, brand's use of social media tends to be just another form of broadcast: not TV, but equally broad-scale, one-to-many messaging in the form of Tweets and posts. In other words, brand-to-users, instead of focusing on what community is all about: user-to-user interaction. Only if you enable rich and frequent interaction amongst customers can you expect intense loyalty, material contributions, participation, and proselytizing.

To create real community, either build your own platform as Airbnb and Yelp have done, or license and customize one that offers the full range of possible interactions outlined on the commitment curve.

Here are some of the key differences between community and *social.*

Community	**"Social"**
Members	Fans/followers
Range of commitment actions (see the Commitment Curve)	Lower commitment actions
Materially contribute	Update
Mutual responsibility and support	Like/comment
Rich two-plus engagement	Broadcast
Relationships with other members	"Conversations"
Of the members, by the members, for the members (horizontal relationships)	Leader/brand/person to many (vertical relationships)
Slow, steady, but sticky growth	Rapid growth (sometimes)

WHAT IS THE ROI OF COMMUNITY?

Community has now become a well-accepted strategy for brands. Inevitably, and correctly, the question is beginning to be asked about its ROI. It should be said that investment in community programs is never likely to approach the huge sums traditional marketing and advertising budgets have demanded. Nonetheless, this new growth and loyalty strategy should be proving its existence.

It's early days, though, both for the strategy and especially for determining how it contributes to the bottom line. Those using Community claim it binds customers to the brand like no other strategy. They tell me it can improve the customer experience, and raise net promoter score (NPS) and, indirectly, revenue. It enables fast feedback so problems can be addressed and customer-driven ideas implemented. Community members are superb brand advocates because they are passionate. They tend to spend more than noncommunity members. They tend to answer each other's questions, thus saving customer support dollars.

This all makes logical sense. But now we're seeing data emerging that supports it. Michael Wu at Lithium (a community platform used by many brands) outlined to me three ways in which he's seen his clients' Communities affecting the bottom line: revenue growth, cost saving, and innovation/co-creation.

1. *Revenue growth.* Community members tend to buy more and tell their friends to buy more: loyalty and advocacy. Susan Wassel at Sharpie told me that: "We track loyalty in many ways on the Sharpie brand and our data indicates that our approach [Community] has created a very loyal user base." Sephora community members tend to spend 2.5 times the amount spent by an average customer—they know this because they can cross-reference community members with store cardholders. *Superfans* (highly active and engaged Sephora community members) tend to spend 10 times more. (Lithium)
2. *Cost saving.* Using your community of users to answer each other's questions can save dollars spent on customer support staff.

   This is often the most immediate and obvious reward of Community. It's normally the case that the customers, especially committed customers who are engaged with other customers, both know your product better than you do and are even more motivated than employees to support fellow community members. Not only are calls deflected from the call center (Linsky's estimates $7m saved annually, Best Buy $5m annually, Tom had 20,000 cases handled by the community in one month saving $150k in support costs—source: Lithium), but also the experience of getting your problem solved by a highly engaged peer is often better than that by a paid employee.
3. *Innovation and co-creation.* The community can not only play the role of an engaged customer service function, but can also collaboratively create content, develop new product ideas, and vote up or down those they would most like to see in the marketplace.

   Verizon has had 1,700 ideas submitted in less than a year. Two hundred fifty are actively being developed and 31 are already in the marketplace (Lithium). Not only are they getting *free* new product development (NPD), they're getting highly invested customers who are proud to be having a say in the direction of the company. And, of course, *free* market research in terms of prioritization of products to be developed.

WHERE DO YOU START?

By now you might be considering Community as one of your key business strategies. But how do you start? These are the two basic things you should do next that will set you in the right direction:

1. *Identify the thing that's shared ...*
Get to know your users and find out what unites them. Do this before you even think of building or using any community technologies or tools.

Without exception, at the heart of every successful community is a shared passion, values, belief system, or worldview. It's not enough to say your members share a love for your brand (even if you're lucky enough for that to be true). You need to dig deeper and find out what they do, or could share at the most profound level: the things that define themselves to themselves and to each other. For Harley it's rebellion. The CEO and the guy on the lam that I spoke to were united in this self-identification. It's what binds the Harley tribe together. This emotionally based self and tribal identity is the true source of Harley's stickiness, not just that they share a passion for the product (which they do too).

Where do you find that thing? A good place to start is the brand's point of view or values that you have already figured out. If they are not especially inspiring (or if you have not identified them yet), then see if your users identify with each other in some distinguishing way. Surface their mutual identity and that can potentially become the worldview that is shared between users, and between users and the brand.

... and declare it.

Once you've determined what members truly share, then you should declare it. Political parties declare their worldview with a manifesto. Religions do it with a holy book or creed. Some brands also have manifestos or creeds (such as Lululemon and eBay). What is more likely is that they will declare their worldview through the brand's communications, design, and distribution strategy.

Steve Jobs did this with the original *Think different* commercial that relaunched the brand after his second coming. It never showed a computer and did not talk about the features. It simply showed famous people who changed history by being nonconformist and creative. In others words, he celebrated the brand's and the community's shared identity, which in turn became a siren call to others who believed they also shared these defining characteristics. This worldview was expressed in everything the brand did: the stores that are temples to design and innovation; the gorgeous packaging; the advertising; and the beautiful form-meets-function products. As one young Mac loyalist told me: "This community, it's literally based around a machine. But actually it's based around a certain way of thinking."

2. *Enable your customers to interact, interact, interact*
This is the most important ingredient of a community. If your members don't engage with each other, you have no community. They need the opportunity to build relationships *with each other*, not just with your brand. It's not enough to have something in common. They need to share it, form relationships, and create strong bonds. If you're starting from scratch, you should look for a platform that will enable your potential members to find each other and interact at every point on the commitment curve. You can:

(a) Build your own platform, as Airbnb has done. It's often the best route (you can design it to suit your users' and brands' needs, and your business goals). But it can be expensive.
(b) Use an existing platform, such as Facebook Groups. They're not bad, but can come with the limitations that result from the platform's own business goals.
(c) Customize one of the many very good, white-label platforms designed exactly for this task—supplied by the likes of Lithium, Jive, or Ning.
(d) Or check whether there are existing communities around the brand. Enable them to function better and then determine how the brand can be useful to them, just like Sharpie did.

Finding the right platform is just the start. Then you need to recruit members to it and stimulate them to interact with each other by posting content, commenting, following, messaging, helping each other, and meeting up face to face. This is an art and science in and of itself.

ARE SOME PRODUCTS OR CATEGORIES SIMPLY MORE PREDISPOSED TO COMMUNITY THAN OTHERS?

Surely passionate communities are easier to create around inherently interesting products or categories such as motorbikes, computers, or travel. Isn't it impossible to pull it off for a rudimentary cleaning product, say, or a commodity category? Not necessarily. Sharpie is an interesting case history for Community precisely because it's *not* an interesting product: it's a cheap-to-produce bit of plastic and ink—it's a commodity product in a utilitarian category.

The trick is to find the shared identity that does or could exist between the product and its users—and especially between its users. And this is most likely to be founded on a worldview, a belief, or a set of values. If a brand and its users stand for the same thing, such as *self-expression* in Sharpie's case, then it really doesn't matter how functionally ordinary or interesting the product is.

For Saturn owners (in its day, the No. 2 best selling small car in America despite a humdrum product that was at parity with its Japanese competitors) it was the core human values of decency and respect that the brand and the customers shared. It was expressed in everything from its launch campaign to the experience in the store. As one owner said to me:

> The car was nice enough looking and I needed an economical car. But I liked the idea of the company … I really went because of the message … it's a sort of a democratic car, a Midwestern car … full of substance. I felt stupid buying into the whole "Saturn Family" thing, but I bought in hard … they were going to be a different kind of company.

CONCLUSION

In 2004, I wrote in *The Culting of Brands*: "The next big thing in business will be community." I suppose I can enjoy a certain amount of *told you so*, but truthfully, I didn't anticipate the growth of social networks. They are responsible for making business aware of the potential of connected customers. After a certain amount of undignified headless-chicken-type activity in response to these platforms, brands (the smart ones) have begun to realize the power of *true* community to transform their existing business or start a new one.

This next era is going to be exciting. New brands will emerge like Airbnb, Yelp, and Tough Mudder that will make Community the core brand experience. Established brands, such as Sharpie and WebMD, will rework their businesses to give it a central role, acknowledging that Community as a business strategy builds loyalty and advocacy like no other. But what we should all acknowledge is that your customers are likely to connect anyway, with or without your help. What a superb opportunity this new connected age presents for brands to adopt the role of intelligent, nurturing community enablers. At last, here's a business and marketing strategy that actually does some real good—as well as being good for the bottom line!

Chapter 5

What It Really Means to Be a Challenger in Today's World

Adam Morgan

In 1997, I began The Challenger Project, an in-depth study looking at how Challenger brands succeed across a variety of different categories. Over the last 17 years this project has launched the term *Challenger brand* into the everyday business vernacular and we see growing reference to it daily (Google displays about 9,250,000 results in 0.22 seconds as I write this).

Despite this widespread use of the term, however, much of the dialogue and analysis about Challenger brands, all too often, offers a superficial and clichéd view of what being a Challenger is actually about: the little guy calling out the big guy, or the crazy upstart that turns everything on its head. While these stereotypes are still valid for some, the reality is that the world of business and brands has evolved considerably over the last decade or so, and so have Challengers.

In this chapter, then, I would like to go back to first principles, to revisit the original eight Challenger Credos in the context of a new generation, and to look at how they are creating a new world of opportunity for what it means to be a Challenger today.

So first to the Challenger principles …

ESCAPING THE MEPHISTO WALTZ

Let's go on a trip.

We're going to travel 400 billion light years to a galaxy called NGC 6240. What distinguished NGC 6240 when first discovered in 2002 was that it contained two supermassive black holes—previously it was thought impossible for the two to coexist within the same galaxy. Yet that coexistence comes at a price for both of them: astrophysicists observe that these two massive forces of suction are gradually pulling each other closer and closer together until eventually they get sucked into each other and become one and the same thing. Astrophysicists refer to this mutually assured dance of death as The Mephisto Waltz.

But as business leaders and marketers we don't need to travel 400 billion light years to see The Mephisto Waltz—we can see it in the high streets around us all the time. We can see brands in the same category obsessively watching what each other does, and responding like with like. One brand does a stripy version, so the other does a stripy version; one does twisty caps, so the other does twisty caps; one brand has a close-up shot of a radiant woman with flawless skin, then they *all* have a close-up shot of a radiant woman with flawless skin. They are, albeit unwittingly, locked in a Mephisto Waltz all of their own, one that brings them closer and closer to each other. As a result these brands get less and less differentiated, and more and more similar—with a consequent erosion in price differentiation, profitability, and loyalty.

If you are a market leader, being locked in The Mephisto Waltz is not necessarily a threat. You don't really want a highly differentiated competitor whose success would be difficult for you to counter; you are in many ways much more comfortable with a second-rank player who does essentially the same as you; they will always be vulnerable to the superior cost-efficiencies and marketing budgets your scale can create, and the pricing, distribution, and communication dominance you can drive through the consequences of that scale.

But if you are a Challenger, somebody who wants to grow by changing the way consumers think about the category, rather than simply being a fast follower, success lies in actually reversing The Mephisto Waltz and putting some clear distance between ourselves and the establishment brand. We cannot compete against the scale and reach of the market leader by allowing ourselves to simply respond to what they do. We have, by definition, to find a new set of reference points and introduce new criteria for choice to the consumers, which they won't find satisfied by the existing players.

This means that we won't become a successful Challenger by studying market leaders, and just emulating them on a smaller scale. We will need to find an entirely different kind of *Operating System.*

A CHALLENGER'S BASIC OPERATING SYSTEM: THE EIGHT CREDOS

When people hear the term *Challenger,* they often misconstrue its meaning, assuming that it relates to a brand's relative size in the market—a brand that is No. 2, 3, or 4 in a given market, in essence. But market position is no definer of being a Challenger—there are, after all, plenty of second-rank brands in large categories which make no real attempt to challenge any aspect of the market leader or the category, yet are still able to maintain a comfortable enough business to survive and even enjoy modest growth.

A Challenger then is defined primarily by a state of mind rather than by a state of market. It is a brand, and a group of people behind that brand, whose business ambitions exceed its conventional marketing resources, and who are prepared to do something bold and different in order to overcome the implications of that gap. And whilst the overall *marketing model* may indeed have significantly changed since we first identified this model in 1998, a new generation of Challengers have continued to show us that there are still a number of core principles that Challengers live and thrive by:

1. Embracing Intelligent Naivety
2. Building a Lighthouse Identity
3. Taking thought leadership of the category
4. Creating symbols of reevaluation
5. Sacrifice
6. Overcommitment
7. Using PR and communication to enter social culture
8. Becoming Ideas Centered

Let us look briefly at each of these in turn.

Embracing Intelligent Naivety

We view experience as valuable in business. We tend to think that the longer you are in a company, the longer you work on a brand, or the longer you've been working in a category, the more insightful you become at seeing the opportunities around you, and understanding where a brand or a business should go. Yet, while this is a natural assumption, the first thing that strikes one when studying Challengers is that deep experience of a category is rare. The Challengers who have shaken up the categories around us, in fact, seem to prize something different: inexperience and naivety—intelligently applied.

You yourself have experienced Intelligent Naivety in starting a new job. In those first few days you see things with blinding clarity; you are able to ask all sorts of fundamental and upstream questions, and feel free to do so. You see entirely new sources of solutions and possibilities. You can do this, quite simply, because you haven't learnt *the rules* yet—rules written and reinforced by others with the *benefit* of experience.

Let's focus on three of the most common applications of Intelligent Naivety here.

The first and most basic practice of Intelligent Naivety is to ask upstream questions about the category that you are in. Why does the category have to behave in the way that it does? Why are the drivers of this category what they seem to be? What are the so-called rules of the category and do I have to stick to them? Just having the opportunity to ask those very upstream questions is enormously liberating and a great way to start a strategic process.

Premium cleaning brand, Method, started from this point. Eric Ryan and Adam Lowry, the founders, asked themselves questions like "Why are cleaning products so poorly designed?" "Why do people buy soap and then have to spend $15 on an aluminum pump to make it look nice in their home?," and "Why does green have to mean your things won't get clean?" In doing so, they spotted an opportunity that blindsided the well-funded and well-experienced incumbent leaders. In the 12 years since they first asked those questions, Method has grown to be a beacon of Challenger success in both America and Europe and has been voted one of the most innovative companies in the world by both *Fast Company* and *Time.*

The second key practice of Intelligent Naivety lies in looking outside (rather than inside) your category for inspiration. Many Challengers have taken the rules of an entirely different category, sometimes a category quite unrelated, and imported them into their own in order to create something entirely new.

So, for example, let's imagine you were trying to break into the cosmetics market, a very well-established market with well-known codes and rules. What if you took inspiration from the world of greengrocers and delicatessens instead? What might the rules and codes of those categories look like if they were applied to yours? Well, perhaps they would give you more color, a very different kind of language, much more theater, and engagement—in fact, a multisensory experience that will bring something literally fresh to the category. An approach that ensured Lush cosmetics stood out from their competition to become a huge success on the U.K. high street; they now have 830 stores in 50 countries.

By overlaying the rules of an entirely different category onto our own, you can see how we might be able to create new possibilities and opportunities. To continue the story from Method, Eric Ryan calls this *Appropriation.* He points out that Method's innovation in hand soap was inspired by appropriating ideas and conventions from the homeware category for their own; it was from this that their iconic teardrop-shaped bottle came to be created, and remains one of their bestselling products.

The last Intelligently Naive practice I'm going to talk about here, and one that we are currently exploring even more deeply in our research, is how Challengers question what is *possible* and what is *impossible* in practice. As experts and businesses we find our own ways of doing things—very often over time these ways come to define how we see the world: sociologists call this Path Dependence—and very often, along with this ingrained set of habits, a set of beliefs develops about what can and can't be done.

Challengers refuse to do things just because *this is the way that things have always been done.* They constantly fight falling into the trap of Path Dependence. Ingvar Kamprad of IKEA summarized this beautifully when he wrote: "By daring to be different, we find new ways. By refusing to accept a pattern just because it is established, we get further." A Challenger's ability to question what is possible is fundamental to maintaining true Intelligent Naivety. Why can't we build a table that can be sold for 5 euros? Why couldn't we use every square inch space on our packaging that is currently devoted to legal copy as a place to project what our brand is about? Why couldn't we take half the time it normally takes to launch this product?

After the fledgling Southwest Airlines, back when it was still only a handful of planes, found a revolutionary way to create a turnaround time that was half that of their competitors, the rest of the industry expressed astonishment at their achievement. "We didn't know it couldn't be done," they said, "so we did it."

Build a Lighthouse Identity

Most brands take a consumer-led approach to finding their position in the market: let us call it the "That's why" approach. It will go something like this:

> I understand how tiring it is reading chapters about Challenger brands at the end of a full day at work. *That's why* Morgan's Mineral Water has six times the amount of caffeine of any other mineral water in the market, to help you stay awake while you get ahead.

What these brands are doing is navigating by you—the consumer. They've gone out, they've done their consumer focus groups, and they've really understood your need states. Armed with this insight, they've produced the solution to a particular problem and issue. They've told you about that solution, and the circle is complete—"please buy me," they say. They are navigating by you: a very natural kind of communication.

The interesting thing about Challengers, though, is that, while they understand their consumers very well, they don't overtly navigate by them. Instead, they take their own position and have a very clear sense of where they stand and why they stand there. Like a lighthouse, they tend to project that sense of where they stand in the form of a point of view about the way the world is, or the way the world would be if they ran it. They project that point of view insistently and consistently in everything they do. And, in doing so, instead of navigating by the consumer they invite the consumer to navigate by them.

Before exploring the lighthouse analogy a stage further, we need to lay one particular misunderstanding to rest—the myth that Challengers pay no attention to the consumer at all, but simply sail by their own star. This is not actually the case at all. Most Challengers have a very good, very strong, and often very personal understanding of their consumers, because they, including and especially their senior management, spend a lot of time face-to-face with them. They have an almost visceral understanding of what drives, motivates, and characterizes their consumers as human beings, and not simply as purchasers of a category. But they don't confuse understanding their consumers very well with simply *playing back* that understanding to the consumers, and mistaking that for a positioning. As Tom Chappell remarked, "Success means never letting the competition define you. Instead, you have to define yourself based on a point of view that you care deeply about."

We need to care deeply about that point of view; we need to be personally invested in some kind of way—because unless we care deeply about it, how can we project it with the kind of intensity that the consumer is going to respond to, an intensity that will create strong preference and loyalty amongst our consumers? Blake Mycoskie created TOMS Shoes and his *One for One* movement (the company donates one pair of shoes for every pair sold) because he strongly believes that *giving is what fuels us, giving is our future.* Kulula, the low-cost South African airline, firmly believe that flying should be for everyone—they are for the people of South Africa, and this passion for demystifying air travel, and making it more accessible to a new generation of South African flyers goes to the heart of everything that they do.

Lighthouses, to play out this metaphor a bit more, are built on rock, the hardest kind of rock you can find. What that means for us is that we are looking for a product truth or a brand truth on which to build our identity, for two reasons. One is that by rooting our Lighthouse Identity in that product or brand truth it will give it credibility and *ownability* in the marketplace. The second is that internally, with our own people, it will give us conviction that this is innately and absolutely us. It will allow us to go out as marketers and project everything that comes out of that product truth with a conviction evident to everybody who comes across us. That product or brand truth will be the rock on which our lighthouse is built.

Once we have defined the elements of our Lighthouse Identity—our product truth, values, and point of view—how we choose to project that lighthouse and the narrative we build around it will be discussed in the second part of this chapter.

Taking Thought Leadership of the Category

There are two types of brand leaders in every category: the market leader and the thought leader. Market leadership obviously relates to superior mass, and all the benefits that come with scale and establishment—from distribution to social acceptability to trust.

However, very often in the category there is another kind of brand leader, the thought leader. The currencies of thought leadership are different to those of the market leader, and revolve not around superior mass but superior momentum—the sense that a brand is coming through, that it is the one that people are talking about, the brand that is setting or resetting the agenda in the category.

If a Challenger can't be the first of these kinds of brand leader, they need to be the second. Consequently, rather than lying in a single activation or campaign idea, the recognition of the need for thought leadership represents the start of a longer term ambition to be seen as a brand that is constantly at the forefront of a fresh way of seeing and thinking about the category and its possibilities.

This is best achieved by surprising the consumer with behavior that (selectively) breaks with consumer expectations around certain kinds of category conventions.

While there are several kinds of conventions that Challengers can choose to play with in order to take thought leadership, we're just going to focus on three here: those of representation, experience, and relationship.

1. *Representation.* Conventions of representation are those surrounding how a brand portrays itself, including naming and product descriptors (think of the playfulness of Australian hair care brand Aussie's Aussome Volume Shampoo—and how very different to the seriousness with which most hair care products take themselves). This sometimes even extends into a visibly different brand architecture, like cosmetic brand

Benefit's *Fixing it* and *Faking it* ranges. Critical here is to recognize that these brands do not break convention for the sake of it: instead they do so both to signal their distinctive identity and to prompt consumers to consider the category in a fresh way.

2. *Experience.* Conventions of experience are those surrounding the product or service experience beyond pure product performance—Ray Davies, CEO of Umpqua Bank (a chain of groundbreaking banks on the West Coast of America), talks about differentiating through the experience his bank offers to their customers. Defining themselves as "a service company who happens to sell financial products" was central to then defining their banks as *stores* rather than branches, and making those stores a local community space that hosted local artists and musicians in evening events when banking hours were over. Their desire to behave like *good neighbors* led to them offering simple but strikingly different experiences such as bowls of water for customers' dogs, and trucks that offered the community free ice cream in the summer and hot chocolate in the winter. The sustained sequence of these fresh initiatives successfully positioned Umpqua as a group of people dynamically resetting the agenda for what a great banking experience could be.
3. *Relationship.* As the fundamental relationship between brand owners and consumers continues to evolve, there exists an opportunity for brands in categories which still observe a *barrier* between brand and consumer (whether physical, such as a bank counter, or informational, such as lack of transparency). Challengers can become thought leaders by transforming those barriers and thereby opening up an entirely new kind of relationship with their consumer. Online retailer Zappos (acquired by Amazon in 2009 for $1.2 billion) is an example of this thought leadership in action: while other call centers are measured on how short a call can be, Zappos employees are encouraged to spend as much time as possible on the phone with their customers—the current record for a Zappos customer call is over 5 hours long. This reflects their commitment to revealing the people behind the brand—who according to Tony Hsieh, the CEO, make the business what

it is—and building a human connection with their customers. In large part through this consumer "wow" (in their words), Zappos boasts a model of 75 percent repeat business, with 20 percent new customers coming through as referrals.

Creating Symbols of Reevaluation

Challengers are brands in a hurry. Natural ambition is frequently linked to short windows in the eyes of trade or investors for the Challenger to prove themselves. So they frequently seek to shake up a consumer's comfortable or habituated perceptions of the status quo through dramatic acts of theatre—acts which we'll call symbols of reevaluation.

We might want to prompt a significant reappraisal of how consumers view the brand, for instance. Audi of America did this with the launch of its $120,000 R8 supercar during the 2011 Superbowl in dramatic opposition to *Old Luxury*—a reframing of the *tired* category incumbents. Besides image and consideration shifts, the car lured people into Audi showrooms who had not previously taken the brand seriously as a luxury car.

Equally the area of complacency we need to puncture might not be consumers' perceptions of our brand, but of the category as a whole. Few people in the United Kingdom gave much thought to school dinners until campaigning TV chef Jamie Oliver pointed out that Britons spent less on lunches for their school children (the future of society) than they did on lunches for their prisoners (the threat to society). Suddenly, he had a nation's attention and support for his national campaign for better meals in schools.

It is said that a rocket to the moon uses half of its entire fuel supply just to leave the earth and reach its desired speed. The same is true of getting a brand off the ground—the real effort and difficulty lies in achieving that initial critical momentum.

Sacrifice and Overcommitment

The Challenger practices that we are going to focus on next are actually two interrelated principles: that of Sacrifice and that of Overcommitment.

Let's first look at sacrifice. The thing about Challengers is that they do not recognize rejection as the biggest threat to them, it's indifference. Rejection is quite an easy thing to spot; indifference is the really expensive problem. One can spend a lot of money, passion, and energy tweaking indifference without moving the needle at all.

As a Challenger we clearly cannot accept weak preference because if that is all that we have, then once all the other big advantages a market leader has on their side—ubiquity of distribution, social acceptability, and trustworthiness—kick in, we have no preference left at all. Instead the only currency we are interested in creating is strong preference, and in order to create strong preference, we are going to have to do things that reach out and bind certain groups of people strongly to us. To do this we must accept, in turn of course, that there are sacrifices we will want to make—certain kinds of targets we will want to give up, certain kinds of messages we will want to give up, certain kinds of places we choose not to be.

What we choose to sacrifice, what we chose to give up, is as important a part of being a Challenger brand as knowing what your Lighthouse Identity is in the first place. A really strong Challenger brand knows its edges: being clear on what you are not, throwing even more light on what you are going to stand for.

And of course, one of the reasons that as Challengers, with limited resources and budgets, we choose to sacrifice is to allow us to genuinely drive success within the three or four key thrusts that will define us. When a karate black belt attempts to smash a brick into two with his/her bare hand, he/she aims not at the brick itself, but at an imaginary point two feet below it. In other words, it is a triumph not of commitment, but of *overcommitment.* The same approach is required of Challenger brands; it is only overcommitment which will push through the inertia and resistance our desired initiatives will inevitably encounter—anticipating all the reasons it might not work in practice, and solving them before they arise.

The New Zealand super premium vodka brand 42BELOW is a good case in point. When they wanted to break into New York's nightclub scene, they knew they had a fight on their hands. They were too small to buy their way in and, with 100 vodkas launching every year, the marketplace was already saturated. Starting to think about ways of making their brand stand out, they came up with the idea of the 42BELOW Snow Patrol. When it started snowing (this was, after all, New York in January), two of them turned up outside nightclubs in 42BELOW branded jackets, unasked and unannounced, and simply started shoveling the snow away from the pavement outside. The bouncers loved them for it, as did the clubbers and the club owners.

So, when they subsequently approached those same clubs about stocking 42BELOW, they were already known, liked, and respected as a determined Challenger who knew how to create new kinds of relationships and publicity for themselves. Mere commitment to a killer sales presentation would never have taken them there; it was overcommitment that sent them out onto the streets on those freezing cold nights and, ultimately, won them the business.

Using PR and Communication to Enter Social Culture

Young Challengers don't have the luxury of large communication budgets, or indeed any budgets at all—but they clearly still want to get people talking about their brand and what they are trying to do. Too often in establishment thinking, the desire to use PR is represented simply by an appointment and briefing of a PR company. Challengers, though, recognize that the responsibility for generating stories that spread begins with us and that we—monthly, weekly, daily—need to become relentless makers of ideas that can travel. Irish budget airline Ryanair, for instance, which is still the most profitable airline in the world, reputedly insists on producing three PR releases a day. Such an explicit requirement demands that the organization thinks and behaves in very different ways to deliver that: from the people it recruits to the way it manages its lawyers.

Whether we have the money for mainstream communications or not, our ambition as Challengers should be to create conversations which take on a life of their own in social culture. To do this, we will have to think about employing some techniques that help us create that broader social ripple. Are we going to identify a debate that's already in the popular culture and attach ourselves to that debate in a unique and stimulating way, for instance, or are we going to create a different conversation altogether?

Perhaps we can pick a fight with a new wave in popular culture and, by taking a contrary view, make that debate entirely our own. Mini famously did this when launching their little car into the American market. While they could have gone for the generic *small on the outside, big on the inside* small car positioning, they wanted to genuinely be a Challenger that created conversation. And so, instead, they chose to attach themselves to (or *grip* against) a much bigger issue in the wider world—climate change and big cars. At launch they proclaimed that the *SUV backlash* had begun, placing Minis cheekily on top of SUVs and driving the two around together in 25 cities across America—positioning themselves as the car that *sipped*, rather than *guzzled*, gas.

Becoming Ideas-Centered, Rather Than Consumer-Centered

Successfully entering a category as a Challenger is one kind of problem; continuing that success is another one entirely. Challengers need momentum—actual momentum (the source of return on investment) and perceived momentum (the sense that this is the brand to watch). The reason most Challengers lose momentum after initial success is that they fail to realize that they have to change to stay the same. Changing in this sense doesn't mean changing their core identity or what they stand for, but rather changing the way a consumer experiences it.

This refreshing of the experiential relationship is one that is fed by a consistent stream of ideas—not just technical innovation and product news (although these can be important) but also marketing and communication ideas that stimulate the consumer's imagination. While we must stay true to our core values and Lighthouse Identity, should the flow of ideas slow, become predictable, or die, the Challenger's grip on the emotions and imagination of its current and future consumers will grow stale and fade. Being clear on where to change and where to remain the same in this regard is one of the key long-term challenges for the owner-driver of a Challenger brand.

BRINGING THE LIGHTHOUSE TO LIFE: EMBRACING A CHALLENGER NARRATIVE

The Eight Credos are the foundational behaviors and practices that any Challenger needs to adopt in order to succeed. Whilst these principles have remained relevant through the huge swathes of change in the communications and business environments over the last decade or so, *how* Challengers project what they stand for—*how* they tell their stories, and the character they assume to do this—has evolved significantly.

As I previously mentioned, the enduring myth about Challengers is that it's always about David against Goliath, the little guy against the big guy—the underdog narrative. But a new generation of Challengers has taught us that the competition is only one of the kinds of challenges we can use to break through, and explicitly challenging the market leader is, in reality, comparatively rare—one will more often find a recent generation of Challengers taking a broader aspect of contemporary culture, or the way a consumer experiences using a product, and weaving a story around that, which engages and draws us in.

The anthropologist Bob Deutsch once commented that the common assumption was that Bill Clinton's continual success with the electorate, in spite of the various scandals that attended his presidency, was because people *just liked him.* Deutsch observed that this was not actually the case—the reason Clinton remained popular was not because people liked him, but because they felt *he liked them.* The same is true with many of our new generation Challengers: we feel at some level they like us. We are not just target markets and demographics and commercial objectives—they share their stories with us, fight for (or against) something that is meaningful to us, and invite us to participate with them in their journey to do so.

To "invite us in" Challengers instinctively and deftly employ narratives that resonate with us. These narratives bring "What We Stand For" to life. They have to be dynamic—they have to move the narrative of the category forward, and indeed ideally move the personal narrative of the consumer forward. Each has an inherent tension and conflict which gives it human interest for us: their cause is our cause, we want them to succeed—we are part of their journey.

HARNESSING THE ENERGY IN NARRATIVE

If we are to explore how to tell the compelling story of our Challenger brand, we must first identify what the main elements of narrative are and see how they might be useful to us in developing our own story to project our Lighthouse Identity.

(This theory forms part of a joint exploration of this theme for Challengers with Brian Lanahan, an expert in applying the principles of story to brands.)

Unexpectedness

The essence of a compelling story is one where life goes in a different direction from the way we expect. To quote Brian Lanahan: "In story we concentrate on the rare moment when the world reacts in a way we did not expect. That's when life gets interesting ... Stories that demand our attention never focus on the banality of life conforming to expectation."

Clearly this will need to be the case with any Challenger in a category: the market leader succeeds by the category continuing to evolve in the way we would expect—given that the market leader has educated us to think their drivers, codes and conventions are the most important ones for us to consider. So in itself, any Challenger must introduce a new narrative, a new story, where the consumer is invited to think of the category as progressing in an unexpected way.

Key questions for a Challenger here are: What is the *normal* evolution of the category? What is the unexpected course we are looking to take it in? Why should that command the consumer's attention?

The Importance of the Inciting Incident

When you see Challenger founders interviewed, one of the topics that always arises is why they started doing this new and fresh initiative with this new and fresh Challenger brand. Usually it relates to a very personal incident, be it a frustration that they had (James Dyson's frustration with his own vacuum cleaner), or something inspiring that had happened to them (Flickr's founders suddenly seeing the real potential of their game application). This is known in narrative as *The Inciting Incident*—the moment that causes the people involved to start the brand or change its direction, and thus makes the story of what it is trying to achieve uniquely theirs.

In our case, if we are founders, we may well have such an inciting incident—an *aha!,* or a *there must be a better way of doing it than this*—and in this case it will simply be a question of putting that at the center of our story. For most of us, as people working to launch or relaunch brands within larger companies that are not our own, we will still want to find an inciting incident—whether by going back to why the brand was originally started and reinterpreting what the inciting incident for its birth had been, or through a moment of personal recognition that something was wrong with the world, that something needed to be done about it and the role our brand could play in that. Some truth, in fact, about why we embarked on our current course that makes it more than just this year's new positioning.

Key questions here, then, include: Why are we a Challenger? What has set us on this course? What is the moment we can point to that has shaped this narrative and direction?

The Objective—The Desire Created by the Inciting Incident

The protagonist in a compelling story—in our case our Challenger—has to be driven by a personal desire, ideally coming from this inciting incident, an objective that propels him or her forward. He or she wants something to happen, wants to achieve something specific, and this has to be visible to us, the spectators (and increasingly participants) in the story. To quote Lanahan again, "We need to really feel what the character wants, and it has to be worthwhile. Boredom in a story is watching a character pursue an objective that is too easy or without meaning." Remember Tom Chappell of Tom's of Maine?—You have to define yourself (as a brand) based on a point of view you care deeply about.

So perhaps when we talk of having a visible cause that we are rallying around, it is not a piece of marketing gimmickry—it is in fact a fundamental part of creating a Challenger narrative that a broader community can all be engaged by. If we want people to engage with us as a Challenger, we have to be visibly pursuing something more than a brand share alone.

So what is it we want to achieve or change as a Challenger? How is this objective visible to those who are watching us? How could we make it more so?

Conflict

All good stories are driven by conflict—not necessarily (or indeed usually) in the sense of fighting, but in the sense of struggle. The protagonist faces one or more key adversarial forces against which he/she must struggle to realize his/her desire. If there is no conflict in a story, it doesn't move forward. And the way he or she deals with that conflict or struggle is where his or her true character is revealed. The challenge that we publicly choose as our reason for being in a market is exactly this struggle; it is and will be the source of energy for our narrative and how we engage with it.

One thing many Challengers do is identify a *monster* to slay, rather than an enemy to fight, that is, a threat to the entire community, rather than just the Challenger themselves, and therefore of compelling interest to that community as a whole. This monster can be anything from a confining convention to the perniciously prevailing wisdom of the day to a behavior which undermines our essential humanity. Focusing on a Monster involves the consumers in the conflict because we are clearly fighting for them, or for a cause they feel strongly about.

Some questions that an ambitious Challenger must embrace include: What are we struggling to overcome to realize our ambition and vision? What monster is standing in our way? How can we unite our community to overcome it?

EVOLVING THE CHALLENGER NARRATIVE FOR A NEW GENERATION

So much for the principles of narrative—how do we see those combined in the most successful challengers of the last decade?

In researching the latest generation of Challengers, a rich palette of stories has emerged—a number of different ways that bring a Lighthouse Identity to life and find a place in the world. Each different kind of narrative provides a critical filter for helping us decide how to use thought leadership and communication ideas, for example, and helping us find our voice in the market. They capture new ways that an Identity can be used publicly to make the target sit up and take some notice of us, getting them to understand why our story and our ambition really matter to them.

We have identified 10 common Challenger Narratives, which we will discuss in more detail below:

1. The Feisty Underdog
2. The Irreverent Maverick
3. The People's Champion
4. The Missionary
5. The Democratizer
6. The Enlightened Zagger
7. The Real and Human Challenger
8. The Visionary
9. The Next Generation
10. The Game Changer

The Feisty Underdog

This is what many automatically think of as the classic Challenger stance. Avis and The Pepsi Challenge, these two iconic Challengers, which in many people's minds (wrongly) define the totality of Challenger thinking, both fit this *David vs. Goliath* model.

This narrative aims to *reduce the world to binary*—that is, present just two brands for the consumer in a crowded category to choose between. It offers at least an emotional reason to support the underdog (they admire our cheeky attitude and nobody really wants to root for Goliath), and perhaps a rational product or service reason as well.

Many Challenger brands start out as a feisty underdog, first, because that is genuinely the position they find themselves in at the beginning and, second, because it is a good way to accelerate the salience of their offer—particularly if they are not in fact No. 2 in the category, but a more distant No. 3 or 4.

Whilst most Challengers then move on from this, as they grow to expressing their identity through other narratives, a small number of brands continue to find their strength from the Feisty Underdog narrative. Men's grooming brand King of Shaves for instance, who position themselves as always striving to give you, the consumer, *50 percent more* than the goliath of a market leader they are taking on.

The Irreverent Maverick

This Challenger narrative is one of provocation, a poke in the ribs, deliberately setting out to create controversy. Irreverent Mavericks are, in effect, counterculture in a box.

How close to the wind they choose to sail defines whether they genuinely polarize the world, at least at the outset, or whether they appeal to a little of the irreverent in everybody. But they exude the kind of energy and character most of us would like more of: think of the sparkling irreverence of the South African casual dining brand Nando's, for example, or the madcap energy of Scotland's favorite soft drink IRN-BRU.

While this narrative might once have been regarded as essentially for small or niche challengers, Red Bull has shown that it doesn't need to be. Red Bull started as a caffeine and energy *hit* in a cold drink, like nothing the market had ever seen before. The initial grassroots marketing targeted usage occasions and user groups such as the nightclub and party scene. If you wanted to stay up all night, a vodka and red bull (or three) would see you right. In effect, it was a better and a cooler product story.

But as the brand image developed, our understanding of this brand became more three dimensional. With its off-center experiential events such as Flugtag and its irreverent sponsorships (notably its recent sponsorship of Felix Baumgartner's record breaking parachute jump from space), we have now come to understand the *Irreverent Maverick* stance it represents and wraps around the product much more clearly. Of course, since Red Bull, more than 150 new contenders have thrown their hats and their products into the energy ring, many matching to a greater or lesser degree the functional performance of the Austrian brand's product. But Red Bull's ability to build an ongoing, enduring narrative around its Irreverent Maverick stance has seen it stride effortlessly clear of all its imitators, and continue to challenge the giants of the soft drink category.

The People's Champion

The People's Champion makes a very specific claim—it is standing up for the consumer who has been undeservedly, and perhaps even actively, exploited by the players in the category so far. It is fighting to succeed because, it says, in doing so the real winner is you, the consumer—and if we both join together, we can overcome the cynical fat cat(s) who have been using us and the category for their own ends.

This is an increasingly popular stance in a number of markets, and we are starting to see some important variations in the overall theme, of which we will mention just a couple here. The first is where the brand takes it upon itself to stand up for the people, or a particular group of people—think of Virgin Atlantic, apparently fighting the restrictive practices created by the dominance of the big airlines on behalf of the ordinary flyer.

The second variation is where the brand is *of the people* in a rather different sense—namely in that it presents itself as a conduit for people themselves to collectively and collaboratively solve an issue that needs addressing, as instanced by groups such as Change.org, which scales petitions for change through its active community.

giffgaff, the British mobile network, is a People's Champion example that bridges both of these meanings. It has very explicitly set itself up as a mobile network *run by you.* On the one hand, they deliberately call out the *fat cats* that have been profiting from the conventions of the mobile phone category by offering a much lower cost model, and on the other the customer support is delivered by other customers themselves, who in turn get rewarded with lower tariffs.

The Missionary

The Missionary Challenger is very open about its desire to bring a new way of thinking to the category. This tends to consist of putting right something in the category which has, in its view, gone seriously wrong. It talks in terms of having a *cause* or being *an agent of change.*

Premium jeans brand Hiut Denim Co. is looking to build a business that gives the skilled jeans makers in Cardigan, Wales, back the jobs that they lost to outsourcing abroad. Their co-founder, David Hieatt, explains their mission to get the town working again:

> Cardigan is a small town of 4,000 good people. 400 of them used to make jeans—they made 35,000 pairs a week for three decades. Then one day the factory closed. All that skill and know-how remained without any way of showing the world what they could do. That's why we have started The Hiut Denim Company—to bring manufacturing back home, to use all that skill on our doorstep, and to breathe new life into our town.

For a Missionary, communicating the *Why* is as important as communicating the *What.* It is the *Why* that converts us to the cause, rather than simply the purchaser of their products.

The Democratizer

One could argue that this is a variant of The Missionary, indeed a cross between The Missionary and The People's Champion. But it is such an important role, and the brands that have built their business models around this stance have had such a profound impact on their categories and the other brands around them—particularly the more expensive ones—that it has to take a place in the typology in its own right.

"Once and forever, we have decided to side with the many," wrote Ingvar Kamprad, in *The World Is Full of Opportunities,* an internal guide for IKEA employees.

The Democratizer believes in taking not from the *rich* and giving to the *poor,* but taking from the *few* and giving to the *many*—opening up the beauty of great design, or the latest catwalk clothing, or the ability to become a broadcaster or news editor, and making it available to everyone. Sometimes this is done with an overtly idealistic flag flying above it (One Laptop per Child, One World Futbol), sometimes without (European fashion brand Zara bringing catwalk looks to the high street).

It is often characterized by remarkable pricing (surprisingly low or free) and/or the deliberate sharing of knowledge that was previously only known by a few.

The Enlightened Zagger

The Enlightened Zagger is deliberately swimming against a prevailing cultural current. Essentially brands of opposition, rather than proposition, are not simply zagging while the world zigs for the hell of it: the Enlightened Zagger reveals to us *why* they are taking the stance that they are. Frequently it is a narrative that says, in effect: "I know a lot of the world seems to think this trend is OK, but in reality it's BS, and I am calling it out for what it is."

Historically, for example, the Spanish shoe brand Camper implored us to *Walk, not run*—fighting the speeding up of the world, and the loss of deep humanity that comes from living slowly. They encouraged us instead to join The Walking Society.

The Real and Human Challenger

At some level, one of the qualities that many Challengers share is the ability to give their consumers a sense of the people behind the brand. They appeal to us at a more personal level than the market leader, partly because they are making a human-to-human connection, rather than a brand-to-consumer connection, and the tone of voice they adopt reflects that.

With this particular stance, the real, human presence of the people behind the brand is made much more explicit in nature and implications. And by being explicit about the people behind the brand, their highly emotional relationship with the creation of their product, and sometimes their ambitions, this kind of Challenger looks to create more than simply a personal emotional connection, valuable though that is. It also implies a much greater emphasis on personal commitment to quality and service—one is given a sense that there is a small and idealistic group of people fighting to bring you something new, good, and special, rather than a faceless production factory with a glossy brand front doing something solely in order to maximize shareholder profits.

Very often there is a handwritten, handmade feel about these kinds of brands and their communications. The tone tends to be either playfully conversational, or ardent and passionate. Ben & Jerry's ice cream and Zappos (mentioned earlier in the chapter) would all be examples of brands using this kind of stance as a key narrative.

The Visionary

While the Missionary is looking to put a newer, better *religion* within the category, the Visionary sees what it offers and represents as transcending the way that the category currently thinks and talks about itself. This narrative is characterized by innovative Challengers such as the hydrogen car company Riversimple, whose vision is to reimagine our relationship with the car and fossil fuels to create a cleaner world; a future to strive for that rises above how we think about the category now.

Zipcar and Whole Foods would be other contemporary examples of Visionary Challengers—Zipcar through its desire to replace car ownership, rather than simply offer a different way of renting them, and Whole Foods through its *Declaration of Interdependence*—a sense that a retailer (and all of us) needs to have a higher view about the relationship with and between *Whole Foods, Whole People and Whole Planet.*

The Next Generation

It may be thought that positioning oneself as *the Next Generation* is simply an executional tactic, but there are specific circumstances which can make this a very strong strategic option for aspirant Challengers who want to accelerate the discussion about the improvement they offer. Sometimes, for example, the market leader is so popular that one may not be able to challenge it head-on.

Silk Soymilk, a brand effectively challenging milk itself, faced the problem that this was not a market leader that consumers wanted to see deposed. People love milk (whatever it may contain)—so one can try to reframe and deposition milk in all kinds of ways, but consumers don't want to hear it criticized directly. Adopting a "Next Generation" Challenger narrative—presenting itself as *the new milk*—was the most powerful one open to them.

As we have already seen with Audi of America's use of their R8 supercar as a symbol of reevaluation, Next Generation brands explicitly aim to show that times have changed, and the choices of brands should evolve with those times. In Audi's case, framing the existing choices in the category as *Old Luxury* allowed them to get greater traction in positioning themselves as a Next Generation brand for an America that has moved on.

The Game Changer

Of all the narratives instanced here, the Game Changer is the one most focused on product. The Game Changer offers us a significantly different service or product experience, wrapped up in a differentiated brand offer and positioning as well.

Airbnb offers a strong example of this: a hospitality experience that, unlike the hotel business, allows you to stay in a local's property, and indeed through them gain a real insight into how to enjoy the city you are staying in like a local, rather than as a tourist. It's not just a cheaper place to stay, but it also has the ability to transform your relationship with your destination. As Christopher Lukezic of Airbnb puts it, "[we are] not only offering them economic value, but also an incredible social and experiential value, that for many has fundamentally changed their outlook on the world"—a Game Changer in hospitality indeed.

BEING CLEAR ON YOUR MAIN NARRATIVE

Of course, the narrative that a Challenger adopts is not always quite as *clean* as separating it into these 10 typologies would suggest.

We clearly see positions being taken from time to time which combine two (or more) of these different elements: a core narrative being colored by combining it with the elements of another.

But the virtue of teasing them apart is to invite us to think clearly about where our main Challenger narrative will be focused, and where our energy and dynamism will come from as we project our Lighthouse Identity out into the world.

FINAL THOUGHTS

So what does it means to be a Challenger in today's world?

We have seen that being a Challenger is primarily a state of mind, rather than a state of market. We have also seen that as a new generation of exciting and inspiring Challengers have emerged over the last few years, the core practices and principles of what it takes to be a Challenger—the Eight Credos—have remained a guiding light, regardless of the changing business and communications landscape. And we have explored a much richer source of Challenger narratives than simply *David vs. Goliath*—new ways to bring our Challenger Identity to life and tell a story that people want to become a part of.

These models have emerged over the course of our ongoing study of Challenger brand behavior, but it is also worth noting that successful Challenger brands do not stand still—they must constantly evolve and adapt in order to challenge the market and the social and economic landscape of the time.

So what is the next key area of research and focus for The Challenger Project?

The Nobel Prize-winning physicist Sir Ernest Rutherford, when asked how he had achieved so much in the field of science with such scant resource, famously remarked: "We had no money so we were obliged to think." The next stage of The Challenger Project is focused on exploring in more detail the relationship between constraints and breakthrough, and how the constraints a Challenger faces can be turned into advantages—whether the constraints are those of budget, resource, or time. The published output, called "A Beautiful Constraint," does, of course, have an eye on marketing and brands, but also explores that thinking in relation to some of the bigger challenges that we, as individuals and as a planet, will need to lean into if we are to secure for ourselves a more positive and opportunity-filled future.

The need for a robust, rather than superficial, understanding of what it means to adopt and pursue a Challenger mindset has surely never been more important.

Chapter 6
Building Brand Authenticity

Michael B. Beverland

INTRODUCTION

Under the stewardship of Quaker Oats, Snapple shouldn't have failed—not if you believe in branding and marketing. Quaker's strategy was simple—take a brand that had been built by amateurs to the next level through an intense professional marketing push. The Quaker team did a superb job of developing customer-driven innovations, accessing mass distribution, and mainstream advertising. How was it that four years after buying Snapple for US$1.7 billion, Quaker sold the brand at the markdown price of US$300 million? Simple, Quaker forgot that consumers drank Snapple because of its quirks and as a reaction to impersonal mass production and mass marketing. The very marketing amateurism evident in the pre-Quaker days gave the brand, authenticity and its value.

Contrast Quaker's approach with Australian-based Pacific Brands' revival of the Dunlop Volley shoe. After starving the brand of marketing investment, Pacific Brands decided to reposition the shoe as an entry-level quality brand that people were not ashamed to own. These seemingly modest expectations belied the extent of the challenge facing the marketing team at Pacific Brands. Although the shoe had once been the only choice for Australian consumers and sportspeople, Nike and others had outflanked functional Dunlop by focusing on quality and fashion, dramatically shifting consumer expectations of athletic footwear. From No. 1 seller in the early

1970s, by the 1990s, the Volley was viewed internally as a commodity by low-priced retailers as a loss leader, by specialist sports retailers as an anachronism, and by consumers as something the "old man wore when mowing the lawns." In short, the brand was a cash cow fast turning into a dog. The Pacific Brands team aimed to turn this around, although never in their wildest dreams could they have planned for what happened next.

During the late 1990s, Australian teens "borrowed" their fathers' worn-out Volleys and proudly began to wear them. Hip teens were wearing this shoe as a semipolitical statement—a rejection of Nike's and Adidas' big budgets, high prices, and large sponsorship deals. The Dunlop team started to receive requests from editors of street magazines run by and for innovative teens, for advertising and free shoes. Suddenly, the Volley was the hottest item on the street and in dance clubs. Dunlop could have exploited the shoe's sudden cool with a retro-inspired mass-marketing campaign. Such a campaign would have had short-term benefits, but no lasting effect. Instead, Dunlop listened to its new fans, providing free shoes to street artists for sculptures and giveaways at raves. They also worked with up-and-coming teen designers on new models. The effect was obvious—the brand was seen as a reborn local icon—an authentic object reflective of the Australian way of doing better with less. The authentic response of the Dunlop team to teens resulted in increased brand equity at little cost (Beverland and Ewing, 2005).

The contrast between these two brands sets the scene for this chapter. Why did the lack of marketing at Dunlop work, whereas Quaker's heavy marketing investment fail? I maintain that certain brands are imbued with authenticity, and that such brands require a different marketing management approach than those positioned solely around functional, emotional, or experiential benefits. However, building brand authenticity is not easy. After all, the two examples above identify that on the face of it, authenticity is something given to a brand by consumers, not something that marketers can create and manage. Closer examination of other brands reveals a more complex picture, with marketers playing an important role in feeding the cultures surrounding these brands.

WHAT IS AUTHENTICITY?

Historically when marketers talked of authenticity, they meant "the genuine article" as opposed to counterfeits. Thus, marketers effectively conferred authenticity to the product, usually through branding, trademark protections, legal force, and recently through DNA markers. However, in today's market, the consumer primarily determines what is authentic. Therefore, authenticity is perceptual—that is, what is real or genuine is in the mind of the consumer (e.g., whether Jack Daniels was a gentleman is irrelevant—all that matters is that consumers buy into the mystery of the brand story and can confirm enough of it fits their desired truth; Beverland and Farrelly, 2010). The following example taken from an interview with Chairman of the Morgan Motor Company, Charles Morgan, illustrates this change in how authenticity is determined.

> Rather than a brand, I think it's more an attempt to interest the cult and keep the cult going. We like providing stories that people can tell in the pub and feel that that makes them part of the family. And so our brand is made up around a series of myths, some of which are true, some of which are owned. The one about the wooden chassis in France, we have tried and tried to get rid of that, but it still persists. And I think eventually we're going to have to say, ok, yeah, yeah, yeah, it's true.

Charles' quote identifies the subjective nature of brand authenticity. Morgan hand builds traditional English sports cars. Part of the body is made of wood, although the chassis certainly is not. Despite this, French fans of the brand continue to believe the chassis is made of wood, a point Morgan no longer sees any reason in denying. As Charles notes, central to Morgan's brand story are myths—some that are true, and others that are created and *owned* by consumers. The French consumers' view is an example of a story that is not strictly true, but provides an element of mystique that is alluring—that is, it works.

Why does brand authenticity matter? First, consumers desire it (Arnould and Price, 2000). Because consumers' brand choices are an extension of their desired self (Belk et al., 1989), they use certain brands to achieve self-authentication (or confirm their desired identity). Brands are chosen because traditional markers of identity such as race, religion, community, and culture are breaking down due to increased globalization, decreased barriers between states, and the increasing ubiquity of branded spaces (including schools, churches, political parties, universities) (Arnould and Price, 2000). Because consumers still desire communal connections, brands that enable them to connect to people, time, place, and culture are viewed as genuine partners, resulting in increased emotional bonds between customer and brand. Since research identifies a link between a desire to connect and brand authenticity, authentic brands are critical to the identity of today's consumer (Beverland and Farrelly, 2010).

Second, research indicates authenticity increases brand equity (Napoli et al., forthcoming). Consumers view authentic brands more favorably. Authentic brands have a higher status among consumers, thus resulting in greater loyalty and price premiums, and not surprising, higher net promoter scores (or word-of-mouth advocacy) (Principals-Synovate, 2008). Also, consumers form greater bonds with authentic brands than other brands (Beverland and Farelly, 2010). This results in greater loyalty, word-of-mouth support, the formation of brand communities, tolerance for failures, and support in tough times. Brand managers also benefit from building authenticity. Third, research reveals that brand authenticity is a better predictor of purchase intentions than brand love, trust, and credibility (Napoli et al., forthcoming). Finally, since a unique brand relationship is the pinnacle of brand equity, brands rated as "authentic partners" are more likely to have higher levels of equity (Keller, 2003). Such results have led many marketers to invest in "authentic branding strategies."

Authentic brands are also remarkably robust. Many of the brands examined in this chapter are decades old, or more. Iconic Bordeaux winery Château Margaux has a brand history stretching back over 600 years. In 2009, the Morgan Motor Company celebrated its 100th birthday—at a time when large car companies such as Chrysler and General Motors required government handouts to survive. Authentic brands can stumble and even go bankrupt. However, such brands also attract consumers dedicated to their survival. Throughout the Steve Jobs' free period at Apple, consumers continued to rally around the troubled brand out of a desire to retain the creative spirit it epitomized. Following the Jobs' led return to its roots Apple has increased its market capitalization and share with the iMac, iPod, iPad, and iPhone.

Finally, as the rest of this chapter will demonstrate, authenticity is not something that can be faked or copied. In contrast to functional performance, lifestyle claims, and experiential marketing strategies, the authenticity of a brand's story is something that provides an ongoing point of difference vis-à-vis competitors. Authenticity has other benefits too. Such is the interest in authenticity that certain brands often garner more press attention than their size merits and therefore can increase their awareness at little expense. For example, despite the performance superiority of Toyota's beautiful Lexus cars, high-profile programs such as BBC's *Top Gear* prefer to cover smaller brands such as Aston Martin, Ferrari, and BMW because they "have soul." Although Lexus is viewed as technically excellent, it is also seen as boring, and must rely on marketing spend to build awareness. The great wine estates of the world enjoy similar benefits, garnering most of the news coverage while accounting for less than one percent of global wine sales.

Can Marketers Manufacture Authenticity?

Although brand authenticity is critical, building it is not easy. In fact, authenticity is often seen as the polar opposite of mass marketing, advertising, and brand building (Beverland et al., 2008), and has become such an overused term that firms must work harder than ever to prove they are authentic (Mack, 2009, p. 10). Authenticity is believed to be natural, unforced, and unstaged, free from self-interest and commercial considerations. Klein's *No Logo* (2000) and antibrand organization Adbusters attack brands for their very inauthenticity, while Seabrook (2000) and Harris (2003) characterize commercial culture as superficial and meaningless. Big brands such as Starbucks may also be attacked for shutting down small neighborhood coffee shops that promote a more authentic atmosphere and genuine dedication to producing quality coffee, despite the fact that historical analysis reveals authenticity is often manufactured by small manufacturers as a competitive response to mass producers (Thompson et al., 2006).

Part of the problem relates to how marketers promote authenticity. Research reveals that explicit statements such as "I'm Authentic" have the opposite effect. Furthermore, marketing *per se* is not the problem; rather research suggests the *appearance* of commercial motivation is the real issue (Beverland, 2006). For example, self-taught artist, the Reverend Howard Finster lost authenticity when he adopted 1–800 numbers, explicitly targeted artworks to customer segments, and produced branded lines of paintings to expand his market (Fine, 2004). Brands judged insincere may also struggle to gain authenticity. American beer brand Coors struggled to gain traction with the North American gay community because its owners sponsored antigay causes. The brand was viewed as attempting to exploit the gay community while at the same time undermining the rights of community members (Kates, 2004).

Marketers can therefore play a role in the creation of brand authenticity despite the aforementioned difficulties. Perhaps it is because of these difficulties that so few brands are considered in the same vein as great artists and given iconic status. The next section identifies the six stories managers use to lend their brands authenticity.

SIX STRATEGIES FOR BUILDING BRAND AUTHENTICITY

My 12-year research program on brand leadership (Beverland, 2009) has identified six ways in which marketers can reinforce consumer perceptions of authenticity: embedding the brand in a community, challenging conventions, sticking to one's roots, loving the craft behind the product/service, downplaying one's marketing expertise, and ignoring direct customer input into innovation. Although brand managers may place greater emphasis on one characteristic at a particular time, consumer research suggests all six are required over the long term in order to be seen as an authentic brand (Beverland, 2005).

Being Part of the Community

When bands such as the Rolling Stones visit Auckland in New Zealand, they all pay a visit to Real Groovy Records—the iconic Upper Queen Street store with its famous neon sign. Real Groovy stocks a vast range of new and used LPs, CDs, and music memorabilia. No history of the local music scene could be written without mentioning this brand. Part of the authenticity of this brand is that it sides with musicians and lovers of music whereas other stores report to shareholders. The team behind the store has made many decisions that seem to defy commercial sense while reinforcing their role in the music community.

For example, when New Zealand music was struggling for radio play in the early 1980s, Real Groovy decided to sell LPs by local artists at cost. This resulted in improved chart performance for New Zealand musicians, forcing radio to play local music in order to remain relevant to their listeners. It's difficult to imagine how artists such as Crowded House would have achieved the success they have without this initial support. Real Groovy again demonstrated their commitment to the community when they bailed out cash-strapped bFM—the University of Auckland's student run station. When the student union was looking to cut costs, Real Groovy stepped in with advertising support, thereby keeping alive an important independent voice on the radio scene. Again, many local musicians gained their first airplay on bFM because mainstream radio rejected more alternative acts.

Such immersion in the local music community has several benefits. First, consumers remain loyal to the brand even though prices may be higher. Real Groovy has higher costs than mainstream retailers because of its generous loyalty scheme and its second-hand trade policy that allows consumers to trade in old music for store credit. The store's owners are also reluctant to engage in widespread discounting because they believe it insults artists. Real Groovy has seen off many larger competitors and maintained sales even in the face of competition from large discount category killers. Being part of the community has one further benefit—community members rally around the brand in times of trouble. In 2008, Real Groovy was forced into receivership because several partners retired and removed their capital. After little more than one-month new partners, many of who were leading members of the local recording industry and had grown up with the brand, recapitalized the business. Their reason was simple—it was impossible to imagine the New Zealand music scene without Real Groovy.

Authentic brands assimilate into the psyche of nations and subcultures. Can we imagine an Australia without Vegemite, France without Champagne, America without Harley Davidson, and Britain without Harrods? Importantly, if we turn the relationship around, we also get a sense that something is wrong. When brands become a part of a community, purchasing them becomes an act of loyalty and identity. Other brands may enter the market with better performance, better pricing, or more marketing, but they lack the necessary authenticity to compete against entrenched locals.

The loyalty shown to local brands is driven by the belief that these brands are in the community for the long term. Bigger, flashier rivals may stay in the community while times are good, but are likely to close stores, lay staff off, and move production when times get tough. While authentic brands stand up for the community, other brands seek to exploit subcultures when market conditions are right or when it is safe to do. For example, Coors attempted to target the gay community when homosexuality was seen as acceptable, whereas Levi's had stood by and supported the community when it was socially unacceptable to do so (Kates, 2004). The snowboard brand Burton is held in high esteem because of its role in developing the sport. Burton continued to make snowboard gear and to support and publicize the sport, even though many ski runs initially banned snowboarders. Subsequently, ski brands such as Rossignol have struggled to enter the snowboard market. In making the cult movie *Dogtown and Z-Boys,* Vans focused on producing a movie about the joys of skating, but did not engage in any product placement, fully aware that their core fan base would whiff the "stink of commercialism." Instead, viewers responded to a company implicitly giving back to the community that had adopted them.

Challenge Conventions

Being authentic has long been associated with going against convention. The Romantic Movement in the 19th century desired an authentic life by rejecting the rational order of the day (associated with industrialization and the triumph of reason over emotion). Authenticity for the Romantics was to be found in nature, craft traditions, and emotion. Punk and new wave artists were similarly inspired, rejecting the overblown music of the early 1970s in favor of a return to simple song structures laced with raw emotion. Although they rejected the dominant norms of the day, these artists created a body of work that endures and continues to inspire new generations. This spirit is embodied in authentic brands.

Apple's playful advertisements challenge people to "Think Different," while their stores feature images of rebels such as Gandhi, John Lennon, and Martin Luther King. Apple's famous 1984 advertisement played during the super bowl captured this rebellious attitude, attacking the conformity and sterility of life under IBM. The flying of the skull and crossbones flag over their headquarters further enforced this position. Despite the success and growth of Apple, the brand continues to present itself as a more humanistic, creative, playful entity in contrast to the "system" as represented by Microsoft, Dell, and IBM.

Sir Richard Branson is a regular late entrant into concentrated mature markets such as airlines, banking, rail, and mobile phones. Every time he does so, experts predict failure. And Virgin has failed, but we continue to love Branson because of his entrepreneurial spirit that seeks to shake up the convention and "stick it to the fat cats." Branson takes on entrenched competitors and in many cases not only wins, but also forces market leaders to offer better deals to their customers. As a result, formerly mature categories start to grow, often increasing returns for everyone.

James Dyson was angered by the fact that the basic technology behind vacuum cleaners had not changed since the first vacuum was invented. Modern vacuum cleaners continued to lose suction after a few uses, resulting in poor cleaning performance. What angered Dyson more was the consumer was being exploited by large, lazy corporations who instead of innovating, engaged in superficial stylistic changes. Every major vacuum cleaner manufacturer who saw no potential in his cyclone design turned Dyson away. To see his vision come to life, Dyson took on considerable debt and founded his own firm. So successful has he been that a new generation of consumers no longer uses the word "Hoover" to refer to vacuum cleaners.

Authentic brands embody the contrarian spirit of great artists. Since the choice of brand often reflects our desired self, authentic brands capture the rebellious spirit that all of us have, but often feel we can't act on. Typical of many of them is the desire to retain important traditions, operate on old world business models that produce great products rather than support poor ones with marketing (e.g., Microsoft's approach to Vista [so playfully pilloried by Apple]), and capture the rebellious spirit. Importantly, they often refuse to accept tradeoffs—for example, between performance and design (Apple), performance and sustainability (The Bodyshop), service and low price (Virgin), and innovation and tradition (Morgan and Château Margaux). In doing so, these brands often approach things differently at a time when others converge around accepted practices, thus reinforcing a sense of sameness and me too-ness in the mind of the consumer.

Stick to Your Roots

Authentic brands seem stubborn when viewed through the lens of "customer is always right." While marketing theory suggests the need to adapt to customer needs, changing societal standards and competitor tactics, the brands covered so far seem to reject new trends, new technologies, and new ways of doing things in favor of sticking to their roots. The people behind authentic brands stick to their roots because they believe they are right—which is also why they rate highly on sincerity.

Australia's greatest wine, Penfold Grange, provides a sobering lesson for marketers keen to mess with a brand's roots. Grange is truly regarded as one of the world's iconic wines. The story of Grange is one of a passionate craftsman battling against the odds to produce something truly unique. Max Schubert (then Penfold chief winemaker) desired to produce a wine that expressed the uniqueness of Australia. Critically, he desired to produce a wine that would rightfully take its place among the great wines of the world. At the time, local wines were pale imitations of European products (often labeled as "Burgundy" or "Hermitage" even though they bore no relation to these wines). Schubert labored to produce Grange, a dry-wine style that blended the best red grapes from Penfold vineyard holdings in South Australia. Initial results were so discouraging that Penfold board ordered Schubert to cease his experiments. Undeterred, Schubert continued on in secret.

Entered in a local wine show under a nondescript code, the wine won several awards (Grange simply takes time to mature in the bottle to be at its best). Feeling vindicated, Schubert continued to produce Grange in good years, ultimately producing Australia's greatest red wine. Emboldened by this, the Penfold team under new owner Southcorp decided it was time to exploit the franchise. Suddenly Grange was released every year, and a new wine—white Grange (or Yattarna)—was released. In 2001, Grange was being discounted in bottle shops and critics were voicing concern that the wine was no longer as good as it should be. White Grange also received unfavorable reviews and was often passed in at auctions.

Grange was in trouble because the marketing and winemaking teams had turned their back on its roots. Schubert desired to produce a world-class wine that was a unique expression of Australia at its best. He was not motivated by high prices or record auction prices. In contrast, the motivation behind the extension to White Grange was profit. Far from being a unique wine, White Grange was simply another expensive chardonnay. As well, changes to Grange had been made to appeal to the American market, thus alienating traditional fans. Now under new owners, the brand attempted to return to its roots with a new marketing campaign featuring a contemplative Max Schubert and his initial experimental bottles under the tagline "To the Renegades: Max Schubert, winemaking legend and creator of Penfold Grange. To those who do thing for love not money."

The history surrounding brands is critical to its authenticity. Research identifies that heritage, sincerity, and love of production are central to consumer judgments of authenticity. Mess with a brand's roots, and consumers are likely to leave in droves. By extending into mass fashion, surf brands such as Ripcurl run the risk of alienating their core constituency because surfers don't like seeing nonsurfers wear "their gear" (Beverland et al., 2010). Remaining true to one's roots does not mean simply repeating past practices because this results in products that quickly become obsolete. What is crucial is to retain the original spirit of the brand. Although Morgan Motor Company rejected the advice to adopt mass production techniques, outsource production of core parts, and use modern materials, they did adopt Japanese quality methods, invested in safety and emissions standards, and built new models such as the Aero, Aeromax, and hydrogen-powered Lifecar. Likewise, every new product released by Apple reinforces its original mission of creating insanely great, user-friendly products.

Love of Craft

Rand's (1943) novel *The Fountainhead* involves two characters of relevance to our discussion on authentic branding. The first, Peter Keating, loves the fame and trappings that come with architecture and therefore gives up everything he loves in order to make buildings people want. Peter is not a very good architect, but he is an excellent impression manager, being whatever people want him to be. At the end of the novel, he is a man destroyed—a soulless individual who realizes how meaningless all the temporary trappings of fame are.

His opposite, Howard Roark (the hero and Peter's friend), drops out of architecture school when it no longer has anything to teach him, works for a fading architecture practice run by iconoclast Henry Cameron, and survives on small commissions given to him by individuals who want something different. Eventually, Roark's radical architectural vision (the character is based on Frank Lloyd Wright) gains acceptance and ends the novel as a successful architect. In a critical passage of the novel, Howard tells Peter that to achieve true happiness in work, one must "love the doing" rather than fame and wealth. The people behind authentic brands embody this spirit.

Authentic brands are staffed with people passionate for the product or service and run by leaders heavily involved in all aspects of production. Charles Morgan (of the Morgan Motor Company) continues to race Morgan's at Le Mans and other events. The firm is staffed with classic motoring enthusiasts, many of whom restore and race their own cars. Real Groovy is run by, and for, music lovers. It is not uncommon for staff to spend a third of their pay at the store on music and movies. Richard Branson requires all staff, from management to front airline check-in counters, every month to keep in touch with the main job at hand. Ralph Lauren is known for walking the floors of Bloomingdales, to ensure his clothes are presented just right. Steve Jobs was well known for being involved in all aspects of production at Apple, often overruling designers or delaying product releases until they met his exacting standards. Levy (2000, p. 139) recalls Steve Jobs's reasons for rejecting the first Macintosh circuit board on aesthetic grounds.

New Zealand film director Sir Peter Jackson loves the art of film making so much so that no detail is too small. For example, in the opening battle scene of *Fellowship of the Ring*, an alliance of dwarves, elves, and humans desperately fight the armies of darkness. The scene is set thousands of years before the formation of the Fellowship. Weta staff were aware that over time, technologies would change and evil creatures such as orcs and goblins would also evolve. As such, there are subtle differences in the features and technology of the different races (Sibley, 2006). Many filmmakers would have reused the same props to save on time and budget. They would have rationalized that most people wouldn't know. Not Jackson—he would know, as would fans.

Love of production is central to consumer-based brand authenticity. Authentic brands sit in contrast with the majority of brands on the market. Just as we switch companies and jobs for better pay and conditions, few brands inspire employees to turn down a better offer. Most employees view their current firm as a means to an end. We usually try and make it through the week so we can engage our passions in the weekend. As such, few brands staffed by such employees inspire consumer loyalty. Just like Peter Keating, many of us have been told to get a practical job, instead of following our passions. Just as we secretly admire artists for having the courage to do what they love, so we admire brands that are run and staffed by true enthusiasts—people who will do whatever it takes to ensure the survival of the brand. As a result, such dedication results in innovative products that become a part of history—such as the Apple Macintosh, Chanel's little black dress, Dyson cyclone vacuum, Hermès Birkin bags, Louis Roederer Cristal, or Manolo Blahnik shoes.

Business Amateurism

Marketers love to revel in their cleverness and professionalism. They love recalling successful efforts at targeting consumers, extending brands, responding to customer needs, benchmarking against competitors, and adopting scientific methods of analysis. They make no secret of their motivations either—they are there to make money and crush the competition. In contrast, authentic brands seem to be run by amateurs that reject customer research and marketing, in favor of gut feel, intuition, and craft techniques. Yet amateurs have some redeeming features. First, they are unpaid. Because of this, they usually do things because they want to. Second, they often think differently because of their lack of training. Third, they are unencumbered with concerns of fame, paying bills, and meeting next quarter's targets. As such, amateurs are often remarkably grounded, humble, and playful.

A great example is Altoids—the popular brand of mints. In a remarkable example of corporate maturity, Claudia Kotchka (VP of Design at Procter and Gamble [P&G]) identified why P&G couldn't produce brands with the authenticity of Altoids. Recalling Snapple, Kotchka (2006) noted how Altoids brand authenticity would be destroyed by the "P&G effect." First to go would be the Altoids tin. Tin is more expensive than plastic, is heavier, is old fashioned, and the unique molded design is difficult and expensive to change in response to changing trends. Second to go would be the high-quality paper inside the tin that protects the mints from breaking. Again, too many parts, too much expense, and paper would be unnecessary in a newly designed plastic container. Third to go would be the wacky flavors—after all, no market test would highlight mass interest in liquorice mints, ginger mints, and cinnamon mints. Fourth to go would be the strength of the mints themselves as this puts many people off. Finally, the shape and size of the mints would be standardized with new production processes because focus groups disliked their rough, seemingly hand-cut shape. Kotchka concluded that the result of this attempt to "smooth out the edges" of Altoids would be to destroy the product's value in the eyes of its customers (in fact, she labeled the new brand "Proctoids").

In-N-Out Burger provides another example of amateurism. This cult hamburger chain from Southern California charges low prices, offers few items, produces everything fresh- to-order (and still hand-cut fries), pays the highest wages in the fast food sector, and enjoys cult-like devotion among consumers. Despite having relatively few stores, high cost, and strong competition, In-N-Out Burger has some of the highest returns in the industry. Also, as a fast food provider, its burgers do not suffer the same poor-quality associations endured by other brands. And, in an industry where staff turnover is rampant, In-N-Out enjoys extremely high levels of loyalty (Moon, 2003). How has this seemingly, old time burger chain outperformed its larger, smarter, more customer-focused rivals? Simple—because it emphasizes on old-fashioned things like quality, care for product and staff, friendly service, and community. In-N-Out is not successful in spite of its lack of professionalism; rather its very amateurism gives the brand its charm as well as a focus on what really matters—taste and service.

Although these brands seem amateurish, don't take this as evidence the people running them have no commercial understanding. Many of the managers of these brands are MBAs and are interested in commercial success. Nothing captures this more effectively than Steve Jobs's quip that "Real Artists Ship" in relation to getting the original Apple Macintosh in the market on time. Take a tour of one of the great wine houses of Bordeaux such as Château Margaux and you'll come away thinking the wine is produced by intuitive artists with ancient hand-made equipment, and recipes passed down through generations. This, however, is just a part of the story. Behind closed doors, these wineries use state-of-the-art technology and have a detailed scientific understanding of raw materials and technological processes.

"We Ignore Customers"

Behind every authentic brand is a creative genius, whether it is James Dyson, Steve Jobs, Steve Wozniak and Jonathan Ive, John Galliano, Marc Jacobs, Peter Jackson, Miuccia Prada, Coco Chanel, and so on. These geniuses regularly solve problems that mere mortals cannot, and they usually do so in innovative ways. These designers and leaders embody a paradox. They regularly produce products that people love, yet reject marketing, consumer research, and consumer-espoused needs. They heretically believe that customers rarely know what they want. Worse than that, they blame customer research for their failures.

In his book *The Pursuit of WOW!* (1994, p. 108), Peters discusses how Miuccia Prada's one flirtation with conventional, customer-driven market research resulted in clothes that Prada was ashamed of, which critics savaged, and customers ignored. As Peters states: "The clothes were over-designed, and it seemed that commercial considerations and self-consciousness were leading her." Prada now immerses herself in the market, constantly on the lookout for emerging trends, small details, and global styles. This information adds to Prada's already famed memory and provides an ongoing source of creative ideas as new knowledge is combined with old for each new season's line. Hardly the stuff of market orientation!

Bought a bottle of Château Margaux lately? Lucky you! It costs around US$500 per bottle in a good year and is nearly unobtainable, as it has been for the last 300 years. Such desirability must be driven by constant customer-driven innovations and changes, right? Wrong! Estate Manager Paul Pontallier has little time for segmentation, targeting, and positioning. His *raison d'être* is simply to offer the best possible expression of the estate, given the seasonal conditions. He is adamant that he doesn't not make wine for a consumer, nor adapt anything he does for segments. His main concern is living up to the esteemed heritage of the brand (sentiments echoed by business-savvy owner Corinne Mentzelopoulos).

Marketers are taught that brands should be developed to meet customer needs and adjusted in line with customer insights from brand-tracking studies. Firms are encouraged to alter structures and systems to ensure they are at one with the all-powerful customer. Yet, authentic brands openly reject the slavish worship of customers and treat conventional marketing tools, such as segmentation, targeting, and positioning, with a degree of contempt (in fact some such as Morgan go so far as to state "the customer is often wrong"). However, taking such statements at face value would be dangerous. Many authentic brands suffered in the past when they traded on their status instead of offering market leadership. So how did they maintain market relevance?

The staff behind authentic brands are totally immersed in their markets and are avid collectors of general information. But market immersion is different from being market driven. Indeed, Peters (1994) contrasts being "of the market" (market driven) with being "in the market" (market immersion). Market immersion involves key employees being active members in the marketplace as a way of sourcing valuable insights and trends. Fashion designers provide great examples. LVMH's Bernard Arnault encourages his designers to travel widely, not because he wants them to adopt the looks of a particular subgroup within a culture, but because the smallest details provide designers with inspiration.

Such activities are vital for three reasons. First, immersion provides marketers of authentic brands with a vital source of new performance standards and stylistic trends. The information collected is often qualitative, experiential, and diverse, in contrast to what many of the more conventional brands gather. Second, this information can be filtered into product styling or brand marketing to ensure ongoing relevance without diluting the brand. Third, and most importantly, the information enables designers such as Jonathan Ive (Apple), or other product developers (from brew masters to car designers) to swear that their products are derived from personal inspiration or the indefinable (and seductive) creative spirit rather than "formal" market research.

FIVE LESSONS FOR BRAND MANAGERS

Authenticity Is Shown

Consumer research reveals that overt claims of authenticity are viewed as marketing hype. Worse, such claims may render genuinely authentic brands fake (Beverland et al., 2008). Wrangler jeans' 2004–5 billboard campaign featured two denim-clad models under the tag line "Born Authentic." Just as consumers may wonder whether something is wrong when brands talk constantly about quality, saying you're authentic may raise concerns in the minds of consumers. Like quality, authenticity must be shown, not stated. To project authenticity, brands can draw on a number of attributes including historical associations, relationship to place or subcultural space, noncommercial values, and the creative process. The Penfold campaign to return the brand to its roots provides a good example of this approach.

Cultural Immersion

The owners and managers of authentic brands collected vast amounts of diverse information and filtered this down to employees. While not all firms rejected formal market research techniques, they did not give precedence to this form of information: small details or one-off experiences were accorded equal value to or greater value than brand-tracking research or focus groups. For example, Quiksilver management routinely asks their staff (and staff ask their children) what they think about the latest surf fashion lines, as their decision to buy (or not to) is considered a crucial litmus test. Marketers of authentic brands need to encourage direct observation gained during staff travel and information gained via personal experience with the products, and place great weight on the much-maligned "gut feel." Importantly, they need to seek information gained via immersion in the market or through membership of a subculture rather than formalized research with specific demographics. Ideas that inform about the practices of such brands should come from *in situ* experiences, tangential sources (viewing other cultures), and involvement in industry-specific forums.

Employ a Brand Historian

The brands mentioned above drew directly on their histories as a form of competitive advantage. Too few companies retain records of their past. Early in my career, I was contacted by firms wanting to reclaim their history, only to find that too many past employees had moved on, or passed away, and too few records were kept. These brand managers often have tantalizing evidence to suggest they are the oldest brand in their class, or country, or the first brand of their type, but have seen such claims usurped by others with the evidence to back them up. Likewise, many brands have colorful characters or associations in their past, yet too little information exists to build a rich, multifaceted story around them. Brand managers should view their brands as historical documents and retain every record, every press clipping (good and bad), and regularly engage writers to provide a historical record (if only for internal training purposes). Vespa has developed a Piaggio Historical Archive, which contains more than 150,000 documents from the company's past. Volkswagen (VW) and Jack Daniels have done likewise.

Don't Be Afraid of Letting Consumers In

Although the owners of authentic brands may not worship the customers' viewpoint when developing new innovations, they do welcome customers into the cult. On the outside, In-N-Out appears unchanged since founding, avoiding demand for chicken and vegetarian burgers as well as salads and larger burgers. However, In-N-Out also has a secret menu. After customers started asking for Neapolitan milkshakes (a mix of chocolate, strawberry, and vanilla) and burgers with three patties or above, the owners rekeyed all the firm's cash machines to allow for these innovations. Although no four–four burger is offered on the menu (four patties and four slices of cheese), in the know consumers may ask for it, service staff can process such requests without problems (Moon, 2003). (In-N-Out's secret menu is now a "not so secret menu" as it is advertised on their webpage.)

Make the Most of Lucky Breaks

The Pacific Brand's marketing team got lucky when teens started wearing the Volley. They were even luckier because their inexperience with this market made them cautious in responding to the Volley's sudden change of status. Authentic brands make the most of these lucky breaks. The marketing team behind Islay-based whiskey brand Bruichladdich are master storytellers. Their famous WMD (whiskey of mass distinction) whiskey arose from a misunderstanding due to CIA paranoia. Fans of the whiskey can watch the manufacturing process live online. The CIA (unbeknownst to Bruichladdich staff) contacted the distillery when one camera went down, inquiring when it would be back up. On inquiring whether the "customer" was a single malt fan, Bruichladdich received the following reply: "No we are not single malt fans; we are the CIA and believe you are making weapons of mass destruction." Bruichladdich used this story as a motivation for a new product—WMD.

CONCLUSION

Can any brand be authentic? I often get asked whether authenticity is relevant to business-to-business brands, or new brands, or fast moving consumer goods brands? Often there is a sense that authenticity is particular to certain categories of products or services, or something that only very old brands have. In response to these questions, it is important to remember authenticity is a product of the consumers' relationship with the brand (marketers play one role in building and reinforcing this relationship). Since the search for authenticity is an enduring theme in much philosophical thought, art works, and individual life goals, there is no reason to think that authenticity cannot apply across a range of contexts (from fast-moving consumer goods such as Altoids mints, fast food such as In-N-Out Burger, through to automotives, technology, household cleaners, services, industrial raw ingredients, fashion, and high-end luxury goods). And, I have studied an enormous range of brands that challenge these beliefs—Innocent Smoothies presented themselves as authentic from Day 1 and reinforced this with a range of stories that distinguished them from competitors. Simply put, every brand can be authentic (regardless of context, age, ownership structure, or country of origin).

Likewise, although business-to-business buyers are often characterized as rational (as opposed to more emotive consumers), the reality is often very different—buyers may make choices based on risk reduction, personal relationships, aesthetic appeal, and so on (at best, organizations try and make purchasing managers more rational). Research also reveals "reputation" is one of the main drivers of business-to-business purchases (Beverland et al., 2007). Since business-to-business branding efforts are relatively new (with noted exceptions such as IBM, Caterpillar, not to mention the vast array of professional services), buyers' relationships with suppliers are defined by past interactions and levels of trust. That is, the relationship between a buyer and a seller is already genuine or authentic. And, such interactions as well as the benefits of long-term supplier–buyer partnerships provide a rich resource for storytelling and brand symbolism.

Creating an authentic brand represents a challenge to modern marketers and brand managers who revel in their marketing skills constant updating, customer service, and scientific understanding of the marketplace. To commercialize, authentic brands must develop open-ended and rich stories rather than mere positioning statements. They must espouse enduring values, become part of the cultural landscape, emphasize their love for the craft behind their product/service, and develop a powerful organizational memory that acts as a repository for their enduring brand story. The brands presented here are those that have lasted the test of time (some trace their lineage back 600 years). By adopting the principles identified here, brand managers can tap into a universal and human yearning for authenticity and, potentially, also assist their brands to endure for hundreds of years.

REFERENCES

Arnould, E.J. and L.L. Price. (2000). "Authenticating Acts and Authoritative Performances: Questing for Self and Community," in S. Ratneshwar, D.G. Mick, and C. Huffman (Eds), *The Why of Consumption: Contemporary Perspectives on Consumer Motives, Goals, and Desires* (pp. 140–163). London: Routledge.

Belk, R.W., M. Wallendorf, and J.F. Sherry, Jr. (1989). "The Sacred and the Profane in Consumer Behavior: Theodicy on the Odyssey," *Journal of Consumer Research* 16(June): 1–38.

Beverland, M.B. (2005). "Crafting Brand Authenticity: The Case of Luxury Wine," *Journal of Management Studies* 42(5): 1003–1029.

———. (2006). "The 'Real Thing': Branding Authenticity in the Luxury Wine Trade," *Journal of Business Research* 59(February): 251–258.

———. (2009). *Brand Authenticity: The Seven Habits of Iconic Brands.* London: Palgrave Macmillan.

Beverland, M.B., A. Lindgreen, and M.W. Vink (2008). "Projecting Authenticity Through Advertising: Consumer Judgments of Advertisers' Claims," *Journal of Advertising* 37(1): 5–16.

Beverland, M.B. and F.J. Farrelly (2010). "The Quest for Authenticity in Consumption: Consumers' Purposive Choice of Authentic Cues to Shape Experienced Outcomes," *Journal of Consumer Research* 36(5), 838–856.

Beverland, M.B., F.J. Farrelly, and P.G. Quester (2010). "Authentic Subcultural Membership: Antecedents and Consequences of Authenticating Acts and Authoritative Performances," *Psychology & Marketing* 27(7): 698–716.

Beverland, M.B., J. Napoli, and A. Lindgreen (2007). "Industrial Global Brand Leadership: A Capabilities View," *Industrial Marketing Management* 36(8): 1082–1093.

Beverland, M.B. and M.T. Ewing (2005). "Slowing the Adoption and Diffusion Process to Enhance Brand Repositioning: The Consumer Driven Repositioning of Dunlop Volley," *Business Horizons* 48(October): 385–392.

Beverland, M.B. and S. Luxton (2005). "The Projection of Authenticity: Managing Integrated Marketing Communications (IMC) Through Strategic Decoupling," *Journal of Advertising* 34(4): 103–116.

Booker, C. (2004). *The Seven Basic Plots: Why We Tell Stories.* London: Continuum.

Fine, G.A. (2004). *Everyday Genius: Self-Taught Art and the Culture of Authenticity.* Chicago, Illinois: University of Chicago Press.

Harris, D. (2003). *Cute, Quaint, Hungry and Romantic: The Aesthetics of Consumerism.* Cambridge: Da Capo Press.

Kates, S.M. (2004). "The Dynamics of Brand Legitimacy: An Interpretive Study in the Gay Men's Community," *Journal of Consumer Research* 31(September): 455–464.

Keller, K.L. (2003). *Strategic Brand Management: Building, Measuring, and Managing Brand Equity.* New York: Prentice-Hall.

Klein, N. (2000). *No Logo: Taking Aim at Brand Bullies.* New York: Picador.

Kotchka, C. (2006). "The Design Imperative in Consumer Goods," *Design Management Review* 17(1): 10–14.

Levy, S. (2000). *Insanely Great: The Life and Times of Macintosh, the Computer that Changed Everything.* New York: Penguin Books.

Mack, A. (2009). "Betting on the Uncertain." *Brandweek,* January 5, p. 10.

Moon, Y. (2003). *In-N-Out Burger.* Harvard Business School Case 9-503-096.

Napoli, J., et al. (forthcoming). "Measuring Consumer-Based Brand Authenticity," *Journal of Business Research.*

Peters, T. (1994). *The Pursuit of WOW! Every Person's Guide to Topsy-Turvy Times.* New York: Random House.

Principals-Synovate (2008). *2008 Authentic Brand Index Study.* Melbourne.

Rand, A. (1943). *The Fountainhead.* New York: Bobbs-Merrill.

Seabrook, J. (2000), *Nobrow: The Culture of Marketing + The Marketing of Culture.* Random House: New York.

Sibley, B. (2006). *Peter Jackson: A Film-Maker's Journey.* Auckland: HarperCollins.

Thompson, C.J., A. Rindfleisch, and Z. Arsel (2006). "Emotional Branding and the Strategic Value of the Doppelganger Brand Image," *Journal of Marketing* 70(1): 50–64.

Chapter 7

The Most Important Brand Question: How Does It Make Them Feel?

Daryl Travis

I admit it. I pay more for things than I should. I can't explain why but I do. Take salt, for example. Morton is my salt and I refuse to buy any other brand even though it costs about 30 percent more than other brands. It's silly but if my market is out of Morton, I go to another store or put off buying salt until it is available. I tell myself, "It's just salt." Technically speaking, salt is salt—just simple molecules of sodium chloride. It truly is the perfect example of a commodity since every brand, by necessity, is made from identical molecules.

It makes no sense that I won't even consider another brand. But I have positive memories of Morton that make me feel good. My mother uses the brand exclusively; I've never seen another brand in her cupboard. Each time I reached for salt during a family dinner, every time my food needed more flavor, Morton met my needs. Yes, any other brand would have worked fine, but Morton now occupies a permanently positive place in my brain, even though, for decades, the company has spent very little on advertising. Still I know the Morton slogan, "When it rains it pours." For me, the brand is like a familiar old song; I know the lyrics and melody by heart, and I feel like I know the brand better than any other. That familiarity creates favorability and I make my choice of salt automatically. I don't have to think about it. I just have a feel for it.

It also makes me feel better knowing Morton Salt consistently maintains about a 50 percent share of the market in the United

States. During consumer research, participants were told a competitive store brand was the exact same product, even packaged by Morton, and many chose Morton nonetheless. Apparently, the brand makes them feel better, too. I know it makes me feel good that so many other people share my irrational preference for Morton salt. This should also make every senior executive—even those in commodity businesses—feel better realizing it is possible that their brands can overcome *me-too* brand status and command higher and more profitable margins. Seriously, if it can be done with salt, it can be done with any product.

Mercedes is one of the most iconic premium brands in the world, but are their cars really worth two or three times as much as any other vehicle that transports us just as well from one point to another? Every brand has a motor and four wheels that capably meet our needs. Are Mercedes vehicles actually better or are they more desired because the brand has created an irrational demand? Obviously, many people feel Mercedes are worth substantially more than basic transportation.

And, I must include myself among them.

There are hundreds of ink pen brands available. Bic pens sell for less than a dollar, mid-price brands such as Parker retail for hundreds of dollars, while luxury brands such as Montblanc cost thousands. All three brands of pens put ink on paper quite well, and it is nearly impossible to distinguish one brand's writing from another. In some cases, the argument could be made that the inexpensive Bic is more reliable than the fancy high-priced brands. Practically speaking, there is no logical reason to ever buy anything other than the perfectly functional, value-priced Bic pen. Yet, both Parker and Montblanc are highly successful brands that find sustainable competitive advantage in creating emotional reasons to buy their products. As proudly stated on their website, "Celebrated for generations as the paramount creator of writing instruments … Montblanc supports the conviction of preservation and opulence." Thank you. Now, I feel even better about my Montblanc.

I believe Richard Branson, of Virgin fame, summed up quite well the business benefits of creating an emotional brand in the foreword to my book *Emotional Branding: How Irrational Brands Gain the Competitive Edge.*

> The idea that business is strictly a business affair has always struck me as preposterous. For one thing, I've never been particularly good at numbers, but I think I've done a reasonable job with feelings. And I'm convinced that it is feelings—and feelings alone—that account for the success of the Virgin brand in all its myriad forms. It is my conviction that what we call *shareholder value* is best defined by how strongly employees and customers feel about your brand. Nothing seems more obvious to me that a product or service only becomes a brand when it is imbued with profound values that translate into fact and feeling that employees can protect and customers embrace. These values shape my rather simple view of business, but they are (or should be) universal … (Travis, 2000)

THE IRRATIONAL EDGE

Irrationality prevails whether the brand is salt, or cars, or ink pens; in fact, it is true of the leading brand in almost any product category. And don't think for a moment this is only true with consumer goods. On the surface it seems counterintuitive and some still want to believe everything in business is coldly rational and completely logical. Yet, in thousands of deep Emotional Inquiry™ interviews with business people and professional audiences, we've discovered business-to-business customers are even *more* emotional about the brand choices they make. Actually, we have yet to discover a category of business-to-business goods and services in which this is not true. Think about it; do you have more emotions involved in your career, your livelihood, even your very identity, or your toothpaste?

We frequently conduct research and consult for highly commoditized product categories and brands in which the product itself may make little difference to the customer—when products are equivalent and decisions can be made on pricing alone—but the desire for service and personal relationships with sales people quickly turn the selling process into an emotional experience. The need to feel confident and to sense that someone has you covered if anything goes wrong consistently trumps price. Engineers, for example, prefer sales people who have engineering backgrounds, so they can help validate the engineer's ideas. Unfortunately, it is also very easy to get it wrong and create negative brand feelings when we fail to think through the psychological affect of messages. It seems innocent enough when medical product brands claim to improve patient results but healthcare professionals resent this approach. Clinicians do not want brands to claim credit for patient care because the doctors, nurses, and technicians provide care and create better outcomes for patients, not the brands. They expect brands to help *them* care for patients not supplant or invalidate their role.

Often a brand commands higher margins and market share simply because a professional audience feels more validated by using the brand. Fluke is an international brand of electronic test tools used by electricians, engineers, and electrical contractors. The brand claims to be the world leader, and a dominant market share confirms it. Their products are excellent and priced accordingly but, most importantly, their signature—yellow color—sends a clear and distinct message that the user can afford the gold standard in testing instruments and is thus seen as a consummate professional. I work with many top consumer and business-to-business brands throughout the world and have seen firsthand that Fluke is among the leaders in creating customer passion and brand loyalty—all based on the emotional premise of elevating the status of their professional audience. Fluke's continued market dominance provides ample evidence that emotional brand resonance is the key to delivering significant and sustainable market share, margin, and profitability.

AB Sciex is a leading brand that does business with scientists whom you would expect to be completely rational. Yet the company's most technical products—mass spectrometers for the molecular analysis of chemicals and substances—elicit highly irrational behaviors from customers. The customer's mass spectrometer allows them to do amazing things and answer questions no one else can. It helps them feel very good at what they do, so much so that they begin to depend upon their mass spectrometer as a trusted friend, and even calling their machines by pet names. AB Sciex sales and service people are well aware of this attachment and use it to the brand's benefit whenever they can. They don't show-up to service the spectrometer; they show-up to see how Maggie is doing today.

When brands make their customers feel something personal—confidence, validation, connection, reassurance, or any other positive emotion, brand loyalty benefits. This is true for any kind of product in any category, be it business-to-business or consumer. It's also true the success and profitability created by these emotionally resonant brands makes shareholders feel good too.

These basic human truths begin to explain why, like most people, I am more loyal and willing to pay extra for brands I trust. It helps us understand why the most important brand question is, "How does it make them feel?" It also helps us see the very clear reality that brands are about feelings, not facts demonstrating why successful brands tend to gain an irrational edge. Given these realities, most executives agree it is time to change the way we think about how people think about brands.

THINKING ABOUT THINKING

Pardon my indulgence for a bit of science and biology here, but it is too important to ignore. Everything about what a brand says and does is reviewed and evaluated in the brain via the exact same mechanisms that drive all human thought and behavior. The choice of one brand over another occurs as a result of the complex interactions of human brain cells. Logos, taglines, colors, and advertisements are all parts of the equation, but the final calculation of value and need is purely a mental exercise—electrochemistry really—based on experiences and memories. Once and for all, we need to recognize that brands exist only inside the human mind.

Each human brain has about 100 billion neurons or brain cells. Day-to-day and moment-to-moment experiences of life cause small clusters of these cells to activate. The activated cells retain or store the experience for future reference. We can think of them as tiny memory cells. Researchers have conducted neural scan studies demonstrating that an iconic public personality, politician, or actor can cause even one brain cell to turn on (Viskontas et al., 2009).

When a similar or related experience occurs subsequently—one day, one year, or decades later—the same cells activate again.

Thoughts are processed and decisions made about everything, including brands, when neurons connect and interact with other neurons. These combinations can store about 1 million billion bits of information—the library of your life. What will you do with all this data unless you are planning a career as a trivia champion? Actually, you need this much information because life is complicated. (As if,

I needed to remind you.) You have to process billions upon billions of data points just to survive a single day.

The ability to process all that information is what makes it possible for you to know what to do each time a decision must be made including whether to choose this brand or that one. Every day people typically make over 200 choices about food alone (Wansink, 2006). Your brain's rapid and automatic access to its stacks of information makes it possible to make decisions. For example, the memory you encoded about how the package of a particular brand was difficult to reseal reminds you to not purchase that brand again.

In this way, your brain is like vast library shelves with endless living volumes of information written and continuously rewritten by weaving together your life's experiences. Every little thing you have ever encountered—including a particular brand experience—whether you were conscious of it or not, is recorded in the neural patterns that comprise these collections. Every single decision you make in the present is filtered, reviewed, and assessed by your past experiences and memories.

Day-to-day survival requires that you access this information immediately, effectively, and effortlessly. In fact, so easily you can do much of it without thinking about it. There is no time to think through every volume in your mind's library when you feel something strange crawling on the back of your leg. You do not need to think; you just react. Fortunately, your brain can navigate tall stacks of information faster than you can blink an eye and maneuver instantaneously from volume to volume to sort out the information you need to survive in that moment.

PATTERN MACHINES

Your brain can do this so well because, unlike a library, it doesn't store subjects per se. Instead, it stores patterns. Jeff Hawkins makes a compelling case that human brains are pattern machines in his book *On Intelligence* (Hawkins and Blakeslee, 2004, p. 62). Your brain effortlessly detects patterns in all of its stored data and helps you recognize what's happening, good or bad, moment by moment. These schemata can be accessed instantaneously to help interpret present experiences and anticipate future ones. Your brain constantly scans your world, looking out for what's going on and what's coming next. It compares every minute thing happening in the moment against past mental models looking for any differences. When it senses only familiar things, all is well. But let your brain sense something different—like that bug on the back of your leg—and every alarm in your body goes off and every defensive system instantly springs into action.

This remarkable capacity for pattern recognition provides us with an automatic way of sensing and doing. This is all very primal behavior for human beings; we cannot change regardless how much we might want to. Imagine, if we actually had to think about every single decision and behavior, our heads would explode! Thankfully our mental models automatically, constantly, and, for the most part, subconsciously send signals to do this or do that. Through these mental models, created from neural patterns, your mind "remembers the future based on what occurred in the past" (Siegel, 1999, p. 30). Using mental models to predict what may happen next is an exquisitely elegant tool for survival (and an ingenious technique for building brands). Otherwise, humans might never have learned crocodiles are faster than they look or discovered the Baristas at Starbucks would happily whip-up just about anything you need.

When brands cause us to frame positive mental models, we don't have to think about which brand to choose. When our reaction is automatic, it drives brand loyalty. It works to a brand's distinct advantage and to its detriment if the pattern is broken. In January 2009, Tropicana Pure Premium Orange Juice, a leading Pepsico brand, released a new package design substituting a generic-looking glass of juice for its iconic brand imagery of a drinking straw protruding from an orange. Not that risky on the surface. But consumers were irate about the change, sending letters, phoning, emailing, twittering, and complaining, "Do any of these package-design people actually shop for orange juice? Because I do, and the new cartons stink" (Elliot, 2009). Consumers were so emotional and vocal about the change that Pepsico had to reinstate the original packaging in less than two months or continue to suffer tremendous sales losses. The moral of the story is, don't mess with the consumer's deeply engrained mental models—advice I had explicitly given the juice maker a few years prior to the incident.

Mental models automatically influence and determine everything we do. You know your phone number, or more accurately you know the pattern of your number. Probably, you recite it so quickly that it forces the person who got your voice message to play it back twice to copy it. But try saying your phone number backwards. It is the same seven digits—you know them perfectly—but you don't have the reverse pattern encoded and cannot reel it out at the same incomprehensible speed. When we speak or listen, we use patterns and mental models of language and grammar. When we watch television commercials or notice an advertisement, we use mental symbols to represent objects, names, emotions, and stories. Mental models make it possible for us to function in everyday life without having to consciously think about everything we do, including choosing one brand or another.

Marketers can use this knowledge of patterns to tremendous advantage by studying and deeply understanding the most important mental models customers hold for their brands. The most emotionally salient mental models are the ones that most influence the customer's connection to the brand. For example, Apple spends lavishly on their product packaging because they know the out-of-box experience creates one of the most powerful mental models for customers. I recently lost my iPhone while traveling and had to purchase a new one. Later that day I had to have a long, serious conversation with myself about whether or not to keep the box—"It's so beautiful and elegant but I don't want to carry it home in my travel bag." Finally, I tossed the darn thing, but when I tell people about my episode, many of them say, "Oh, I have all of my Apple boxes on the shelf at home."

Sometimes the moments that matter most are sensory experiences driven by products, packaging, and even merchandising (Frijda, 1994). Other times, the experiences become salient because someone—even a service person—reinforces the customer's decision. "Those glasses make you look smart." Or, it might simply be a pleasant and easy ordering process. It literally can be anything, any touch point on the customer's journey with your brand. The charge for modern marketers is to identify and understand the patterns and mental models that create the customer's feelings as they become aware, engage, acquire, use your brand, and importantly, what they tell their friends about the experience.

FEELINGS NOT FACTS

We like to believe our behavior is completely rational. We cling to the idea that we think everything through logically and reasonably. If this were true, we would never eat too much or consume anything unhealthy, and no one would ever be even the least bit overweight. Everyone would diligently save money and have enough put away for rainy days and a worry-free retirement. We would exercise regularly, refuse to buy higher-priced products that don't provide value, and always make the right choices. (You've got all those covered, right?)

The higher prices we willingly pay represent perfect examples of the power of brands. If people were rational beings, we would only choose the lowest priced goods. Yet, low-price brands are almost never the leading brands in any category. It is difficult to think of a leading brand that is also the lowest cost brand. Consider Apple or Adidas. Computers and shoes are categories in which there are many, many less expensive, perfectly adequate choices, but these brands are preferred because we feel they offer us something more. Clearly, people buy brands for implicit, intangible, even irrational reasons beyond the pragmatic. We buy brands because of how they make us feel.

The legendary economist John Kenneth Galbraith once said that an ordinary person, wheeling a shopping cart through the aisles of a supermarket, is in touch with his or her deepest emotions. This is true even if he or she tries to fill the cart with only the cheapest items. It appears rational, but the person is not motivated as much by the actual price as the feelings of confidence, capability, and control he or she gains from getting good deals.

This is because the vast amount of information in our brain is not just randomly stored away in the neurons. According to psychologists, emotions influence what customers remember and how we construct mental models (LeDoux, 1991). The data of our lives is filed and catalogued based on the nature and intensity of the emotion associated with it. We can think of emotion as the Dewey Decimal system of our brains. Memories are encoded with emotions and retrieved with the emotion intact, which in turn activates and influences our mental and physiological responses.

Antonio Damasio, one of the leading neuroscientists in the world, has confirmed emotion is integral to the processes of reasoning and decision-making. His research utilizes magnetic resonance imaging to analyze a patient's brain at the same time behavioral or cognitive observations take place. Studies of several individuals who experienced neurological damage to emotion centers of their brains demonstrated the subjects became completely incapable of making rational decisions when their emotions were not functioning properly (Damasio, 1999). Damasio's work has, in many respects, slammed the door shut on the notion that pure rational thought is ever independent of emotion.

In *The Marketing Power of Emotion*, John O'Shaughnessy, distinguished Professor Emeritus of Business at Columbia University shares, "Emotions are the energizers of meaning. It is the emotions that signal the meaning or personal significance of things, whether these things are objects like a sports car, events like a holiday, or the actions, say, of doctors and waiters" (O'Shaughnessy and O'Shaughnessy, 2002).

Daniel Kahneman, winner of the Nobel Prize in Economic Science and widely regarded as the father of Behavioral Economics, has spent the better part of his distinguished career debunking the rational model of judgment and decision making. Throughout the years of study and dozens of experiments, his research convincingly demonstrates people use patterns, rules of thumb, heuristics, and mental models to simplify thinking and that most of our decision-making is intuitive, automatic, and beyond our awareness. Even more interesting and potentially alarming, his work reveals people rarely do any real calculation to make a decision. Instead, we rely on how we feel in a given situation (Kahneman, 2011).

Once again, in real world research, our work for leading brands confirms what the scientists claim about the irrationality of human decision-making and behavior. We've seen over the course of thousands of deep Emotional Inquiry ™ interviews around the world that respondents are not fully aware of why they do what they do, and are decidedly emotional in making decisions. In spite of what people want to be true about their behaviors, the actions they take betray their beliefs. People claim to do substantial research before making purchase decisions, but we have discovered they rarely do—even when buying homes, cars, or making critical investment decisions. For all the talk of getting a second medical opinion, it is troubling to reveal how many people rely on the diagnosis of a single physician to decide on critical surgery or long-term care for chronic, life-threatening illnesses. And it turns out physicians—who we hope make only rational decisions based on clinical data—are humans too and utilize the same fatally flawed rationales that we all do. If there is one universal finding in all of our work around the world, it is that human beings are anything but rational beings.

CHANGE THE WAY PEOPLE THINK

In the fall of 1992, the Office on Smoking and Health at the Centers for Disease Control and Prevention (CDC), got advance data from a study conducted by the Environmental Protection Agency (EPA) revealing dramatic findings on the effects of tobacco smoke in everyday environments. Based on scientific analysis of the respiratory health effects of environmentally transmitted smoke (ETS), the EPA would start to classify ETS as a Group A carcinogen that causes cancer in humans. This put tobacco smoke in the same category as radon, asbestos, and benzene—substances widely known to be environmental dangers.

At the time, the public was well aware of the harmful effects of smoking and its impact on personal health. But antismoking messages had become wallpapers and people were blasé about them. People had seen so many messages and heard so many warnings that they had grown numb to the subject. The brain does not process the same message over and over. Once it gets it, it gets it. The pattern is established, and the brain simply scans over it. There were also other more urgent public health threats that warranted more media attention and emotion including HIV and AIDS.

The marketing team was challenged to communicate this new EPA information. They would most likely have only one chance to make news and create a stir with it. It too would fade into the background unless the team came up with a new and compelling way to get the public's attention. It would be essential to find an emotional flash point that would draw people into the message and create enough emotional velocity to motivate them into action.

Among the reams and reams of research of CDC data was one small data point claiming more than 90 percent of the population, at that time, believed public smoking posed a health risk for anyone exposed to it. However, another question in the study revealed the same people who were convinced of the risk never raised their concerns to smokers. Someone in the marketing team suggested, "Cigarette smoke at work, on airlines, in restaurants and at home is so normal no one ever thinks to say or do anything about it." Another offered, "Maybe people simply don't have the knowledge about just how bad it is? Once we give them the cold hard facts, surely they will respond." Someone else rebuffed, "People know smoking is bad, they're just afraid to say anything about it." That's when the room went silent and everyone knew at that moment this was the insight they were looking for. It was the breakthrough that might change the public's thinking. It was clear and simple—people knew environmental smoke was bad but didn't do anything about it because no one wanted to confront smokers directly. The message needed to overcome that negative emotion and reframe the whole messaging proposition if it was to succeed.

As a first step, the team recognized that ETS was not a well-known term nor did it invoke any emotional reaction whatsoever. ETS would need to be rebranded in a way that could promote communication and stoke the desire to take action. The marketers landed on the term Second Hand Smoke that communicates succinctly while serving to make the point that this is not just a personal health decision. This emotional insight also leveraged the opportunity to turn the communications from a personal health message to an environmental warning that ignites passions—it's fine if I choose to smoke but it's wrong for you to put me at risk with your smoke—and give people permission to initiate the conversation about the dangers of Second Hand Smoke.

The EPA facts would inform people about the dangers of Second Hand Smoke. That was obvious. But, it was also true, no matter how compelling the message was, people would not confront smokers face to face. It would need to help overcome the psychological and emotional barriers preventing people from taking action. That was the insight that would motivate change. To bring it to life, the team created a tagline warning, "We're All at Risk." This helped reframe the message and focus on the broader environmental dangers. The CDC also created a printed kit with various messages and specific directions about actions people could take to join the cause and spread the word about the dangers of second hand smoke. The kit included letters and brochures that could be sent to those who control environments—owners, bosses, union stewards, public officials, and press releases for the local media. All of our messages offered the materials free of charge to anyone who called a toll free number—something the CDC had never before done.

This approach to branding Second Hand Smoke has been very successful in the United States. The emotional message raised awareness and enlisted the nonsmoking public in ways never imagined. The Second Hand Smoke branding efforts empowered and equipped the nonsmoking public to join the conversation and drive awareness. Of course, the tremendous outcome is that it is no longer possible to smoke in offices, restaurants, airplanes, and most environments that expose nonsmokers to tobacco smoke.

Any brand that recognizes the opportunity to understand and change the way people think can create competitive advantage. What is coffee if not another example of a commodity product? Though every day, millions of people drive by millions of places to get a cup of coffee on their way to Starbucks where they enjoy the privilege of paying several times what they might pay elsewhere. Sure you can argue the coffee is better, but is it, really? Many people in the United States will argue Dunkin' Donuts coffee is better. I think a case could be made that coffee is coffee, but nevertheless, both brands have connected with people on a deeper emotional level and changed the way they think about coffee.

CHANGE YOUR MIND

Even in the face of overwhelming evidence of the power of emotional branding, many marketers remain stuck in the mindset that consumers make brand choices for rational, pragmatic reasons. Much of this is caused by how consumer research is commonly practiced. Mark Earls (2009) warns, "We ask individuals what they think, what they do now and what they will do in the future; they tell us what they think and what they do and what they plan to do, and we count the hands and report the data back on this basis. As if it was objective truth."

There is an argument that consumers don't know what they want and that research is pointless. When a reporter asked Steve Jobs about the market research that went into the iPad, he famously answered, "None. It's not the consumers' job to know what they want." Obviously, he meant the traditional market research not the empathy-based insight that comes from deeply understanding customers. He was right. Simply asking consumers what they want is an exercise in futility. Instead, you have to get into their heads to learn what's really motivating them. That's why I urge clients to forget about the *voice of the customer* and focus on the *mind of the customer.* Jobs clearly understood this. He didn't bother obsessing on market data and analytics. Instead, he spent a lot of time thinking about consumers and being an active consumer of technology himself. That's how he knew what to do next.

There were a number of excellent MP3 players on the market long before iPods were introduced. Yet, Apple struck on an amazingly simple emotional insight—it's about the music stupid. Apple recognized they could vastly improve upon the experience of music players by actually making a vast selection of music available. So, they developed and launched iTunes to make it easy and affordable to select and download your favorite songs. Apple tried the competitive products, felt the unmet needs, and smartly figured out a way to, quite literally, change the music business and the world. It was the emotional insight that would create huge market advantage. It was the emotional insight we might expect from a company who urges us to *think different.* It was the emotional advantage that would propel Apple's brand meaning and status even higher. It's the emotional leverage that delivers almost 80 percent market share for the company. They make quite a bit of money with that little emotion-based insight. Oh! Incidentally they have built the largest company in the world leveraging one emotional insight after another.

The most successful brands think and behave this way. What customers feel is never far from their thoughts and finds its way into every aspect of their operations. Harley-Davidson is a good example. When the weather is nice, several hundred Harleys line the parking lot at corporate headquarters in Milwaukee. When executives ride their own Harleys to work, they become the customer and it changes how they feel about features for new models and living their brand promise at every touch point.

I call this *method marketing*. Everyone knows what a method actor is—someone who completely immerses themselves in the character while striving to become the character. In the same way, we all need to become *method marketers*. We're convinced the most innovative companies do this instinctively. They become the customer, so they can feel what the customer feels. They get into the customer's head. They know exactly who they are, the intimate details of how they live their lives, and their deeper unarticulated desires and needs. Then the most successful brands become quite intentional about meeting those needs.

Zappos studied consumers and realized they would have to completely remove the emotional risk of buying shoes online. So, their shipping is free and they allow you to return unworn products even months after purchase. It's worry and hassle free, and it makes customers fall in love with the brand. Starbucks built an empire by deeply sensing the emotional nuances of the experiences consumers seek. And, mind you, it's an empire of coffee shops, another commodity business. Other legendary brands including Southwest Airlines, FedEx, Facebook, and Nordstrom are all built on sensing and meeting customers' emotional needs. In fact, almost every successful brand finds a way to understand and meet their customers' emotional needs.

A. G. Lafley, retired Procter & Gamble CEO, makes it abundantly clear in his book *The Game Changer:*

> It requires deep understanding of what drives the consumers' *emotions*. It requires understanding not only their need but, also their *aspirations*. You must get an appreciation for who they are, how they live, and—yes, of course—how your product can best improve their lives. (Lafley and Charan, 2008)

THINK MIND OF THE CUSTOMER, NOT VOICE OF THE CUSTOMER

We think we think about everything, but an overwhelming body of science indicates more than 95 percent of our mental functions are driven by nonconscious influences and automatic cues derived from the familiar patterns, mental models, and heuristics imprinted in our brains. Quite simply, our mental functions are designed in such a way that we don't have to think about everything. The mental influences that drive our behaviors are emotional and processed outside of our conscious awareness. But, while this is great to help us get through the day, it creates a lot of problems for marketing researchers and strategists. If customers aren't aware of what drives their choices and behaviors, it's practically useless to ask them what they think about why they do what they do or choose one brand over another. They simply don't know. Oh, they'll give you rationalizations—what they think is the right answer—but the truth is they don't consciously know why.

What people think is the right answer does marketing researchers and strategists very little good. In fact, it frequently leads them astray. People will tell you they buy on rational reasons such as price, but then the low-price brands are never the leading brands in the category. People obviously make purchase decisions for more intangible, irrational reasons they often cannot articulate. This is why more and more we see leading brands turning toward emotive approaches to find competitive advantage. Rational benefits work when there is nothing else, no other brand to compare it to, but that is rarely the case in today's crowded marketplace. The old rational product benefit approach also no longer works because time to market has been so reduced that a successful new product will be copied and often improved upon before the original has time to gain any real advantage. The only real chance of sustainable success a modern brand has is to engage customers at an emotional level.

This is why we must utilize research methods that allow us to explore nonconscious motivations, people's unarticulated desires, and emotional needs. It means we have to get into people's heads. But it's dark in there and we don't know our way around, so it makes us uncomfortable, so much so that it becomes acceptable to settle for superficial, one-dimensional research that provides answers to what is happening but never why. Yet, if we don't discover why people do what they do, we'll never meet their unarticulated desires and needs and fail to find any advantage in the marketplace.

That's why I am convinced marketers need to also become passionate social scientists and develop expertise for getting into people's heads. And, it is why I advocate so strongly that marketers, who want to discover deep insights and true advantage, need to shift their own mental models to the *Mind of the customer* because that's where the real answers are.

We must also recognize that people are not interested in the bells and whistles of our brands unless those features make them feel something. Brands need to make them feel cool, confident, beautiful, smart, successful, and, in many respects, they just want brands to make them happy. So if you only ask one question, ask, "How does our brand make them feel?"

REFERENCES

Damasio, A. (1999). *The Feeling of What Happens: Body and Emotion in the Making of Consciousness.* Orlando: Harcourt Books.

Earls, M. (2009). *Herd: How to Change Mass Behavior by Harnessing Our True Nature.* Chichester: Wiley.

Elliot, S. (2009, February 22). *Tropicana Discovers Some Buyers Are Passionate about Packaging.* http://www.nytimes.com/2009/02/23/business/media/23adcol.html?pagewanted=all

Frijda, N. (1994). "Emotions Are Functional, Most of the Time," in P. Ekman and R. Davidson (Eds), *The Nature of Emotion* (pp. 112–122). Oxford: Oxford University Press.

Hawkins, J. and S. Blakeslee (2004). *On Intelligence: How a New Understanding of the Brain Will Lead to the Creation of Truly Intelligent Machines.* New York: Times Books.

Kahneman, D. (2011). *Thinking Fast and Slow.* New York: Farrar, Straus and Giroux.

Lafley, A. and R. Charan (2008). *The Game Changer: How You Can Drive Revenue and Profit Growth and Innovation.* New York: Crown.

LeDoux, J.E. (1991). "Systems and Synapses of Emotional Memory," In L.R. Squire, N.M. Wienberger, G. Lunch, and J.L. McGaugh (Eds), *Memory: Organization and Locus of Change.* New York: Oxford University Press.

O'Shaughnessy, J. and N.J. O'Shaughnessy (2002). *The Marketing Power of Emotion.* Oxford: Oxford University.

Siegel, D.J. (1999). *The Developing Mind: How Relationships and the Brain Interact to Shape Who We Are.* New York: The Guilford Press.

Travis, D. (2000). *Emotional Branding: How Successful Brands Gain the Irrational Edge.* New York: Crown.

Viskontas, I.V., R.Q. Quirogab, and I. Fried (2009). "Human Medial Temporal Lobe Neurons Respond Preferentially to Personally Relevant Images," *Proceedings of the National Academy of Sciences of the United States of America* 106(50): 21329–21334.

Wansink, B. (2006). *Mindless Eating: Why We Eat More Than We Think.* New York: Bantam Dell.

Chapter 8
Brands and Innovation

Jean-Noël Kapferer

NO INNOVATION NO BRAND

Essays and books on brands rarely talk about innovations. As a rule, they present branding as an answer to questions such as "how should companies name or identify their innovations/their new products?" This is nothing but tunnel vision because in reality one cannot separate branding from innovation.

Innovation is critical to branding and is the only way in which brands that follow a premium pricing strategy can sustain their pricing strategy. Innovation is equally relevant to brands that follow low-cost business models. Companies such as Southwest Airlines in the United States and Ryanair or easyJet in Europe were only possible because they rewrote the rules of the game by innovating in their domain.

We live today in a world of brands and generics. This is as true of FMCG companies (just browse through the aisles of Wal-Mart or Carrefour) as it is of services, such as B2B, IT, pharma, Internet companies, etc. Our minds are full of "names" that represent value propositions in the marketplace. One must remember that every "star" brand that easily comes to mind started off small, often as a one-man company. But this one-man company had a golden nugget in the form of an innovation that the owner believed could change the world.

In a way, startups are optimists—they feel anything is possible. The founding inventions were sometimes invented in a garage

(Apple) or just as a solution to a very simple problem for oneself like how to get rid of old furniture or products (eBay), a means of talking to friends on campus (Facebook), or even as a way to reduce the costs of transportation (Ikea furniture packed in separate parts for one to assemble on their own).

THE PREREQUISITE: THE BRAND PLATFORM

All the brands in the world are nothing but names of innovations that not only succeeded at first, but also maintained their edge, thanks to constant innovation. Obviously, branding is more than just "naming," it is also about defining the long-term characteristics (both tangible and intangible) of this chain of innovation.

Brand building is the process by which this long-term meaning is conveyed and shared by the potential buyers in the market. The twin engines of brand building are innovation and communication. Consistency is the key to managing these dual engines. Innovations build brands if and only if they create a consistent picture of what the brand is about. This does not mean that they should always stick to the same product category; most companies end up doing things very different from what they did when they first started (think of IBM, Louis Vuitton, or even P&G). To survive, brands need growth sectors just as surfers need waves!

Central to brand strategy is the task of building trust, respect, and even love vis-à-vis the brand, based on it consistently delivering on its promises and sticking to its core values. When a brand owner does this, he/she can capitalize on this asset—a brand with advocates, fans, loyalists, and engaged clients. This can then be used to enter entirely new sectors and derive a competitive advantage from the existing brand awareness and image. However, this is only possible as long as the innovations that the brand introduces are meaningful to customers and stay consistent with their existing image of the brand.

All the diversifications that Apple undertook since it was created have followed this virtuous path. They surprised competitors, delighted clients, and reinforced the brand for they embodied the long-term discriminating core values of the brand, which were about making everything radically simple and easy to use while being mentally highly stimulating thereby providing a great user experience.

Brands in their modern meaning are business models and names. This business model aims at creating value by placing emphasis on the brand's intangibles (how much trust, consideration, loyalty, passion, advocacy, engagement, etc., the brand has built in the market) and leveraging these in growth markets. This model will work as long as the original "core brand values" remain constant.

This is why one of the first things companies should do when they start their business is to identify what core values they want their brand to stand for (Kapferer, 2012). These values should be restricted to very few, well-described, differentiating values. The articulation of these values provides the "brand platform," the "charter" of the brand, its very own holy commandments which are sacred that are never to be betrayed. This is the nature of focus and discipline with which "love brands" are built.

BRANDS AND PATENTS

If a brand does not patent its innovations, it loses the key benefits of innovation. Disruptive innovations not only delight clients in FMCG and B2B, but radically also change the rules of the category. To not adopt them quickly is to sentence one's own brand to death. The entire patent case between Samsung and Apple is proof of this. Samsung could not compete with Apple without immediately adopting some of the unique features that make iPhone such a delightful object (that smartly encompasses all the core values of Apple). But Apple patented these features precisely for this reason.

There are close links between brands and patents, and these need to be analyzed in depth. First, both can be posted in the balance sheet, in the very same section as intangible assets. Let us remind ourselves what an asset is: *sensu stricto* an asset is something that is owned by a company, which is separable from the company (i.e., it can be sold or licensed), and that produces extra profits beyond the accounting time period (one year). Patents are legal ownerships that create entry barriers for competition, thereby defending the temporary monopoly created by the innovation and allowing/sustaining the price premium that forms the source of enhanced profitability for the company. Patents can be sold and hence have an economic value.

The entire pharmaceutical industry lives on patents that were either created by the companies themselves or acquired from other companies which in most cases are startups (Moss, 2007; Sudovar, 1987).

Interestingly, brands too can be posted in the balance sheet. According to the IFRS new norms, they are truly intangible assets. Their financial value is that of the net additional expected cash flows that their usage will bring to the company. To follow the accounting rules of prudence and credibility, only those brands that have been acquired can be posted in the balance sheet.

Through this method, Pernod Ricard, the world's second largest spirits and wine company posted €3.9 billion in its balance sheet when it acquired Absolut Vodka in 2009. According to the IFRS norms, to build a credible and accurate figure, this amount cannot be amortized but should regularly be compared to the present fair economic value of the brand and in case of any discrepancy these figures must be corrected accordingly.

It is highly significant that the IFRS norms consider brands as nonamortizable assets (unlike plants or buildings for instance). This means that, in theory, brands are resilient. They are not expected to lose their value over time, unless they are poorly managed.

It is the task of management not only to grow sales and profits, but to simultaneously also build brand capital, which is called "brand equity." This is a very interesting term, for it uses both a marketing term (brand) and a financial concept (equity). The financial treatment of not amortizing brands is the big difference between brands and patents. The latter offer protection is only for a maximum period of 20 years. Many countries such as India do not even wait that long when the nation's health is under threat. The Indian government believes that if an epidemic threatens millions of Indians, it is fair to allow the production of generics of vaccines that are technically still under patent protection.

What happens when patents come to an end? Often the patent holding brand continues to create a halo of exclusivity and desire despite the presence of competition. Brands can actually be said to possess a "mental patent" that lives on in their audience's mind beyond the duration of the patent.

From the argument presented till here, the relationship between brands and innovation is apparent. Both work together and enhance the creation of value for their investors through their mutual interaction. The PIMS study provides strong evidence of this; see Figure 8.1.

This figure demonstrates the relationship between R&D investments and value creation for brand-intensive companies (black) versus nonbrand-intensive (generic) companies (gray). As is to be expected, investment in R&D creates value, at least in the sector analyzed in this study (FMCG). The higher the R&D investments per employee, the higher the added value per employee!

It is important to note that this is not as true today of sectors where innovation can come from sources other than R&D such as customer feedback, research-based insights, etc. Professor C.M. Christensen (1997) believes that mega corporations are managed too carefully and are risk-averse so as to protect investors, and it is this mindset that prevents the rise of strong innovations. This is

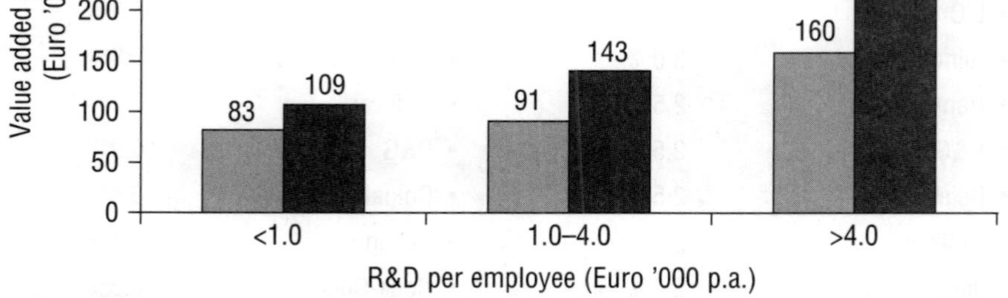

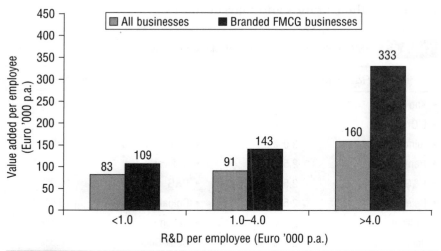

Figure 8.1 How Branding Enhances the Value of R&D

SOURCE: PIMS (2004).

in striking contrast with Apple where Steve Jobs said that Apple's continued success lay in its ability to take risks and to "endanger its life" with each new product it launched (CNNMoney/Fortune, November 9, 1998).

In the pharmaceutical sector, the link between R&D investments and success has been disappointing amongst mega corporations. As a result of this, in 2012, Sanofi, the world's fourth largest pharma group, slashed its R&D investments after realizing that these were not as productive as they were before and that they no longer were able to create new blockbuster drugs. Instead, the company decided to invest in external growth by acquiring several startups that had developed very promising innovations.

Revisiting Figure 8.1, one can see how much branding enhances the value added by R&D. In fact, this additional impact grows with the level of R&D investments. This is why the companies that invest a lot in R&D are also those that invest a lot in marketing so as to create the long-term brand associations in the market. It can be said that R&D "invents" progress and brand is the name of this "progress" as it reaches the market.

The figures of Table 8.1show how brand companies invest heavily not only in R&D but also in marketing (OC&C, 2010) in order to build both their brands and market shares.

Table 8.1 FMCG Stars of R&D and of Marketing Investments

R&D/Sales		*Marketing/Sales*	
• Kao	3.8%	• L'Oréal	30.9%
• L'Oréal	3.4%	• Estée Lauder	25.9%
• Ajinomoto	3.0%	• Pernod Ricard	17.8%
• Henkel	2.5%	• Uniliver	13.7%
• P&G	2.5%	• P&G	10.9%
• Beiersdorf	2.5%	• Colgate Palmolive	10.6%
• Uniliver	2.1%	• Kellogg	9.1%
• Japan Tobacco	2.0%	• Coca-Cola	8.3%
• Nestlé	1.7%	• Kao	7.3%
• Colgate Palmolive	1.6%	• Japan Tobacco	6.6%

SOURCE: OC&C (2010, Paris).

THE ERA OF COPYING

Companies live in an era of hyper competition based on the widespread prevalence of copying (legally or illegally) as a business model. This is why brands find it so important to quickly harvest the returns of one's innovations as these may soon be copied, imitated if not counterfeited. Here are some examples to illustrate this fact.

In Europe in 2012, 50 percent of all products sold in supermarkets or hypermarkets are copies of the bestselling SKUs from "A" grade brands. These copies are sold by the trades' own brands, at a price that is lower by 25 percent to 50 percent or even less than the "A" grade brands! It should be remembered that the reason that trade brands can be priced so low is that they neither have to invest in R&D nor in marketing (Hoch, 1996; Kumar and Steenkamp, 2007). All they have to do is invest in shelf space (that too in their own shelves), in price, and in leveraging the trust attached to the store name (Tesco, Carrefour, Asda, Decathlon, etc.) that is used to endorse these products.

The goal of most hypermarket chains is to have their own brands represent more than half their sales. This is a prerequisite for their profitability. Branded "star products" are now being sold without any margin because of the price competition between retailers. The winning SKUs from trade brands are mere copies of the winning SKUs from the "A" brands. Sometimes they are even manufactured by the "A" brands' manufacturers themselves! Only companies such as the L'Oréal Group, Procter & Gamble, and Sony refuse to manufacture for their copiers.

Trade brands are complete lookalikes of the original "A" grade brands in their outlook, and this serves to create consumer confusion (Kapferer, 1995a, 1995b) to the disadvantage of "A" grade brands. So, why aren't the main multinational companies suing these trade brands for their trademark infringements?

Multinational companies resist the temptation of such law suits because they know that the power of retail concentration works against them. In France, for instance, six retailer groups represent 70 percent of the sales of each of the multinational companies. No local CEO of a multinational will risk losing 10 percent of his brands' sales to a temporary boycott of his brands by a mega retailer, and this is a distinct possibility if he tries suing them.

Zara is one of the most exciting business successes in the last 20 years. It created the "fast fashion" industry, a fantastic business model based on a cluster of small subcontracting companies located in and around Spain, which have the logistical efficiency to reasonably replicate any new product and bring it to retail shelves in just 15 days after it was originally conceived and designed.

But does anyone know the names of the designers at Zara? It's not worth the effort of trying to look them up because they are unknown! Zara is remarkably good at using other designers' catwalks as a source of inspiration for the fashion designs that Zara sells. Zara's designs sell at just about the same time that fashion magazines announce about the new fashions displayed at these designers' catwalks. Thankfully, high fashion designers aim at people who want authentic designer brands and are willing to pay for them. Zara, however, aims at those who cannot afford authentic designs. The presence of Zara stores in the high fashion streets of Paris, Madrid, Milano, or Shanghai tells an interesting story that even the rich like to buy low-cost imitations!

Let's go back to the Silicon Valley where copying is the norm. In an interview with *Rolling Stone* magazine (January 17, 2011), Steve Jobs said that Microsoft had reduced the gap with Apple because the Mac had not upgraded fast enough, thereby making it easy for Microsoft to imitate the Mac. Even the authorized official biography of Steve Jobs (Isaacson, 2011) mentions how the brilliant innovations brought by the Mac were themselves based on a visit to the ultra-secret Fundamental Research Center of the Xerox Corporation.

What lessons can one draw from these multisectorial examples? First, that innovation is necessary for survival and that it is an ongoing, everlasting process. It is the crucial edge that sustains price premiums, the buzz around the brand on social networks, in the blogosphere and in mass media. Brands are there to create people's agenda that sparks renewed desire and creates economic growth in mature markets.

Brands become the source of dreams of consumers in emerging nations because of the assured quality that they bring to the market at an accessible price. China and Russia have been starving for quality products for 50 years, and since the fall of communism, consumers of these countries have wanted to catch up on all that they've missed in terms of products and services. They even want to experience the best quality products if they can, such as products of Michelin Tyres, Toyota, Schneider Electric, or even Siemens electrical equipment.

The second lesson is illustrated in Figure 8.2. The best defense against fleet-footed imitators lies in the speed of innovation (Schnaars, 1995). This is typically measured by the percentage of sales coming from the products that weren't in existence three or four years ago. As shown in Figure 8.2, there is a straight negative correlation between the rate of innovation by brands and the market share of trade brands and price brands.

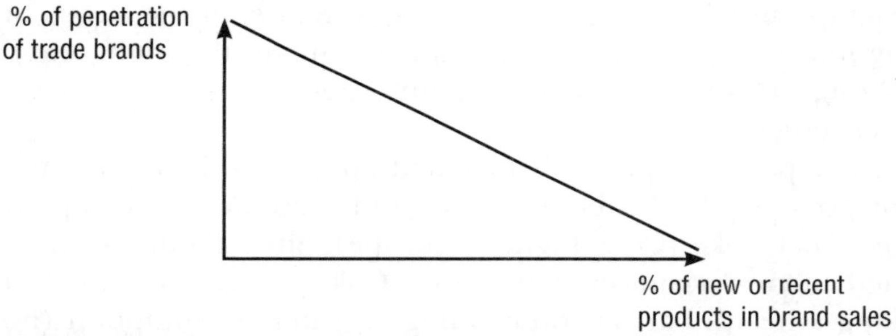

Figure 8.2 How the Rate of Innovation Protects from Store Brands

CAN COMPANIES GROW WITHOUT INNOVATION—COKE?

Whenever one talks about brands and innovation, the common question people ask is: "Aren't there companies that have grown without innovating?" Coca-Cola is a prime example of this. The erstwhile No. 1 brand in terms of brand valuation and current No. 6, Coke's brand name itself was estimated to be $73 billion by Millward Brown in 2011. This brand introduced its first new product almost 100 years after the brand was first launched. The first Coke glass was served in Atlanta in 1886, but Diet Coke was launched only in 1988!

Realizing that Coke contains the equivalent of four sugar cubes per glass and that it is not good for the health when drunk in large quantities every day, the Mayor of New York has banned the sale of all soft drinks in big formats on streets and in public places.

The Coca-Cola Company was bound to have known that a large number of Americans' health was endangered by a high daily intake of sugar; however, they did not make a move to address this problem for a century. Instead, year after year, they focused their marketing strategy on increasing the consumption per capita of the highly sugary classic Coke. They maximized customer equity long term (Blattberg, 2001).

It is estimated that the per capita consumption of Coke is 200 liters per year in the United States (in Mexico it's a staggering 225 liters!). This high level of consumption was achieved through the significant multiplication of packaging formats. A well-thought-out strategy saw each format adapted to the exact moment and situation of consumption that it targeted (at bars, at home, in the street, at vending machines, at a picnic, at a discotheque in the night, etc.). Even though this was not a striking innovation, it was undeniably extremely efficient.

The company was probably prodded into action by the mounting concerns worldwide about obesity, and therefore the company launched Diet Coke (Coke Light in Europe). Since then, they have launched many variants of the Classic Coke, each one aimed at unlocking a health barrier to encourage greater consumption (no carbs, no sugar, no caffeine, etc.).

But innovations go beyond the product itself. One should also consider commercial innovations as a part of brand innovations. Burberry, the English fashion brand, is proud to say that they have the largest number of friends on Facebook. This brand has been a consistent trend setter in the area of using digital marketing. Burberry has catwalks that one can watch online or in stores with the facility to order all the designs seen on the catwalk though a simple click on the giant in-store touch screen.

Many car brands have innovated, not just in the product itself but in the area of service too. The Korean car manufacturer Khia, however, is the only one to offer a seven-year guarantee. Facom, the tool-work brand, proposed a lifelong guarantee! Afflelou, an optical retail chain, created a promotional breakthrough; buy one pair of glasses and get one pair free. Afflelou's innovation created total disruption in the market and led this retail chain to market leadership. These examples demonstrate that innovations are not restricted only to products but to any aspect of the brand that can deliver value.

WHAT COMPANIES EXPECT FROM INNOVATIONS

What do individual companies expect from new products and innovations?

Table 8.2 presents the answers from four major companies from the FMCG and B2B areas. Interestingly, there is much more homogeneity in B2B expectations. B2B companies typically sell ingredients for a process or another product. For them, innovation is the only source of competitive advantage, albeit temporary. Also, B2B is plagued by copycats, generic me-toos that are made in China and imported at a low cost by wholesalers or Internet suppliers. And finally, innovations can justify a higher price. The B2B company actually sells office stationeries—for it, even the slightest innovation is the only way to generate growth in the very mature markets that they operate in where price is the only argument that buyers listen to. B2B1 company is an ingredient brand producer: tubular electrical engines for awnings.

In comparison, B2C companies realize consumers' tastes are always changing and must be met, if not preceded by new products. Strangely enough, the objective to put store brands at a distance

Table 8.2 Why Are Innovations So Strategic for Brands?

	FMCG1	*FMCG2*	*B2B1*	*B2B2*
Consumers' tastes keep on changing	1	2	6	6
Source of temporary competitive advantage	2	4	1	1
New products can be sold at higher price	3	5	3	3
They give a modern image to the brand	4	3	4	7
New products provide higher margins	5	1	7	4
Only way to keep store brands at a distance	6	6	2	2
Only way to keep being listed in superstores	7	7	5	5

seems minor. It is a fact that FMCG1 sells only cheese specialties, with a very strong differentiation. As to FMCG2, they sell biscuits with also a high level of sub-branding (each product of the range has a specific brand name).

All these companies stress the fact that innovation is the only way to grow markets that are saturated. People have run out of wants, and new products need to spark fresh desire for consumption in them. The high technology markets have many examples of how new products render the earlier ones obsolete—yesterday's niche products, such as iPhone or Samsung Galaxy, will soon constitute the majority of the market. This is the only way to protect profit margins. It is also a good way to achieve brand growth when entering new countries/markets.

The fact that innovations allow brands to charge high prices is demonstrated by large-scale studies comparing the price of new products according to their level of success (see Table 8.3). Data from the market research company SymphonyIRI reveals interestingly that the "champions" are also the most expensive ones.

Success in this case is measured by the ratio of the sales of "innovation" against the category's average sales. Indexing the ratio of the price of the new SKU versus the average price of the category, one finds impressively that the "champions" are above 130, whereas failures are only around 110. This could appear like a contradiction with consumers' price sensitivity especially in times of recession; however, in fact, it is not.

Why are some innovations highly priced? This pricing is based on their owners' belief that these innovations will create value for their consumers. An innovation with a low price is an implicit statement that the innovation is not really meaningful. The consumers tend to respond in agreement to this by abstaining from buying the brand.

Table 8.3 Price Index of Successful FMCG Innovations

Superstars	133
Stars	124
Just pass	118
Fail	110

SOURCE: Adapted from IRI/Symphony, 2011.

CLASSIFICATION OF BRAND INNOVATIONS

Of course, all innovations are not alike. Some of them are just new product variants (such as Cherry Coke or Vanilla Coke), which are also known as line extensions. Many innovations are termed incremental innovations, but this does not mean that they are useless. In fact, most brands engage in a continuous flow of incremental innovations, the car industry being a typical case in point.

Year after year car manufacturers add new (mostly electronic) features to their car models, but once every decade comes an innovation that changes the rules of the market. The Toyota Prius was once a niche product, just for the affluent few; however, it is now the world's third bestselling car of 2012. The Toyota hybrid engine has become the standard of the 21st-century car (at least the early years of the century) that all competitors have had to follow. This is an example of "disruptive" innovation.

The term "Blue Ocean" (Dru, 2002; Kim and Mauborgne, 2005) was coined to describe innovations that create markets that did not exist before. These innovations are also called "value innovations" because they propose a bundle of added values of the nature that were never seen before; innovations that were unimaginable in the past.

Dyson invented the vacuum cleaner without a bag. Before this, all vacuum cleaners had bags. A vacuum cleaner without a bag was inconceivable to the extent that none of the major brands accepted the Dyson's innovation. He was forced to create his own company and brand in order to sell his innovation. Today all vacuum cleaner brands offer two versions of the product, either with or without bags. There are many other examples of Blue Ocean strategy, such as easyJet and Nespresso.

The essence of the Blue Ocean innovation is the suppression of a value that everybody in the sector considers mandatory (like "vacuum cleaners by definition need bags") so as to give a lot more than competition on some other value. If easyJet or Ryanair suppresses all services or makes the services (that are no more included in the flat price so that if one desires to fly without any service, he/she can access a very low-cost flight) payable, they can then propose a Paris London flight at £10!

Now, as in the case of all *ex post facto* theories where authors select only the successes, Blue Ocean oversells its case. In many instances, it does not work because there simply is no demand. It is very revealing that all extensions of easyJet outside of the airline industry have failed! easyRent a car is a good example of this.

Bic, the famous ball pen maker, introduced a no-frill fragrance with excellent natural floral components for the youth. The fragrance failed, because the youth wanted the same glamorous fragrance with extravagant packaging and celebrity associations as their parents, albeit under new brand names.

Recently, Bic produced a mobile phone with only limited functions (no email!) aimed at the elderly who cannot follow the pace of technological progress the way their grandchildren do. This is a typical Blue Ocean strategy, but it has not yet met with success. But Bic is a family company and enjoys taking risks as they did when they introduced the first disposable razor against Gillette, the first disposable lighter, and more recently a Bic windsurf board (which has gone on to become the No. 1 in volume in France). Interestingly, Bic has always named their innovations after the parent brand "Bic."

To understand why they followed this naming strategy, one needs to look at the logic of branding of innovations.

THE BRANDING OF INNOVATION—THE ISSUE OF BRAND ARCHITECTURE

Consider what could have led Samsung to name its Smartphone Galaxy? Was it just an attempt to differentiate it from other smart phones within its own range? Or was it to position Galaxy as the only global competitor against Apple's iPhone? Nokia never branded its products, but only gave them alphanumeric codes!

These issues are not about the process of naming but pertain to the issue of brand architecture. The key questions are:

1. How to create order within a wide range of products or services?
2. How to facilitate the flow of image and value between the Master brand and the new product in both directions—

top-down for trust endorsement and bottom-up for displaying modernity?

These issues can become complex in vast conglomerates such as Nestlé, P&G, or Saint Gobain. These have been dealt in detail elsewhere (Kapferer, 2012). For the sake of simplicity, architecture can be divided into two families (Aaker, 1995):

> *Branded house* architecture refers to those companies that use only one name, which is their own, as a Masterbrand name. They designate their many product or service lines with simple generic words, such as Samsung 3D television. If they use special names, these do not aim at becoming sub-brands, but are merely signals to describe some product (like Ikea uses several Swedish names to describe their furniture).
>
> *House of brands* architecture instead recommends the creation of many different product brands, each catering to a particular segment. It does not name products after the Group name. This is typically the approach of P&G (Ariel, Tide, Pampers, Tampax, Gillette, Braun, etc.), of the L'Oréal Group (Lancome, Biotherm, L'Oréal Paris, Garnier, Maybelline, The Body Shop, Kiehl's, etc.), and of LVMH (Louis Vuitton, Moët, Hennessy, Bulgari, Berluti, etc.).

"Branded house" is typical of B2B groups, as in these cases the stature of the group name is leveraged across all its business units and sectors. The strategy is to present the aspects of trust and respect that the brand has. This can be seen in the cases of GE, IBM, Schneider Electric, etc. The "House of Brand" architecture is necessary when the brand's identity reflects that of their own specific target. As a result, companies create a portfolio of brands. For instance, ITW (Illinois Tool Works) never uses its own corporate name, but holds a vast portfolio of niche brands all aimed at a specific professional target.

The same reasoning can be applied at a brand level. For instance, take one of the brands of L'Oreal Group—Biotherm or Lancôme—how should these brands name their new product innovations? Should they use generic terms or invent new brand names such as they did with "Genific"?

Most of the times, modern brands mix the two architectures. Take the example of 3M corporation. When their R&D department came out with a fancy invention (small sticking paper notes), this gave rise to many issues. The first one was the obvious marketing question of whether there was a market for that product and if so, where was it situated?

The second was a branding issue which was whether to place this radical innovation under the mega-brand Scotch (which itself needed to be revamped, modernized, and decommoditized)? Or should the innovation be a standalone brand? If put under the Scotch name, should it be named in a generic way (removable sticking notes) or with a nickname to become a sub-brand (Post-it)?

In addition to these issues, there was also a real need to visibly depict this brand as coming from 3M.

EVALUATING DIFFERENT NEW PRODUCT BRANDING SCENARIOS

Examining the issue of the link of Post-it with the Masterbrand (Scotch), three scenarios were evaluated at 3M headquarters.

1. *A no link scenario.* 3M could launch Post-it besides Scotch as a standalone brand, another new Masterbrand.
2. *An umbrella link scenario.* It means using one brand only (Scotch); therefore, this innovation would be named by a generic name. This would lead to creating a name like "Scotch removable stickers."
3. *An endorsed link scenario.* "Post-it" by Scotch (which means two levels of branding).

Further questions that need to be addressed would be as to whether the packaging and the ads should carry the logo of the corporation 3M, and if so, where.

Now, as everyone knows, the decision was made to launch Post-it not as a sub-brand of Scotch but as a new standalone brand. This was because it was not only a new product but also a real innovation that unveiled a whole new market. It was crucial that this new market had its own significance and its own leader.

THE NAMING OF BRAND EXTENSIONS

Many innovations are in fact brand extensions. All through its existence, Apple has made brand extensions a key driver of its growth. All new products from Apple from the iPod to the iPad have been brand extensions. Nestlé too started as baby milk powder and now has extended to chocolate, coffee, confectionary, and a variety of other foods and drinks. Some of these extensions carry the name Nestlé as the Masterbrand name (Nestlé chocolate or Nescafé), while some are just endorsed by Nestlé (like Lion or Nuts bars). Others are standalone brands (Buitoni for instance, Herta ham, Perrier water).

What decision framework should be used to help managers decide on how to name their extensions? First, it should be remembered that a brand is not just a name, but a promise of remarkable (core) values, which are central to the brand that it will never compromise on. The branding of any brand extension will depend on the ability of this extension to deliver on all the brand's core values.

If any brand values are absent, based on the price level of the offering, then these values are called peripheral or conditional values.

Figure 8.3 depicts some typical cases from the total overlap of values to the total difference if there is no contradiction of values.

Case 1 refers to extensions that carry all the Masterbrand's core values. In such a case, there is no need for a separate sub-brand, but for a descriptor. Take the case of Apple's extensions that carry all the values of the Apple Masterbrand; all they needed was a product descriptor and hence their mobile was called iPhone, their tablet iPad, etc., without Apple going in for new brand names.

On the other hand, Samsung which had not built a strong brand in the West chose to build a separate brand (Galaxy) with added perceived value when it launched its Smartphone (and

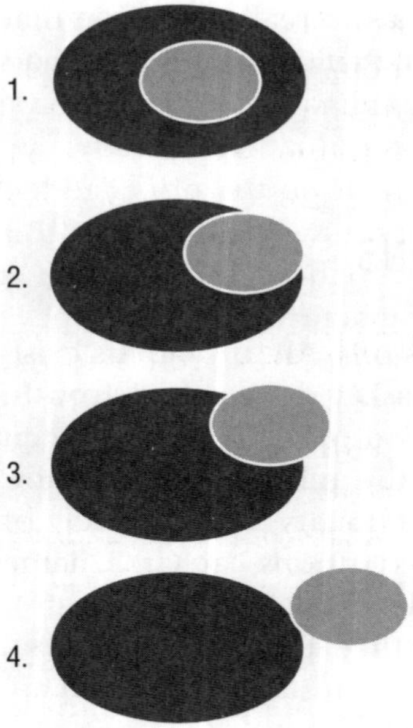

Figure 8.3 The Relationship of Brand Extensions to the Core Values of the Brand (Extension in Gray Ellipse and Brand Core Values in Black Ellipse)

subsequently tablet) with connotations of high technology, power, and aspirations.

Case 2 refers to innovations that carry most of the brand values but which add one more of their own. Since the majority of their core values are conveyed, this extension can still be launched under the umbrella of the Masterbrand's name. Armani Casa or Armani Cafè is the example of this. Remember that elegance and "Italianness" are core values of Armani even if flavor is not.

Case 3 refers to situations where the extension is conveying only half of the core values and adds many more of its own with one extension value that actually might conflict with one core brand value. At such times, one needs a sub-brand that is backed by a simple endorsement. Gillette's core values are typically excellence but also include virile machismo (the best a man can get). To target women, it was impossible to name this new product line as Gillette for women. A sub-brand had to be created (Venus) with a small endorsement by Gillette on the pack.

Case 4 refers to situations where the brand should not use its name on an extension for they are in contradiction of the brand's core values, unless this extension precisely aims at changing the core values (Balachander and Ghose, 2003). This situation typically happens when the brand wants to move up or down the price ladder. Dom Perignon was at first endorsed by Moët & Chandon, but this hampered its ability to move up the price ladder. The reverse is equally true. So should BMW, the manufacturer of MINI, have called it the mini BMW? Of course not, since MINI refers to the swinging London culture and BMW is a typical German brand!

NEW LINES AND OLD LINES: THE VIRTUOUS CYCLE OF BRAND SUSTAINABILITY

There is a virtuous circle between the brand's new lines and old lines. Innovations bring new blood (new consumers, new uses, new peripheral values, etc.) to the brand that sustains the brand's long-term relevance (Figure 8.4). Old product lines bring in profits and cash flow that finance these new product launches. However, care must be taken to realign the old lines with the new brand positioning, as this directly influences the focus of R&D for future innovations.

For instance, Danone's new positioning is "active health." This led the group to exit the beer market. Former dairy lines have had to change their advertising body copy and now talk about the calcium or the cereals that they contain. Danone's new products are all advanced innovations that do good to the health—Activia for digestion comfort, Actimel with pro-biotics, Essensis for the skin, and Danacol for cholesterol.

Beyond the halo of modernity that they bring to the mother brand, some extensions can also directly impact the sales of the old products. Thus, Smirnoff Ice boosted the sales of Smirnoff standard bottle. The iPod and iPhone brought new consumers to Apple stores and made that brand more known, understood, and desirable to many PC addicts, leading to a positive spill-over feedback effect on sales of I-Macs. It has also been demonstrated (Lei et al., 2008)

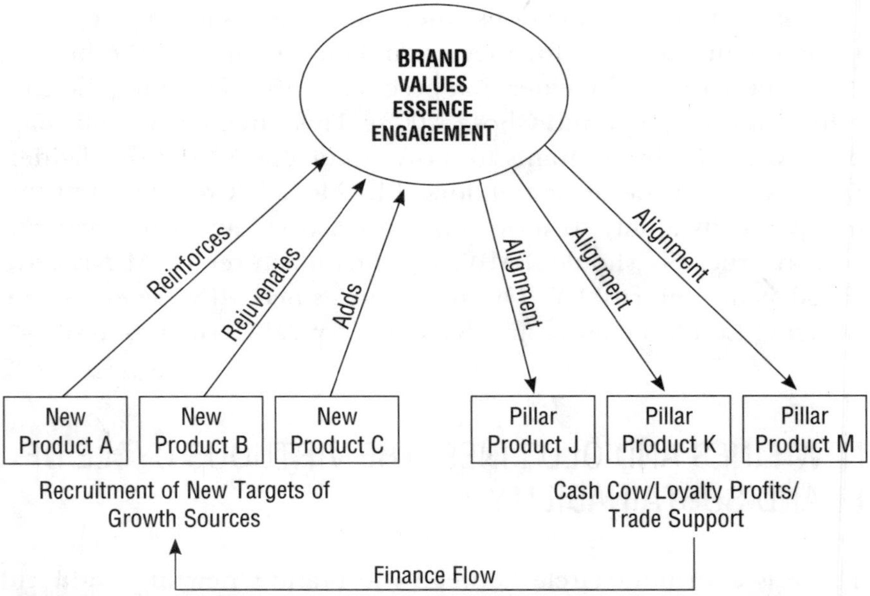

Figure 8.4 Building Brand Resilience: The Virtuous Circle of Innovation

that advertising new products of a range boosts the sales of older products of that range more than the direct advertisement of these old products.

CONCLUSION: INNOVATION AND BRAND COMPETITIVENESS

Where does innovation fit in the assessment of brand competitiveness? The ability to compete is a function of (a) the present status of the brand (measured by brand strength and market growth rates) and (b) its inner resources to resist obsolescence. Innovativeness is the second pillar (Figure 8.5). So, many brands have lost their future because they lack this key driver of success. Recently, Adidas announced that it would relaunch Reebok by positioning it in the fitness market and by drastically increasing its rate of innovation reflected in terms of the number of its new product launches.

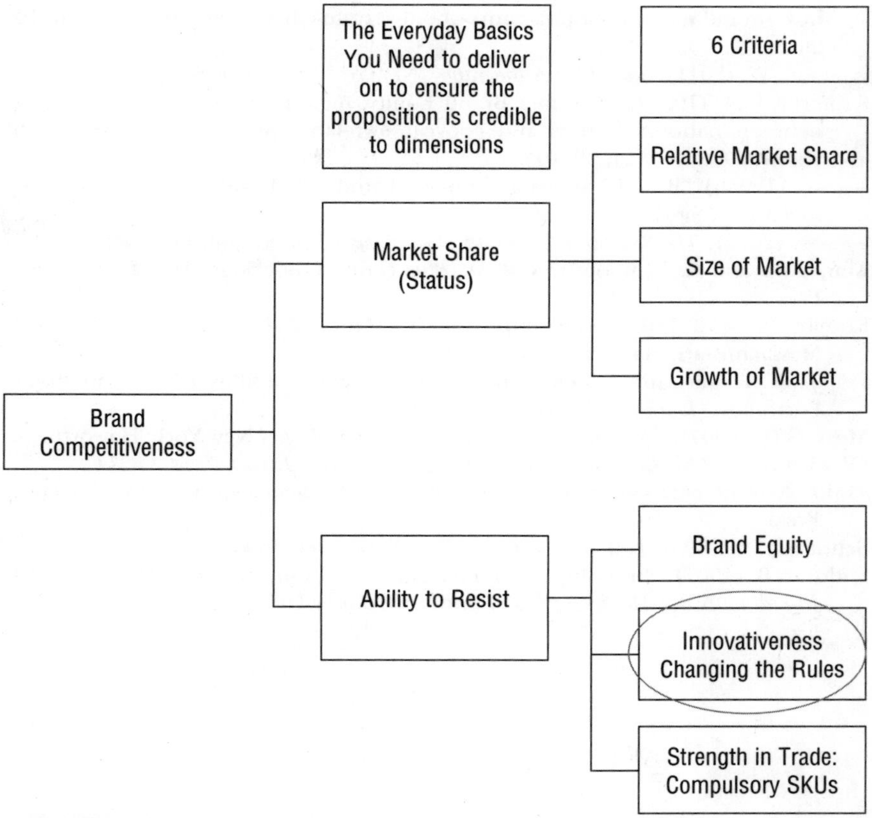

Figure 8.5 Dimensions of Brand Competitiveness

REFERENCES

Aaker, D. (1995). *Building Strong Brands.* New York: Free Press.

Balachander, S. and S. Ghose (2003). "Reciprocal Spillover Effects: A Strategic Benefit of Brand Extensions," *Journal of Marketing* 67(1[January]): 4–14.

Blattberg, R. (2001). *Customer Equity.* Cambridge, Massachusetts: Harvard Business School Press.

Christensen, C.M. (1997). *The Innovator's Dilemma.* Cambridge, Massachusetts: Harvard Business School Press.

Dru, J.-M. (2002). *Beyond Disruption.* New York: Wiley.

Hoch, S. (1996). "How should National Brands Think about Private Labels?" *Sloan Management Review* 37(Winter): 89–102. http://sloanreview.mit.edu/article/

how-should-national-brands-think-about-private-labels/, accessed March 13, 2013.

Isaacson, W. (2011). *Steve Jobs: A Biography.* New York: Simon & Schuster.

Kapferer, J.-N. (1995a). "Stealing Brand Equity: measuring perceptual confusion between national brands and copycat own-label products," *Marketing and Research Today* 23(2), 96–103.

———. (1995b). "Brand Confusion: Empirical Study of a Legal Concept," *Psychology and Marketing* 12(6), 551–568.

———. (2012). *The New Strategic Brand Management,* 5th edition. Kogan-Page.

Kim, W.C. and R. Mauborgne (2005). *Blue Ocean.* Cambridge: Harvard Business Press.

Kumar, N. and J.-B. Steenkamp (2007). *Private Label Strategy.* Cambridge, Massachusetts: Harvard Business School Press.

Lei, J., N. Dawar, and J. Lemmink (2008). "Negative Spillover Effect in Brand Portfolios," *Journal of Marketing* 72(3): 111–123.

Moss, G.D. (2007). *Pharmaceuticals: Where's the Brand Logic?* New York: Haworth.

OC&C (2010). "An Analysis of World Brands," *Internal Report.* Paris: OC&C.

PIMS (2004). *Profit Impact of Market Share.* Boston, Massachusetts: Harvard University Press.

Schnaars, D. (1995). *Imitation Strategies.* New York: Free Press.

Sudovar, B. (1987). "Branding in the Pharmaceutical Industry," in J. Murphy (Ed.), *Branding: A Key Marketing Tool.* London: McGraw-Hill.

Chapter 9

Branding with a Cause

Kartikeya Kompella

In today's world we are surrounded by brands, and in turn brands too are surrounded by people. In an increasingly transparent world, every brand is being examined for what it says or does. Take a step down the wrong path and expect to be exposed sooner or later. Make a wrong policy and listen to social media reverberate with displeasure.

Greater affluence in developing countries, greater strife in developed countries, increased awareness through the Internet, as well as the ease and instantaneity of communication through social media have given rise (and voice) to a more purposeful segment of consumers who now evaluate brands *also* on how they treat disadvantaged groups, the environment, and other stakeholders.

The question "How good are you when no one is watching?" which traditionally has been applied to individuals to introspect about moral standards has been replaced for brands with the question "How good are you toward those whose interests don't directly affect your business?"

This question which has always been important is now gaining even more importance because it gives strong cues in terms of what values brands need to stand for and what actions they need to take responsibility for.

It's important to understand the context that has led to the greater scrutiny of brands. Let's take a quick look at how, with the passage of time, the mantle of social responsibility has shifted across institutions, leading to today's debate on the social responsibility of business.

It is one of life's unhappy truths that there has always existed an inequality of fortune across men. There always have been the rich and the poor, and in times of strife, the poor have turned to the most powerful people in their region for aid.

For a long time monarchs were the most powerful people in any land and distressed people often turned to their king for help. In most countries, with time, the power of the monarch diminished but the Church gained power and in turn took responsibility for the welfare of the people. Again, over a period of time, the Church ceded its power to governments, which took the responsibility for the good of the people.

Today in most countries, business is the most powerful institution that exists and people are looking at this large and wealthy institution to take some responsibility for society (Cohen and Greenfield, 1997). This expectation exists and is being expressed strongly. However, a majority of businesses do not want to take responsibility for society as they neither recognize the need to do so nor do they want their resources to be used for what they consider to be unprofitable/non-business initiatives.

CONFLICTING VIEWPOINTS

There are two differing viewpoints as to who business needs to direct its responsibility toward, and most businesspeople are polarized between these viewpoints.

These viewpoints differ in their definition of who the stakeholders of a business are and therefore where the responsibility of business lies:

1. The investor-oriented argument (which is understandably very popular) says that the responsibility of business is toward its shareholders alone. As Milton Freidman is famously to have said: "The business of business is business."

   The advocates of this philosophy believe that investors take all the risks and therefore business is only responsible to them (of course, after paying bills and taxes). This group clearly interprets the term "stakeholders" literally as only being investors.

2. The society-oriented argument is based on a broader definition of stakeholders. As per this argument, the term "stakeholders" also includes employees, vendors, local communities, and the society at large. This definition looks at everyone who is impacted by business including local communities which may neither be employees nor be associates.

   This argument contends that business is a part of society and uses social resources and hence has a responsibility to society. Business, in fact, uses a disproportionate amount of social resources and has a powerful impact on man and environment that cannot be ignored just because it pays its taxes and bills.

   Importantly, many of the ills of the world whether obesity or environmental degradation are due to business and it cannot ignore the collateral damage it causes.

BUSINESS IS UNDER TREMENDOUS PRESSURE

Business recognizes that it cannot exist "as an island" and that it needs to have a good reputation across audiences. Despite business' reluctance, more and more companies are adopting social responsibility initiatives because the overall image of business is suffering.

There are of course a growing number of enlightened businesspeople whose motives are based on their personal interest to help society but these still constitute a minority.

Trust is integral to the success of brands; however, distrust toward business today is fairly deep-rooted. The impersonal nature of business (corporation versus people) makes it easy for corporates to be seen as cold and unfriendly.

This unfriendly image turned toxic when the world economy took body blows in 2001 and 2008 due to the greed of some highly reputed brands. Understandably the Edelman Trust Barometer 2009 (a global study on trust in institutions) showed a 62 percent drop in trust in business among survey respondents over the previous year

(Edelman Editions, 2009). The Edelman Trust Barometer 2012 shows that trust in business had not risen significantly since 2008 (Edelman Editions, 2012a).

Despite the bad news, there is hope for corporates too. Respondents state that demonstrating greater care for customers, employees, local communities, the environment, and society can help corporates build trust (Edelman Editions, 2012b).

Consumers today are increasingly looking at organizations and brands to show purpose. The Edelman Good Purpose study 2012 reveals that 87 percent of the respondents felt that business should place at least as much emphasis on societal issues as they do on business (Good Purpose, 2012).

Consumers may not be as impractical or unrealistic in their expectations as the data might suggest—76 percent of the respondents in the Edelman Good Purpose study 2012 stated that it is acceptable for companies to support good causes and make money at the same time (Good Purpose, 2012). Consumers aren't asking business to give up on profits—they are just asking them to do business in a smarter manner.

WHERE CORPORATE SOCIAL RESPONSIBILITY STRUGGLES

The traditional model of Corporate Social Responsibility (CSR) has its merits, but unfortunately it does appear ponderous, preachy, and boring to most businesspeople. It looks only at what the business can give and nothing that it can get, and this approach doesn't rest well with many businesspeople.

The traditional model of CSR does not offer inspiration as the concept has been poorly marketed. Various scandals have shown, however, that business reputation is fragile and that CSR is a powerful reputational tool that is worth investing in.

Businesses are adopting CSR and making it work for them. They've taken a more responsible stance toward their supply chains, local communities, and the environment and seen the benefits of this approach.

It bears noticing though that many CSR initiatives revolve around areas that have been traditionally reputational weak spots and so CSR appears to be operating as a pre-emptive reputational tool. There does, however, seem to be a more fundamental strategic approach/opportunity that many businesses have missed.

A BRAND SOLUTION TO CSR RESISTANCE

All businesses are brands each using a different combination of values and associations to identify and differentiate themselves in competitive marketplaces. Brands provide meaning and direction to businesses through what they represent.

Support for a cause is a powerful way of demonstrating that the brand stands for a particular principle, belief, or ideology because it goes beyond *talking* about it to actually putting resources behind this belief. The very act of standing up for something meaningful is indicative of principles, beliefs, and other positive differentiating virtues for a brand. These lead to building trust and affinity among stakeholders who share such beliefs or principles.

If the cause is a logical extension of the brand or a reinforcement of its purpose, then it works even better for the brand. As long as the cause is seen as being in the realm of social responsibility (and not all causes necessarily are), the cause would be the "social responsibility" expression of the brand and therefore be serving brand and society at the same time.

CAUSE-RELATED BRANDING—WORKING FOR SOCIETY AND BUSINESS

Cause-related branding is a manner of aligning social responsibility initiatives to a brand through the identification and support of an appropriate cause to make such an initiative work for both brand and society. The right alignment gives social responsibility initiatives direction and makes them contribute directly toward business (brand) objectives, something that CSR does not normally focus on.

Cause-related branding has all the image benefits of CSR while being more authentic as it emerges directly from what the brand stands for. Not enough brands practice cause-related branding, and only few of those who do, have perfected their cause-related branding efforts. However, there is enough evidence now to show that it is an approach with great potential.

Dove from Unilever is a great example of cause-related branding. Dove identified a cause that flowed directly from the character of the brand and made it the backbone of their brand efforts. They sustained it, built on it, and it paid off wonderfully for the brand. Let's look at this in detail.

In 2004, Unilever commissioned a global study called "The Real Truth about Beauty" (Etcoff et al., 2004). The study aimed at understanding what beauty means to women and why. The study also sought to understand whether there were new ways to discuss female beauty that were more "genuine, satisfying, and empowering to women" (Findings of the Global Study on Women, Beauty and Well-Being, September 2004, Etcoff, Orbach, Scott & D'Agostino—StrategyOne).

The study revealed that only around 2 percent of the women surveyed defined themselves as "beautiful"; however, a majority chose to call themselves "natural" or "average" (Etcoff et al., 2004). When it came to evaluating themselves, most women used the terms "beauty" and "physical attractiveness" interchangeably; however, when it came to interpreting these as separate concepts, they were able to make a clear distinction that "physical attractiveness is about how one looks, whereas beauty includes much more of who a person is." Beauty as defined by women included personal characteristics such as kindness, happiness, and confidence (Etcoff et al., 2004).

Interestingly, 48 percent of the respondents strongly agreed with the statement "When I feel less beautiful, I feel worse about myself in general," demonstrating the impact of their self-concept of beauty on their feelings (Etcoff et al., 2004).

Sixty-eight percent of the respondents agreed with the statement "The media and advertising set an unrealistic standard of beauty that most women can't achieve," and 47 percent of the respondents strongly agreed with the statement "Only the most physically attractive women are portrayed in popular culture" (Etcoff et al., 2004).

These findings revealed a rich vein of emotion that marketers may have suspected existed but hitherto not tapped into. Dove realized that media and advertising defined beauty in a very limited, physical manner that makes women feel inadequate and that this in turn negatively affected their self-esteem.

Dove itself had followed the tradition of using "regular" people in their advertising to promote their brand. It was the ideal brand to champion the *cause* for a new definition of beauty.

In 2004, Dove started its iconic "Campaign for Real Beauty" with the aim of "changing the status quo (of beauty) and offer in its place a broader, healthier, more democratic view of beauty … a view of beauty that all women can own and enjoy every day."

Dove's "Campaign for Real Beauty" attempted to dispel the media-created myth that beauty is purely to do with physical attractiveness. In the campaign, Dove celebrated "real beauty" that recognized physical attractiveness but defined real beauty as being more than just physical so as to also capture a beautiful spirit.

Dove was telling women that "they're beautiful just the way they are" and women loved the brand for that. Here was a brand with a history of using regular people to endorse it standing up for the average woman. It was genuine, heart-felt, and empathetic, and consumers roared their approval. Sales for products featured in the campaign ads increased 600 percent in the first two months, with an overall sales increase across the entire brand reaching 20 percent in 2005 (Cone and Darigan, 2007).

This was not a one-off campaign—the brand had truly understood the spirit of the cause and was living it. In 2006, recognizing that many girls and young women develop low self-esteem due to dissatisfaction with their looks, and that this stops them from reaching their full potential in life, Dove established the Dove Self-Esteem Fund. This fund was created to inspire and educate girls and women about a wider definition of beauty (http://www.dove.us/Social-Mission/campaign-for-real-beauty.aspx, accessed June 13, 2013).

In 2010, Dove launched a stirring initiative to *make beauty a source of confidence, not anxiety*, with the Dove Movement for Self-Esteem (http://www.dove.us/Social-Mission/campaign-for-real-beauty.aspx, accessed June 13, 2013).

Dove's depth of involvement with the cause of building self-esteem in girls and women is admirable. In addition to running powerful campaigns that build awareness of the need to build self-esteem (Evolution, Onslaught, Little Girls, Daughters), Dove has also created self-esteem-building educational programs and activities that inspire and motivate girls around the world.

To their credit Dove has reached over 7 million girls so far with these programs and targets reaching 15 million girls by 2015 (http://www.dove.us/Social-Mission/campaign-for-real-beauty.aspx, accessed June 13, 2013).

Dove's "Campaign for Real Beauty" is a wonderful example of cause-related branding for four reasons:

1. It built a cause from a powerful brand attribute that was unique to the brand—"real women."
2. The cause resonates powerfully and personally with women.
3. The brand and the cause are strongly linked to one another. Cause promotion helps the brand and vice versa.
4. The brand lives and promotes the cause in an enduring manner.

ACHIEVING BRAND OBJECTIVES USING CAUSE-RELATED BRANDING

Brands can achieve various brand objectives using a clear understanding of branding and some imagination. Let us look at some of these.

Increased Preference and Advocacy

One of the key tasks for marketers is to build preference for their brands. Edelman's "Good Purpose 2012" shows that (social) purpose builds brand preference. Fifty-three percent of the respondents saw purpose as the trigger for purchase while choosing brands when quality and price were equal (Good Purpose, 2012). These findings are similar to the findings of other surveys that examine consumer attitudes toward social initiatives such as the Cone Citizenship Studies, BITC's Brand Benefits Study, etc.

It is a marketer's dream to have a large number of consumers recommending their brand to others. It is a privilege reserved for relatively few brands that enjoy a special status with consumers. Edelman's "Good Purpose 2012" shows that purpose can be a strong driver for brand advocacy. Seventy-two percent of this survey respondents opined: "I am more likely to recommend a brand that supports a good cause than one that doesn't" (Good Purpose, 2012). This figure has moved up from 52 to 72 percent in five years, indicating that this mindset is spreading (Good Purpose, 2012).

Establishing Differentiation

Brands such as The Body Shop and Ben & Jerry's powerfully differentiated themselves from competition on the basis of their affiliation with different causes.

The Body Shop has associated itself with several causes (against animal testing, supporting community fair trade, building self-esteem, etc.) each built around the brand's umbrella theme "Beauty with a Heart." Arguably, The Body Shop's most popular initiative was its campaign against testing of cosmetics on animals. This program served to build awareness of an important issue while also making a strong values-based statement that powerfully repositioned competition.

The Body Shop is a good example of a brand that built differentiation and stature using cause-related branding. In 1998, The Body Shop ran its first self-esteem campaign. The campaign featured a voluptuous doll they called "Ruby." The doll debuted in The Body Shop windows in the United Kingdom, along with the slogan "There are 3 billion women who don't look like supermodels and only 8 who do."

As Anita Roddick mentioned in her website, Ruby was a light-hearted yet thought-provoking way of addressing a serious subject that women felt strongly about. The campaign resonated with consumers who resented beauty companies' strategy of using thin models to make women feel inferior thereby making their products all the more necessary (Roddick, 2001). Through Ruby, The Body

Shop had challenged the stereotypes of beauty and started a worldwide debate on body image and self-esteem.

Through these causes and others, The Body Shop established itself as a cosmetics company that had a serious, humane view of beauty that differentiated it from more vacuous competition.

Enhanced Relevance

Cause-related branding can establish brand relevance extremely well. Saffola, a brand of safflower oil in India, has attached itself to the cause of people taking care of their heart. This is a relevant cause in India where obesity and sedentary habits are forming a lethal combination.

Saffola has been promoting the cause of healthy hearts in India, every year, on World Heart Day. Its many promotions include a habit change campaign to encourage people to walk to work, use the stairs, and adopt a more active lifestyle. Saffola offers free cholesterol tests and even a means of people determining how old their heart is! Saffola has a website full of advice on how to be heart-healthy with site visitors having the option of getting advice from dieticians and other health experts (http://www.saffolalife.com/young-at-heart-age-of-your-heart/, accessed June 13, 2013).

Saffola's cause-related branding efforts have made its products even more relevant to Indians. Saffola's entire stance of stressing the importance of having a healthy heart has served not just the social cause of building awareness and encouraging heart-healthy behavior but has also made Saffola's heart-healthy offerings even more relevant to consumers.

Higher Sales

Cause-related branding is used very often to drive sales; however, there are instances of brands doing more than just that.

In the United States, a lot of fire departments operate on very tight budgets and are underequipped in terms of protective clothing, breathing apparatus, and other necessary equipment.

TUMS, the antacid brand, tied up with the First Responder Institute to support these fire departments. The brand developed a program that would impact firefighters in a very direct and tangible way.

TUMS ran a promotion campaign, "TUMS put out more fires than you know!," that promised a donation of 10 cents on every can of TUMS sold during the cause promotion period.

The brand saw a 16 percent increase in sales volume during the promotional period and generated $238K for the Institute (Cause Marketing Halo Awards Archive, 2004). These figures are impressive in the context of the low-involvement category that antacids operate in. The program was well thought-out enabling the brand to build an association with a relevant cause and using the connection well.

The campaign line "TUMS put out more fires than you know!" gave the brand stature beyond its product attributes in a category known mainly for product benefit and attributes.

Coke experienced even more dramatic results in their cause-related marketing promotion run at select Walmart stores with the nonprofit MADD (Mothers Against Drunk Driving). Coke promised to donate 15 cents to MADD for every case of Coca-Cola sold during the promotion period. The sales of Coke surged by 490 percent during the six-week promotion period (Cause Marketing Forum, 2010).

Building Trust

Standing for a cause speaks a lot about a brand's values. When stakeholders see that the brand is willing to play a larger role in society and not base all their decisions purely on business, they are likely to believe that the brand has the principles and willingness behave responsibly and this engenders trust.

Various surveys (Edelman Trust Barometer, Cone Citizenship, Lintas MSN Crosstabs) have shown that people trust companies that are socially responsible more than those who are not. Social responsibility is at the heart of cause-related branding, and so its ability to build consumer trust is in-built.

The key tasks of most brand marketers are to build preference, relevance, differentiation, trust, and drive sales. The above examples demonstrate that cause-related branding can be used successfully to achieve all of these and thus offers a good opportunity for brands to grow while benefitting society.

TYPES OF ASSOCIATION WITH CAUSES

In their book *Good Works,* Kotler, Hessekiel, and Lee have classified social initiatives for Doing Well by Doing Good into six types (Kotler et al., 2012). In this chapter, these initiatives have been interpreted in the context of cause-related branding.

Cause Promotion

In this form of association, brands (corporate or product) build awareness, concern, or recruitment for a cause in order to build greater support for the cause. The means of building support for the cause could be through a communication campaign launched by the brand or the brand may support a nonprofit that runs the campaign.

Cause promotion can produce powerful results for brand and society. Lifebuoy from Unilever is the world's largest selling "health" or "germ protection" soap brand and has a very real and relevant connection with the cause of hygiene, specifically hand hygiene. Started in 1894 as a response to the frequent outbreaks of cholera in Victorian England, Lifebuoy was created with the intention of being a lifesaver (http://www.lifebuoy.com/about-us/, accessed June 13, 2013).

True to its social mission, Lifebuoy has played a sterling role in building awareness of the need for hygiene. Lifebuoy has campaigned strongly and consistently about the need for people (especially children) to be protected from germs. Their sustained, well-thought-out promotions have increased the brand's relevance in no small way, resulting in its growth as a brand leader. Lifebuoy's campaigns on hand hygiene have also helped prevent millions of children from falling ill and saved countless lives.

Another powerful cause promotion initiative is the movement to "End Child Hunger" from ConAgra Foods. As a corporate brand that owns several food brands, it was logical that this brand should target a hunger-related issue.

Most people associate the concept of "child hunger" or "hungry children" with third world countries; however, few realized that the United States could be home to many poor, hungry children. When ConAgra brought to public awareness the fact that one in every five children in the United States lives with hunger, it shook public conscience. "Nearly 17 million children in America face hunger," says its website in a chilling statement of reality (http://www.conagrafoods.com/our-company/our-commitment/foundation/child-hunger-ends-here, accessed June 13, 2013).

From a brand marketing perspective, their selection of the cause was more than brilliant. The cause area was neither so broad for the brand to get lost nor was so niche that it was insignificant. The cause was such that the brand could play a significant role and grow with the cause while tapping into the hugely emotive issue of Child Hunger.

The cause "End Child Hunger" had a positive impact on brand and society. Through their promotion of this cause ConAgra has mobilized millions of dollars of support and tonnes of food for hungry children as well as built immense stature for its brand.

Cause promotion needs to be planned well to deliver powerfully. The better the fit between cause and brand, the better for both as their growth too then is interlinked. The more the public support for the cause grows, the better for the brand and vice versa leading to a virtuous circle.

Cause-related Marketing

Probably the most common form of cause-related branding programs—cause-related marketing—sometimes provides examples of cause-related branding at its worst.

The cause-related marketing program structure is mostly designed around the brand pledging to pay a fixed sum of money (or donation of an in-kind product) to a specific nonprofit or cause based on consumers' purchase of the brand. The duration of the program is normally specified, the payout is predetermined, and the cutoff volume of sales up to which level only the brand will contribute to the nonprofit is stated.

It is the lure of sales and the cap on the marketers' outflow that encourage some marketers to run such programs; however, it is the cap on the outflow that can also cause stakeholders to suspect the brand's actual commitment to the cause. Cause-related marketing on its own can often be a poor way for a brand to demonstrate genuine intent toward a cause unless there is a more enduring strategic dimension to the program.

The ease with which cause-related marketing programs can be set up, coupled with the linkage to sales, makes them an easy choice for marketers. This often leads to poorly thought-out programs in which there is no connection with the brand and the cause, or programs that appear to have more of a sales orientation than any genuine interest in the cause.

Cause-related marketing programs have been misused by unscrupulous businesses that either did not pass on their contribution to the concerned nonprofits or drove sales by claiming association with a fictitious nonprofit. For this reason, cause-related marketing programs are sometimes viewed with slight cynicism.

From a brand perspective though, cause-related marketing makes the brand an enabler, giving the consumer the satisfaction of doing a good deed simply by choosing to buy the brand. This satisfaction is important to consumers who often don't have the time or money to get involved in as many meaningful initiatives as they would like to. There is some merit in this approach, but cause-related marketing programs need to be planned well so that they don't taint the consumers' satisfaction of participation in any way.

Not all cause-related marketing programs are suspect. TOMS Shoes and Newman's Own are two extremely good examples of cause-related marketing done by for-profits. Newman's Own (of the legendary actor Paul Newman) donates all its profits to nonprofits of its choice (http://www.newmansown.com/charity, accessed June 13, 2013). The satisfaction that consumers get from choosing Newman's Own over competition and the stature that the brand enjoys is remarkable.

TOMS Shoes commits to donate a pair of shoes to the needy for every pair of shoes that people buy from them and one pair of glasses for every pair of glasses bought from them (http://www.toms.com/our-movement/l, accessed June 13, 2013). This brand too enjoys enormous following because of its large-hearted, open-ended cause marketing strategy.

In both these cases, the brands have built immense differentiation and respect through their cause-related marketing strategies. The large-hearted approach of these brands has lifted their initiatives from being viewed as sales promotions to being the defining aspect of these brands.

Corporate Social Marketing

In these types of programs, the objective is to make people change their behavior in a manner that is good for the individual/society. This could be in the form of more healthy living (Saffola—"take the stairs, don't take the lift"), the environment (Patagonia—"Don't buy this shirt unless you need to"), safety (Safeco and making people more aware of how to prevent wildfires), etc.

Lifebuoy does a lot of laudable work in the area of hand hygiene. They go beyond cause promotion to actually trying to create behavior change. Their "handwashing" campaign has touched several millions of people with the sole aim of making them wash their hands more often especially before or after events that could lead to spread of germs. Lifebuoy globally monitors diseases that can be spread through touch and urges people to wash their hands to prevent transmission of these diseases. This change of behavior helps society irrespective of which soap the stakeholders use; however, consumers are likely to prefer this brand for the role it played in protecting them.

Philanthropy

The oldest form of social responsibility practiced by corporate houses, philanthropy, is the donation of money or in-kind donations to a cause or nonprofit. This could be in the form of awards, scholarships, free products, etc. Brands such as the Tatas, Ford, and Microsoft have earned a wonderful reputation from their generosity over the years. Society too has benefitted immensely from their sustained largesse. Most causes face a shortage of funds, and philanthropy is a simple but important solution to such problems.

Often brands think that it is enough to just make donations, and hence little thought goes into designing these programs to make them cause-related branding exercises that work for both the brand and society. Ideally every *strategic* social program done by a brand should look at doing something for the brand too.

Tide's Loads of Hope is a philanthropic initiative from Tide (P&G) that recognizes that inconsequential as it might seem, disaster stricken people too need their clothes to be washed and folded. The availability of clean clothes is often an important step for people to actually start rebuilding their lives. Tide drives a mobile Laundromat to places in the United States where disaster has struck and relief work is going on.

The Tide team washes clothes, dries them, and folds them free of cost. Where they don't actually travel, they send in free cases of the product. The Tide's Loads of Hope team have traveled over 40,000 miles in America and washed over 58,000 loads of clothes helping over 27,000 families in 31 cities (http://www.tide.com/en-US/loads-of-hope/about.jspx, accessed June 13, 2013).

From a brand perspective (depending on the brand's image and track record), philanthropy can be seen by stakeholders as an easy, uninvolved means of "buying" involvement with a cause. It's important for brands to guard themselves against such cynicism by designing their philanthropic programs well, to deliver for both society and the brand. Sustained painstaking efforts like Tide's Loads of Hope can counter negative perceptions and work effectively for brands.

Volunteerism

Corporate volunteering programs involve corporates encouraging their employees to volunteer time to a cause or nonprofit. This could be in the form of giving employees time off to do community service for a cause or nonprofit. Other stakeholders such as associates, the trade, etc., may also be encouraged to volunteer time.

Volunteerism is extremely important for society because a lot of nonprofits either do not have enough people to help out for special occasions or lack the specialist management skills required to scale up their projects.

Volunteerism often does not get much visibility because the scale and extent of such efforts are far more limited than other cause-related branding programs. However, the impact of volunteerism on the brand can be very significant because it is seen as a hardworking and strong demonstration of intent, which adds a lot of credibility to the brand.

The volunteerism efforts of brands such as Disney and Home Depot show that this is a very powerful tool for brand and society.

Let us look at Disney. This brand is about bringing joy to families and what better way to do cause-related branding than by directing their social responsibility initiatives toward making children happy.

Disney employees collect new toys for distribution to underprivileged children. The employees of Disney support "The Toys for Tots Foundation," a nonprofit organization whose mission is to collect new, unwrapped toys each year and distribute these as Christmas gifts to less fortunate children. In 2011, in an extremely hardworking effort, Disney employees collected 3,000 toys for distribution by Toys for Tots (Prihoda 2011).

(Disney's involvement with Toys for Tots is not a new form of involvement but a tradition that spans over 60 years. In fact, Walt Disney and his animators designed the original Toys for Tots logo, which the campaign still uses today.)

Home Depot is the world's largest home improvement specialty retailer and espouses a do-it-yourself philosophy. Its associate-led volunteer program Team Depot is quick to volunteer its members' skills to help build or rebuild projects that help society. In 2012, Team Depot completed more than 1,200 projects across the United States (The Home Depot Foundation, 2013, Homedepotfoundation.org).

Socially Responsible Business Practices

These are voluntary business practices that companies adopt to support causes that are good for community. Many people believe that this is the fundamental area of business responsibility to society and that genuine intent starts by doing business in a socially responsible manner.

Socially responsible business practices, as their nomenclature suggests, are good for society—they take care of the environment or people in some way or the other. Such business practices imbue the brand with positive associations that strengthen the brand.

Starbucks pioneering Fair Trade Practices is a good example of how socially responsible business practices can help both society and brand. Starbucks does a lot for its suppliers by paying a fair price for the coffee they buy, ensuring that workers in their vendors' coffee plantations are well taken care of, etc. The knowledge that their coffee has a lot of "good karma" attached to it sets its consumers' minds at rest and contributes a lot to the brand's "fine-coffee" drinking experience.

360° ADOPTION OF CAUSES

Each type of association with causes has its own benefits for both brands and causes, and most well-planned cause-related branding programs use more than one type of cause association. ConAgra is a great example of a brand that uses different types of cause approaches to work with great focus toward a single cause, helping both brand and society.

ConAgra promotes the cause of Ending Child Hunger across America. This is its core cause area. ConAgra promotes this cause in several ways including a national public-service advertising campaign to raise public awareness of child hunger.

As a step toward achieving its goal of an America that is free of hunger, ConAgra sponsors nonprofit Share Our Strength's Cooking Matters. In their program, Cooking Matters uses culinary and nutrition experts to teach its course participants how to select nutritious and low-cost ingredients and use these in ways that provide the best nourishment possible to their families. Importantly, Cooking Matters also teaches people how not to waste food.

Through its cause-related marketing campaign Child Hunger Ends Here, ConAgra's brands invite consumers to support the movement by entering codes found on specially marked packages. In 2013, for every code entered at www.childhungerendshere.com (for a prespecified period), ConAgra pledged to donate the monetary equivalent of one meal to Feeding America, a hunger-relief charity up to a maximum of 3 million meals (Feeding America, 2013, Feedingamerica.org).

ConAgra donates the equivalent of 1 million meals in product every month to Feeding America (ConAgra Foods, 2012a). Since 1993, ConAgra Foods and its brands have contributed over $37 million to nonprofits and more than 310 million pounds of food to support Feeding America programs (ConAgra Foods, 2012b).

ConAgra's employees have played a large role in supporting the cause of ending child hunger. In March 2012, nearly 2,000 employees participated in 125 volunteer projects and volunteered more than 3,400 hours of service to community-based programs. More than 108,504 meals were packed or served, and 69,954 pounds of food was donated to families in need (ConAgra Foods, 2013c).

What makes ConAgra's efforts so impressive is not just their intent and the scale with which they have adopted the cause but also their understanding of the cause and how they have kept stakeholders' interest in it alive. What started close to a decade ago as Feeding Children Better lives on today as the cause of Ending Child Hunger. The campaign expression has changed with time, but the intent has remained constant.

Their understanding of the nuances of child hunger is impressive—the fact that many children face hunger in summer when school is closed because they don't get the school provided lunch is insightful and heart-tugging. It's this combination of insights and their interesting branding of programs such as "Hunger-Free Summer," "Hungry to Help," and "Nourish Our Community" that keep their programs memorable, inspirational, and fresh.

CAUSE-RELATED BRANDING—STRATEGIC ASPECTS

There are some key strategic aspects that need to be considered while developing a cause-related branding program.

Understanding the Purpose

The first step before considering a cause-related branding program involves deep introspection into why the brand wants to do this program. This would require debating a variety of issues ranging from the brand's stance on social responsibility, the motivations behind the program, stakeholders expectations, how the program success would be measured, etc.

A clear reason as to why the brand is adopting a cause and a charter by which the program will operate is critical for structuring a good cause-related branding program. While clarity of purpose will determine the direction of the program, the charter will define the boundaries of its operation. The charter is especially important because it determines the balance of the program between brand and cause.

Without a clear charter there can be inconsistency in decision making that can impact the brand and expectations from the brand. Cause-related branding programs are long-term initiatives, and if the purpose is not clearly documented, then it is easy for stakeholders to lose sight of the initial purpose over time as business circumstances change.

Understanding the Brand

Developing a cause for a brand is based on what the brand stands for. Armed with this understanding, brands can build effective cause-related branding programs even with a small budget.

Take the example of Nike, a brand that's about personal physical performance. The Nike Employee Grant Fund has awarded $20,000 to De Paul Treatment Centers to help create a health and fitness program in what is a small but interesting initiative.

This health and fitness program aims at enabling youth who are undergoing rehabilitation to get into a healthy life that is free from drugs and alcohol. This program helps restore the health of former addicts and show them a healthier way of enjoying their lives (Nike funds De Paul treatment centers youth fitness project, 2011, Depaultreatmentcenters.org). The idea of replacing the consumption of drugs with the joy of exercise is excellent. A program of this nature and nuance could not have been designed without an appreciation of what the brand stands for.

Kraft's philanthropic initiative the "Delicious Difference" week where Kraft employees serve free nutritious, delicious hot meals to hungry people takes on key aspects of the brand—flavor and nutrition.

It is critical to have a keen understanding of what values and associations the brand stands for, who its stakeholders are, the basis of the brand's relationship with its stakeholders, the basis of the brand's differentiation, and the brand's personality and ideology when developing a cause-related branding program so that the program is in sync with the different nuances of the brand.

Choosing the Cause

The selection of the cause for a cause-related branding program is based on the brand's larger purpose and the brand's objective in associating with a cause. Most cause-related branding initiatives are consumer-facing initiatives, and so the causes often are designed to build or reinforce the brand's relationship with the consumer.

A good way of identifying a "cause" that works for the brand is this seven-step method:

1. Identify all the key associations of the brand and category, both negative and positive. For example: A fast food chain's associations can be *taste*, hunger, nutrition, spices, *freshness*, MSG, ingredients, family, children, etc.
2. Identify all the issues that are related to these associations. Based on the above example, this could be *obesity*, lifestyle diseases, malnutrition, genetically modified food, unsustainable farming practices, soil depletion, chemical fertilizers/pesticides, etc.
3. Identify brand nuances that are specific to the brand such as Cajun, spicy, baked, *low fat*, etc., for a fast food chain.
4. Identify a combination of association, an issue, and a brand nuance. For example: Subway speaks of their *fresh, tasty low fat* sandwiches. The brand's cause-related branding programs flow in the same direction as the brand stance.

Subway uses sponsorship (philanthropy) to fight obesity. Through their association with the American Heart Association's Jump Rope for Heart and Hoops for Heart, the brand engages children in physical activity and raise money for lifesaving research in the area of stroke and heart care.

5. *Crafting the cause*: ConAgra could have chosen to take up the cause of ending hunger in the United States; however, the size of the cause would have been extremely large and ConAgra's role in this cause would have been much smaller given the many other brands supporting this cause. By crafting the cause to address only child hunger, ConAgra was able to be a large player in a smaller, more specific, emotive cause.

   The crafting of this cause allowed ConAgra to be able to "own" this cause while also making it different (hence memorable) from the other hunger-related causes in the United States. Designing a cause-related branding program requires an understanding of how to make the cause more "brand-friendly" without losing the essence and appeal of the cause.
6. *Gauge internal stakeholder commitment*: It's important to know what your internal stakeholders think of the program—if it doesn't inspire them or make them feel good, then it's unlikely that this will work with customers either.
7. *Test*: Research is not be-all and end-all of decision making but provides important inputs. It's important to see how stakeholders view the cause and what it does for their perception of the brand. Ascertaining brand fit, relevance, memorability, distinctiveness, and stakeholder resonance are key aspects to be studied through research.

Getting the Balance Right

To get the most from their cause-related branding programs, brand custodians need to ensure that these are designed in a balanced manner. A program that primarily focuses on a cause may not get enough organizational support, whereas a program that is one-sided in favor of the brand may not get consumer and employee support. Ideally the brand and cause should be linked together so that the success of one leads to the success of the other as demonstrated in the earlier mentioned cases of Lifebuoy and Dove.

Choosing the Resources

Great cause-related branding programs are built through great partnerships. In the absence of well-managed nonprofits, sensitive promotion agencies, and committed stakeholders, most cause-related branding programs would grind to a standstill.

The credibility of the nonprofit, its understanding of the cause issues, its understanding of the brand's objectives, etc., all play a role in determining the partners' fit with the cause-related branding program. Choosing between setting up a trust/foundation and running the program in-house or choosing a partner is like a "make or buy" decision and has several strategic implications.

Setting the Metrics

The difference between a cause-related branding strategy and a brand idea that uses a cause often lies in the metrics for success. If success is only measured in brand scores without an attempt at measuring the impact or progress of the cause, then the program is only working for the brand which is unfair and is likely to affect the brand's credibility in due course.

Portfolio of Causes

There are times when for certain tactical reasons, brands need to support causes unrelated to their brand purpose. It is best that these causes are promoted only to the relevant target group to the extent required so that they fulfill their tactical requirement only. This will allow the brand to shift focus back to its cause-related branding program quickly without distracting the core audience from the main brand cause.

Ben & Jerry's were able to promote several diverse causes to their consumers without causing confusion or eroding their equity because their brand was not seen as aligned to any particular cause alone. In fact, their positioning as "a brand with a heart" allowed every cause that they promoted to become yet another reminder to their consumers as to what the brand stood for.

CONCLUSION

Cause-related branding is a very powerful tool because it engages stakeholders on values. It is for this very reason that it needs to be handled with care.

Cause-related branding programs need to be approached with belief and intent—belief that the program will work and the intent to make it work for both society and brand. Belief is the cornerstone for success and intent reflects the brand's commitment to the cause, and this forms the basis for stakeholder engagement.

Cause-related branding is an underutilized tool and offers as much to brands as it does to society. It needs to be pursued with a sense of partnership, creativity, and a long-term perspective for it to yield powerful results.

REFERENCES

Cause Marketing Forum (2010). *Proving That Cause Marketing Is a Win Win.* http://ww2.causemarketingforum.com/page.asp?ID=345, accessed June 13, 2013.

Cause Marketing Halo Awards Archive (2004). *TUMS Helps Put Out More Fires Than You Think, TUMS and First Responder Institute.* http://www.causemarketingforum.com/site/apps/nlnet/content2.aspx?c=bkLUKcOTLkK4E&b=6431039&ct=8971919, accessed June 13, 2013.

Cohen, C. and J. Greenfield (1997). *Double Dip.* New York: Simon & Schuster.

ConAgra Foods (2012a). *Citizenship Report: Impacting Child Hunger.* http://www.conagrafoodscitizenship.com/good-for-the-community/our-cause/impacting-child-hunger/, accessed June 13, 2013.

——— (2012b). *Millions of Children May Go Hungry This Summer without School Provided Meals.* http://www.conagrafoods.com/news-room/news-Millions-Of-Children-May-Go-Hungry-This-Summer-Without-School-Provided-Meals-1823786, accessed June 13, 2013.

——— (2012c). *Citizenship Report: Our People.* http://www.conagrafoodscitizenship.com/good-for-the-community/our-cause/our-people/, accessed June 13, 2013.

Cone, C. (2012). *Introducing Good Purpose.* http://purpose.edelman.com/slides/introducing-goodpurpose-2012/, accessed June 13, 2013.

Cone, C. and K. Darigan (2007). *Cause & Affect.* http://www.contributemedia.com/opinions_details.php?id=182, accessed June 13, 2013.

Edelman Editions (2009). *Business's Fall from Grace: Where to from Here?* http://edelmaneditions.com/wp-content/uploads/2010/11/edelman-trust-barometer-full-report-2009.pdf, accessed June 13, 2013.

——— (2012a) *NGOs Remain Most Trusted Institution Globally, Despite Decline.* http://edelmaneditions.com/wp-content/uploads/2012/01/Final-Brochure-1.16.pdf, accessed June 13, 2013.

——— (2012b). *New Dynamics in Play to Build Trust in Business.* http://edelmaneditions.com/wp-content/uploads/2012/01/Final-Brochure-1.16.pdf, accessed June 13, 2013.

Etcoff, N., et al. (2004). *The Real Truth about Beauty: A Global Report.* http://www.clubofamsterdam.com/contentarticles/52%20Beauty/dove_white_paper_final.pdf, accessed June 13, 2013.

Feeding America (2013). *ConAgra Foods Child Hunger Ends Here Spring 2013 Campaign.* http://feedingamerica.org/how-we-fight-hunger/our-partners/promotional-partners/child-hunger-ends-here.aspx, accessed June 13, 2013.

Good Purpose (2012). *Introducing Good Purpose.* http://purpose.edelman.com/slides/introducing-goodpurpose-2012/, accessed June 13, 2013.

Kotler, P., D. Hessekiel, and N. Lee (2012). *Good Works.* Hoboken, New Jersey: Wiley.

Nike funds De Paul treatment centers youth fitness project (2011). *Exercise Program Will Help Teens Recover from Drug and Alcohol Addiction.* http://www.depaultreatmentcenters.org/PDFs/DePaul.Nike.pdf, accessed June 13, 2013.

Prihoda, K. (2011). *Disney VoluntEARS Donate 30,000 Toys to Families in Need at Walt Disney World Resort.* http://disneyparks.disney.go.com/blog/2011/12/disney-voluntears-donate-30000-toys-to-families-in-need/, accessed June 13, 2013.

Roddick, A. (2001). *Ruby, the Anti-Barbie.* http://www.anitaroddick.com/readmore.php?sid=13, accessed June 13, 2013.

The Home Depot Foundation (2013). *How We Help: Lending Hands Serving Others.* http://homedepotfoundation.org/page/volunteerism, accessed June 13, 2013.

Section 3

Branding beyond Marketing

Chapter 10

Living the Brand

Nicholas Ind

INTRODUCTION

The traditional approach to brand building emphasizes the importance of marketing communications. This orientation made sense in the past when advertising was trusted and organizations had better control of their brand messaging, but as brands become increasingly fluid due to the active involvement of consumers, it is no longer viable. As Merz et al. (2009) note, "the logic of brand and branding is also evolving and has shifted from the conceptualization of brand as a firm-provided property of goods to brand as a collaborative, value co-creation activity of firms and all of their stakeholders." Now it is services—or at least service thinking—that dominates, and dialogue that matters. In many developed economies, services already represent about three quarters of gross domestic product (GDP). Even where manufacturing still holds sway, it is not the act of purchase but the consumption over time that determines the relationship with the brand (Vargo and Lusch, 2004). Consequently, it is experiences of usage and interactions with representatives of the company that are often most important in defining brand meaning and determining value. The implication of this is that brands are not immutable abstract things but rather constantly evolving entities that are defined by, and for, people.

The Importance of Employees in Building Brands

It is employees who interact with the outside world and converse with external stakeholders. It is employees who share knowledge with each other and create the experiences (sometimes together with consumers) that generate value. It is employees who help to drive the consumer loyalty that strengthens the brand and secures future cash flows. In this perspective, the brand is created in a space of dialogue where the organization and the individual meet. Increasingly, consumers are involved with the brands they buy through communities and social media and equally employees are participants in consumers' lives through ongoing interaction both online and offline, such that consumers "become partial employees and employees become partial consumers" (Cova and Dalli, 2009). This connectivity is opening up organizations and serves to reemphasize that it is employee–consumer relationships that define brands and help to generate knowledge that can be used to adapt and develop products and services. As an IBM study of more than 1,500 managers (2010) notes, "[T]he most successful organizations co-create products and services with customers, and integrate customers into core processes."

ENGAGING EMPLOYEES WITH BRANDS

If, as some research suggests (Baumgarth, 2010; Berry, 2000), employees are essential to stakeholder perceptions of the brand, then employees need to both understand and engage with the idea of the brand. Employees need to know what the organization stands for and be capable of delivering it in their everyday work both in their behavior toward their colleagues and in how they behave and communicate with consumers so that experiences live up to (and exceed) expectations. As King and Grace (2008) note, "there is an inherent power in having an informed workforce that is both able and committed to delivering the brand promise." Yet, this seems to be a challenge in many organizations because the brand itself is not central to decision making. Rather it is often seen as the province of the branding or marketing department and of little wider consequence for employees.

To move the brand to an organization-wide role requires that branding be recognized as more than just communication and instead becomes the unifying idea that creates a focus for business planning, HR, research and development, operations, and marketing. When this happens, there is clear benefit in terms of profitability, "the more brand-oriented a company is, the more profitable it is" (Gromark and Melin, 2005), and in the quality of the brand–customer relationship (Burmann et al., 2009). The question that emerges then is: How can an organization affect the transition to become more brand oriented? The answer lies with the approach to living the brand.

Clarifying the Concept—Living the Brand

The idea of "Living the Brand" is clearly different to some other terms that swirl around the area such as Live the Brand, Internal Branding, Internal Marketing, and Employer Branding. "Living the Brand" implies something that employees willingly engage with (rather than the exhortation of "Live" that says it is something employees must do). It also suggests that it is something culturally defined that occurs day in and day out, whereas Internal Branding and Internal Marketing are more oriented toward persuading employees to act in certain ways. Living the Brand also makes the point that there should be only one definition of the brand idea, whereas a concept such as Employer Branding creates a separate entity aimed at a specific target audience.

If employees choose to participate in living the brand, it is because they identify with the brand and are able to internalize the values it represents. Managers can certainly inspire employees in the process and they can act as a role model, but it is a mistaken assumption that they can either command people to do it or sell it to them. To really bring the brand to life inside an organization, there needs to be high levels of participation, not only in the implementation but also in the definition process. As the management pioneer

Mary Parker Follett argued, the important aspect of common thought is not that it is held in common, but that it has been produced in common (Holland, 2006).

DEFINING THE BRAND: PARTICIPATION AND SIMPLICITY

There is a view that the articulation of the brand needs to be a top management exercise and that wider employee engagement in the process is slow and leads to consensus-seeking blandness. The top-down approach may be easier and quicker and perhaps more prevalent, but it probably reflects the preferences of CEOs and their advisors.

The managerial approach is flawed in several respects. First, a coterie of managers drawn perhaps from Marketing, Branding, and HR (as they often are in these processes) is rarely reflective of the source of real influence inside an organization. In a branded goods company, often the most influential people can be found in sales; in telecoms, it might be engineers and technologists; and in banks, it will be the bankers themselves. Second, although managers often have good access to research reports as to the behavior and attitudes of employees and consumers, the higher one is in the organization, the more one becomes removed from the day-to-day reality of blocks in the system, complaining customers and internal politics. As van Riel (1995) points out, "The picture that the managers have of their company ... is not necessarily the same as the view of the company held by other employees or members of target groups." Third, when there is a lack of participation, the onus is then on managers to sell the resulting idea to an often disinterested organization (and it is not unknown for organizations to reject such an idea outright). For engineers, pharmacists, and civil servants, the notion of brand values is probably seen as ephemeral, "fluffy," and largely irrelevant. It is often a feature of organizations that go down the top management route, that many years after the brand was first formulated, managers in internal communications are still creating booklets, films, and other mechanisms in an attempt to generate awareness and engagement.

Aligning Key Stakeholders

In place of the small group of senior managers, the definition process should try and engage as many people as possible, both inside and outside the organization. This is more complex and time consuming, but it does ensure that the resulting idea is inclusive of all key points of view; that the brand reflects the reality of the organization; that the language of the definition is appropriate; and that employees learn about the meaning of the brand through participation in the process.

Typically, the participative approach will incorporate the views of all key departments within the organization and also external stakeholders either through research or through direct involvement. To illustrate the process, here are some examples of organizations that have worked to be inclusive.

In 2003, IBM chose to redefine its mission and values. The quest was led by the then CEO Samuel Palmisano. As IBM was (and is) a strong believer in collaborative innovation, it made sense to ensure the active involvement of employees in the process:

> We couldn't have someone in headquarters sitting up in bed in the middle of the night and saying "Here are our new values!" We couldn't be casual about tinkering with the DNA of a company like IBM. We had to come up with a way to get the employees to create the value system, to determine the company's principles. (Hemp and Stewart, 2004)

Consequently, more than 300 executive interviews were conducted, 1,000 employees took part in focus groups and during a 72-hour webjam, there were some 10,000 postings. The resulting statement of the values was not something that was invented, but rather grew out of the dialogue.

Similarly, when Kraft Foods acquired its independence as an organization in 2007, it went through an eight-month process to determine its corporate brand that included events in Chicago, Paris, and Shanghai that involved managers, staff, and customers and an internal online community of 10,000 people that helped to generate and evaluate ideas. The resulting brand idea clearly resonated with employees in that several thousand opted to become ambassadors for the brand. Also participants in the process were twice as likely as non-participants to support the solution.

Eight months after the brand launch, 94 percent of staff believed the work was worthwhile, 83 percent believed in what the company was trying to accomplish, and 86 percent knew what they were expected to do to make Kraft Foods successful.

Finally, to show that the process can also work for noncommercial organizations (indeed may be particularly appropriate for NGOs as their cultures tend to encourage participation), when Greenpeace International decided to review its identity—the word "brand" was rejected as culturally wrong by the organization—there was a requirement that all 40 executive directors that represented the different geographies would have to agree the resulting definition.

Research was undertaken first with key external audiences and then there was a program of workshops around the world involving people from different functions. At certain key points, the emerging identity definition was tested back on the organization and the final recommendation was evaluated in research. Francesca Polini, the director who steered the process, says,

> The rolling workshops, international meetings and brainstorming sessions enabled the project to develop momentum. Initial ideas were refined, developed, or discarded at each stage of the process. Participants at each workshop were invited to build on the outcomes of the previous ones, or to suggest alternatives. As a result many people came to question received wisdom and assumptions surrounding the Greenpeace identity.

The value of the involvement of diverse viewpoints and a questioning approach was that the resulting definition of a vision and four values was concise, relevant to people, and supportive of the strategic intent—it was also signed off by the 40 executive directors at the first attempt.

The Need for Simplicity

While participation is an important driver of employee understanding, the resulting definition must be simple enough for people to engage with. If the definition ends up with several layers (corporate, brand, behavioral) and/or with too many words, it both prevents the focus that the articulation is working toward and creates an idea that is too complex to use every day.

Communications and branding staff may be comfortable working with complex ideas about the brand, but a salesperson or bank teller is unlikely to absorb three of four layers and 16 value words (the most I have come across). To generate the necessary focus, the process of definition should be robust and adhere to the following basic principles.

First, the definition should feel authentic in the sense it should build on the organization's history and heritage (Stagis, 2012). This is about uncovering what is true to the organization rather than creating something new. Second, it should have aspiration and stretch the organization toward its strategic goals, yet the stretch should not be to such a degree that the idea begins to lack credibility with employees (van Rekom et al., 2006). Third, it should feel inspirational, in that the idea itself is sufficiently motivating for people to exert brand citizenship behavior—in other words behavior outside defined roles that builds the brand (Burmann et al., 2009). Lastly, the result of the previous three points should be a brand definition that incorporates a sense of tension between what is and what can be in the future (Ind, 2007).

Tension is valuable because it both drives discussion about the meaning of the words and pushes the organization forward. If the definition lacks this tension, it will only tend to reinforce the current way of doing things and will consequently lack a strategic relevance.

If we look at the outdoor clothing brand Patagonia and its purpose statement "to use business to inspire and implement solutions to the environmental crisis" and its four values of "quality, integrity, environmentalism, and not bound by convention," we can see that it is true to the company's long-term commitment to the environment, pushes the company toward its future goal, and inspires its employees. As Casey Sheahan, CEO, says of the company's staff, "They enjoy an all day, all night love affair with the brand."

Similarly, the software company Mozilla espouses an inspirational idea: "to promote openness, innovation, and opportunity on the web," which motivates not only the 600 people that are employed by the company to develop software, manage processes, and market products such as Thunderbird and Firefox, but also the thousands of volunteers who work for the brand for free.

At Greenpeace International not only does the purpose of the organization to protect and conserve the environment and to promote peace give focus to employees and 3 million members, but seemingly contradictory values such as "nonviolence" and "confrontation" generate sometimes vociferous debate about the meaning of what people do.

The Importance of Interpretation

One plausible criticism of these definitions is that the same words—quality, environmentalism, innovation, and integrity—all keep appearing. Partly this is because the choice of words that can be used is limited. Occasionally, there is something out of the ordinary such as Orange Telecom's "refreshing" or Virgin's idea of being the "People's Champion," but mostly there is a cluster around the obvious. However, it can be argued that brand distinctiveness comes about not because of the uniqueness of the words, but because of the way they are used and interpreted.

The semiotician Umberto Eco (1999) draws a distinction between dictionary and encyclopedic knowledge. In the case of the former, the understanding of a word such as "quality" would be constrained by a concise definition of the word. However, in the case of the latter, experience among a community counts for more than linguistics and the encyclopedic knowledge of "quality" for the organization grows (becomes) fuller through exploration and action, such that a law firm and a software company both might use the same word, but understand it in different ways. In this sense, we might argue that brand definitions are not really definitions at all until they acquire contextual meaning by being adopted and used in a "ceaseless flow of living language-interwoven relations" (Shotter, 2005). In other words, a number of brands might proclaim that they stand for quality, but this remains an abstract concept until employees and then customers experience it.

BRINGING THE BRAND TO LIFE

To move the brand from abstraction to reality, organizational members have to engage with the idea it represents. This is both a top-down and bottom-up process. Organizational initiatives come around all the time and very often employees sit and wait to see which initiatives are most important. One of the key signals for this is symbolic leadership. In other words, if the leaders of the organization seem to be embracing an idea, then it might just be worth paying attention to. Leaders can play an important role here by embodying the brand, in setting organizational priorities, explicitly linking the brand to business strategy, and inspiring employees through their actions. As an illustration, Harris (2007) narrates the experience of two strategy executives presenting to the Executive Board of Orange—a company that was built around a strong customer orientation and a set of brand values that focused clearly on customer benefits. Although the executives were only at the early stages of their presentation on the company's strategy, the CEO Hans Snook interrupted them, thanked them for their efforts, and asked them to leave. The presenters pointed out that they hadn't finished and had many more slides, but Snook told them that they had already said quite a bit without ever mentioning the customer. Consequently, they were finished and could go.

Harris points out that the consequences of the experience were immediate and far-reaching,

> First, it concentrated the minds of the strategy team for that particular presentation and for every subsequent piece of work undertaken. Secondly, the board members too took away additional insight that day into how the CEO was absolutely determined to represent the customer at all costs. Finally, stories about that day meandered throughout the organisation, establishing a firm body of lore about the importance of remembering the customer and it served as a constant reminder to the whole of the company.

In addition to symbolic action, we should also note that engaging employees with the idea of a brand is not something that can be imposed through the diktats of leaders. People will not suddenly become "innovative," "trustworthy," and "team players," or whatever the brand values are, simply because leaders tell them to be. Rather, leaders have to adopt a transformational leadership style by showing commitment to the brand and by empowering their staff to deliver it (Morhart et al., 2009).

If the brand is used well by leaders, it can help to create the boundaries within which people can be set free to utilize their knowledge and creativity in the service of customers and other stakeholders. For example, film animation company Pixar encourages its leaders to provide direction and support when needed, but otherwise it sets people free and lets them have control over every stage of idea development. Given the high risks involved in film production, the temptation for leaders is to try to avoid or minimize risks, but Pixar understands that this temptation should be rejected if an idea is to flourish (Catmull, 2008).

The principle of trust runs throughout the Pixar approach, as it also does in companies such as Patagonia, Mozilla, Bangladeshi telecoms company Grameenphone, and Dutch bank Rabobank, but many companies struggle with trusting employees and customers and as a consequence empowerment tends to be cosmetic (Argyris, 1998; Kim and Mauborgne, 2003).

While the active involvement of leaders is vital to bringing the brand to life especially at a more strategic level, by itself it is insufficient. The brand will lack a deeper relevance if it remains the preserve of a few senior people or only head office employees. People at all levels, business units, functional areas, and geographies, need to have the opportunity to build the brand. Thus, employees need to participate in creating brand meaning and humanizing the abstraction of the brand idea through what they say and do.

There are mechanisms such as brand books, events, and videos that can help communicate the idea of the brand to employees, but the brand idea needs to move from being something people are told about to something that they use. Therefore, the meaning of the brand idea needs to be explored not just as a means of generating enlightenment but also as a way of inspiring relevant change. This shifts the orientation away from talk to action. In practical terms, this means involving people in discovering what lies beneath the words that describe the brand. Although there are different ways of doing this, one tried and trusted method is through implementation workshops.

At workshop events, people are brought together for either a half-day or full day to create and refine initiatives that align with the brand vision and values, help achieve business goals, and are implementable and measurable. The process normally encourages people to be adventurous and uncritical in the idea generation phase and then more critical as filters are applied and ideas are refined.

The goal should be to focus on a limited number of initiatives to which a real commitment can be made. The outputs depend on the participants, inputs, and goals, but as an illustration, the initiatives might include a more brand value-based approach to recruitment and induction, overcoming siloization through cross-functional projects where brand values are an input and a measure of accountability, online and offline mechanisms designed to enable early-stage customer involvement, more open approaches to innovation involving universities and entrepreneurs, and better use of tacit and explicit knowledge in sales management.

The danger here is that people involve themselves in workshops and in contributing their ideas and then implementation is poor. It is important that there is thorough and rapid feedback from the organization on ideas that are rejected and those that will be developed. The ideas that progress then need to be visibly supported by managers and properly resourced. One other means to help ensure effective implementation is for a brand champion to be selected from each team that has participated in the process. The role of champions is to help implement the selected initiatives, to communicate progress back to the team, and to share best practice with other champions across organizational boundaries.

An example of an effective bottom-up approach is the Women's Institute in the United Kingdom. Formed in 1915 as a means of revitalizing rural communities and developing the skills and knowledge of women, the WI, as it is known, enjoyed many decades of growth and then a more recent challenge of an aging membership and a decline in relevance.

In 2008, a goal was set to boost membership and to achieve an overall younger and more diverse membership profile that better reflected modern Britain. Part of the resulting process was the development of a new brand idea based around "Inspiring Women" and three core values: principled, active, and creative. The values have not only steered a new approach to identity and communications, but also to the activities of WI advisors—the individuals who help bring in new members and establish new WI branches.

Here implementation workshops were used to inform the advisors about the philosophy of the brand and to generate ideas together with them as to how to change and improve current practices to deliver the brand at local and regional levels during day-to-day interactions. The success of the program is that there has been a rapid acceleration in the number of new branches (30 in one month during 2012) and membership is growing and becoming younger.

CULTURE IS EVERYTHING

In discussing the commitment of the Patagonia staff to the brand, CEO, Casey Sheahan, says that "culture is everything." It seems a powerful statement, but what does it mean? Sheahan's point is that in Patagonia the brand comes to life because the idea behind the purpose statement and values really lives inside the organization. The brand attracts people to join the company, it defines how they behave to each other and toward customers, and it helps them to make key decisions.

The Patagonia brand is something tangible and deeply felt. The point about the culture is that the definition of the brand, which was developed in 1996—nearly 40 years after the company started—was the result of a collective process where a diverse group reached back into the past to understand and to connect with the heritage of the business. In this sense, the words merely make explicit what was tacit before. Consequently, the brand feels true to the culture. However, the brand is not merely backward looking. It also creates a framework for innovation in the use of materials and the way products are made. When, for example, Patagonia decided it wanted to create a range of wet suits, it rejected the use of petrochemically derived neoprene and instead opted for neoprene made from limestone rock. The environmental impact was further limited by using recycled polyester and chlorine-free wool in the lining. This ongoing search for more environmentally friendly yet high-quality fabrics occurs because the idea of the brand is an integral part of the culture. Here we might also note that the brand meaning itself evolves (and with it the culture) as innovations are implemented.

The cultural cohesion of Patagonia doesn't happen automatically. It comes to life because of the people that join the organization.

This signifies the importance of the brand in the development of human resource practices. People seek out Patagonia as a place to work because the organization is very explicit and consistent about its purpose and values in all its communications. This is not just about baldly stating what the company's belief system is about, but rather bringing ideas to life through an open and honest approach based on sharing as much as possible with both internal and external audiences.

Once people join the company, they are trained on the meaning of the brand and encouraged to support it. As a way of reinforcing the brand, employees can also take time off to work for environmental charities of their choosing and they have the opportunity to go and work in the Estancia Valle Chacabuco park in Patagonia, which is owned by a former chief executive of the company and is being restored to something like its natural state from fenced farmland. Typically, employees spend three-week stints in the park.

The value of this work is clear in terms of the restoration of the park land, but it also has a profound effect on employees. Former PR Director Tim Rhone says of the Chacabuco visits, "There's a willingness to do that and give people that experience. They (employees) understand what the brand is and instead of 'environmentalism'—just a word—it becomes Patagonia. It becomes something you can hold."

Patagonia is not unique in its commitment to its values and their incorporation into HR practices. Companies such as IKEA and Google incorporate their brand ideas into all aspects of the recruitment, appraisals, development, and reward processes. Being explicit about the brand helps to ensure that new people have a good propensity to identify with the brand and have the skills and knowledge that can be nurtured in line with it. However, we should be aware that overly dominant brands do carry a danger in that they can become cult-like organizations where only on-brand activity is allowed and individuality is denied (Hochshild, 1983; Land and Taylor, 2011).

While managers might desire the comfort of unity, organizations should avoid the perils of groupthink and encourage diversity, not least by connecting employees with customers and sharing knowledge with them.

MANAGING AND MEASURING

"Stop asking how you can get employees behind the brand and start thinking how you can put the brand behind your employees" (Hatch and Schultz, 2008, p. 127).

There is a tendency to think that employees can be made to live the brand, but as Hatch and Schultz point out, managers can foster greater commitment and creativity, if the brand becomes the framework that supports employees and their aspirations. This is a subtle yet important shift for it reminds us that we have to move beyond simply telling people about the brand and instead engage them with living it in their relationships with each other and with stakeholders. This is a more complex process because it involves the whole organization and the need to address issues such as leadership, cultural fit, human resource practices, structure, and resources (Burmann et al., 2009).

The idea of the brand in this perspective is no longer just the responsibility of the branding team, but rather a unifying concept that supports the overall direction of the business and helps to overcome the silos that bedevil organizations. Therefore, managers and employees from all disciplines need to engage with the brand and help deliver it. This shifts the primary role of brand managers from communicators to connectors: helping to bring insight and creativity into the organization from the outside, connecting people from different departments and geographies, sharing best practice, and ensuring that brand and business strategies are intertwined.

Inside the organization, connections need to be fostered through the unifying potential of the brand idea—something that Rob BonDurant, chief marketing officer at Patagonia, says helps to "really tear silos down" and a willingness to create the mechanisms, such as high-level brand councils that bring together personnel from key operating functions. Externally, the coming together of employees and external stakeholders is important because it enhances knowledge and improves the perception that employee contributions are valued by the organization (King and Grace, 2008). However, what is experienced through interaction has to be shared and it is not always the case that organizations are adept at listening. This reinforces the need to acquire good feedback through both offline interactions and online communities and to use this knowledge to create something of value.

From Brand Equity to Brand Valuation

The purpose of engaging employees with the brand is clearly about value creation, but this raises the issue about how easily this can be measured. It is possible to determine the engagement and satisfaction of employees and to link this to the experience of customers and other stakeholders. Rucci et al. (1998) used such an approach based on causal pathway modeling to demonstrate the connections at U.S. retailer Sears between employee satisfaction, customer satisfaction, and revenues. The writers note, "It is our managers and employees, who, at the moment of truth in front of the customer, have achieved this prodigious feat of value creation."

It is also possible to see that engaged employees can make a significant contribution to the widely used concept of brand equity—the "differential effect that brand knowledge has on consumer response to the marketing of that brand" (Keller et al., 2008). Brand equity comprises several levels of knowledge: salience, performance, imagery, judgments, feelings, and resonance. Particularly at the higher level of resonance, which features loyalty, engagement, attachment, and community, we can observe a potential contribution from employees who through their interactions help cement relationships with customers. Yet, the difficulty with this brand equity model is that it tends to underplay the role of the employee. To tackle this, King and Grace (2010) have turned inward to specifically investigate employee-based brand equity (EBBE). Their model shows that employees who have clarity about their role and demonstrate commitment achieve high levels of satisfaction and are able to exhibit brand citizenship and spread positive word of mouth. The EBBE is a valuable addition in the quest to demonstrate the benefits of living the brand. However, as employee/customer involvement brings both sides closer (Ind et al., 2012), we should ideally seek to link internal and external measures.

Brand valuation methodologies whereby predicted future cash flows for each brand segment are evaluated in terms of the contribution from the brand and brand strength can help provide insight into the contribution of brand engaged employees. In particular, brand strength is a good indicator of the impact of employees, because its core constituents are awareness, consideration, preference, and loyalty. While the first two constituents are important, it is preference and loyalty that really define the likelihood that planned cash flows will actually materialize. As preference and loyalty are much more about brand experience than communication, we can argue that in most product categories it is employees and their connectivity with customers that drive relationships and brand strength. The quality of brand valuation processes is highly dependent on the quality of the inputs: the more assumptions that have to be made, the more questionable the results. The virtues of it are that it provides an insight into which brand segments are valuable, the relationship of the brand with its customers, and a metric that matters in the board room.

CONCLUSION

An effective living the brand process helps to enhance the worth of the organization's brand, generates fulfillment for employees, and creates value for customers. Yet to achieve this potential, organizations need to see living the brand not as a project but as a way of life. It needs to reflect the organizational culture and also influence its evolution as the business stretches toward its goals. From this perspective, it might seem an inward-looking process, but the real quest here is to better connect the organization with its customers. Rather than rely primarily on the abstraction of market research to bring the voice of the customer inside, we should encourage employees to identify with the brand and to internalize it, so they can be set free to listen to customers, engage with them, and work together to provide relevant and brand aligned experiences.

Companies such as Mozilla, Patagonia, and Grameenphone are adept at doing this, because they have the confidence to blur the boundaries between the inside and outside, and to create a bazaar of possibilities (Raymond, 1999). While living the brand tools are helpful enablers in realizing the opportunity for participation, we would argue that its achievement is much more to do with attitude—a belief in the intellect and creativity of employees and customers. It is recognition that amidst all the definitions of brands, that truly, brands are about people.

REFERENCES

Argyris, C. (1998). "Empowerment: The Emperor's New Clothes," *Harvard Business Review* 76(3): 98–107.

Baumgarth, C. (2010). "Living the Brand: Brand Orientation in the Business-to-Business Sector," *European Journal of Marketing* 44(5): 653–671.

Berry, L. (2000). "Cultivating Service Brand Equity," *Journal of the Academy of Marketing Science* 28(1): 128–137.

Burmann, C., S. Zeplin, and N. Riley (2009) "Key Determinants of Internal Brand Management Success: An Exploratory Empirical Analysis," *Journal of Brand Management* 16(4): 264–284.

Catmull, E. (2008) "How Pixar Fosters Collective Creativity," *Harvard Business Review* 86(9): 64–72 .

Cova, B. and D. Dalli (2009). "Working Consumers: The Next Step in Marketing Theory," *Marketing Theory* 9(3): 315–339.

Eco, U. (1999). *Kant and the Platypus: Essays on Language and Cognition* (Trans. Alastair McEwen). London: Secker and Warburg

Gromark, J. and F. Melin (2005). *Brand Orientation Index: A Research Project on Brand Orientation and Profitability in Sweden's 500 Largest Companies.* Göteborg, Sweden: Label.

Harris, P. (2007) "We the People: The Importance of Employees in the Process of Building Customer Experience," *Journal of Brand Management* 15: 102–114.

Hatch, M.J. and M. Schultz (2008) *Taking Brand Initiative: How Companies Can Align Strategy, Culture and Identity through Corporate Branding.* San Francisco, California: Jossey-Bass.

Hemp, P. and T.A. Stewart (2004) "Leading Change When Business Is Good: The HBR Interview," *Harvard Business Review* 82(12): 60–70.

Hochshild, A. (1983) *The Managed Heart.* Berkeley, California: University of California Press.

Holland, E. (2006) "Nomad Citizenship and Global Democracy," in M. Fuglsang and B.M. Sørensen (Eds), *Deleuze and the Social* (pp. 191–206). Edinburgh: Edinburgh University Press.

IBM (2010). *Capitalizing on Complexity* (Research based on 1541 face-to-face interviews with CEOs worldwide between September 2009 and January 2010). IBM.

Ind, N. (2007) *Living the Brand: How to Transform Every Member of Your Organization into a Brand Champion,* 3rd edition. London: Kogan Page.

Ind, N., C. Fuller, and C. Trevail (2012). *Brand Together: How Co-creation Generates Innovation and Re-energises Brands.* London: Kogan Page.

Keller, K.L., T. Aperia, and M. Georgson (2008). *Strategic Brand Management: A European Perspective.* Harlow, England: Pearson Education.

Kim, W.C. and R. Mauborgne (2003). "Fair Process: Managing in the Knowledge Economy," *Harvard Business Review* 81(1): 127–136.

King, C. and D. Grace (2008). "Internal Branding: Exploring the Employee's Perspective," *Journal of Brand Management* 15(5): 358–372.

———. (2010). "Building and Measuring Employee-Based Brand Equity," *European Journal of Marketing* 44(7): 938–971.

Land, C. and S. Taylor (2011). "Be Who You Want to Be: Branding Identity and the Desire for Authenticity," in M.J. Brennan, E. Parsons, and V. Priola (Eds), *Branded Lives: The Production and Consumption of Meaning at Work* (pp. 35–36). Cheltenham, UK: Edward Elgar.

Merz, M., Y. He, and S. Vargo (2009). "The Evolving Brand Logic: A Service Dominant Logic Perspective," *Journal of the Academy of Marketing Science* 37: 328–344.

Morhart, F., W. Herzog, and T. Tomczak (2009). "Brand-Specific Leadership: Turning Employees into Brand Champions," *Journal of Marketing* 73(5): 122–142.

Raymond, E. (1999). *The Cathedral and the Bazaar: Musings on Linux and Open Source by an Accidental Revolutionary.* Sebastopol, California: O'Reilly.

Rucci, A., S. Kirn, and R. Quinn (1998). "The Employee-Customer Profits Chain at Sears," *Harvard Business Review* 76(1): 82–97.

Shotter, J. (2005). "Peripheral Vision," *Organization Studies* 26(1): 113–135.

Stagis, N. (2012). *Den Autentiske Virksomhed: gør indre styrker til fremtidens vækststrategi.* Copenhagen: Gylendal Business.

van Rekom, J., C. Van Riel, and B. Wierenga (2006). "A Methodology for Assessing Organizational Core Values," *Journal of Management Studies* 43(2): 175–201.

van Riel, C. (1995). *Principles of Corporate Communication.* Englewood Cliffs, New Jersey: Prentice-Hall.

Vargo, S. and R. Lusch (2004). "Evolving to a New Dominant Logic for Marketing," *Journal of Marketing* 68: 1–17.

Chapter 11

Employer Brand Management

Richard Mosley

Considering the 80-year history of brand management, the concept of employer branding is still a relatively new concept, but it has now become very widely adopted. The term was originated in 1990 by Simon Barrow when he moved into the recruitment advertising business and began to apply the disciplines he had learnt from his previous experience in consumer brand management. The first academic paper on the subject appeared in 1996, and the first book in 2005 (Barrow and Mosley, 2005). When Simon Barrow and I conducted research for this book, there were still only a handful of companies such as Unilever and Shell, which had adopted the thinking and the terminology. However, over the next three years the idea took root, and it quickly became a more widely used lens through which companies across the world sought to tackle the increasingly fierce competition for talent in the boom years before the bust in 2008. During these early years, application of the concept was largely limited to employer brand identity management and proposition-based recruitment advertising. However, over the last five years, the discipline has broadened to include a much stronger focus on all aspects of the employee experience from candidate management through to people management processes and practices, with every "touch-point" aligned to deliver against the employer brand promise.

From the organization's perspective, the employer brand sums up the key qualities current and prospective employees identify with you as an employer, whether economic (compensation and benefits), functional (e.g., learning new skills), or psychological (e.g., sense of identity and status). Whether you've defined it or not, you already have an employer brand. The key question is whether you're clear about the distinctive benefits you'd like people to associate with you (commonly described as your employee value proposition [EVP]), proactive in communicating and delivering against this promise, or happy to live with an unclear and inconsistent employer brand by default.

How people feel about their employer brand is increasingly critical to business success or failure. Leading companies realize its importance in attracting and engaging the people they need to deliver profitable growth. They are also beginning to recognize that creating a positive brand experience for employees requires the same degree of focus, care, and coherence that has long characterized effective management of the customer brand experience. This has led many of the world's leading companies such as GE, HP, IBM, Microsoft, Nokia-Siemens, PepsiCo, P&G, RBS, Shell, and Unilever to pursue active employer brand development strategies.

Alongside a more integrated (internal–external) approach, there has also been an increasing desire for employer brand development to be aligned more seamlessly with the corporate and customer brand. This approach sees the HR-led role of employer brand management as a reinforcing counterpart to the marketing-led role of customer brand management, with the role of leadership to maintain the overall integrity of the corporate brand through appropriate communication and behaviors.

A good example of this is Microsoft whose corporate brand proposition focuses on enabling both personal and business customers to realize their full potential. Reflecting this core purpose, Microsoft's employer brand proposition focuses on employee development, ensuring that the people who work for Microsoft can "come as you are, and do what you love."

This has helped to move the agenda on a step from the generic focus on becoming an "employer of choice" that dominated HR efforts for a number of years, before it became apparent that aspiring toward an ideal blueprint of employment was unlikely to deliver on the more distinctive fit for purpose requirements of the customer brand and business strategy. This progression toward a more integrated view of the brand has also promoted a recognition that employer brands need to play a dual purpose. The employer brand proposition needs to clarify what both prospective and current employees can expect from the organization in terms of rational and emotional benefits. However, it also needs to clarify what will be expected of employees in return. Microsoft promises employees that it will help them realize their potential. In return (in accordance with Microsoft's core values), it expects employees to "take on big challenges and see them through." Inherent in most "integrated" employer brand propositions is a "give" and a "get" that aligns the employer brand promise with the customer brand and corporate performance agenda (Figure 11.1).

As for the customer experience, being consistent is good, but being both consistent and distinctive is even better. If you want to deliver a distinctive customer brand experience, and that experience depends heavily on interpersonal interactions, then you need to ensure that your employer brand attracts the right kind of people and your employer brand management reinforces the right kind of culture (from the customer-facing frontline to the deepest recesses of every support function).

To ensure your culture is aligned with the desired customer brand experience, it clearly helps to have a distinctive "brand of leadership," but it is equally important to ensure that your people processes are also distinctively in tune with your brand ethos.

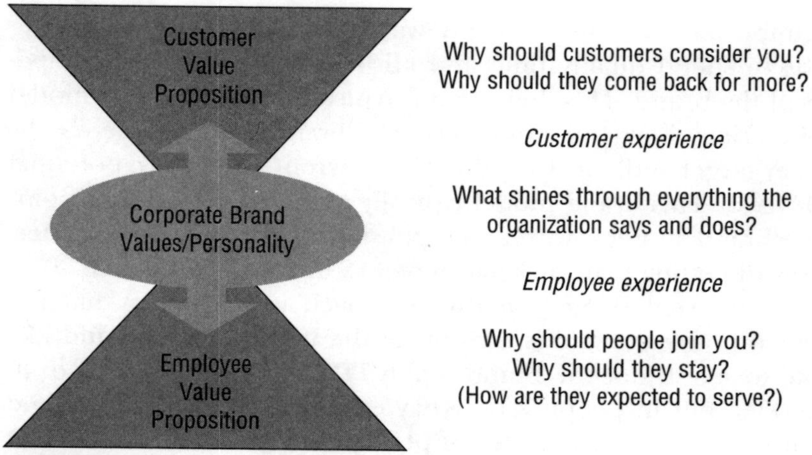
Customer Value Proposition
Corporate Brand Values/Personality
Employee Value Proposition
Why should customers consider you? Why should they come back for more?
Customer experience
What shines through everything the organization says and does?
Employee experience
Why should people join you? Why should they stay? (How are they expected to serve?)

Figure 11.1 Integrated Brand Model

SOURCE: Author.

These "signature" employer brand experiences help to engender a distinctive brand attitude, generate distinctive brand behaviors, and ultimately reinforce the kind of distinctive customer service style that will add value to the customer experience and differentiate an organization from its competitors.

A number of years ago, the global retailer Tesco's customer satisfaction scores began to plateaux. Realizing that the solution to this issue did not rely solely on the price, quality, range, and display of its product offering, but also on the satisfaction and engagement of its front-line employees, Tesco developed an EVP that committed the organization to improving the Tesco working experience in a number of key areas. For example, Tesco's research revealed that employee engagement was closely related to the amount of time and quality of recognition they received from their managers. By providing managers with better people management training and freeing up more of their time to coach and encourage their employees, Tesco made a significant impact on the company's engagement scores. In turn, this was correlated with a 5 percent improvement in customer satisfaction, and 2.5 percent like-for-like growth in sales.

GETTING TO THE HEART OF BRAND MANAGEMENT

It is important for those tasked with developing and managing brands to spend quality time and effort defining the key components of the brand. This definition is typically enshrined in a model that describes how you would like the brand to be perceived by your key target audiences (in this case, current and future potential employees). This brand model typically provides the starting point for the brand strategy, with an emphasis on finding the most effective way of getting your message across to the target audience.

The inherent danger in this approach is forgetting that the model you have defined is a vision of the brand as you would like people to see it, not the brand reality. The real brand lives not in the model, but in people's everyday experience of the brand and the rather more untidy cluster of perceptions and associations that they carry around in their heads. The reason this is important is that if brand communication strays too far from the perceived reality of the brand, it can feel phoney or worse, setting up expectations that fail to be delivered.

This has been a significant issue in a number of emerging markets such as China where recruitment marketing is still a relatively recent phenomenon and very prone to enthusiastic overclaim. A report from the Corporate Executive Board (2008) from a number of years ago suggested that only one in five employees joining multinationals felt that the recruitment promises they had been made accurately reflected their working experience. It is therefore no surprise that attrition levels within multinational companies in China have been consistently among the highest worldwide.

People are understandably cynical about brands which promise much, but fail to live up to expectations, brands that are all show and no substance. These are the brands that give branding a bad name.

This gap between vision and reality is extremely pertinent to employer brands. Corporate policy and value statements appear particularly prone to aspirational overclaim. It is not only the expensive gloss of the paper that makes employees feel that corporate literature is out of touch. It is also the tendency of corporate communication to gloss over the everyday realities of the employment experience in their assertion of what the company claims to stand for or offer its employees.

I recently came across a classic example of this in a company undergoing a significant period of transformation. The communication package extolling the benefits of this change program was grandly entitled *Genesis* (the first book of the Christian bible describing the creation of the world). However, since the reality from an employee perspective was a significant downsizing of the workforce, the program soon picked up another name amongst the employee population: "Exodus" (the second book of the bible describing the mass flight of the people from tyranny). As you can imagine, this did very little to build the company's employer brand.

The task of most brand managers who inherit an existing brand is to close the gap between the current brand reality and the brand vision. This requires them to steer a course between what may initially appear to be two contradictory goals. The first goal is to maintain the clarity, consistency, and continuity of the brand. The second goal is to introduce changes that will help to develop, stretch, and refresh the brand. Striking the right balance between these two tasks is a constant challenge. Change too much and the brand will lose focus, change too little and the brand will lose relevance.

While brand models vary from company to company and it makes sense to adopt a similar model to the one used for your corporate and/or customer brands, we believe the key components of a successful EVP are as illustrated in Figure 11.2.

Corporate Brand Essence
Core purpose, values and personality
The core brand DNA of the organization reflected in everything it says and does
Employee Value Proposition
Core Positioning
The one quality you most want to be famous for as an employer
Pillars
The distinctive qualities that further define the employment experience
The "Give and Get"
The balance of expectations between employee and employer that define the employment "deal"
Reasons to Believe
The tangible proof points that make the proposition credible
Qualifiers
The everyday basics you need to deliver on to ensure the proposition si credible

Figure 11.2 The Core Components of an Effective EVP

SOURCE: Author.

DO YOU KNOW WHAT YOU NEED TO KNOW?

The world's most powerful brands are built on great insights into the human condition, but as anyone in marketing soon recognizes there is far more to developing and managing a successful brand than understanding customers' needs and aspirations. When I started my career as a market researcher, I recall a well-worn marketing director advising me: "If all you did was respond to what customers asked of you, you'd soon go out of business." As my experience extended into marketing consultancy, I eventually realized that this sentiment was not driven by hubris, but humility in the face of the complex, multilayered varieties of insight required to successfully manage a brand.

To get it right, the brand owner must not only listen carefully to what customers say they need, but also find a way of understanding their latent and implicit needs (that is to say, the needs they have difficulty expressing or are simply unaware of). In addition to understanding the customer, they must also understand the overall shape, size, and dynamics of the market; the underlying organizational or technical capabilities supporting the brand's competitive edge; the investment required to launch and sustain the brand; and how this fits within the overall investment portfolio and business goals of the organization.

Within the employer brand context, we believe that there is significant value in taking a similarly multifaceted approach. Understanding the explicit needs and aspirations of your employees is a good starting point, but it is not enough to ensure an effective internal brand strategy. As with customers you also need to develop an understanding of employees' implicit needs, and the organizational, cultural, and labor market context within which the employer brand will operate.

Leading employers often make use of a wide variety of qualitative and quantitative research techniques, including:

- Labor market mapping (where can we best find and target potential candidates?)
- Attraction analysis (what are people looking for from potential employers?)
- External image research (how do people regard us in relation to other employers?)
- Joiners' surveys (what expectations do new joiners have, and are we meeting them?)
- Employee engagement surveys (how engaged are our current employees?)

- Engagement driver analysis (what drives employee engagement in our company?)
- Segmentation (how much do employee needs and aspirations vary from group to group?)
- Appreciative inquiry (what characterizes our organization at its best? What makes us distinctive?)
- Best practice benchmarking (how do our current HR practices compare with other leading companies?)

If you are setting out to strengthen the employer brand, it is important to understand not only the immediate "climate" of employee opinion, but also the longer term culture of the organization.

Culture, like personality, is often a difficult concept to pin down precisely, because it describes general patterns and tendencies rather than a reliable objective reality. Nevertheless, like brand personality, the notion of organizational culture can be very useful in getting a handle on how people generally perceive things work within an organization. What do people regard as normal within the context of the organization? What kind of behavior tends to be frowned on? What kind of people tend to do well within the organization or struggle to fit in? (Microsoft used to define its ideal target profile as "natural communicators, with a passion for technology," which meant that even in a technical environment, technical proficiency is not enough to do well, you also have to be good at sharing your ideas with others to fit in and get on.)

All of these are particularly useful questions to ask if you are trying to define and develop the employer brand, because the culture of the organization is a good way of describing the current brand reality, as opposed to its value statements which tend to be more closely related to the brand vision. More simply put, culture is descriptive (the way things are); values are aspirational (the way things should be).

What Do You Want to Be Famous for?

Every brand is surrounded by alternatives competing for their share of attention, interest, and loyalty. Brands need to be focused to compete effectively in this crowded space, and brand positioning represents the art and science of targeting the right audiences with the most compelling benefits and brand messages.

To be compelling most brands need to emphasize what makes them different and better at fulfilling the needs of this target group. This is a tricky business since most functional benefits are soon copied. This means that in addition to delivering constant improvements to the functional performance of the product or service to remain competitive, brands also need to develop and defend a position in the marketplace that they can uniquely own. This is where the brand image and personality plays a critical role in both anchoring the brand (what stays the same as the functionality changes) and differentiating the brand in the people's minds.

Creating a distinctive proposition is particularly challenging in the employment market as the range of potential employment competitors is vast, and the range of basic features (e.g., financial compensation, learning and development, career opportunity) is relatively narrow. However, the rules of differentiation are no different to any other crowded marketplace. You need to highlight the one or two features within your overall employment offer that you believe you can excel in, rather than try and cover every angle. You also need to be specific rather than generic in defining these "special" features. Claiming to be an "innovative" company would be largely generic. You would need to be more specific about your particular approach to innovation to stand out. For example, innovation at GE is largely focused on continuous, incremental quality improvements, innovation at Ikea is focused on delivering attractive designs at very low cost, at the LEGO Group the focus is on "open innovation," which involves collaborating with their worldwide community of LEGO product enthusiasts, and at Disney, they even have their own special word for innovation, which they call "imagineering."

RECRUITMENT MARKETING

Once the EVP has been defined, the next step is typically to bring the underlying proposition to life with some form of creative expression. It used to be the case that an EVP would inevitably be translated into some form of creative recruitment campaign, with a tagline, visual style, and core messages developed to feed into a range of advertising templates.

The standard format for many years was the print advert, but this has now changed dramatically with the waning influence of print media. With the growing dominance of online media, particularly career sites and social networks such as LinkedIn, Facebook, and Twitter, this templated campaign style of thinking has become increasingly outdated. Employer branding has become both simpler in terms of "brand framing" (the consistent identity components of visual and verbal expression, such as color, design, and taglines) and more complex in terms of the more fluid demands of "brand content" (stories, profiles, HRPR, etc.) and format (video, interactive dialogue, gamification, etc.).

While campaign headlines and images may still provide consistent framing, the content in the frame increasingly needs to be authentic, real-time, and constantly refreshed to command people's attention. In this new world of recruitment marketing, the EVP plays an even more fundamental role in providing the thematic underpinning behind a much wider range of communication content.

Brand communication management now needs to be delivered on four levels:

1. Brand-managed identity and advertising (*visual design/campaign messages*), for example, P&G's long-running employer brand campaign "We hire the person, not the position"
2. Brand-managed stories (narrative content, generally sourced from employees but edited and produced by the employer brand team); for example, the way in which P&G's employer brand team developed a range of video profile stories to reinforce the above campaign message on its career site, YouTube channel, and Facebook career pages
3. User-generated content (narrative content, stimulated and monitored by the employer brand team), for example, Deloitte's "Film Festival," which involved employees creating their own videos to express what it's like to work for the organization
4. Published word of mouth (monitored and occasionally responded to by the employer brand team)

INTERNAL COMMUNICATION OF THE EVP

Whether you opt for a major internal launch, or take a more gradual approach to introducing your employer brand to employees, the clarity and focus of the communication is key. The overwhelming evidence from external brand research is to "keep it simple." Consumers receive thousands of brand messages a day, and advertisers need to keep their core messages simple and direct to cut through. While employees are sometimes regarded as a more captive audience, in reality they are just as likely to suffer from information overload.

Employer brand messages, therefore, need to be equally simple and direct. Ensure you are absolutely clear about the two to three core messages you want potential candidates and current employees to consistently associate with the employer brand, and put 90 percent of your attention into getting these core messages across. This may mean sacrificing some of the more detailed information you would ultimately like to communicate to employees, but if you take the longer term view, there should be time to build this up over time.

You also need to ensure relevance. As some of our early research with the London Business School revealed, the use of brand language can be off-putting to many employees. This is not just a question of being cynical about marketing; it is more a question of people's natural tendency to disengage from overcomplicated and unfamiliar language. You would never use brand jargon in communicating the benefits of your brand to customers, so why use it with employees?

In this respect, it is far more effective to frame your communication in terms that employees will more readily understand as relevant and meaningful to their everyday working lives. Fast track development, flexible working, and forward thinking are all worthy and attractive claims, but these promises will be a lot more persuasive if you can also demonstrate what this looks like in practice.

Employees will pay as much, if not more attention to your external marketing than your target customers. If handled well, this can provide your organization with a boost to employee engagement in addition to any further benefits you derive from improving your external brand image and driving sales. You should make sure your employees are well briefed on any high-profile marketing activities.

Employees should understand what, if anything, is expected of them to support new promises or claims. If, as is increasingly common, your advertising incorporates "employees," you should also make sure that this representation is well researched internally as well as externally. Are they credible role models or merely dancing to the tune of the advertising message?

ARE YOU PREPARED FOR THE TOTAL JOURNEY?

It is one thing to establish the nature of your employer brand—what it is and what it needs to be to achieve your business objectives, but it is quite another to ensure that it is managed with the same care and coherence as you would a customer brand. If you fail to put in place the management systems and the senior management support for them, then the whole employer brand initiative may wither and result in nothing more than some tinkering with recruitment advertising.

The marketing concept of the brand "mix" (incorporating all of the controllable elements that contribute toward people's experience of a brand) is just as useful to apply internally as externally. From this perspective, recruitment and internal communication represent only two aspects of the employer brand mix that you may need to address.

While the employee experience is far more complex than any service experience, there is a recognition that organizations would benefit from adopting a similar approach. People management involves a wide range of ritualized processes and HR "products," which can be described as employee "touch-points." The term "customer corridor" used to describe a relatively predictable sequence of touch-points can equally be applied to the recruitment process, orientation, employee communication, shared services (including HR and facilities management), reward, measurement (e.g., employee engagement surveys), performance management, and employee development. Likewise, core values and competencies can be seen as a framework for governing the everyday experience of employees through the communication and behavior of their immediate line managers and corporate leaders (see Figure 11.3).

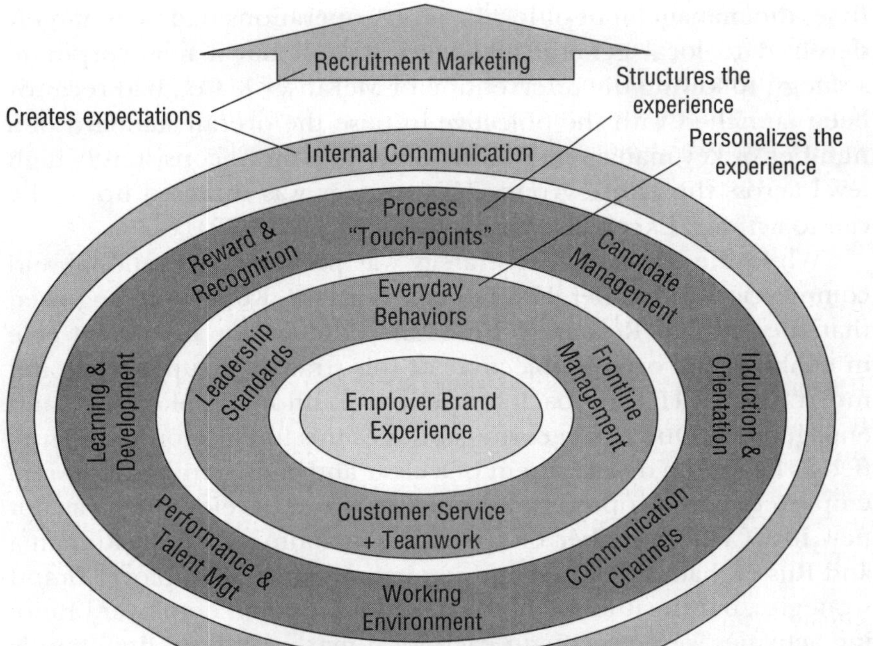

Figure 11.3 Employer Brand Touch-points

SOURCE: Author.

CASE STUDY—COCA-COLA HELLENIC

One of the early adopters of this more strategic and integrated approach to employer brand management has been Coca-Cola Hellenic (CCH), the second largest company within the Coca-Cola Company's global "system" of bottling and distribution partners. When their employer brand development work commenced, CCH's operations extended across 27 countries, including most of Southern, Central, and Eastern Europe (including Russia), and Nigeria. At this time, they employed 33,000 full-time staff, mainly working in production, distribution, and sales. Up to this point in time, the management of local country operations had been largely devolved to local general managers (GMs), but a new corporate strategy, following the intervention of McKinsey & Co., had recently been launched with the objective to raise the overall standard of a number of key management disciplines to a more consistently high level across the entire group. This strategy was summed up by the call to action: "Excellence across the Board" (EATB).

While the focus of this strategy was primarily operational and commercial, the Chief HR Officer Bernard Kunerth recognized that the Human Resources function could play a significant role in enabling the overall objectives of this strategy by upgrading and integrating CCH's approach to talent acquisition, development, and engagement. One of the cornerstones of this integration was identified as being the development of a clear and consistent, group-wide, employee value proposition. Employer brand development was not new to CCH. A number of countries, including CCH in Romania and Russia, had developed and implemented local employer brand strategies, but the underlying EVPs and subsequent employer branding activities were specific to each local market and predominantly external in focus. In order to raise the overall standard of employer brand management across the group, and create greater consistency, Bernard Kunerth decided that it was necessary to pool the learning from these local initiatives and create a common "masterbrand" EVP for the whole of CCH.

THE EVP DEVELOPMENT PROCESS

From the very start of the initiative, it was recognized that for the new group-wide EVP to win ownership across both geographical and functional divides, the development process would need substantive involvement from marketing and communications, as well as validation across a number of local operating companies. With this in mind, the process was divided into three key stages, each of which involved significant participation from a broad range of stakeholders.

Stakeholder Consultation and Evaluation of Relevant Existing Data

Interviews were conducted with a range of senior stakeholders from HR, marketing/communications and senior line management to identify shared needs and aspirations. These interviews revealed a number of highly relevant considerations relating to the organizational improvements sought to deliver on CCH's performance enhancement strategy (EATB). The most important of these were: improving the leadership pipeline and "bench-strength"; improving talent mobility across geographical borders; breaking down silos between countries to share best practice and deliver greater cost efficiency and effectiveness through more consistent and more integrated HR processes (including recruitment and learning and development); and addressing the need to recruit a significant number of young (Gen Y) sales people, particularly in fast growing emerging markets.

The second key research component at this stage was analysis of a company-wide culture survey recently conducted across the group, to identify their perceptions of what it's like to work for CCH and corresponding people management strengths and weaknesses.

EVP Development Workshop

This took the form of a one-day session with a representative selection of key stakeholders from HR, Marketing/Communications, and Line Management. During this workshop, the key insights derived from the research conducted earlier were translated into a shortlist of potential EVP attributes, identified as desirable in terms of: current or potential CCH strengths; appeal to internal and external target groups; features that would differentiate the company from competitors for talent; and qualities that would support organizational performance. The five key themes that emerged from this workshop were:

1. CCH's passionate focus on quality (which in addition to being closely aligned with the overall corporate strategy was also felt to be distinctively strong in relation to other organizations)

2. A winning team spirit (clearly credible at the local level, if not so evident across organizational boundaries)
3. The ability of CCH employees to make a personal impact on the performance of the company
4. A shared aspiration to improve CCH's performance in relation to personal and professional development (currently inconsistent, but a strong focus of planned future investment)
5. The reflection that, at its best, CCH was a fun place to work, but highly inconsistent in terms of creating a healthy balance between the company's intense focus on commercial performance and the "sociability" associated with a relatively young and highly dynamic organization

From the EVP development workshop, two core positioning options were also identified. By core positioning, we mean the overarching "umbrella" theme, which would be used to inform the creative expression of the EVP through recruitment advertising and internal communication. These were:

- "Passion for excellence"—focusing on the strongest current strength and differentiator. This positioning was also selected because of its clear alignment with the overall corporate strategy, "Excellence Across the Board."
- "More than just the world's leading brand"—focusing on the iconic global status of Coca-Cola, and the wide variety of opportunities offered by "the company behind the brand."

Validation and Final Recommendation

Questions covering the four defining attributes identified earlier were incorporated into a group-wide engagement survey, in order to test both the potential of each factor to drive engagement and current levels of CCH people management performance in relation to each attribute. The engagement survey served to validate the employer brand project team's attribute assumptions and recommendations. Following further additional input from the Operating Committee (CCH Group board) and a representative group of five country managers, the final Employer Brand Platform (with accompanying validation data) was defined as follows.

> ***Passion for excellence (core positioning)***
>
> *"A passion driven organisation sharing a commitment to excel in everything we do."*

The validation survey identified that 75 percent of employees believed that "we demonstrate a passion for excellence at CCH" (with other quality- and performance-focused questions making up five of the top seven overall favorability scores).

> ***Making a difference (EVP Pillar)***
>
> *"There's no passion without progress. CCH believes in setting clear goals and letting people get on with taking action. There's always a challenge, every opportunity to prove yourself and very little chance of getting bored."*

The survey identified that empowerment was both a top 5 ranking driver of employee engagement and a significant current strength, with 75 percent of employees claiming that they "feel empowered to get things done," and 87 percent that "the work I do makes an impact."

> ***Part of a winning team (EVP pillar)***
>
> *"Coca-Cola's status as the world's no. 1 brand has been achieved through a relentless passion to win. Whatever your role in CCH, you're part of a team that enjoys competing and never settles for second best."*

The pride that people felt in being associated with Coca-Cola was strongly evident in the validation survey, alongside a relatively strong perception that "we work well together across departments."

> ***Realizing your full potential (EVP pillar)***
>
> *"CCH is as passionate about bringing out the best in people as it is about getting results. With growing investment in training and an emphasis on home-grown talent, there are thousands of career success stories at CCH."*

The survey identified that professional development was a top 5 ranking engagement driver, but currently weak in terms of delivery, with only 46 percent of employees claiming to be given "ample opportunity to grow professionally."

> ***An enjoyment business (EVP pillar)***
>
> *"CCH brings enjoyment to millions of people through its market leading brands and the many community activities our employees participate in each year. We try and ensure people enjoy their work as much as consumers enjoy our products."*

Having fun at work was also identified as a consistently important engagement driver at CCH, with relatively average perceptions of CCH being "a fun place to work" and "celebrating success" suggesting significant room for improvement across the group.

EMPLOYER BRAND ACTIVATION AND MEASUREMENT

Following final sign-off from the CCH senior management team, the EVP was communicated to the wider HR community at a "Passion for Excellence" conference, and to the wider line management community at the company's annual Country Managers' event. These events also provided an opportunity to provide a briefing on related group-wide initiatives that would support the employer brand promise, and kick start the local action planning process, which served to address some of the more locally specific strengths and weaknesses highlighted by the employee engagement survey.

One of the initiatives following the creation of the EVP was the development of the first group-wide external recruitment campaign, but the most significant focus in terms of HR management time and attention was to bring the employment experience at CCH more closely into line with the four key employer brand promises (pillars), which in turn the company believed would drive both higher levels of employee engagement and organizational capability (by means of improved employee development and quality focus).

The main focus for internal action centered on the two most significant aspirational stretch areas, identified by the survey and encapsulated by the new EVP. These were: "Realizing Your Full Potential" (professional development) and creating an "Enjoyment Business" (fun at work).

The first of these stretch areas was supported by three interlinked, group-wide programs: the introduction of a new career pathing and leadership development model (supported by a new management development curriculum); a new performance management framework; and a new front-line leadership training program (the first step in the new leadership curriculum), called "Passion to Lead." It was believed that placing the immediate focus on front-line managers would deliver a double dose of support for the "Realizing your full potential" attribute, both directly, through an increased training investment in developing the most populous group within the overall "leadership community," and indirectly, through the impact on employees associated with the following improvement in team leaders' coaching and development skills. In 2008, this progress was maintained through the introduction of a further leadership training program targeting the "Managers of Managers" called "Leadership Excellence," and the development of a team of internal coaches.

The second, "Fun at Work" focus, was devolved to local country managers. This involved a wide range of initiatives from improving social facilities, focusing greater attention on team recognition and celebrating success, to improving work–life balance.

The impact of these targeted employer brand initiatives was measured in several ways. Since the launch of the new employer brand, CCH has conducted two further employee engagement surveys over a period of four years. Within this survey full engagement was defined in terms of employees claiming discretionary effort (going the extra mile), advocacy (recommending CCH as a good pace to work), and loyalty (intent to stay). Over the first year, the percentage of fully engaged employees across CCH improved from 36 percent to 43 percent, and three years later had risen to 55 percent. This was achieved over a period during which CCH rightsized its headcount across the entire organization (from a peak of 47,000 employees one year after the employer brand launch to 43,000 three years later), and maintained a firm control over salary rises.

There were also significant improvements in relation to the more EVP specific questions (aggregated to represent an overall Employer Brand Index).

	+1 year	*+ 3 years*	*Diff.*
Passion for excellence			
Q – We demonstrate a passion for excellence at CCH	75	79	+4
Part of a winning team			
Q – I feel I am part of a team at work	75	80	+5
Q – We work well together across departments	66	72	+6
Making a difference			
Q – The work I do makes an impact	85	88	+3
Q – I feel empowered to get things done	70	82	+12
Realizing your full potential			
Q – I am given ample opportunity to grow professionally	51	60	+9
Q – There are excellent job opportunities available for me	50	54	+4
An enjoyment business			
Q – CCH is a fun place to work	64	71	+7
Employer Brand Index (double weighted)	67	74	+7

The senior team at CCH believe that investing in the company's employer brand significantly improved their ability to attract, engage, and retain key talent, and in turn helped maintain their performance through the economic downturn.

CCH's approach represents a good illustration of the wider trend toward more joined-up employer brand thinking and practice. The key to success, in CCH's case, was the recognition that their employee value proposition needed to provide a balance between current credibility (winning team/making a difference) and achievable aspirations (realizing potential/an enjoyment business), twinned with an appreciation of the tangible investment required to convert stated aspirations into observable progress. In the authors' experience, organizations that demonstrate improvements are far more likely to make significant gains in employee engagement than those that simply highlight current positives, and this was certainly the case with CCH during this period.

It was also important that the case for the employer brand as a strategic enabler was established early on in terms of reinforcing a group-wide internal focus on quality, leadership development, engagement, and talent retention, and not simply as a shop-window for attracting external talent. Once line managers understood this, the employer brand became not only an HR initiative but a leadership imperative, reflected in the fact that the employer brand tagline "Passion for Excellence" has subsequently been adopted by the business as the corporate brand tagline.

THE OPPORTUNITY FOR HR

The employer brand approach can potentially help to address two of the key challenges at the heart of HR management. As Dave Ulrich (1997) pointed out in his book *Human Resource Champions*, the first of these is HR's requirement to be both a partner to the business and employee champion. The tools of brand management are designed to address this balancing act by helping to define and mediate between the value of the brand to people and to the business. It's generally in the customer's interest to demand more for less. It's generally in the business' interest to offer less for more. If this sounds familiar in the context of employee pay negotiations, we believe there is a distinct benefit in extending this conscious and explicit balancing act to the broader relationship (the "psychological contract") between the employee and the organization.

The second challenge is the requirement for HR to be both agents of change and guardians of stability. As Ulrich points out: "Businesses must balance the past and the future ... the benefits of free agency and control ... efficiency and innovation." This second balancing act is also a central feature of effective brand management, and we believe that the well-honed tools associated with this discipline can be of great benefit to the HR profession in addressing this complex and highly demanding task.

A further major benefit of adopting the employer brand approach is the scope it provides for more seamless integration with the "external" business agenda. For example, the marketing and HR functions often fail to see eye to eye because they tend to use different language and models to describe very similar objectives. Adopting a "joined-up" model of internal and external brand relationship management can help to clarify and resolve many of these apparent conflicts and ensure that both the internal and external agendas can be brought into closer alignment.

THE BENEFIT TO THE MARKETING FUNCTION

One of the most common complaints that we hear from marketers within service businesses is that their sphere of influence is seldom allowed to extend beyond brand communication. The employer brand perspective can provide an effective platform for transforming this notion of brand as communication to something more deeply rooted in the structure, process, and behavior of the organization. We also believe that it can help to deliver greater impact and credibility to internal marketing programs by joining up the employee's experience of the brand with the desired customer experience.

WHY EMPLOYER BRAND THINKING IS HERE TO STAY

Many new management disciplines have risen to prominence over the last 20 years. The pattern is now familiar. First there is the seminal book heralding a new dawn of management effectiveness. Consultancies appear on the market with well-packaged implementation programs. There are a flurry of articles, conferences, and guidebooks featuring competing models and pioneering case studies. In some cases, there may even be an award program. And then, just as people are settling down to await the results, the fickle wheel of management fortune takes another turn, and there's a new game in town. So is this just another fad? We believe there are three fundamental reasons why employer brand management is here to stay.

Organizations Increasingly Recognize That They Cannot Take the Commitment and Loyalty of Their Employees for Granted

Despite the desire to ensure that employees are broadly satisfied with their working conditions, it has largely been taken for granted that if you give people a decent job they will gratefully do your bidding. This view is increasingly at odds to the growing reality of employment. The companies that regularly populate the top end of the global top employer league tables (such as Google, P&G, KPMG, and Microsoft) have long realized that valued employees, such as profitable customers, are free to make choices, to join, to engage, to commit, and to stay. They also realize that to attract the right kind of people, to encourage them to remain loyal, and to perform to the best of their abilities requires a far more focused, coherent, and benefit-led approach than companies have been used to providing. Given the long-term trend for organizations to treat their valued employees more like valued customers, we believe that the logical conclusion for most will be to sharpen up the way in which they manage the brand that these people work for—the employer brand.

Employer Branding Provides an Effective Commercial Bridge Between HR, Internal Communications, and Marketing

People management has long been the poor cousin of marketing management, with HR regarded by many organizations as an administrative cost center rather than as a vital component in the creation and delivery of business value. This is fast changing. Most businesses have woken up to the vital importance to the business of recruiting, retaining, and developing the right people. The service sector, particularly, has woken up to the fundamental importance of engaging employee commitment in delivering customer satisfaction and loyalty. The growing commercial emphasis of these activities is bringing HR and internal communication practice increasingly in line with the approaches and disciplines more commonly applied to the creation and delivery of external value, namely marketing and brand management.

Employer Branding Draws on a Discipline That Has Proven Lasting Value in the Marketplace

Branding and brand management have evolved over time, but the central tenets of the discipline: close attention to the needs and aspirations of the target audience; focus on benefits; competitive differentiation; and the marshalling of a coherent and consistent brand experience are as central to brand management today as they have ever been. The foremost reason why employer branding is here to stay is that in driving and sustaining people's commitment and loyalty there has been no more effective approach than brand management. No doubt it will involve a further evolution in brand management practice. We believe that HR has as much to offer marketing as marketing to HR. Both sides can learn, both sides will benefit, and if, as we believe, the greatest net benefit will ultimately be to the business, employer branding will be here to stay.

REFERENCES

Barrow, S. and R. Mosley (2005). *The Employer Brand.* London: Wiley.

Corporate Executive Board (2008). "Introduction to Building a compelling EVP in China," Teleconference, October 15.

Ulrich, D. (1997). *Human Resource Champions.* Boston, Massachusetts: Harvard Business School Press.

Chapter 12

Global Branding: Strategy, Creativity, and Leadership

Sicco van Gelder

Over the past decades, people around the globe have become increasingly discerning and have been offered much more choice. This is due to three factors that have worked both simultaneously and in tandem. The first is that trade liberalization and subsequent global competition have increased the supply of goods and services to consumers and have driven down their prices.

The second is that people around the world have, overall, become richer, especially in places such as China and India. The third is that, due to increased competition, many product life cycles have shortened dramatically, which means that people are offered new, innovative, novel, and better products and services all the time. Just take the example of the relentless advance of computer and telecommunications technology, which has transformed the way many people live and work, and not just in rich countries.

In their roles as consumers, citizens, workers, decision makers, policy makers, and investors, people will look carefully at what brands have to offer them. They will choose those brands that clearly offer them the most value, and demands for value are increasing rapidly. How will global brands cope with these demands? How will they be able to continuously increase their value to fickle stakeholders? How will they do that in a world where people are becoming more and more conscious of their national, regional, and local identities?

As a reaction to these above-mentioned global developments, companies have mainly been concerned with improving their operational efficiencies. This may seem obvious, considering the pricing pressures they are under; however, it is a supply-side solution that can jeopardize their ability to compete in the future. Unless companies can find ways that will persuade their customers to pay more or buy more of their products or services, they will only be engaged in a race to the bottom. In the PC business, HP, Dell, and Lenovo slog it out as their products and brands become increasingly irrelevant to both consumers and businesses.

Some brands have reacted by improving their offers to their customers. For instance, Apple has shown relentless innovation. Rituals, a Unilever offshoot that is fast expanding from its home base of the Netherlands, offers a highly stylized home and body care products. Tesla is at the forefront of electric cars. Such examples show that global competitiveness is less about efficiency than about creating new and inspiring value for customers.

CREATING VALUE: THE COMBINATION OF STRATEGY, CREATIVITY, AND LEADERSHIP

This chapter argues that the combination of strategy, creativity, and leadership will determine the competitiveness of global brands in the coming decade. It does not matter whether these brands are products, services, NGOs, corporates, or places. All need to build their global competitive advantages, and no advantage is more powerful than a compelling brand. A compelling global brand is one that offers exceptional value to its stakeholders who live in very different countries, under different circumstances, in different cultures, and often with different needs.

Strategy, creativity, and leadership are to a brand what fuel, heat, and oxygen are to a fire: reduce one and it flickers, remove one entirely and it extinguishes. It is in the combination of these three that the energy of a brand relies upon. Interbrand's list of top brands for 2012 gives an indication of the power of this trinity. Comparing 2011 and 2012, the biggest winners in the brand value increase are:

- Apple (+129 percent)
- Amazon.com (+46 percent)

- Samsung (+40 percent)
- Nissan (+30 percent)
- Oracle (+28 percent)
- Google (+26 percent)

These six are well regarded for their vision, their ability to innovate, and the quality of their management. As a result, they provide value to their customers worldwide well over and above what their rivals are capable of. Now look at the biggest losers on this list:

- Blackberry (–39 percent)
- Nokia (–16 percent)
- Goldman Sachs (–16 percent)
- Yahoo! (–13 percent)
- Moët & Chandon (–13 percent)
- Citi (–12 percent)

These six have either lost their way and/or are stuck in a product category that is under severe pressure. They have all come up against competition that can provide more value to their customers. Although the computation of brand value is always open to discussion (there is always the matter of the purpose for which a brand is valued), this list does illustrate the importance of getting the mixture and balance of strategy, creativity, and leadership right. Strategy, creativity, and leadership are examined separately below, before looking at their combination and before looking at them in a global setting.

Strategy

There are three forms of strategy that are pertinent to brands, namely business strategy, brand strategy, and marketing strategy. The significance of business strategy to branding is that it determines the vision, purpose, objectives, business model, resources, competencies, and motivations for the brand. What the business strategy sets out to achieve is turned into a value proposition by the brand. Thus the brand strategy deals with what makes the brand unique, inspiring, believable, trustworthy, and likeable or even admirable.

None of this is worth a thing unless this translates into the brands' products and services, and their pricing, promotion, servicing, and delivery. The brand functions as the organizing principle for the entire strategy process, because it is the definition of the value to be created for the organization's stakeholders. In other words, the stakeholders must be offered an experience that is on brand. IKEA's business strategy is concerned with global expansion through stores offering low cost, (largely) self-assembly furniture of reasonable quality. The brand permits the world's (growing) middle-class entry to a modern home-based lifestyle. IKEA's marketing aims to turn customers into fans through guerrilla marketing (e.g., home decorating bus shelters in New York and the Kobe monorail), in-store design (e.g., turning the staircase in its Kuala Lumpur store into a set of drawers), product design (e.g., new iconic products such as the Billy bookcase), and the in-store routing (e.g., by family life stages as well as products).

Creativity

Creativity is about ideas. This can be about thinking in a different way about familiar issues or even coming up with absolutely new ideas. Creativity can and must be applied throughout the entire strategy process from the formulation of a vision for the brand right down to the design and delivery of its products and services. Truly creative organizations break down the barriers within the organization and with the outside world and engage all stakeholders in a continuous creative process.

Creativity is therefore not something that is limited to brainstorming sessions, but rather a habit that is embedded in the organization. Creativity is not the same as innovation, which may be termed "applied creativity." Creativity is also not the same as improvement, which may be termed "routine creativity." However, both innovation and improvement require pure creativity to function.

The brand functions as the inspiration for creativity, it gives direction and provides the parameters within which the creativity must take place. In other words, the creativity has to be on brand. Swatch's creativity for example is entirely on brand. The design of the "second watch" is always meant to show off who the wearer is: elegant, emotional, and sometimes provocative.

Leadership

Leadership is about creating the vision, structures, systems, trust, and clarity that inspire people in the organization to achieve its strategy and apply their creativity to the things they do in their work. Leading a brand entails setting a context and a culture within which employees live the brand and stakeholders perceive the brand. In other words, the employees' behavior and demeanor must be recognizable on brand. Yvon Chouinard, the founder of outdoor brand Patagonia, is a leader who committed his company to being an outstanding place to work, and to be an important resource for environmental activism. The commitment included paying employees working on local environmental projects so that they could commit their efforts full-time.

Leadership is also about involving employees in the planning and implementation of the actions required to fulfill the organization's vision. This means inspiring the workforce to contribute creatively to a common goal and aligning their personal values to those of the brand. Increasingly, leadership involves creating (temporary) partnerships with other stakeholders of the brand. These can take various forms, such as public–private brand partnerships for places, brand development partnerships, marketing partnerships, and product or service development partnerships.

Leading such partnerships involves joint strategizing, joint development, and joint implementation. This puts an added strain on leadership, because it involves negotiating with partners. The brand that the partnership develops and manages helps to keep it on track, because it provides the partners with a clear guiding purpose to fulfill. In Amsterdam, ING, Shell, the municipal government, and several other local partners developed a brand for the former Shell Research Area (now known as Overhoeks) that was used as the guiding principle for the urban planning, the architecture, the strategy for attracting key tenants, and the management of the area.

The Combination of Strategy, Creativity, and Leadership

It is clear from the above that strategy, creativity, and leadership all have an important part to play in branding. The new leadership agenda has introduced creativity into the mix where the focus has so far been on strategy—devised by the leadership and handed down to the organization.

As explained, strategy without creativity (Nokia) and creativity without leadership (Sony) are not meaningful. However, it is in their combination that these three become imperatives to the branding process. If the links between the three are strong, they reinforce, inspire, and interact with each other.

Traditionally, strategy, creativity, and leadership have been separated in organizations, because it was felt that these were processes suited to particular departments, organizational levels, or even certain individuals. This has led many corporations, such as GM, Philips, and Xerox, to develop uninspiring brands, which lose their luster over time. All were originally strong innovators, which compartmentalized disciplines in such a way as to eradicate synergies between strategy, creativity, and leadership. Some brands even came a cropper, such as Kodak. Consumers had no qualms about abandoning Kodak's photographic film for digital cameras from Nikon, Canon, and Sony.

It has generally been young and imaginative companies that tended not to separate the disciplines, such as Apple, Amazon, Dyson, Virgin, Quiksilver, Red Bull, and Google. It probably came naturally to their founders to appreciate the linkages between strategy, creativity, and leadership and to apply branding as the guiding principle of all they do. Yet, the kinds of brands and the way they combine strategy, creativity, and leadership differ significantly.

But even old-fashioned giant conglomerates can learn to be nimble and apply the disciplines across their organizations. Take the example of Samsung, an organization that is traditionally hierarchic and nontransparent has shown that it can be flexible and innovative.

Characteristically, the decision to switch from developing "me too" consumer electronics products to innovative ones was made by Samsung Group Chair Lee Kun Hee in 1996. This decision has meant untying Samsung managers from corporate red tape and allowing them to use all the resources under their own roof.

Mr Lee launched an effort to focus the company on a new competitive advantage: design innovation. He committed $126 million to develop a global-design program and established the company's first-ever in-house design school. Before long, the company's top designers, and in later years, marketers and engineers, were taking full-time classes, six days a week, in fundamentals such as mechanical engineering and marketing.

THE IMPLICATIONS FOR GLOBAL BRANDING

Global branding is a complicated matter that requires management to understand the various internal and external factors that affect their brand as it stretches across the globe. Global and international brands are affected by differing structural, motivational, and cultural influences across the countries (and sometimes even within the countries) that they operate in. For the purpose of this chapter, the discussion is limited to the influence that these factors have on strategy, creativity, and leadership.

Global Strategy

A company's strategy can differ significantly between markets because of various local circumstances. Initially management's vision of the future of the market may differ significantly between countries. This has an immediate impact on the organization's future purpose. For example, Toyota's vision of a market for hybrid powered cars is directly relevant to developed markets where people are willing and able to spend money on a "green" car and where environmental legislation makes such cars almost inevitable. Such a vision has little or no relevance to fast developing markets such as those in Africa. There Toyota's vision is probably more about the potential of the market for regular cars with rising consumer purchasing power.

Business models may also differ between markets, due to local circumstances. Some business models will just not work in certain countries due to matters such as low Internet and credit card penetrations, legislation against direct selling, differing business hours, differing technological standards, and low levels of disposable income.

In each market there are conventions, the unwritten rules of the product, and service categories that can affect the brand. There are structural conventions—the way almost all players in the market act—there are cultural conventions—the things most people believe and the way they behave to one another—and there are motivational conventions—the way that people commonly fulfill their needs.

For example, brands often unwittingly carry the values of their country of origin in them as part of their brand identity, which can be entirely inappropriate to a host country. A typical American social value such as equality will be totally inappropriate in a hierarchical society such as Indonesia. That is why McDonald's offers a clear-up service in such countries rather than letting its patrons dispose of the remains of their meals themselves. This example shows that brands can play different roles and have different meanings in various markets.

Finally, marketing strategies may differ between markets. This can be due to a differing brand strategy, as discussed above, but may also be due to legal, religious, competitive, infrastructure, purchasing power, and personnel limitations imposed by a country. Examples of this are lamb burgers in India, the difficulties of efficiently distributing wares into the Chinese hinterland and the subsequent lack of control of product shelf displays, and the mini packs in which personal care products are often sold in many developing countries.

It is clear that all such factors should force management to be highly creative when devising global strategies. With such a multitude of factors to take into account, it is an enormous achievement to be able to create the greatest value for the brand's stakeholders in each and every market.

Global Creativity

Although creativity is lauded by academics, consultants, business leaders, and politicians the world over, it is actually not considered to be the same thing in every society nor is it regarded equally highly in every society. Culture and education have a significant impact on creativity in various parts of the world.

In Europe, creativity is often considered to be limited to specific individuals, departments, or organizations. In addition, creativity is generally confined to specific creative industries or research and development functions. Thus, European brands are often well known for their product design and their marketing creativity, such as Alessi, IKEA, Heineken, L'Oreal, Audi, and Prada. Technological and business innovations are generally not the strong points of European brands.

The value of design to European audiences has often been underestimated by Japanese and U.S. brands. Japanese and Korean car makers have had a tough time matching the European brands, but are catching up. U.S. fashion brands have also found it tough to compete in the European marketplace. Erstwhile venerable jeans brands such as Levi's and Wrangler have not been able to respond adequately to the marketing creativity of Diesel, G-star, or Gsus.

In the United States, technology, entertainment, and entrepreneurship are highly regarded and it is no wonder that the country has produced most creativity in these very powerful areas. A lack of sensitivity to local circumstances has sometimes played havoc with U.S. brands, especially when they tried to forcefully challenge local beliefs, values, and customs. What was considered creative or innovative at home was not much appreciated elsewhere.

East Asian countries, that have an education system geared to rote learning and societal values of obedience and respect for elders, do not encourage young people to stick their necks out. A lot of stock is often placed on perfection. This is an aesthetic need that in particular encompasses many aspects of Japanese society, ranging from manufacturing to sports and from religion to food. Examples of brands that cater to this need for perfection are Lexus and Shiseido cosmetics.

In Japan, creativity in business is often focused on process improvements, such as just-in-time production, lean production total quality management, and continuous improvement. Although these innovations led to an almost worldwide quality revolution in the 1980s, it did make Japanese brands take their eyes off foreign consumers who value other things. Arguably, the most creative area of Japanese business has been in what is commonly called gadgets, such as Sony's Aibo robot dog.

The significance to global branding of these differences in creativity not only has to do with different consumer preferences, but also with the fact that global organizations employ people with these differing mind-sets. In other words, the creativity of a Korean employee is going to be quite different from the kind of creativity one may expect from an Italian employee and different again from one in the United States. This is a benefit when it comes to localizing the brand and fulfilling its potential across markets, but it makes the brand difficult to manage globally. However, culture is not a strait-jacket and that creativity can be encouraged by creating the right structures, environment, and rewards for people in the company.

Global Leadership

Leading a global brand is about providing direction, structure, inspiration, and opportunity to the people who manage the brand in various parts of the world. Not only do they themselves have different cultural backgrounds, but they also manage the brand in environments that are often (totally) unknown to global management. It is essential that global management realizes this and understands how these differences affect the brand as it stretches across the globe. On the one hand, this means implementing a common brand strategy and management framework that is comparable across markets. On the other hand, it means getting to grips with how leadership differs in various parts of the world.

In collectivist societies, such as most Asian ones, leadership is about managing groups rather than managing individuals. This means that as a manager it is more important to ensure group performance rather than individual performance. This has an effect on strategy and creativity because in a collectivist society these become group processes aimed at achieving consensus. Voicing personal opinions is considered bad behavior. Strategy is, therefore, often stated in "group language." Similarly, individual creativity is not encouraged, yet group creativity is often found in the shape of continuous improvement.

In Europe, leadership is often about a multistakeholder environment whereby management spends time and energy trying to keep everyone on board. Management is about various kinds of partnership performance, such as co-development, co-branding, and public–private partnerships.

Strategy is often stated in language about the vision, purpose, and ambition of the organization. Creativity is often undertaken in R&D centers, which are more and more connected with partner R&D centers. For example, Philips and Douwe Egberts jointly developed the hugely successful Senseo coffee machine by putting their knowledge of electronics and coffee brewing together. The emphasis among European brands is frequently on sharing and the evolution of technologies and knowledge.

In the United States, leadership may be about driving an organization to achieve specific firm goals: for example, increased shareholder value, ROI, and market share. Strategy is often stated in terms of growth, being market leader, and financial results. For example, HP talks about its corporate objectives in the following order: customer loyalty, profit, market leadership, growth, employee commitment, leadership capability, and global citizenship. The leadership of creativity (and innovation) is often a highly personalized matter among U.S. business leaders.

It is about the personal drive of people such as Phil Knight, Howard Schultz, and Jeff Bezos. Creativity for U.S. brands is generally about reinventing the way people work, innovation breakthroughs, and revolutionary technology. The leaders of globally operating companies need to be far more culturally aware than ever before. They need to understand what travels well and what does not, and when and why local adaptations to strategy, creativity, and leadership are required. This requires not only an appreciation of structural, cultural, and motivational differences between markets, but also a clear understanding of how the company can best operate across borders.

CONCLUSION

Getting the mix and balance between strategy, creativity, and leadership right across multiple markets is the most crucial job of global management in the years to come if their brand's flame is to burn brightly and not to flicker or be altogether extinguished. As this chapter explains, it requires a thorough understanding of how these disciplines actually work and, more importantly, how they interact with one another in structurally, culturally, and motivationally different settings.

This is not some intellectual game played by people sitting at their desks in corporate offices, but a contest for entire organizations to determine where they are going, how to do so in original and valuable ways, and how to keep everyone inspired and on track. The best tool available to ensure this happens is the brand, functioning as the organization's guiding, inspiring, and organizing principle.

Chapter 13

Brand Valuation: Identifying and Measuring the Economic Value Creation of Brands

Jan Lindemann

INTRODUCTION

The economic benefit of brands is today widely recognized. However, how this benefit is created within the overall business context and measured in financial terms remains the domain of a relatively small group of specialists. This is surprising given the importance of brands to business value.

On an average about a third of shareholder or company value can be attributed to brand assets, and there is substantial evidence that suggests that companies with strong brands outperform on the stock market with respect to risk and return (see Lindemann, 2004, 2010).

This obviously differs by industry and valuation approach. Clearly, there is a discrepancy between the importance of brands as economic assets and the understanding of their value creation. The reason for this is twofold.

Firstly, in many cases the brand is closely intertwined with the rest of the business, and an operationally clear separation is neither feasible nor desirable. This is in particular an issue with business-to-business brands such as IT or financial services where technology, people, and brand have to feed on each other for the overall business success.

Secondly, understanding and measuring the value creation of brands is complex as it requires mixing financial and market research data. In addition, it requires an understanding of how perceptions are created within the mind of potential and existing buyers. This complexity makes it hard for most audiences to get into the details of brand valuation.

Nevertheless, understanding, measuring, and managing brand value has become a crucial task for management as well as investors. This chapter will therefore explain why brand valuation is relevant, and how it is calculated and ultimately used by businesses around the world.

The focus will be on concepts and application and to a lesser extent on the technicalities of the valuation methods. There are by now plenty of publications that cover in detail the different valuation approaches including calculation examples. So further reading is recommended for those who want to get into the nitty gritty of brand valuation methods (see Lindemann, 2010; Salinas, 2009).

THE VALUE OF BRANDS

The recognition of brands as core business asset has entered the mainstream of the C-suite agenda. Most CEOs will acknowledge the importance of brands for their business. However, this C-suite recognition has not necessarily resulted in the appropriate management of brands.

In the case of companies operating only or mainly through one brand, the holistic nature of brands makes brand management a complex affair as it spans several independently managed departments or management silos.

But managing brands holistically and across functions is most effective for increasing shareholder value, and brand valuation is all about managing the economic value creation of brands and their underlying businesses.

Brand valuation requires a detailed understanding about the specific value creation of brands in a business context. How do brands create value for a business?

Brands contain and represent the higher level perceptions of a company's historic and present interaction with the marketplace, most importantly its products and services. The interaction with the marketplace happens through product and service delivery as well as communication.

In a world where the difference in actual product and service delivery between different suppliers is often hard to identify, perceptions about these products and services play an important role in influencing customers' and prospective customers' purchase decisions.

Brand perception comprises both factual (tangible) aspects and emotional (intangible) aspects. Depending on the brand, the emotional or factual aspects can be more pronounced.

The mix of brand perceptions differentiates one brand from another. This differentiation has two components—firstly, the strength of the perception relative to competitors and secondly the mix of perceptions. Brand management is the active management of these two sets of perceptions.

Today, branding has progressed beyond the consumer goods sectors and features in nearly all businesses. That has made brand management more complex as many corporate brands have a wide range of customer segments and stakeholders.

For example, brands such as Apple and BMW create perceptions for consumers, business customers, employees, shareholders, and regulators. As each of these audiences looks at branding from a different angle, these brands need to be managed through a variety of corporate functions such as marketing, sales, product development and R&D, HR, and investor relations. Each of these functions manages perceptions of the business for different target groups.

While communications play a key role in managing brand perceptions in particular for FMCGs or packaged goods, other elements such as product development, channel management, customer service, and sales personnel can be equally or more important than communications. Some companies have addressed the complexity of brands by putting experienced line managers into brand management functions to make it more business oriented. This makes sense, as the world's most valuable brands such as Apple, IBM, and McDonalds depend much more on customer experience than on media communications. Such brands, therefore, need to be managed with a holistic perspective and not through the conventional dependence on marketing communication.

EMERGENCE OF BRAND VALUATION

The complex nature of brands has significant implications on how to assess their economic value creation, ultimately in financial terms. Brand valuation has become management relevant in the late 1980s as a variety of M&A transactions defied traditional valuation approaches and the stock market value of quoted companies started to outstrip their book value at an increasing pace.

The average price-to-book ratio for the companies of the S&P 500 index ranged over the last 20 years has averaged at around 3.5. Even during the recent stock market crash, the ratio remained around 2.0 (see Lindemann, 2010). This indicates that investors see significant additional value over and above that stated by the accountants.

This has led to the discovery of intangibles as key drivers of shareholder value. The key accounting issue was that goodwill could not be capitalized. Even in M&A transactions where the actual value of intangible assets was implied in the transaction price, they had to be written off!

Finally, the accounting profession overhauled the treatment of intangibles in order to align accounting values with business reality. Standards around the world most notably IRFS (international) and FASB[1] (United States) developed detailed procedures for dealing with intangibles upon an acquisition or merger.

They also categorized intangible assets into different groups such as marketing (trademarks, trade names, Internet domain names, etc.), contractual (licensing and franchise agreements as well as other contracts), technology (patents, software, databases, etc.), customer (customer lists, patents), arts (books, operas, movies, plays, etc.), and related assets as well as goodwill which comprises all other intangibles that cannot be specified (see IRFS 3[2]).

This was done for two reasons. Firstly, the accounting profession had to deal with the then largest accounting issue for most acquisitions, that is, intangible assets. Secondly, accountants wanted to create some type of accountability for the acquisition of highly priced intangible assets. Instead of just writing them off, they would

[1] www.fasb.org
[2] www.irfs.org

remain on the balance sheet and be subjected to an annual impairment test. The capitalized values, however, would stay the same if the value were unchanged or increased or they would decline if the impairment test showed a lower value.

The accounting treatment of intangible assets ended up being a half-baked solution as only acquired intangibles could be recognized on the balance sheet. For that reason, the Burger King brand is included in the balance sheet of Burger King Holding Inc. with a value of US$2.2 billion (Burger King Holding Inc., 2011) accounting for about 41 percent of the company's market capitalization.

The McDonald's brand is in absolute and also in relative terms more valuable than the Burger King brand but is not valued on the company's balance sheet, as it has been organically developed and not been subject of an acquisition.

As a result of these accounting standards, even extremely valuable intangibles such as the Coca-Cola brand or the Apple brand and technology know-how are not recognized. Only through mergers or acquisitions can the value of intangibles be recognized on the balance sheet.

The accounting recognition of acquired intangibles did little to increase the accountability of management. Investors more or less ignored the accounting changes as they did not affect cash flows, the prevailing valuation basis for share prices, or adjusted price/earnings (P/E) ratios to make them comparable. Nevertheless, the accounting debate was an important breakthrough for the management recognition of the value of intangible assets as it provided audited financial values. It was an important influencer to make the C-suite aware of the importance of intangibles and, in particular, brands.

Interestingly, brands were a key driver in kicking off the accounting debate as it was the takeover of brand owning companies such as RHM, Rowntree, and Kraft General Foods that triggered the discussion. However, the standards struggled to properly catch the holistic nature of brands as they often combine a variety of elements. For example, the Coca-Cola brand includes trademarks, designs, and copyrights as well as the famous recipe. In technology, certain patents can also be part of the brand. Nevertheless, since the introduction of the accounting standards on the treatment of goodwill and intangibles, many brands and other intangible assets have been valued and capitalized on balance sheets. Another outcome was the discussion and development of methods and techniques for valuing brands.

BRAND VALUATION APPROACHES AND METHODOLOGIES

Brand valuation is a derivative of established valuation methodologies such as cost, comparable transactions, multiples of key financial data such as annual revenues, and/or different types of earnings, as well as discounted forecast earnings and/or cash flows. These are at different levels of sophistication and expertise adjusted to the valuation of a specific brand or portfolio of brands.

Worldwide, there are easily 50+ different approaches for valuing brands. Although many of these claim to be proprietary, most of them tend to be variations of similar approaches. Many of these variations are more about consulting firms trying to differentiate their offer rather than meaningful differences in the fundamental approaches. While there are a large variety of approaches on offer, the most widely used methods fall into two categories: market- or comparables-based and brand-specific valuation approaches.

Market-based Valuation Approaches

Market-based valuation approaches focus on transaction values for brands that are assumed to be comparable and therefore providing a benchmark or comparable for the brand to be valued. This requires to identify valuations of similar brands in previous transactions such as the sale and purchase of a similar brand, the licensing rate paid for a similar brand, a balance sheet value of a similar brand (which as explained above is based on a previous M&A transaction), or the value generated for different transactions such as brand-asset-based securitization.

These valuations are considered market based because either some third party has paid cash or another financially measurable price in the context of a transaction for use or ownership of a brand or a publicly trusted expert such as an accounting firm or a brand valuation consultant has provided a valuation of a brand that is used in financial accounting or legal procedures. From the valuation of the brand that is deemed comparable, revenue and profit multiples are derived and applied to the brand that is to be valued.

The most widely used market approach is the net present value (NPV) of discounted royalty incomes from brands for which licensing rates are available. This approach is used by the accounting firms to value brands for recognition on balance sheets.

The idea is that a market-based comparable royalty rate most appropriately represents the income stream from the brand to be valued. This is called the royalty relief method as it values the brand according to the NPV of the licensing fees that would have to be paid for the use of the brand. The value of the brand is calculated by forecasting the revenues the brand is expected to generate multiplied with the royalty rate of a comparable brand discounted to an NPV with the cost of capital of a business operating in the brand's sector or category.

The market valuation approach is relatively simple and cost-effective. The trick is to find a reasonably comparable royalty rate or transaction. However, this is also where the market approach is seriously flawed, as it requires the comparable brand to be reasonably comparable with respect to its ability to generate similar revenues and cash flows in comparable markets as the brand to be valued. The comparable valuation method is widely used in finance as it provides the comfort of a (however defined) "market" view.

It is also easy to apply and still forms the basis of most M&A transactions as well as analysts' assessment of quoted companies. It is therefore popular with decision makers in the C-suite as it is easy to understand. Most valuation experts are more cautious about using comparables, as in many cases the comparability is flawed and adjustments need to be made limiting the benefit of using a comparable valuation.

In the case of brands, this is even more the case as brands can operate in the same markets and offer very little actual difference in the product or service offer but can significantly differ in their value creation. Brands need to be different by definition in order to be valuable. Even in categories where nearly everything is comparable, such as cola drinks, the brands are very different. For example, there is little difference with respect to the operational aspects of the underlying businesses of the Coca-Cola and Pepsi-Cola brands. Product, distribution, and marketing of both businesses are comparable. Both fight fiercely for the same consumer. However, the brands of both businesses are extremely different. Coca-Cola is the heritage cola brand. It is perceived as the "original" that created the category even if some consumers prefer other brands. Pepsi, on the other hand, is the challenger brand with a more dynamic youth-focused image.

Today, Coca-Cola is the leading cola brand not only in the United States but also in the rest of the world. Pepsi is still the challenger brand, and other cola brands have not managed to gain significant share of the cola market. Coca-Cola and Pepsi are a good example as to why comparable valuations do not work well for brands.

Although similar and perhaps comparable in all other aspects the brands are very different which is reflected in their value creation. The Coca-Cola brand ranks in all published surveys among the most valuable brands in the world and has done so for the last 10 years. The Coca-Cola brand can generate far more demand and thus revenues than the Pepsi brand. The brand is also less fashion dependent, and thus its revenues and cash flows are more stable and less volatile. The Coca-Cola brand is therefore in absolute and relative terms significantly more valuable than the Pepsi brand. There is no evidence that the Pepsi brand will be able in the foreseeable future to reach or surpass the value creation of the Coca-Cola brand.

A comparable value is therefore of limited value. Similar cases can be made for brands from different categories such as Apple, IBM, Hermès, and McDonalds to name a few. This is not to say that comparable valuations have no use in the case of valuing brands. Some of the derived multiples can provide value ranges and ballpark numbers that are relatively easy to obtain. However, the nature of brands makes it hard to find reasonably comparable values. This means that for valuing brands comparables should only be used as crosscheck for a brand-specific valuation.

In addition to the conceptual difficulty of finding comparable brands, there is the added difficulty of the quality of brand valuations that are disclosed and obtainable. For example, a balance sheet value cannot reflect increases in the value of a brand as accounting standards only allow for downward change in brand value if the annual impairment test results in a lower value for the brand. That means even if one accepts the valuation approach that has been used for the initial balance sheet valuation, chances are that after a couple of years this value may have become obsolete. This suggests that balance sheet values are of limited use as they reflect only a market transaction at a point in time. If the value of the brand has increased since the valuation was conducted, the balance sheet value has lost its relevance.

One of the most widely used comparable market valuation benchmarks for brand valuation is licensing and royalty rates. While these offer a larger amount of market-relevant comparables, they often require creative interpretation.

Many royalty rate agreements bundle in one royalty rate the use of several intangibles, making it very difficult to get a clean brand-only rate that could be used for comparison. This is the case for many franchise arrangements for fast food restaurants where the royalty rate includes the brand as well as certain operational processes. Many of these agreements also require the franchisees to invest in promotional advertising. That means publicly available royalty rates often do not provide "clean" rates for brands as they include also other intangibles.

Acquisitions and disposals of brands are another source of comparable market transactions. However, most transactions that involve prominent and successful brands are a combination of business assets where the brand is the key value driver, but the success has created a whole business asset with other value-driving components. The specific brand value that ends up on the balance sheet will have been prepared by an accounting firm most likely using a market-based comparable transaction. The majority of these transactions tend to happen in predominantly consumer-focused businesses. Examples are Absolut, the leading premium vodka brand bought by Pernod Ricard in 2008 through the acquisition of Vin & Sprit for €6.3 billion or Burger King bought by a private equity consortium that included TPG and Bain Capital in 2008.

Many pure brand transactions involve mostly smaller brands bought by small private equity groups or brand-focused investors such as Iconix. The latter acquired brands such as London Fog or Joe Boxer that are sold in different retail chains. However, as mentioned earlier, taking these transactions as example in order to value other brands can be misleading as London Fog is unlikely to reach the size, relevance, and ultimately value creation of Burberry although both brands have a heritage in waterproof military coats. In many cases, the disclosure of such pure brand transactions is limited, making it difficult to derive meaningful comparable valuation parameters.

As the above examples demonstrate brands are rarely comparable as by their very nature, they need to be different in order to influence the customer's choice. In addition, one of the key valuation parameters is revenue generation, which is a function of volume, price, and frequency of customer purchases. It is in most cases impossible to find a market-valued brand with comparable revenue patterns.

In most cases, the comparability of market transactions is questionable, and most valuations need to be adjusted in more than one way in order to make the market valuations comparable. For that reason, comparables or market-based valuations are of limited use and should be used as a secondary valuation or crosscheck.

The other issue with this type of market valuations is the fact that they provide purely a number but no explanation about value drivers and actions that have resulted in the value. A market-based valuation is therefore of limited use for management actions as it cannot provide a link between management actions and economic value creation. Market-based valuations can be helpful in a transactional context where ultimately only a number for a royalty rate, balance sheet, or acquisition or disposal value is required. However, if you want to understand the drivers of brand value and what actions can be taken to influence this value, then only having a financial value is insufficient.

Brand-specific Valuation Approaches

The severe limitations of comparable market transactions have resulted in the emergence of brand-specific valuation approaches. The advantage of these valuation methodologies is twofold. They deliver a number that is derived based on the specific earnings the brand is expected to generate. They also deliver a financial value of the brand. In addition, many of the brand-specific valuation approaches provide the drivers of brand value as they are built from bottom up from the revenue generation of the specific brand. The brand-specific valuation approaches emerged in the late 1980s as a result of the takeovers of many companies with strong consumer brand portfolios.

In this context, a small brand consulting company called Interbrand became one of the pioneers of brand valuation. In 1988, RHM, a British company that owned a portfolio of strong predominantly national brands, became a takeover target as an Australian buyout company was mounting a hostile bid for the business. RHM's management believed that its business was significantly undervalued as the offer price represented only a small premium over its balance sheet value. As the balance sheet did not include the value of the company's brand portfolio, its management initiated the first properly recorded brand valuation that was included in the balance sheet.

As the accounting firms at the time were opposed to recognizing intangible assets on the balance sheet, RHM's management turned to Interbrand, which created the first brand-specific valuation approach. The model was relatively simple and unsophisticated by today's standard standards. Nevertheless, it was effective as management included the value of the brand portfolio on the balance sheet and used it to fend off the hostile bid. It should be noted that at the time accounting for intangibles was a gray zone and too exotic to warrant the attention of the accounting profession.

Later Interbrand's valuation approach became the basis for the economic use method that values the brand according to its asset-specific value creation. The economic use approach has become the dominant brand valuation approach for management purposes as it is built from the perspective of how brands affect businesses. It is not just a financial calculation but also a thorough assessment on how the brand generates and secures customer demand in different market segments.

There are many variations of this approach due to brand and marketing consulting firms promoting their "proprietary" valuation methods with each claiming to have come closest to the holy grail of brand valuation. Like most financial valuation approaches, brand valuation too is a combination of art and science. While the model has to follow sound economic and financial principles and rules, there are many assumptions that need to be made to produce a useful and meaningful brand valuation on which business decisions and transactions can be based.

From a financial point of view, the valuation should follow a discounted cash flow or DCF model that discounts expected future earnings according to their risk profile to an NPV. From an economic point of view, it needs to reflect the way brands create value.

The key task of a brand is to influence the customer's choice toward purchasing a company's product and services. This influence of the brand has two components. The first one is to secure the purchase and convert a potential customer into an actual one, that is, purchasing customer. The second one is to ensure that the customer continues to buy the company's products and services and thus becomes a loyal customer.

Therefore, brands are instrumental in creating and sustaining customer demand. This demand results in revenues that come from the price at which customers buy, the volume they buy, and the frequency at which they buy. These factor determine the revenue generation of the brand.

The financial impact of brands is mainly on the top line, that is, revenues, although pricing has also a direct impact on profit margins. There are additional cost benefits that a strong brand can achieve such as higher return on R&D investments, better and more predictable asset utilization as well as economies of scale. Nevertheless, revenue generation and sustainability are the predominant areas where brands add value. This should therefore be reflected in the valuation approach. Most brands operate in different market segments. For some, this is narrower, such as soft drinks or beer, whereas for others it is wider, such as certain corporate brands that spread across a range of diverse business activities.

The segment in which the brand operates in has a significant impact on its value creation. For example, the same beer brand will have a different impact on consumers' purchase decisions in a supermarket or similar retail environment versus an on-trade environment. In the supermarket, there will be a wide range of choices of brands and price promotions that will affect the purchase decisions, whereas in an on-trade environment there will be a limited choice of brands but rarely brand-specific price promotion. Each segment differs with respect to the level of choice, pricing, operating costs, etc.

The segmentation can be even more diverse for corporate brands such as HP or GE that cover a wide range of B2B and B2C segments. It is therefore important that the valuation recognizes the market-segment-specific conditions in which the brand operates.

BRAND VALUATION FRAMEWORK

In order to capture the value creation of a brand, the appropriate valuation methodology needs to comprise the following five key steps:

- Market segmentation
- Forecasting of revenues the brand is expected to generate in the future
- Identifying the profits that the business can extract from the revenues generated by the brand
- Determining the earnings that are attributable to the brand
- Calculating an NPV for the earnings attributable to the brand

The valuation of the brand needs to reflect the different market segments the brand operates in. The overall value of the brand will be the sum of the valuations of the different segments the brand is present in. These market segments need to be of strategic size and materially relevant over the forecast period. They also need to reflect significant differences in the purchase behavior of consumers as well as be mutually exclusive.

Most segmentations are multidimensional, including customer attitudes, purchase behavior, geography, product/service, and this approach to segmentation makes the valuation more accurate in financial terms. It also makes it more useful for management as it provides insights for targeted marketing and communications initiatives.

The NPV of future earnings or cash flows is the most widely used and accepted valuation approach in corporate finance and management accounting. This valuation method requires a forecast of revenues, profits, capital employed, and cash flows. For a brand valuation, the first step is to prepare a forecast for the revenues the brand is expected to generate in the future, which is called "Brand Revenues."

The basis of the forecast should be historic trends, market reports, and growth outlooks for the brand with respect to price and volume. Forecasting is more an art than a science, which makes it important to be transparent about the assumptions which are best kept to a minimum. The forecast period should be ten years split into a detailed five-year forecast, which is extended according to long-term trends for another five years.

From the forecast Brand Revenues all operating costs that are necessary to support and deliver these revenues are subtracted to derive an operating profit or EBIT (earnings before interest and tax). From the EBIT, all applicable payable taxes are deducted as well as a charge for the capital employed representing the capital investment necessary for the business to function, that is, fixed assets plus working capital. The result is the economic profit generated from the revenues generated by the brand.

The concept of economic profit is similar to EVA or economic value added, which Stern Steward popularized in the 1990s. Economic profit works better for the valuation of brands and other intangibles than cash flow as it better represents the brand as a separate asset. It is also a more pragmatic approach as it is easier to forecast. After all, a brand's valuation should focus on the brand-specific aspects of the valuation and not get bogged down in forecasting manufacturing capacity. Ultimately, the forecast comprises revenues generated by the brand, operating costs, applicable taxes as well as the capital employed required for operating the business.

The economic earnings represent the return for all intangibles of the business. These include brands, R&D, management, HR, etc. In order to value a brand, the brand-specific earnings need to be identified. Here the proprietary valuation approaches offer a wide range of at times bizarre models.

The consensus approach is that market research data need to be analyzed in a way to identify key drivers of demand, that is, the reasons why customers buy a product and service and then the impact the specific brand perception has on these key drivers. For most businesses, sufficient market research data is available to build such a model. Drivers of demand can be functional and/or emotional benefits. For example, in the case of the purchase of a mobile phone, there will be design, ease of use, display quality, functionality, availability of software such as apps, pricing, image attributes such as "cool image," innovative, user-friendly, etc.

These demand drivers can be assessed according to their impact on outcome metrics such as loyalty, advocacy, and purchase. For each driver, the impact of the brand on each specific driver is assessed. The more the impact of the demand driver depends on the brand perception, the higher is the impact of the brand. For a very functional driver such as price, the brand impact will be marginal, while a purely emotional driver such as "cool image" will completely depend on the communication of the brand. The relative importance of the demand drivers is then multiplied with the impact of the brand to derive the overall brand contribution.

"Brand Impact" is a percentage with which the intangible earnings will be multiplied to derive "Brand Earnings," that is, the profit directly attributable to the brand. The brand contribution varies significantly in particular by industry but also in the same categories as some product or service offers are more brand dependent than others. The brand contribution concept is widely accepted and used albeit each consulting firm has a different name for the same process to brand its approach.

Most of the accounting firms tend to focus on financial valuations for balance sheets and financial transactions. They tend to use a simpler approach as they derive the brand contribution from comparable royalty rates. The issues arising from using comparable licensing or royalty rates for valuing brands have been discussed earlier. They should be used for crosschecking if reasonably comparable transactions are available but not as a primary valuation approach.

The value of the brand is derived from the sum of the discounted brand earnings for the selected segments. Given the longevity of many brands, it is fair to assume that their value creation will exceed the explicit forecast period be it five or ten years. This requires to determine the Brand Earnings of the last forecast year and the growth rate of these earnings into perpetuity. This residual value can contribute to more than half of the overall value. It is therefore important to be transparent about which growth rate has been applied. In most cases a growth rate in line with long-term inflation will be a reasonably conservative assumption.

For most valuations, the NPV effective cash flows will amount to about 30 years (obviously depending on the growth forecast). This assumption is fair as most of the leading global brands are older than 30 years. In fact, brands such as Coca-Cola and Goldman Sachs are older than 100 years. This compares with the average lifespan of an S&P 500 company of about 25 years. With respect to the forecast brand earnings as well as the terminal growth rate aggressive "hockey stick" like growth scenarios should be avoided unless there is compelling evidence for it (which is rarely the case). Once the Brand Earnings forecast and the terminal growth rate have been determined, they need to be discounted to an NPV. This requires applying an appropriate discount rate that reflects the risk profile of brand earnings.

Here the creativity of most brand-specific valuation approaches has resulted in questionable approaches. Most use some type of brand scoring or assessment model to create a factor that drives the discount rate or is added as a premium to the risk-free rate represented by the yield on government bonds. While the notion of assessing the risk of a brand to certain factors is understandable, the implementation of this notion has created financially unsound approaches. After all, brand valuation is designed to translate the value creation of brands into the language of finance. It, therefore, needs to follow sound financial valuation concepts.

Unfortunately, the brand risk assessment models of nearly all brand-specific valuation approaches fail badly in this aspect. They mostly create unsound discount rates that do more harm than good for the art and science of brand valuation. For greater accuracy, the risk aspects of the brand should be factored into the forecast and the discount rate should be kept simple.

In most cases, the cost of capital of the underlying business or industry will provide a more appropriate discount rate than the proprietary approaches. The technical aspects of the valuation illustrate the particular difficulty in valuing brands as it requires sound understanding of financial and marketing aspects. A failure on either side will impair the validity of the overall valuation.

USE OF BRAND VALUATION

As brand valuation is a complex science, the question arises: What is the benefit of going through such an exercise? There are many management and financial applications that require financial values. The most prominent one is brand management. If brands are important business assets accounting for up to 80 percent of company value (and about a third on average), then managing their value creation is a key management task. This includes managing all details of the brand value chain, including customer experience, consistent communications at all levels as well as product and service delivery. Brand valuation is also crucial for assessing the ROI of marketing and branding expenditures overall as well as for specific brand building initiatives such as advertising campaigns or sponsorships.

Strategic and tactical management decisions can be guided by brand valuation. For example, when two institutions with strong brands merge, then brand valuation can guide the decision of which brand to use for the merged business and how to migrate the organization toward the new brand. The valuation provides an objective view on the value creation of the brands involved and reduces the politics, which often lead to choosing the brand of the stronger partner of the transaction.

Brand valuation is also useful in assessing the ROI of a specific initiative and to guide the investment allocation between different brand building initiatives, including marketing and media mix as well as R&D, product design, and distribution channels. In addition, brand valuation provides management accounting information that is crucial for managing the single most valuable asset in most companies. Samsung Electronics is a good example for a company that has used brand value as KPI for senior management and marketing personnel. It has guided the company's marketing investments and has helped to make Samsung one of the fastest growing global brands.

Next to brand management, there are also a wide range of financial transactions for which brand valuation is required. The obvious one is the recognition of brands on balance sheets upon acquisitions as discussed earlier. International as well as most national accounting standards require after an acquisition to split up the acquired goodwill into separate categories of which brand is an important one. These balance sheet valuations are now predominantly conducted by accounting firms using the royalty relief approach.

Brand valuation is also used in M&A transactions where the brand constitutes a key value driver and asset. Over the last couple of decades, there has been an increasing amount of asset-backed securitizations where a brand or a portfolio of brands is used to back bond issues. Some of these so-called esoteric asset-based securitizations have raised nearly $2 billion in financing (see Dunkin Brands, 2007).

Another important area for brand valuation is licensing. There are two areas of brand licensing. The first one is an internal licensing of brands to subsidiary companies to manage the brand assets more consistently and effectively. Sometimes this involves tax-efficient structures where a brand holding company is located in a low tax jurisdiction and receives the royalties from subsidiaries in higher tax location for the use of the corporation's brand assets (e.g., Shell). Then there is the licensing of brands to third parties. (The fashion designer Pierre Cardin has made a business out of only licensing his brand name.) Or a company sells the license for the use of its brand in a different application or market. For example, Caterpillar receives substantial royalty income from licensing its CAT brand to toy and cloth manufacturers.

CONCLUSION

Brand valuation has come a long way since it emerged in the late 1980s. It has changed the perception of brands as key business assets and created recognition among the C-suite that brands are among the most valuable assets a company owns.

Acquired brands are now found on companies' balance sheets, and the management attention to brands has increased significantly. Brand valuation was instrumental in professionalizing brand management and providing a value-based approach to the management of brand assets. Brand valuation is now an established discipline, and the annual brand value league tables published by various branding and marketing agencies still create some media buzz although the initial excitement has subsided.

Although most of these proprietary valuation approaches include finically questionable elements, they follow the method described earlier. There have been several attempts to create some minimum consensus around brand valuation approaches. While this exists for the above-described principles, there is still too much confusion and lack of transparency about the different approaches used. This is evidenced by the difference in the value each consulting firm calculates for the same brand.

At times these differences can exceed 100 percent and are too large to indicate a clear consensus. However, it must not be forgotten that brand valuation like most valuations is as much an art as much as it is a science. Different assumptions result in different outcomes and values. The complexities and discrepancies notwithstanding brand valuation are an established management tool that is now widely used by leading companies around the world. It has professionalized brand management and established brands as one of the most important business assets any organization can have. For that reason, brand valuation can only increase in importance in the future.

REFERENCES

Burger King Holdings Inc. (2011). *Burger King Holdings Inc. Annual Report.*

Dunkin Brands (2007). *Annual Report.*

Lindemann, J. (2004). "The financial Value of Brands," in R. Clifton (Ed.), *Brands and Branding*, 2nd edition. *The Economist.* Princeton, New Jersey: Bloomberg Press.

———. (2010). *The Economy of Brands.* London: Pallgrave Macmillan.

Salinas, G. (2009). *The International Brand Valuation Manual.* New York: Wiley.

Section 4
Together We Stand

Chapter 14

Co-branding

Tom Blackett

In its purest form, co-branding is a collaborative venture designed to advance the interests of two (or more) parties in a considered, strategic fashion. Legally, the parties concerned are independent entities and their intention is to together create something new—a product, a service, or an enterprise—the scope of which falls outside their individual areas of capability or expertise but which jointly is attainable. The choice of the right partner is therefore key, and the marriage of the two brands must be given a clear rationale that underpins the benefit to the customer.

Sometimes this rationale is provided in the uniqueness and appeal of the new product or service thus created; sometimes it lies in the novelty of two (or more) known and trusted brand names coming together, albeit in the provision of a "generic" service or product. Whatever, it is often a feat of conjuring: requiring the skills of the matchmaker, abundant patience, goodwill, and a little luck. Successful co-branding is not easy to pull off, but it can prove to be both rewarding and profitable: moving brands on, taking them into new markets and generally providing the refreshment brands need to keep them sharp and relevant.

Co-brands are now familiar, generally welcomed and usually successful. In a world that has become sophisticated in its appreciation of branded goods and services, their appearance is unlikely to cause undue incredulity—and therefore rejection without trial. This is because the partners involved will usually have gone to great lengths to ensure that their union results in an attractive product, makes sense to their customers, and provides a decent return on investment. Above all, they will have assured themselves that it will enhance their brand.

POST-WAR UNITED KINGDOM: A HISTORICAL PERSPECTIVE AND A VERY EARLY CO-BRAND

I grew up in the United Kingdom in the years following the end of the Second World War. This was a time of austerity: after six years of total war the country was on the verge of bankruptcy and the population exhausted. Food rationing and shortages lasted for several years, into the 1950s, and everywhere was a sense of a country struggling to come to terms with profound economic, social, and cultural changes. For the British, there was no "peace dividend," just slow and painful recovery.

Nevertheless, there were highlights. The Festival of Britain, in 1952, designed to make the British people aware of the technical and cultural achievements of the post-war period; the Queen's coronation in 1953; and the arrival of commercial television in 1955 were all events that in their different ways lifted public morale and helped to forge the new Britain.

It was the birth of commercial television that elevated brands to a level of public awareness that none but a few had previously enjoyed. My generation—the "Baby Boomers" of the 1940s and 1950s—grew up with television advertising, and I think we were especially influenced by this phenomenon. Accordingly, we became the first generation to view brands as quotidian, part of national life: we sang the jingles, chanted the slogans, and came to identify with brands to a much greater extent than did our parents.

Shell and BP were then—and are now—two of the leading petrol and oil brands in the United Kingdom. And they were—for all their intense rivalry—probably the very first example of co-branding in this country. In 1932, ShellMex and BP Ltd was formed, when both companies decided to merge their U.K. marketing and distribution operations, partly in response to the difficult economic conditions of the times. Petrol tankers branded "ShellMex-BP" were a common sight on the roads throughout the country, until 1966 when the joint venture was wound up.

To many in the increasingly brand-conscious world of the 1950s, the "ShellMex-BP" co-brand was a paradox. In common with their competitors—Esso, National Benzol, and Mobil—both Shell and BP maintained individually branded advertising and sold their petrol to customers at individually branded garage forecourts (there were no service stations in those days); yet they shared distribution and marketing under their joint names. Here was an example of a joint venture driven by entirely pragmatic reasons but which largely ignored the rules of brand differentiation, demolishing any claims either party may have made at the time for the superiority of its fuel.

To petrol retailers the purpose of the co-branded distribution service would have been clear, but this would not have been obvious to consumers. For me, at the time, it was my first exposure to co-branding. I was far too young to have anything other than a child's understanding of brands, but I knew that brands signified differences, and here there was something odd going on. In retrospect I now see these were the contradictions that can arise if no clear rationale is supplied for why two erstwhile competitors had come together.[1]

WHAT IS CO-BRANDING?

Back in 1932, when ShellMex-BP was created in the United Kingdom, the term "co-branding" did not exist. So, what is co-branding, and why has its use become so widespread?

Over the last 30 years or so, we have witnessed extraordinary growth in world trade. Much of this has been driven by developments in the "BRIIC" markets (Brazil, Russia, India, Indonesia, and

[1] Many years later, I learned that for some time after the termination of the ShellMex-BP joint venture, a significant proportion of the public, particularly older customers who had grown familiar with the relationship over many years, mistakenly continued to believe that there was some sort of connection between the two companies.

China), where rapidly increasing prosperity has created huge markets for consumer goods and services. In the more mature markets, too, there has been steady growth accompanied by technological developments, which a few years ago would have been quite inconceivable. The onset of the financial crisis, beginning in 2008 and continuing to drag on at the time of writing, slowed this growth in the West but the trend overall remains upward. These factors have helped to create a climate of commercial opportunity that is unmatched in the history of the world.

For many companies in a hurry, the formation of joint ventures with like-minded partners provides a way ahead, and co-branding has increasingly become a way of helping brand owners exploit the equities in their brands at low cost and risk. But the term "co-branding" is relatively new to the business vocabulary and is used to encompass a wide range of partnership activities involving the combination of two (or more) brands.

Thus, co-branding could be considered to include official sponsorship, where Coca-Cola and McDonald's lend their name to the London Olympics, partnering with the Olympics brand; retailing, where in the U.K. Esso forecourts host Tesco stores; financial services, where BA and Amex offer a jointly branded charge card; fine dining, where celebrity chef Gordon Ramsay has his own branded restaurant at Claridge's; or alcoholic drinks, where Gordon's gin is premixed with Schweppes tonic water. The list is endless.

Put simply, co-branding is a form of cooperation between two (or more) brands with significant customer recognition, in which all the participants' brand names are used—and which produces something new or better, over and above the capabilities of the constituent brands. Co-branding is a superior form of joint venture, a collaboration that produces added values for the customer, irrespective of whether the customer is a "middle man" (like a petrol retailer) or the ultimate consumer.

TYPES OF CO-BRANDING

Broadly, there are four main types of co-branding: here expressed in terms of the level of "shared value" they create.

Reach-Awareness Co-branding

The lowest level of shared value creation occurs in situations where cooperation enables the parties involved rapidly to increase awareness of their brands through exposure to their partner's customer base. Many direct marketing-based partnerships are justified on this basis, and co-branding between credit card suppliers and other parties illustrates the principle well.

The American Airlines A-Advantage Visa card, teamed with Citi, is a good example. Both parties leverage their high net worth customer databases, and are complementary and potentially symbiotic (the Holy Grail of co-branding). Purchasers using the card to book flights earn points and get rewards; American Airlines and Citi gain customers: it's a win-win.

Visa is perhaps one of the most successful and well-known innovators of reach-awareness co-branding. With selective partners Visa has gained worldwide recognition with over 1 billion cards in more than 130 countries, supporting nearly $2 trillion in transactions annually.

Values' Endorsement Co-branding

The next level of shared value creation occurs where the relationship is specifically designed to include endorsement of each other's brand values and positioning or both.

Credit cards again provide a good way of illustrating the concept. In recent years, many charities have launched co-branded "affinity" credit cards with a bank or transaction processing company. In the United States, The Nature Conservancy offers cards in conjunction with Bank of America, as does Worldwide Fund for Nature in the United Kingdom. The bank, or processing company, may generally pay the brand owning organization a bonus for each new account generated, plus a percentage of every transaction charged to the card. Corporate sponsorship also illustrates this; the British retailer Tesco co-promotes Cancer Research UK's annual Race for Life fund raiser, paying a fee, and has become a major supporter of the charity. The benefit to Tesco is entirely intangible—a burnishing of its image, if you will—while the benefit for Cancer Research UK is vital revenues for research, and the endorsement of the United Kingdom's biggest and most successful retailer, lifting its image out of the rarified world of the laboratory.

Ingredient Co-branding

The third level of shared value creation is ingredient co-branding, where a brand noted for the market-leading qualities of its product supplies that item as a component of another branded product. Diet Coke with NutraSweet (aspartame) is a famous example of this genre. At one point in the early life of the Diet Coke brand, the manufacturer dropped NutraSweet and substituted an unbranded artificial sweetener; such was the outcry from consumers that the company was compelled to restore NutraSweet. Intel, the supplier of microprocessors to many leading manufacturers of laptops, is another example of a brand that has become an indispensable partner in the product and brand "mix." Without the Intel brand, the value of the branded laptop would almost certainly be greatly diminished.

Ingredient branding features in the performance sector of the automobile market, where technical collaboration is commonplace. The Cooper Car Company, which specialized in designing engines for Formula One motorsport, has collaborated for many years with the manufacturers of the Mini (now BMW). Similarly, Cosworth, another Formula One specialist, has had a long relationship with Ford in the United Kingdom, and Cosworth-adapted engines have featured in many of Ford's saloon cars over the last 40 years. Mini-Cooper and Ford Cosworth are synonymous with performance; as such they add a dash of excitement and glamour at the top of their respective model ranges.

Perhaps unsurprisingly, the range of potential partners for an ingredient co-branding venture is very small in most markets. The product or service must lend itself to a junior–senior combination, and there must be two strong brands already existing that can agree to co-brand. Alternatively, there must be a junior partner, such as NutraSweet or Intel, which is an essential component of the finished product, has the unique product features to sustain a brand, and is willing to invest to build brand strength. In some cases, for example,

Intel, the ingredient brand may grow to be more valuable and powerful than the dominant brand appearing on the finished item. In the clothing industry, Lycra and Woolmark are two such dominant partners. The ingredient brand may in such circumstances be the stronger motivator in the purchase decision.

The essence of ingredient co-branding is that a manufacturer provider, wishing to convey focused messages about the attributes and values of their product, uses and promotes branded components whose own brand image reinforces the desired attributes and values.

Complementary Competence Co-branding

At the fourth and highest level of co-branding, two powerful and complementary brands combine to produce a product that is more than the sum of the parts and relies on each partner committing a selection of its core skills and competencies to that product on an ongoing basis. Whereas ingredient co-branding requires the "junior" partner to contribute a specific tangible component to the "senior" partner's product, complementary competence co-branding involves a range of components, which may be tangible or intangible.

A well-known British example of complementary competence co-branding is the tie-up between Esso and Tesco Express to establish 24-hour mini-supermarkets at petrol stations. It repeats the formula pioneered by 7-Eleven with Mobil in the United States and with Shell in Australia and extends it by using the brand of Britain's leading supermarket chain.

To this venture, Esso brings its brand strength as one of the country's top three petrol retailers, its array of well-sited locations, and its operational expertise in running petrol stations. The benefits it would expect to reap are increased sales volumes compared to operating the petrol stations and shop on its own, plus increased brand loyalty from customers in return for the improved service its stations are able to provide.

For its part, Tesco Express brings the brand strength of the Tesco supermarket group, its knowledge of consumer buying patterns and lifestyles, its purchasing expertise and market power, its distribution infrastructure, and its operational expertise in running supermarkets.

An interesting—and highly contemporary—variant of this type of co-branding can be seen in the United States. Here fast food restaurants such as Pizza Hut and Taco Bell increasingly share the same building—and sometimes the same counter, menu boards, and staff. The motive of course is reduced operating costs in difficult times: Pizza Hut and Taco Bell share the same parent company, Yum! Brands. (This partnership has featured extensively on YouTube.) The two brands also share, to a large extent, similar target consumers. So while the attractions of cost reduction are obvious, these must be offset against the possibility of cannibalization.

It is perhaps worth mentioning one further type of co-branding, which I shall call "implied provenance" co-branding.

To illustrate this: Volkswagen (VW) acquired a stake in the Czechoslovakian motor manufacturer Skoda in 1991; this was increased to a controlling share in 1994. The fortunes of Skoda—once thought of as something of a music hall joke—have improved dramatically since then. VW has invested substantially in design and manufacturing at Skoda and, critically, has made absolutely no secret of its ownership of the former east European brand. Nor has it sought actively to quash rumors that Skoda models have the same platform as those of VW. The connection between the hitherto down-market Czech brand and mighty VW has been hugely beneficial to Skoda, supplying the confidence through association that has succeeded greatly in overcoming consumer skepticism in the West.

In the same way, we have the Smart car, the product of a joint venture between Mercedes and Swatch. Neither partner has sought to conceal its participation in the project, but, equally, neither partner's name appears on the car itself. Perhaps Mercedes feels that an overt association with the idiosyncratic Smart car would not be helpful to the image of its range of beautifully designed automobiles. But Swatch, originally, had no such reservations: as the originator of the concept it argued strenuously for the inclusion of its name; Mercedes, however, refused. It ruled that a neutral name should be used and chose Smart, the acronym of "Swatch Mercedes Art," the original code name for the project.

U.K. supermarkets make no attempt to disabuse consumers of the provenance of their "private label" products. (Private labels are the supermarkets' own brands and account for over one third of all grocery purchases in the United Kingdom.) The retailers would welcome consumers assuming that their private labels were all supplied by leading manufacturers—and have sometimes in the past adopted branding for these products that has come very close to that of the big brands. Most manufacturers, on the other hand, want nothing less, and companies such as Kellogg's have run campaigns to reassure consumers that they do not supply product for retailers' private labels.

But such is the power of the retail trade that manufacturers can feel pressured to acquiesce. The famous toy manufacturer Lego was approached in the late 1990s by a major retailer who asked to be supplied with Lego bricks which it would package and sell under its own brand. Lego's production and finance people were in favor of this proposal—improved factory utilization and return on assets—but the marketing team were strongly against this. So closely associated is the unique Lego brick with the Lego name, they argued, that it would be tantamount to giving away the brand. The retailer's proposal was rejected.

Implied provenance co-branding does not really belong to the taxonomy of co-branding. It is, rather, marketing "sleight of hand." It is certainly connected with shared value creation; but as it relies not upon an explicit link between the brands concerned but upon serendipity, we should rule it out of formal consideration, but keep it very firmly in mind for its undoubted efficacy in image building (and possible image destruction).

THE ADVANTAGES AND RISKS OF CO-BRANDING

It is right that we should spend a little time considering the pros and cons of co-branding. The last few pages have dealt almost exclusively with the successes—or at least those examples of co-branding that have become well known: naturally so, because it is really only the successes which get written about.

My friend and colleague Bob Boad addressed these subjects in a masterly way in our 1999 book *Co-Branding: The Science of Alliance.* I shall attempt to summarize—and where necessary bring up to date—his analysis. This was based upon his many years of experience at BP, which as we have seen has been very active in the field of joint ventures, many of which have resulted in it sharing its brand with a new partner.

Benefits

The chief benefits of co-branding can be summarized as follows:

- For established brands, co-branding offers the opportunity to create an entirely new income stream or to boost earnings of existing products.
- For new brands, it may confer an immediate credibility in a skeptical marketplace. Co-branding may reduce the need for costly investment in targeting new markets, because the partner may already be well established there, or it may be a way of overcoming non-financial barriers to entry, because the partner may enjoy strong popular acceptance.

Similarly co-branding may be a way of gaining additional brand exposure, of reducing risk, of speeding investment payback, of facilitating price-profit maximization, or of providing a novel way of communicating with the market. It can be used to gain short-term tactical advantage as well as for longer term strategic purposes. And when times are tough, larger companies with extensive brand portfolios focused on specific market sectors may cross-promote their brands, thus stretching further their marketing budgets. Let us look at some of these.

Royalty Income

Manufacturers of components or ingredients can find that a co-branding deal offers the possibility of incremental income, as our old friends NutraSweet and Intel have shown. Both these brands have demonstrated their worth by proving that they enhance the overall product offer and are therefore well worth a share of the additional profits forthcoming. They genuinely "add value" and create a premium.

Sales Boost

Co-branding can provide a significant boost to well-established brands. It has already been commented upon that Mini's partnership with Cooper supplies "monkey gland" to an otherwise middle of the road model range. The average consumer may not be able to afford a Mini-Cooper, but their pride of ownership—and importantly the perceptions of their peers—is boosted by the presence of a higher specification model in the range.

New Markets

Co-branding can help a brand owner enter new markets. Volkswagen's long-term strategy is to become a dominant player in the mass market for automobiles. Its initial investment and eventual takeover of Skoda were designed to achieve this strategy in Eastern Europe. It realized that it could not simply march in with its VW brand, but should rather capitalize on familiarity with and affection for the incumbent Skoda. The Czech government, the major shareholder in Skoda, realizing that here was a national asset starved of necessary investment, was glad to sell off its share in return for a healthy premium, the development of a national brand with potential international prestige, and guaranteed jobs in manufacturing (Skoda plants have since also been opened in Sarajevo, Bosnia and Herzegovina, and Maharashtra, India).

Cross-Promotion

Cross-promotion is a popular contemporary concept, driven largely by the need for companies to make their advertising budgets stretch further and leverage their competitive edge. "Brand bundling" is a variant: it is the practice of companies marketing multiple brands at once. Not only can it be cheaper to show a variety of products in one advert, this style of promotion also encourages cross-selling.

In the United Kingdom, this technique has long been used by the retail sector. Tesco, for example, has used the same TV ad to promote multiple products in a range, while River Island might use its ads to encourage cross-selling by showing which jacket matches a certain pair of jeans.

Procter & Gamble has been making the most of this type of collective marketing by buying all the advertising spots in particular programs and showing "makeover breaks," where a woman is made over using multiple P&G brands such as Max Factor make-up, Olay face cream, and Aussie hair products.

P&G has also bundled other brands together with its "Science Behind the Beauty" spots, where entire ad breaks are dedicated to explaining how Head & Shoulders, Oral B toothbrushes, and Olay work, using white-coated technicians to give credibility to the message. P&G insists that brand bundling provides a "great return on investment."

But critics of brand bundling doubt whether consumers know or care that certain brands are made by the same company, and that, misguidedly, the company sponsoring such activity thinks that the corporate brand is more important than individual product brands.[2]

Additional Consumer Benefits

By linking with other, complementary, businesses, companies have been able to offer their customers a variety of incentives for using their services or buying their products. These are generally referred to as "loyalty programs." For example, a very wide range of companies have introduced credit or charge card facilities: retailers, airlines, hotels, charities, oil companies, and utilities; such facilities are a natural fit for retail, airline, hotel, etc., customers, and banks and credit card providers are keen to mine these customers.

Nectar is an interesting co-brand partner and the United Kingdom's largest loyalty program. Over 18 million collectors earn Nectar points when shopping for groceries, do-it-yourself products and holidays, and paying for utilities, flights, eating out, petrol, and car servicing. And collectors can earn Nectar points when they shop online at over 500 leading online retailers. Nectar also offers the Nectar Credit Card from American Express, where use of the card earns bonus points.

[2] I am grateful to *Marketing Week*, August 25, 2011, for these comments on brand bundling.

Integrated Consumer Services

The co-branding relationship between Shell and Tesco Metro in the United Kingdom has already been mentioned, and such relationships have become commonplace. Again in the United Kingdom, Moto, which owns the right to manage certain motorway service areas, now partners with Burger King, EDC (the eat and drink company), Costa, M&S Simply Food, Greggs and WH Smith to supply a comprehensive range of catering and leisure services to travelers, including fuel. Not all of these brands are available at every stop however, and canny Moto, aware of the loyalties and preferences of the traveling public, features signs advertising an M&S stop coming up in one mile, or a Costa stop, etc. The Moto brand benefits through association with these brands and is enhanced accordingly.

The presence of all these brands helps to enhance the image of the main service operator, through offering a range of hospitality services that the operator itself would find it impossible to provide to the quality required and in a profitable fashion.

Internationally, BP has Wild Bean Cafes at many of its BP Connect petrol stations in four continents. Wild Bean Cafes (owned by BP) offer Barista-style coffee and snack foods. The appeal of fresh coffee is universal, while the snacks can be adjusted to suit national tastes. The Wild Bean Café concept is an exciting one, located as it is on major roads and outside the usual urban milieu of the likes of Starbucks, Costa, and Café Nero.

These are just a few of the opportunities offered by co-branding, and the benefits that can accrue. Clearly co-branding can be a powerful and versatile tool, offering major strategic and financial advantages to those who "get it right"—but it is not without risk, as the next section discusses.

Risks—What Can Go Wrong?

Choosing the right partner is fundamental to successful co-branding. Choosing the wrong partner poses considerable risks to your brand's reputation. It, therefore, pays to make sure you thoroughly investigate the background, culture, and values of your potential partner in order to minimize the risk of unexpected problems.

The co-branding agreement must provide for the possibility of termination in the event that your partner suffers a serious reputation problem, to minimize the knock-on damage to your own brand.

Financial greed, corporate incompatibility, shifts in strategy, and sheer market attrition: all these things—and more—can disrupt the partnership. While it is difficult to legislate for these hurdles, it is wise to be aware that they can—and do—arise.

Financial Greed

Co-branding activity ought sensibly to be regarded as something that contributes to the development *of* long-term brand value, not as a way of making a "fast buck." It will often be prudent for the brand owners to accept a modest return in the early stages of a relationship, to allow a reasonable proportion of the profits to be re-invested in building up the co-branded product or service. A fair split of the profits is also necessary because only by allowing the partner to earn a reasonable reward from the project can it be motivated to develop the co-branding as a long-term relationship.

Potential Incompatibility

This is always a risk: businesses have personalities and like humans they do not always find the characters of others to their liking. The attitudes and values of a proposed co-branding partner may differ significantly from those of your own company and the potential for such divergence to cause friction should not be underestimated. Conflicts in relation to day-to-day matters, such as dealing with customer complaints, can prove just as big an irritant as disputes over broader policy issues, such as environmental concerns. However, cultural differences can often prove a major stumbling block.

Major cultural differences dogged the relationship between the Russian oil company TNK, owned by a group of Russian "oligarchs," and BP. The two companies formed an equal partnership, TNK-BP, in 2003, to explore and extract oil and natural gas. After years of acrimony (during which the BP chief executive of the joint venture was at one point forced to flee Moscow and carry on his duties from a secret European location), in late 2012, BP sold its stake in

TNK-BP to the Russian oil major Rosneft. BP has now taken a stake in Rosneft and intends to carry on its Arctic exploration with its new partner.

Shift in Strategy

Since its public listing in early 2012, Facebook has been under pressure from investors to come up with strategies that increase revenues from advertising and partnerships.

Zynga, the maker of "Farm Ville" and "Mafia Wars," makes most of its money selling virtual goods on Facebook, and its growth and success has been tethered to the rise of the social network. (The availability of games on Facebook has been established in a recent survey as a powerful attraction to users.) *Marketing* magazine, November 30, 2012, reported:

> In 2010, the two companies struck a five-year deal, handing Zynga, which was one of the first games developers on Facebook, an advantage over rival games publishers through various aspects of exclusivity.

Facebook and Zynga were effectively a co-brand, due to the very high degree of interdependence between the two.

However, under a new agreement announced in a regulatory filing "Zynga will be free to ditch Facebook's login, ad units and payments services on its site, enabling it to operate as a standalone games business."

According to the filing, Zynga will no longer be required to use Facebook as its exclusive distribution partner for games. Zynga's games will still appear on Facebook, but there will no longer be cross-promotion directing users to its website. It also means that Facebook can now develop its own games, although it says it has no plans to do so.

"The two companies listed within seven months of each other. It became apparent that Zynga was moving out of the shadow of Facebook in March, when it unveiled plans for its own freestanding games platform."

The report ends: "Last month, Zynga announced it was axing 5% of its global staff and closing its UK office."

Did Zynga jump—or was it pushed? Whatever, a shift in focus has clearly taken place whereby Zynga is to pursue its future more as a freestanding business (and brand), and the co-branding relationship with Facebook is now effectively dissolved.

Brand Dilution

Co-branding can have a dilutive effect on a brand if the project fails. This can of course be minimized by careful partner selection, rigorous evaluation of the co-branding opportunity, and high production/delivery standards. But even if these are adhered to, it must be remembered that the two (or more) partners are *sharing* the kudos that success brings, and equally sharing the opprobrium—and reputational damage—that an unsuccessful collaboration may cause.

The joint venture Sony Ericsson was formed in late 2001 to develop, manufacture, and market mobile phones. Sony Ericsson's strategy was to release new models capable of digital photography as well as other multimedia capabilities such as downloading and viewing video clips and personal information. The venture struggled, however, following the launch of Apple's iPhone in 2007, leading to fear that the company was in danger of decline, in common with its stricken rival Motorola.

Despite cash injections by the parents, Sony Ericsson continued to lose volume and market share, and on October 27, 2011, Sony announced that it would acquire Ericsson's stake in the joint venture. Sony Ericsson had been unable to match, let alone exceed the quality of the iPhone and has paid the price of lack of innovation in a market that continues to develop apace.

Time will tell whether the Ericsson and Sony brands will suffer reputational damage as a result of their failed collaboration. Sony has not made a profit since 2008; its brand is spread across numerous electronic products and has little focus—and therefore meaning for consumers. Ericsson is more focused, on telecommunications, yet the brand's ranking in the "Global 500" league table has spluttered along in the last five years. Both brands are lackluster, and their failure in smartphones, while not fatal, is unlikely to advance their reputations.

In summary, the advantages of co-branding outweigh the potential risks. Although there have been some narrow escapes, no famous brand has yet been brought down by an incautious alliance.

DEVELOPING A CO-BRANDING STRATEGY

Unless you are a company whose business is built entirely around forging joint ventures—be they to enhance product development, distribution, or geographical reach—it is unlikely that you will have a co-branding strategy. This is exactly as it should be because, no matter how big is your concern, your approach toward adopting co-branding, appraising opportunities, and evaluating potential partners and their brands should be made on a case-by-case basis.

I have sketched above the different types of co-branding arrangement that exist; these are by no means exclusive to particular sorts of company or within certain sorts of industry. The reality is that companies frequently follow two or more of these approaches, depending upon their objectives, resources, and capabilities. These are largely executional issues, but even the most pragmatic of companies should be aware of the two principal routes that can lead to the adoption of co-branding strategies.

"Top-Down" Route

First there is the "top-down"—systematic—approach where the company decides that it needs a development strategy for its brand(s). The logic runs: we have a brand; this brand has a reputation; can this reputation be leveraged to take the brand into new products, new markets, or new countries? If so, how widely can we "stretch" the brand and where can we market it? And to achieve this, do we have the necessary R&D, manufacturing, and logistical resources—or do we need a partner? And if we need a partner and the partner has a brand, can his/her brand and reputation add anything over and above the practical support he/she can offer? A simple audit of the potential partner's brand, based on customer research, can help to establish whether (a) compatibility and (b) possible synergies exist.

"Bottom-Up" Route

Then there is the "bottom-up"—reactive—approach. Your research and development people have come up with a new product (or service) idea—or you have had an interesting approach from a third party. The financial people run the numbers and, subject to the cost of marketing, the idea is viable. Does the idea fit one of your existing brands, or is it sufficiently distinctive to warrant a brand name of its own?

In terms of execution, there will be pressure to wrap the new idea under an existing brand name (thus minimizing incremental marketing cost)—even though it might represent a significant improvement on or departure from the established brand. This is a perennial issue within companies where innovation is important; do we use the "master brand" approach, proliferating ranges of product variants (such as Kellogg's cereals), or do we opt for "free-standing brands," identifying (frequently similar) products separately (such as Unilever's detergents)?

In a perfect world, the decision should be informed by the degree of originality inherent in the new product idea. But the more original it is, the more risky it may be. Therefore, the inclination—particularly in these austere times—is to position these innovations as "extensions" under master brands, rather than new brands. However, another option is to seek a partner who is willing to put expertise, investment, and, if it adds value, his/her brand name into the project, in order to give it an additional boost.

Both these approaches lead us to the identification and evaluation of potential co-branding partners. This process, which is part subjective, part objective, should be driven by the ultimate goal—the enhancement of your brand through the mitigation of risk and the maximization of the synergies available. How you judge candidates is of course entirely up to you, but "hard" factors such as stability, resources, and reputation are bound to feature high on your list, together with "soft" factors such as culture and compatibility.

Many commentators (I include myself) have in the past likened co-branding to marriage. Up to a point I think this is probably still true. Certainly the injunction from the *Book of Common Prayer* regarding marriage, that it should not be taken in hand "unadvisedly, lightly or wantonly," remains every bit as applicable to co-branding alliances. And like a successful marriage both partners have to keep working on it. But here, perhaps, the parallel ends. Co-branding is essentially a transient activity, and unlike marriage, nobody expects the partnership to last forever. Expectations are therefore shaped accordingly.

Obviously, there must be mutual respect. But neither side should forget that their partner is no more than that: an independent entity, often with very different corporate objectives, and whose interest in collaboration may be driven by very different motives.

Thus, companies interested in forging co-branding relationships should be aware that such relationships are rarely more than a "marriage of convenience." They can in a few instances become something of more lasting duration and in even fewer instances lead to an amalgamation. However, prospective partners should focus overall on (a) the long-term health of the brand they bring to the table and (b) nothing else.

THE FUTURE OF CO-BRANDING

Co-branding has never been, nor ever will be a mainstream marketing activity. But it remains an extremely useful way of refreshing brands, reaching new audiences, and entering new markets.

The developing world offers tremendous opportunities for Western businesses. India is a country of 1.2 billion people, and is set to overtake China as the most populous country on Earth—and unlike China, the population is youthful. Half of all Indians are under 25; this is nearly 10 percent of the world's population. Consider the size of that market, now and in the future. India's growth rate is about five times faster than that of any European Union country. The Indians are young, aspirational, dynamic, democratic, and with a gloriously uninhibited press.

According to Boris Johnson, the mayor of London, writing in the *Daily Telegraph*, November 27, 2012:

> Young Indians these days are like any other global population that finds itself in the throes of embourgeoisement: they are gripped and excited by America and American brands—Google, Coke, Nike, Starbucks, you name it. The biggest foreign food supplier in India is Domino's Pizza, an American firm … Trade between our countries is growing … and there is a natural fit between Britain and India, a cultural and commercial fusion that is growing the whole time. You can see it in cuisine, where restaurants serving Indian food employ more people in the UK than coal, steelmaking and shipbuilding combined … Above all, we can see the fusion in business. Look at the alliance between BP and Mukesh Ambani's Reliance, or at Vodafone's takeover of Hutchinson. Or look at … Jaguar [cars], product of an Indian-owned firm that is made by Brits and exported to China; or look at JCB 3DX backhoe loader, a British machine made by Indians and exported to Africa … India should be one of [the UK's] key partners … Imagine selling a Jaguar to one in every 100,000 Indians. That's a lot of Jags and a lot of jobs.

India is receptive to industrial partnerships and is becoming used to co-branding. There have been co-branded credit cards involving Citibank and Jet Airways, Standard Chartered Bank and Indian Railways, Indian Oil and Citibank, and Citibank and Times of India. There has been Project Drishti, where ₹1 per pack of (P&G's) Whisper has been donated to the National Association for Blind for the benefit of female children. And there have been many examples of Indian manufacturers partnering with "cool" Western brands to attract the burgeoning younger demographic.

And China? In the *Sunday Times* article, June 9, 2013, "Friendless and Cold, the Chinese Dragon Drifts," Michael Sheridan wrote about the difficulties of partnering with China.

> It is no coincidence that the two biggest global trade zones in the making—The European Union's free-trade area with the US, and the American Trans-Pacific Partnership—exclude China. Governments are exhausted by trench warfare over trade. Corporations are weary of intellectual property theft, fraud and haughty officialdom. While the American economy is slouching towards recovery, China's is decelerating.

It would of course be wrong to rule out the possibility of Chinese and Western companies forming co-branding alliances, but at the time of writing the prospect seems distant.

Otherwise, as long as world trade continues to grow so will the opportunities for joint ventures flourish. Co-branding is the lusty infant—occasionally, wayward child—of such partnerships. Those companies who choose to stake their brands in these ventures should think long and hard. NutraSweet had everything to gain and nothing to lose through their tie-up with Coca-Cola. Coca-Cola took all the risk when it allowed the NutraSweet brand name to appear on the can, but the ingredient performed, Diet Coke is now fabulously successful, and the rest is history.

Chapter 15

The Guide to Co-creation

Clare Fuller and Arunima Kapoor

INTRODUCTION

We have been working in the brand space for many years. Over that period, knowledge, experience, and understanding of brands have developed considerably. In the 1970s and 1980s, most people thought of logos, packaging, and advertising when the brand word was mentioned. The world has moved on, and while these disciplines are still important, the concept of brand is now much broader. Others in this book will define brand in their own ways. To us, it means the set of ideas that defines why an organization exists, how it does things, and what it produces.

In spite of access to the growing body of thinking about brands over the years, coupled with substantial investment in research and consultancy advice, as well as increased sophistication in brand management, it was clear to us that many brands were still failing to perform effectively. Too many just didn't achieve what their owners hoped from them. So we stopped to ask ourselves why.

It seemed to us that the key problem was that brands live in a world which is confusing and complex. The people driving brands know this, but the processes they use tend to isolate the different factors or stakeholder groups and understand them separately. What is needed is a way of looking at them together, to understand the dynamics and interrelationship between them.

We realized that existing approaches were not going to achieve this, so we started to explore ways of replicating this messy and complex world in the brand development process. We experimented by bringing different stakeholders together, over longer periods of time, to tackle brand challenges. We invented ways to do this, and at the same time we discovered that consumers—and other stakeholders—are much more motivated and better equipped to help than we might have expected. So, the ideas driving co-creation were born.

It is still quite a new approach that involves moving out of a safe, known, zone. So if you are attracted to the ideas behind co-creation, and you decide to harness them in your business, you might experience some resistance and you may need to be ready to use your arts of persuasion to bring your colleagues on the journey with you.

This chapter explains more about what co-creation is and how it works. It is based on our 10 years' experience working with more than 100 forward thinking and leading brands internationally. They have spanned the B2C and B2B sectors in travel and hospitality, in financial services, in FMCG, in telecom and technology, in healthcare—and beyond.

As you read on, we'll explain how co-creation can help build brands in many different ways. Whether you are starting from scratch, refreshing an established brand, or looking for incremental improvements, co-creation can help you:

- Understand *exactly how your brand is perceived* by people on both the inside and the outside of your organization, and what it means to them
- Decide how your brand should be *positioned* and what it should stand for
- Increase brand *relevance* to stay essential in consumers' lives
- Drive *differentiation* to help your brand stand out and be noticed
- Identify effective ways to *communicate* your brand ideas
- *Innovate* and develop *new products and services* to support your brand and increase revenues and profits
- Build *customer-centricity* internally to make sure everything your brand does adds value to your customers' lives
- Inspire your people—those delivering the brand experience—to *behave* in new and better ways

WHERE HAS CO-CREATION COME FROM?

Over the last 10 years, the term co-creation has been used more and more in the media and on the web.

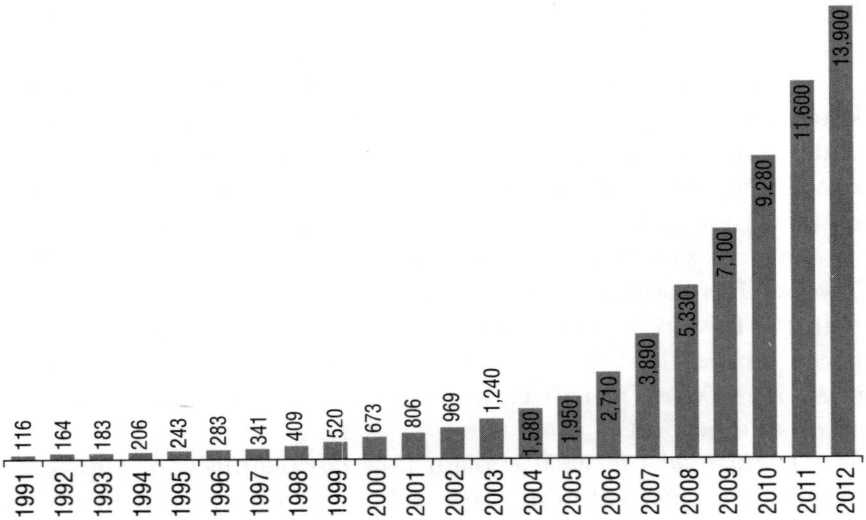

SOURCE: Promise.

As you might imagine given the chart above, it was hard in the early days to convince people that working together with their customers, staff, and management, often in the same room, to build the future of their brand was a good idea. For most companies, customers were statistics, to be watched through a two-way mirror from a safe distance, and heard about in a long report or PowerPoint presentation. All the emphasis was on developing the science of customer understanding and being separate from them to ensure objectivity and avoid contamination of ideas. Co-creation breaches this thinking by blurring, and even removing, these boundaries.

Winning the argument on intellectual grounds was difficult, but there were a few brave clients who were willing to give it a try—often because they operated in very competitive fields and were looking for something different—or because they had tried everything else and were looking for something new. Or, sometimes, because they "just believed."

WHAT CO-CREATION IS ...

We define co-creation as the collaborative process between an organization and its customers, staff, and other stakeholder, which creates mutual value.

Here's a technique to help make sure your dialogue with others is genuinely co-creative.

The Yes, and ... Yes, but ... game

Try discussing your next holiday with your partners. Ask them to make a suggestion about where to go. Try answering all their proposals with something that begins with "yes, but ...."

Let's go to Paris for a holiday!
Yes, but the weather won't be nice at this time.
We can pick the month we like, to ensure better weather?
Yes, but then it will be crowded with tourists and everything will be expensive.

Now try the same exercise, but this time begin your answer with "yes, and ...."

Let's go to Paris for a holiday!
Yes, and we can take long walks by the Seine ....
We can just soak in the city and sit in the cafes.
Yes, and we can go to Monmartre and get our portraits done!

Notice how much difference it makes when you are in "yes, and ..." mode: your partners feel valued, the dialogue is maintained, and you can build ideas together.

This technique is co-creative because it encourages people to build on each other's ideas, rather than shoot them down. It puts people in a collaborative (rather than competitive) mindset and encourages diverse groups to find things in common and work with each other.

True co-creation can be defined by three core principles:

- *It must involve a company and its customers.* From the company side, this doesn't just mean the marketing people: it's important that a broad cross-section of staff from all levels are involved. "Customers" may be consumers or business customers, but the key thing is that co-creation is not something that can be achieved within the company alone, no matter how many different people or functions are involved. More than this, customers are involved as trusted partners or advisors, whose individual opinions are highly valued.

- *It is a two (or more) way dialogue,* where all participants are working together to tackle a challenge, each giving and taking from each other in the search for progress and change. In this respect, it is different from crowd sourcing where a large number of people are invited to contribute ideas and solutions, which are then appraised and evaluated by the brand owners. It is also different from traditional research approaches where customers are placed in a neutral environment, and watched by the "experts" from behind a screen.
- *It is a creative process,* where participants enter into it wanting and expecting something new and different to emerge. Like all successful creative processes, it means exploring the unknown which can feel uncomfortable or make people anxious. This means that the participants need to feel comfortable and secure working together. They need to trust each other, and feel free to try new things and make mistakes.

As you'll notice, people and interaction are key; we use our belief that "relationships are the source of results" to drive the co-creative process. In the early days, it was impossible to achieve all this without getting in the room with people. For a long time, that made co-creation logistically difficult to achieve and expensive. Only the most ambitious and most well-resourced companies could enter into it. But technology has changed all that, and we (by which we mean all practitioners) have proved that companies and their customers can get together, enter into a true dialogue, and be creative online, provided they get proper facilitation and support.

… AND WHAT CO-CREATION IS NOT

When we first started using the word "co-creation," people would often look blank, or ask us what it meant. Nowadays, we are more likely to get the response, "yes, we do that around here." But as we probe, it turns out that people are talking about many different things when they say this.

Some people are talking about the same thing that we are, others simply do not understand, or want to get on the bandwagon without really changing the way they do things. True co-creation can be a difficult and time-consuming process that involves listening—really listening—to other people's points of view and being willing to change. For many companies, the constraints of time, money, or even patience get in the way. People want a sexy solution and their boss wants it by tomorrow. So any process that involves many different stakeholders can attract the "co-creation" label. Calling something co-creation often appears to add value, whatever is under the hood.

Co-creation is different from other approaches which sometimes sound similar. Here are some examples: Mass collaboration (such as Wikipedia) involves many people making individual contributions to help build something. Mass customization (practiced by Dell) is the use of flexible manufacturing systems to produce custom output. Open innovation (such as Lego) is where a company asks consumers to solve a problem (which could be to develop products, services, and paths to market) independently, rather than collaboratively.

A PRACTICAL EXAMPLE OF CO-CREATION IN ACTION

One of the most successful early examples of co-creation by a leading brand was work at British Airways back in the 1990s. The airline was looking for breakthrough ideas that would drive yield and margin growth. They embarked on a series of bold initiatives, working with customers, which led to a string of successful innovations.

How Co-creation Built Brand Relevance and Differentiation at British Airways and Drove Innovation

FLAT BEDS AT BRITISH AIRWAYS

Issue: BA's Club World cabins weren't full. All airlines had the same business class product, the "cradle seat," and customers couldn't see the benefit of flying one airline over another. Attempts to differentiate through service failed to have significant impact on consumers. The British Airways brand was suffering—it was no longer seen as different or special, margins were under pressure, and brand loyalty was slipping.

Process: BA launched a program to define 21st-century air travel, looking to upgrade every cabin. Club World was given prominence (being the most profitable cabin). The process included a series of co-creation workshops with customers, crew, ground staff, travel agents, travel coordinators, and BA management.

Results: Through the co-creation workshops, it became apparent that the resounding customer need was sleep. They wanted the flat beds already available in First Class to be introduced in Club World. This seemed impossible as it had never been done before; BA would have to rip out 1.7 seats to accommodate one flat bed. However, management couldn't ignore what customers were repeatedly demanding. It led to an 18-month program, involving the redesign of Club World seats, cabin layout, and commercial cases, resulting in flat beds in Club World. This made BA the only airline at the time to offer flat beds (therefore sleep) in business class across its fleet.

This breakthrough led to:

- The world's first "Beds in Business" in 2000, increasing revenue per seat by 60 percent and doubling customer satisfaction in the first year.
- Overall yields increased 8 percent and brand loyalty increased 23 percent in a declining market.
- Other long-lasting innovations from the co-creation process include the world's first Arrivals Lounge, Well-Being in the Air, and the "service excellence" positioning.

WHEN SHOULD YOU USE CO-CREATION?

Brand owners often ask us how and when they should think about using co-creation. Clearly, there are some areas of your business where your key inputs will come from professionals with deep expertise in the topic, and co-creation is less relevant. These areas include legal and financial matters, but also other areas within marketing, such as preparing a brief, executing the specifics of a product or service, or designing visual and verbal communications.

For us, co-creation is a philosophy as well as a set of specific tools. We fundamentally believe that in most areas of your business that touch customers, working together with them and your staff will generate superior solutions. However, if you look around you, you will find that co-creation has had a bigger impact in some areas than others.

- It is powerful in the *service* sector because it involves and inspires those people interacting with customers to think and behave in new ways.
- It is powerful in *FMCG* where companies are highly competitive because it can help them find both big breakthroughs and the sort of small changes that can generate a big cumulative revenue impact.
- It is powerful in *highly regulated industries* where people are risk averse and/or feel that change is impossible, because it gives them permission to think beyond their normal boundaries.
- It is a powerful tool for leaders who want to *disrupt* the status quo because it can lead to breakthroughs and totally new concepts.
- It is a powerful way to tackle challenges that require a deep understanding of emotions (money, communications, healthcare, and personal care, for example) through its ability to explore feelings, be creative, and model change.
- It is powerful for *startups*, and for brands which seek *reinvention*, because both seek to change the way people see things, and the process itself replicates the journey that customers and staff need to go on to achieve success.

... and the list goes on. But like any approach, co-creation is not a panacea. In sectors where consumers are outwardly directed and looking for the brand to tell them what to think and feel (high status luxury goods such as watches or fashion are examples), co-creation may have less to offer. In these cases, the consumer wants to believe the brand knows better than they do and desires a level of detachment that the co-creation process could undermine.

WHAT DOES THE CO-CREATION PROCESS LOOK LIKE?

We have talked quite a lot so far about the philosophy and principles driving co-creation, so this is a good time to look more closely at how you can actually do it.

There're two key ways we can co-create.

Live: With all key stakeholders in the same room working together to "build the future" or "solve a business challenge." For example, this can also involve physically building a prototype of what a product or service should look and feel like, with consumers.

Online: In an (typically closed, invitation only) online community, where we invite consumers, specifically recruited to suit the brand and the project requirements, to work collaboratively over a period of months to years. We use our communities to explore questions, create ideas, and develop concepts, using a combination of brainstorms, polls, live online focus groups, etc.

In online co-creation, the online Community is created bespoke for each brand. No two online Communities are identical so that they can truly reflect the brand in question and develop solutions that are relevant and unique.

In this chapter, when we talk about co-creation, we refer to both the "live" and "online" methods. Where we mean one or the other in particular, this is specified.

It is worth saying early on that getting a lot of people together (whether in a room, or online), inviting them to be creative, and giving them a big question is not enough. In order to co-create effectively, everyone involved (customers, staff, and experts) needs skills, tools, and resources. So when you design your process, the term "co-creation" would not be the first thing you actually do with people. Typically there are around five stages in the process, designed to take participants on a journey that most of them have never been on before.

Stage 1: Scoping

This includes the proper definition of the challenge. From the brand owner's point of view, this means being clear about the problem you want to solve, and in particular what your commercial objective is. Do you want to increase sales? Or increase margins? Do you want incremental change or a breakthrough? Or both? You also need to consider what consumer behavior would help you achieve these objectives—is it about changing behavior? Or changing preferences? Making life easier—or something else? Thinking hard about these questions will make sure that your co-creation activity leads to the right result. Management interviews and workshops are

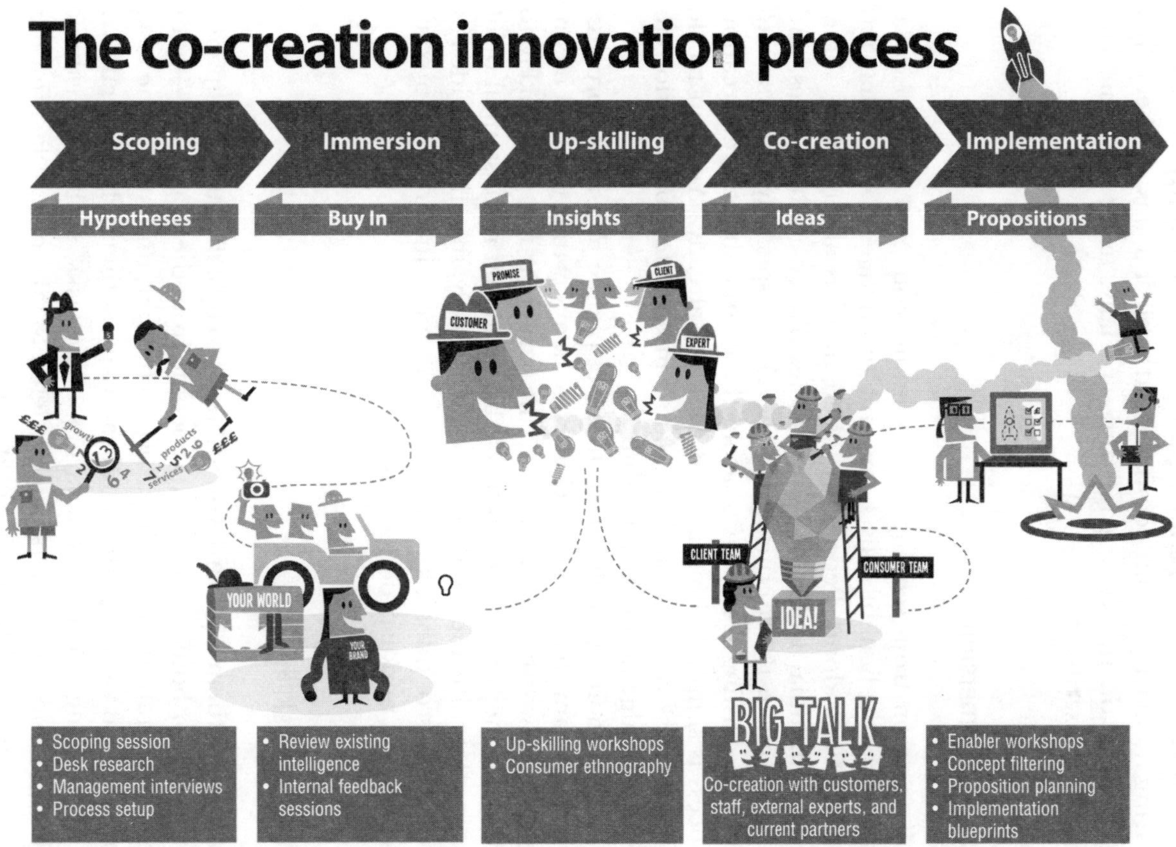

SOURCE: Author.

good ways to explore these questions. And even at this initial stage, it's a good idea to start thinking about some initial hypotheses and sharing them within your company and project teams, to check that everyone is on the same page and, crucially, using the same language to describe it.

Stage 2: Immersion

Following on from scoping, comes immersion. You need to make sure that you benefit fully from any knowledge or work that has already been done. People are often nervous about trying something unfamiliar which breaks the rules like co-creation does, and this can make them critical. It's therefore especially important to build on existing learnings to avoid the charge that the co-creation process is simply "telling us stuff we knew already." You can tackle this with desk research, and by holding internal feedback sessions to test knowledge and understanding.

At this point, you also need to invite people to join the process. It is important to frame your challenge in a way they will find meaningful and worthwhile; consumers in particular are more likely to engage if they are invited to tackle an issue that is substantial or of personal significance to them. Not surprisingly, they find the idea of creating a groundbreaking new product more inspiring than commenting on minor product developments.

Stage 3: Upskilling

Having got them on board, you will need to upskill your participants. This goes for both customers and people from the brand side—both need preparation so that they trust each other, understand the task, know how to work together, and can express themselves effectively.

Upskilling can involve a variety of pretasks, such as consumer ethnographies, consumers being briefed to take part in fact-finding missions or retail safaris, or brand owners being trained in listening skills. During this stage you should also gather as much useful insight as you can.

Stage 4: Co-creation

Only at this point will you be ready to engage in the activities most often associated with co-creation. Whether bringing your participants together in the room (in a workshop format) or online (through a digital community), you will need to develop a detailed plan that helps them on their journey from the "world of the unknown" to potential solutions. They will need activities to help them warm up and get to know each other, to share experiences and insights, and to be creative and come up with new ideas. We introduce some examples of what these activities could be later in this chapter, demonstrating that to get the best possible solutions we need to "access the personal as well as the professional" and encourage our participants to play, experiment, and push the boundaries.

Ultimately we must also be ready to take our participants fully into our confidence. At the end of the day, we want a solution that fits with our idea of what the brand can, or is positioned to, deliver. To get the best out of them, we must be ready to share the ambitions and constraints that frame and shape our ability to implement their ideas.

It is worth adding here the importance of getting the physical surroundings right. In live co-creation, your team needs space to move around, to cluster in small groups, and to express their ideas. Co-creation is more successful in big light spaces than in small dark ones!

They will also need resources to help them express their ideas, including drawing and craft materials, and maybe even a dressing up box (virtual or live)!

Co-creation will generate a lot of outputs: ideas, words, phrases, images, and more. But at this point the answers you are looking for are unlikely to drop into your lap fully formed. It can happen, but it's more likely that you will need to sift through the things that you have collected; think about them; and interpret them, in order to build your solution areas. You will also need to filter and develop the ideas, adding information and insight from the earlier stages. This is the development stage. You may also need to do further work within the organization at this point, to explore which ideas can actually be implemented and learn about what the potential cost implications, enablers, or blockages are likely to be.

Stage 5: Implementation

Finally—and often the process can be fairly lengthy—you will be ready to enter the implementation stage. And while some people may feel like this is the end point of the co-creation process, it is really only the beginning. Taking ideas into the bigger organization involves its own set of activities including detailed planning, pilots, development of blueprints, and eventually, roll-out.

WHO SHOULD YOU INVOLVE IN YOUR PROCESS?

Many co-creation practitioners disagree about the type of consumers needed for successful outcomes. There is a lively and unresolved debate about whether the results are better if you work with "creative" or "expressive" consumers than "ordinary" people. Our experience, supported by a variety of studies, suggests that with the right encouragement all consumers can be creative and the best results are obtained through involving a broad mix of participants.

Other areas of disagreement include the role that experts can play in the co-creative process. We believe that they often have a significant role to play in upskilling the group by building knowledge and understanding. Another is whether co-creation is something that works only in Western cultures. We have co-created successfully in the Middle East and in Asia. Co-creation can work across countries and cultures, when done in the right way and by bearing in mind cultural nuances.

How Co-creation Built a New Brand Positioning for Kraft Foods in Just Five Months

KRAFT FOODS—GLOBAL VISION AND MISSION

Issue: In 2007, Kraft Foods was facing a raft of changes: a new CEO, the acquisition of the LU biscuits business, a bigger workforce of 140,000 people, and a new strategic direction. There was renewed focus on growth, but although margins were good, there was lack of consumer focus and investment in the brand. It was not clear what it really stood for any longer.

Process: The company decided to review its brand purpose and values to help drive further growth and provide a strong and unifying internal direction. The new brand had to not only build off existing internal and external strengths, but also be capable of driving future growth across an extended geography.

Kraft could have opted for an expert-led approach but decided instead to involve customers and employees, in response to a widespread and growing willingness for people to engage and contribute their creativity.

Live co-creation workshops were held with customers and staff in Paris, Chicago, and Shanghai. Each market has very different attitudes to food (e.g., the French are very interested in "balance" while the U.S. people are more concerned with convenience); to "big brands" (an attractive novelty in China but the subject of cynicism in Western markets); and to participating in co-creation (the Chinese like to agree, while the French are happy to argue). In spite of these differences, a clear consensus emerged over the "biggest idea" that Kraft could own in people's lives.

Findings from the live co-creation were then fed into an online community, which brought together the company's leaders worldwide. In total, almost 10,000 staff participated in the solution.

Results: The result was a new mission, vision, and values in just five months. This included the consumer-facing proposition "*Make today delicious.*"

The process delivered convincing consumer support to help build confidence internally, as well as ensuring that employees' voices were heard directly. Eight months after launch, internal surveys showed that 9 out of 10 staff felt that the work was worthwhile and almost the same number felt they knew what they needed to do to make the company successful. The level of support was similar across the Kraft organization.

WHY THE CO-CREATION PROCESS WORKS?

It Involves All Stakeholders

Co-creation works because it involves all stakeholders, who are treated as not only equal to each other, but are also acknowledged throughout the process to be important. Business problems are considered with the people who seek to gain most from the process (staff) and those who benefit from the output of co-creation (customers).

It Values Customers

Organizations that do co-creation well openly share their problem or vision with the customer co-creators. They treat them as partners in the process and tell them candidly what they are hoping to achieve and why they need their help.

Customers in return feel valued in the process; they want to help the company succeed because they feel part of the team. When treated as equals, consumers work very hard for brands, and they delight in the status they achieve by helping to bring something new to life or shaping the future of a business. It is the power of creation—the ability to say—"I did that!" Consumers feel ownership for the ideas they develop, and they push them through, fight for them, and try to make them happen. In the face of their customers' compelling arguments, companies find these ideas hard to disregard.

It is simple really: if someone asks me what I want, and I have the ability to use my energy productively to develop what is right for me (often to my long-term advantage), why wouldn't I want to do it? This is the reason we encourage companies to share what happens next: when the co-creation process is over, feedback to the consumer co-creators is key. Consumers need to know that their ideas are valued, how they will be used or developed, or if they would not be developed, why not.

It Values Staff

Most companies are full of people with ideas, and are often just looking for ways to make sense of the raw "material." When they work with their customers to develop these ideas, they feel confident to stand behind them, and furthermore they now have ammunition to tell their bosses and colleagues why the idea is a good one. And these co-creators have hidden reach: they will be your biggest advocates when their ideas take shape. They may not be in large numbers, but they will influence and advocate their idea in every way they can.

So often we hear staff say: "we develop things all the time, contribute ideas, but then we never know what happens to them."

A good co-creation process takes internal stakeholders on the whole journey, from start to finish.

It Engages People

Simply put, co-creation works because it engages people. Brands have many different stakeholders, each with their own personal view of the brand. Co-creation brings these people together and allows them to work together to build a cohesive brand point of view, leading to greater engagement with the brand.

Engagement is not just another buzzword; it is the reason ideas succeed, because there are people committed to making them happen.

Of course, not all co-created innovations come to life, and there are many things to consider before a business decides to implement an idea. For example, the business case, whether it is brand appropriate, whether the company can deliver it, what needs to be created/changed to make them happen, what do the "experts" say, etc. Nonetheless, companies can be assured of one fact: when something is co-created, it answers a real consumer need. This is different from experts deciding what they think people need.

This is a good place to pause and look at another example to illustrate the power of co-creation.

Refreshing the Proposition Driving a Long-established Brand to Drive Commercial Success

REFRESHING THE BRAND MESSAGE AT KUONI

Issue: Kuoni has long been a leading holiday company in luxury holidays. In recent years it has seen its market share erode due to an increasingly competitive landscape. It needed new compelling customer communications to help the brand clearly articulate and deliver a relevant message, product range, and service to its customer, and to drive more business in a difficult market. Kuoni asked for a powerful and modern brand proposition to communicate what has made them great over the past 30 years. A key requirement was to find a solution that could be implemented at a modest ongoing cost, by adding value to existing communication activities and services.

Process: A co-creative process involving interviews and workshops with Kuoni and competitor customers as well as the Kuoni leadership team and staff to understand where the brand had come from, what it meant today in the market, and what it could offer in the future, to make the brand and its offering more compelling to customers. Followed by an iterative process, working closely with the leadership team and staff to develop a brand proposition and future initiatives to deliver the proposition, which were relevant to the business today, future proof, and could be extended to other markets.

Results

- New brand essence 'with anyone else it wouldn't be the same' came directly from a consumer quote in the workshop process
- New communications campaign 'crafted by Kuoni'
- Kuoni's investment in CRM allows them to isolate the impact of different marketing factors. The work was directly responsible for Kuoni's sales growth in 2012, bucking the trend in a falling market

SOME POWERFUL TECHNIQUES FOR YOU TO TRY

We've talked about consumer engagement and creativity already. But how can you get 300 consumers to care about your business challenge? How do you get them to be more creative and share more of their personal selves? Over the years, we've racked our brains and tried hundreds of ways to get better at this, involving psychologists, social scientists, marketers, communicators, and digital experts, to find the answers to these questions and develop our tools. So here, we are going to share a few of our favorite co-creative techniques. They are taken from the *Promise Method Cards* (a pack we produce to explain our IP to our people and clients), and all of them have been used successfully to solve challenges for brands as diverse as Heinz, Sony Music, Intel, Orange, Bupa, Kraft, Barclays, L'Oreal, and Virgin Media.

An *engagement* tool—to help you motivate all your stakeholders to come up with their very best and most potent "stuff."

engagement
insight
creativity
filtration

Share A Secret

Why?

This is a great way to establish relationships between members who don't know each other and to build foundations for the work to come.

How?

1. Ask members to share something about themselves that few people know
2. As a moderator, go first and share something about yourself
3. Look after members and ensure everyone feels safe rather than judged

promise
communispace

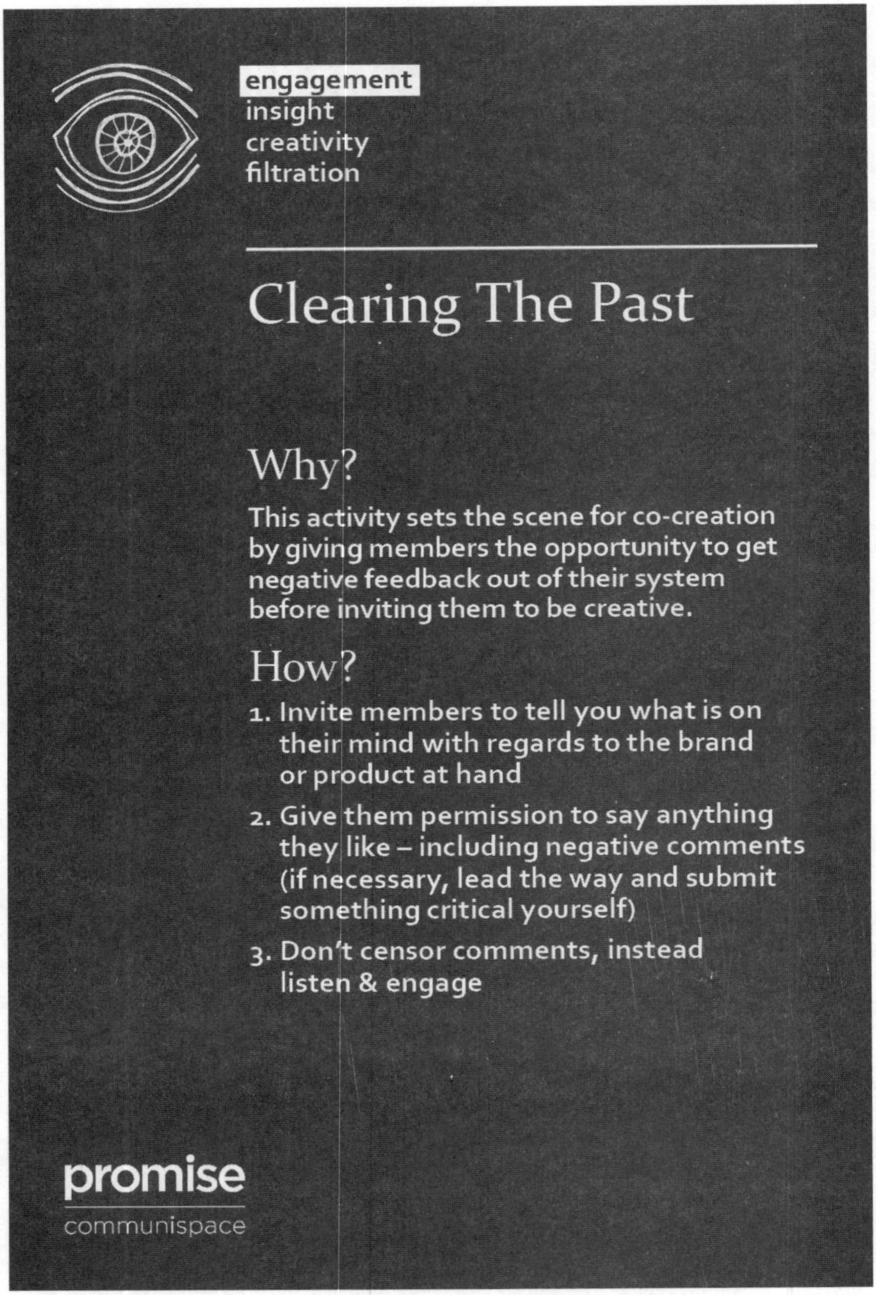

engagement
insight
creativity
filtration
Clearing The Past
Why?
This activity sets the scene for co-creation by giving members the opportunity to get negative feedback out of their system before inviting them to be creative.
How?
1. Invite members to tell you what is on their mind with regards to the brand or product at hand
2. Give them permission to say anything they like – including negative comments (if necessary, lead the way and submit something critical yourself)
3. Don't censor comments, instead listen & engage
promise
communispace

SOURCE: Author.

An *insight* tool—to help you dive deeper and see things that neither you nor your competitors have noticed before.

engagement
insight
creativity
filtration

The Promise Gap

Why?

This is a useful mechanism to identify the gap between a brand's mission statement and consumers' actual perception of the brand.

How?

1. Share the relevant brand promise or mission statement with members
2. Ask members whether they feel the brand or service actually match up to their claim
3. Identify areas of concern and pinpoint issues that need to be addressed

promise
communispace

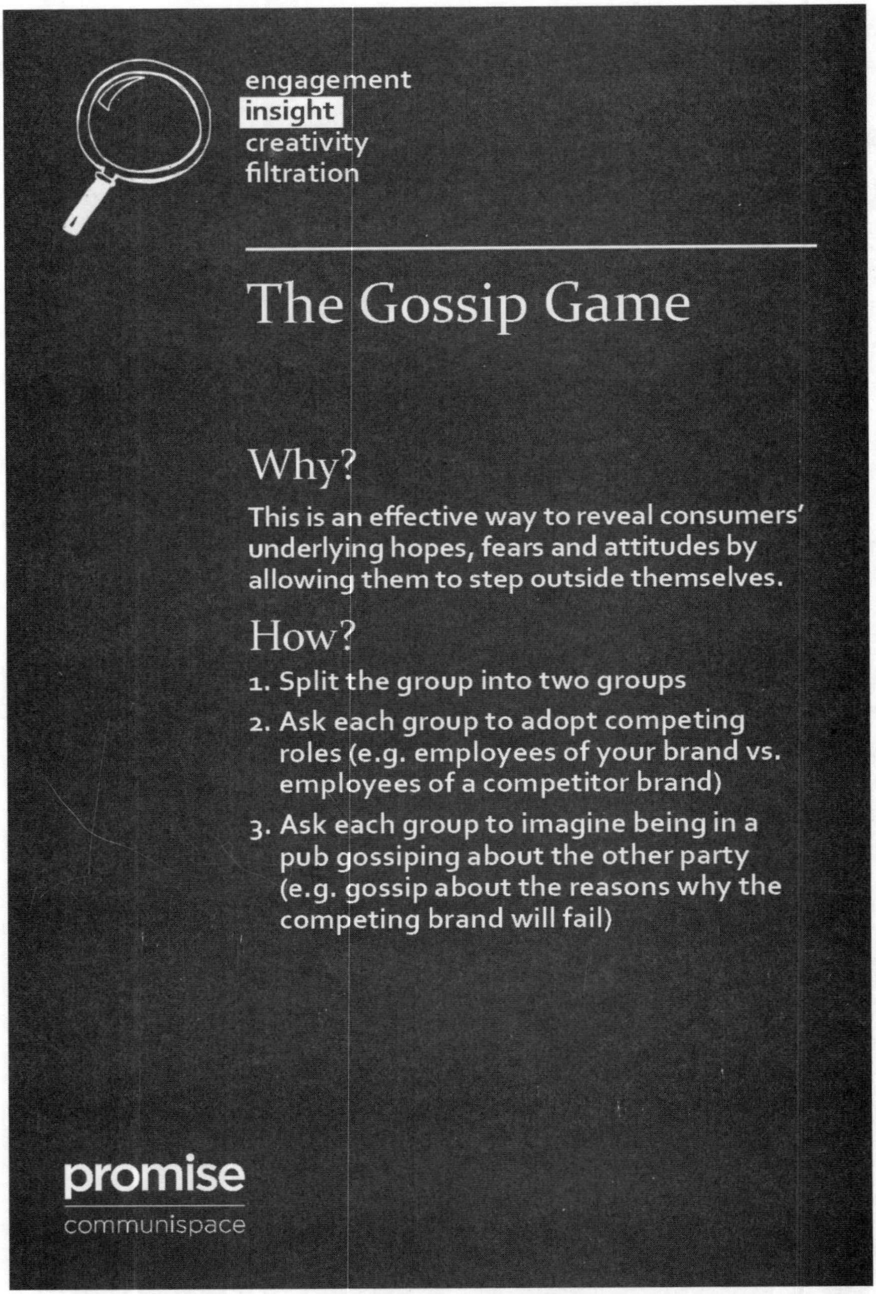

engagement
insight
creativity
filtration
The Gossip Game
Why?
This is an effective way to reveal consumers' underlying hopes, fears and attitudes by allowing them to step outside themselves.
How?
1. Split the group into two groups
2. Ask each group to adopt competing roles (e.g. employees of your brand vs. employees of a competitor brand)
3. Ask each group to imagine being in a pub gossiping about the other party (e.g. gossip about the reasons why the competing brand will fail)
promise
communispace

SOURCE: Author.

A *creative* tool—to help you push back the boundaries and find breakthrough ideas—things that can change a product, service, or category.

engagement
insight
creativity
filtration

Dragons' Den

Why?

This is a great technique to generate a range of competing consumer-centric propositions for a new product or service.

How?

1. Share the detailed brief including criteria that concepts will be judged on
2. Provide guidance up until the deadline
3. Present long-list of concepts to the jury (Dragons) and select winning ideas
4. Share results with members and invite them to use the Dragons' feedback to further improve their ideas

promise
communispace

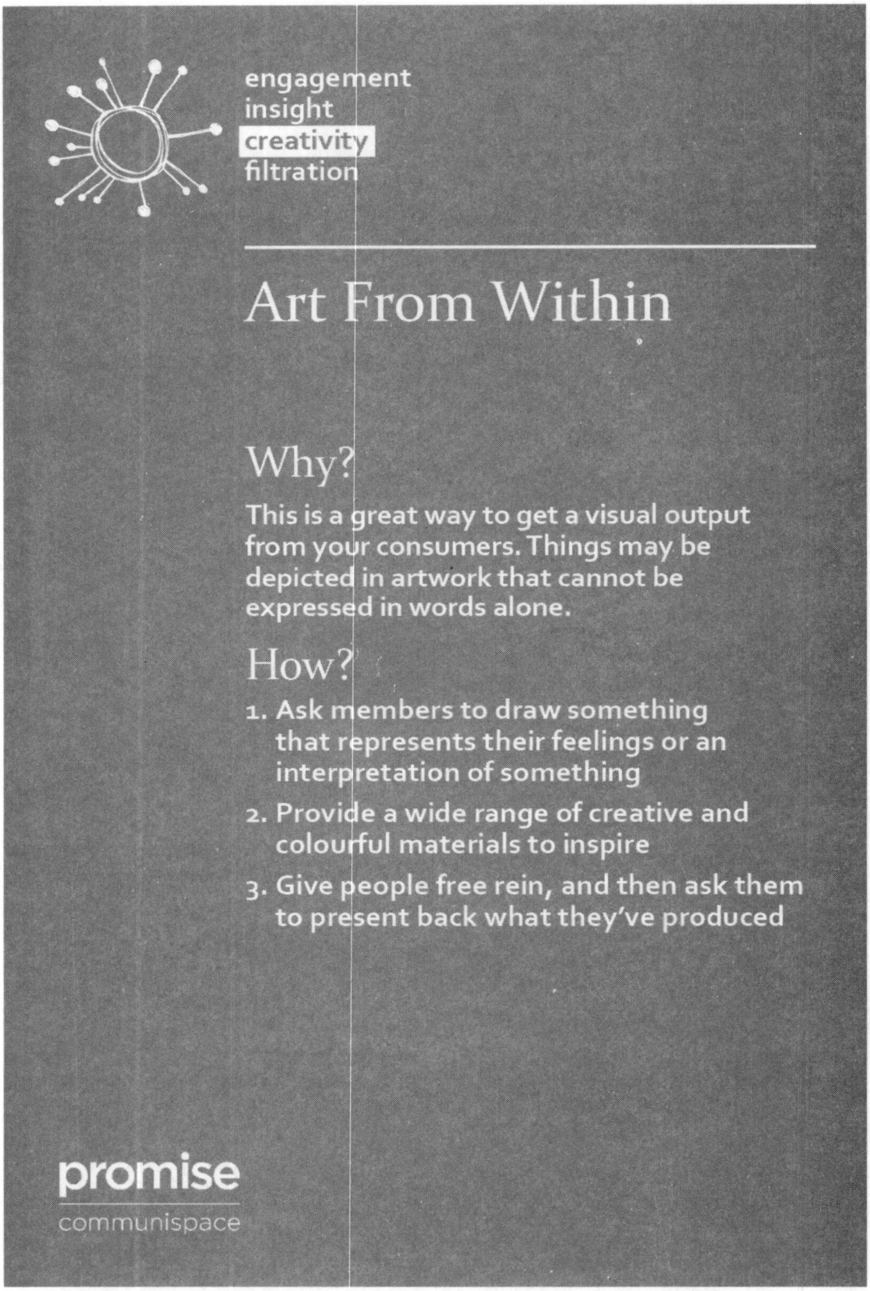

engagement
insight
creativity
filtration
Art From Within
Why?
This is a great way to get a visual output from your consumers. Things may be depicted in artwork that cannot be expressed in words alone.
How?
1. Ask members to draw something that represents their feelings or an interpretation of something
2. Provide a wide range of creative and colourful materials to inspire
3. Give people free rein, and then ask them to present back what they've produced
promise
communispace

SOURCE: Author.

A *filtration* tool—to help you reduce your long list of potential ideas down to the ones that will make a real difference.

engagement
insight
creativity
filtration

One Hundred Points

Why?

This is a great technique to understand a concept's most valuable features.

How?

1. Identify all of your concept's various components
2. Launch a value allocation activity listing up to ten key features
3. Give members 100 points each and ask them to allocate their points according to how much they value each component

promise
communispace

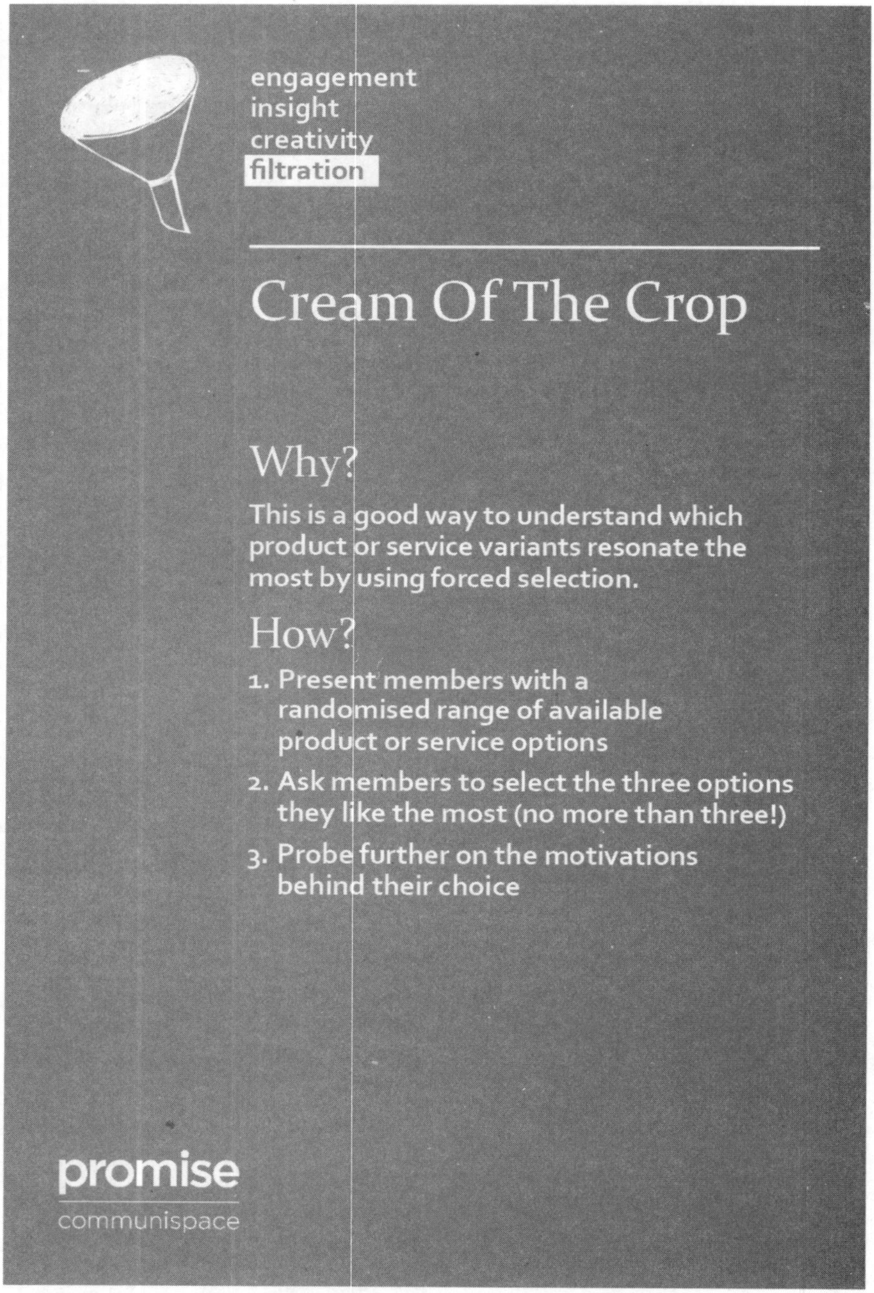

engagement
insight
creativity
filtration
Cream Of The Crop
Why?
This is a good way to understand which product or service variants resonate the most by using forced selection.
How?
1. Present members with a randomised range of available product or service options
2. Ask members to select the three options they like the most (no more than three!)
3. Probe further on the motivations behind their choice
promise
communispace

SOURCE: Author.

WHAT ARE THE BENEFITS OF USING CO-CREATION?

Whether or not you choose to use co-creation will depend on a host of factors, one of which will probably be what your colleagues think and feel. If your colleagues ask you to boil down the key reasons for co-creating, here they are:

- *Speed*: It gets to the right answers sooner because it involves all relevant stakeholders from the very beginning, saving time going back and forth between the relevant parties. This is true both up and down the organization: it can be very frustrating to develop a solution only to have to go back to the beginning with one or more stakeholder groups, to convince them that an idea is robust and workable. The Kraft case study mentioned earlier demonstrates this very point.
- *Internal buy-in*: Immersion and co-creation ensure all internal stakeholders have brought into the ideas developed, because they have been involved in the creative process and often helped progress the ideas personally. The most common reason for ideas failing, even before they have had a chance to develop, is the lack of internal understanding and support, especially at a senior level. For example, being part of the co-creation process convinced senior managers at British Airways to invest in the flat beds in business class—a decision that looked commercially extremely risky as it reduced capacity significantly.
- *Reduces business risk*: Co-creation helps brands respond to the real needs of consumers rather than creating ideas in a vacuum based on what they think people should want. Involving all the relevant people means de-risking the process —many minds provide checks and balances and ensure that the problems and proposed solutions have been considered from all angles. It also helps companies to face truths in a way they cannot hide from. When you hear your customers point out your flaws, or surprise you with insights into how they really live their lives, it is hard to ignore. For example, a major high street bank was convinced to drop its plans for a new paid-for account, in spite of initial enthusiasm for the benefits it offered.

- *Richness*: Co-creation provides a contextualized description of the world of consumers and brings ideas from the outside in, to stimulate thinking. It ensures you benefit from the combined power of many minds, rather than the ability of the "genius" who in practice is a rare breed and may not be possible to identify with confidence. And it is worth remembering that there are always more smart people outside your organization than within it! A new co-created hotel loyalty scheme was built around the idea of rewarding people with unique local experiences rather than points, building an emotional connection (in a very crowded market) rather than a transactional one. It boasts over 2.5 million members in two and a half years.
- *Engagement*: Externally, it connects a group of highly motivated and productive consumers who commit to helping your brand, leading to better solutions and implementation. Internally, it smoothes the way for implementation: often the biggest hurdle brands face is executing a good idea. If the key stakeholders are involved in the journey, and even have a hand in creating the BIG idea for their brand, they will buy into it and help bring it to life. We are constantly amazed at the commitment and time consumers put into helping brands solve problems or build the future. For a leading mobile phone brand, consumers interviewed their friends and submitted results, took pictures and videos whilst they were out and about and posted them online, completed a homework pack involving five tasks, attended four working sessions and, finally, made a presentation to senior management at the company—all of which involved many hours of hard work for little immediate reward.

WHAT DO CONSUMERS WANT IN RETURN FOR THEIR PARTICIPATION?

The relationship of consumers with brands can be ambivalent. On the one hand, they clearly see a benefit to working with a company that is willing to listen to them and create new products and services in response to their ideas. On the other hand, they are not about to give all their ideas away for nothing. This has been true since the market research industry started but co-creation and technology have made the situation more complex.

Consumers are more generous with their time and creativity if they feel the brand is really listening to them rather than going through the motions. The co-creative process, with its emphasis on being open and collaborative, encourages this. Equally, the ability to participate through online communities means that consumers can engage with others, and enjoy the prestige and social interaction this delivers.

At the end of the day, the answer to the question about paying consumers is, "it depends." It depends on the topic under consideration, and it depends on how hard it is to find the right people to involve. And it depends on when you ask. We observe a sort of honeymoon period with consumers right now—they like being involved in co-creation, and these days they especially like doing it online. As this sort of engagement becomes more mainstream, and the novelty value declines, it is likely that we'll have to pay them more, both extrinsically (in terms of money) and intrinsically (in terms of social and other emotional benefits).

THINGS TO WATCH OUT FOR

As you can tell, we are fervent believers in the co-creative process. But there are some watch outs.

- Co-creation is harder to do in companies where the senior teams are dismissive of customer or lack respect for them.
- While co-creation offers solutions, one must be realistic in one's expectations and understand that it can't offer solutions overnight.
- Participants need to develop specific skills to co-create effectively. It is not something you can make up as you go along.
- Co-creation is less effective when a specialist skill is required, for example, in design, copywriting, ad planning, etc. Some problems require expertise and greater control.

- At some point, co-creation must stop in favor of focused action—the implementation and execution of ideas. It must not be allowed to become an endless process.

WHAT DOES THE FUTURE HOLD?

We believe that the world of corporate decision making has changed forever. Both companies and their consumers have discovered how working together generates value—for both sides. Talking to consumers and brands regularly, we do not anticipate going back to the old ways, where the voice of the consumer was detached from—and often subsidiary to—the might of the organization. The "conversation economy," in our view, is here to stay.

Section 5

Building Brands on Belief

Chapter 16

What Chatterjee Said: Designing Brands from the Inside Out

Patrick Hanlon

I am 30,000 feet above the Arctic Circle. The airplane TV screen says the outside temperature is 73 degrees below zero Fahrenheit. People are sleeping, scrunched, cuddled, sprawled, mouths gaping, wheezing, dreaming, snoring, and silent. I am hurtling through thin air on a computer-defined trajectory from Tokyo to New York City. This trip has taken me from New York to Paris to Mumbai to Shanghai to Tokyo and now back to New York City. My head still chatters from dozens of conversations—English accented by Mandarin, Hindi, and French, a smattering of dissonant tongues. My ears buzz with the babble of cart vendors, taxi drivers, airport intercoms, hotel clerks, shop assistants, restaurants, and coffee shops. A thousand thoughts run through my head, which thrums like the aircraft's turbofans thrusting me through the stratosphere. I slide open the window shade and my eyes wince at the chromium blast of morning sun creeping over the arc of Earth. Six miles below a string of mountains unnamed and unknown throw purple shadows over a blue snowfield. A black river scrawls back and forth in loopy graphite curls. The frozen scape glimmers and sheens in the pink brittle frosting of new dawn.

A thought sticks inside my head. Something a marketing manager named Chatterjee asked during dinner at the Taj Mahal Hotel in Mumbai. A turbaned waiter had just scurried away for the hundredth time and Chatterjee stared at me with deep brown eyes as he raised a glass to his lips and sipped Coca-Cola. He placed his heavy glass back onto the smooth white linen. "You are an expert in branding," he said. He paused, turning his glass in the light, and then asked, "Why do you think we believe in some brands and not in others?"

While it is easy to explain how Coke has become an adored beverage brand after 100 years of marketing and advertising efforts, it is difficult to explain how Starbucks has also become a beloved beverage in a fraction of that time, with minimal advertising. Why?

The answer is that brand should not be confused with corporate identity programs or even the product's features and benefits they represent. Instead, we must consider brands as belief systems. Once you create a belief system through a coded construct that includes *creation story, creed, icons, rituals,* a special *lexicon, nonbelievers,* and *leader,* you attract others who share your belief. This creates community. Primal brands radiate with something more than functional utility; they become spiritual magnets that create an incredible sense of belonging. We smile familiarly at strangers wearing white ear buds for their iPhone and at individuals emblazoned with the badges of Nike or North Face or Mercedes. We acknowledge each other, because we are all members of the same tribe. We belong to each other. My people.

Brands often defy rational response and, instead, are intense multisensory experiences that go beyond brand promise or product value. The seven elements of primal code radiate and plunge people into a state of belief and belonging that transcends mere ownership. They not only share products, but also share beliefs. More than merely customers, they are transcendent communities.

At the core of these communities is a system of beliefs: seven elements that are intrinsic to designing the robust brand communities we care about.

We refer to these seven elements as the primal code and will describe them for you now.

The *Creation Story* or mythos is the beginning of the brand narrative. This first piece of code is fundamentally human: we all want to know where we came from, where we were born, who made us. The same is true for products and services, organizations, movements, and civic communities. One of the first things we ask when we see a product that excites us is: "Where did you get that?" or "Who made that?" All belief systems begin with the fundamental human question: "Where are you from?"

The origin story is the first trigger for creating a resonant brand. For example, we know that HP and Apple both started in American garages. Tata, India's largest automobile manufacturer, originally built locomotives. Samsung, today one of the largest consumer electronics companies in the world, was started by the founder Byung-Chull Lee as a small company exporting fish and produce to China. Blacksmith John Deere created his version of the steel plow and founded the company that carries his name, which today is a multinational company that manufactures farm and construction equipment. Levi Strauss invented blue jeans and founded what is still the largest blue jean company in the world, by outfitting gold miners with durable goods. When Toms Shoe company founder Blake Mycoskie saw extreme poverty and barefoot children in Argentina, he had an idea. By recreating traditional alpargata footwear with fashionable materials, he could create a compassionate enterprise as well as clothe a less fortunate population. Other companies have a less compassionate premise. Athletic sport shoe brand Puma was started in Herzogenaurach, Germany, when Rudolf Dassler got into an argument with his brother Adolf over the family footwear business Adidas. The primacy of origins not only holds true for products and services, but for personality brands as well. Mohandas Karamchand Gandhi spent many years in London and South Africa before returning to India and his destiny in 1915; Lady Gaga started out working as an assistant in New York City; and so forth.

Chatterjee shifts uneasily in his chair. "But do people care about history?" he asks. "Who cares about memories of the past?"

This is not nostalgia; it is legacy. For a number of reasons, social, economic, or draped in human psychology, we want to know where people, places, and things come from now more than ever. Before we put our money on the table, we want to know "Who made this?" In today's connected global world, rife with pseudonyms on the Internet, Wikileaks, factory fires in Bangladesh, web stalkers, we want to know the origin of things. We cry out for transparency. In today's global brand economy, consumers want understanding and context before they connect with a global community of strangers. "Where are you from?" and "How did you get here? are fundamental questions that kick off the brand narrative.

The second piece of primal code is the *Creed.* Once we know where you are from, tell us what you are about. Belief systems begin with a statement of core principles. Tell us how you are different from everyone else. For some, this might be tied to features and benefits, like Mercedes Benz's old theme line, *Engineered like no other car in the world.* More likely, it aligns to a higher order purpose and relevancy, for example, Coke's *open happiness,* Apple's *Think different,* Nike's *Just do it,* or the notion of *freedom for all.*

The creed is the reason for being that positions the person, place, or thing in our minds, and stakes your claim in the marketplace. The creed tells us what you celebrate and differentiates your community.

What you believe in—and why—is no simple question. When the software game developer Bungie (the Xbox game developer that created the billion dollar Xbox franchise *Halo*) decided to buy itself back from Microsoft, the stakeholders found themselves in a state of deep introspection. Bungie wondered, *Who are we?* Did they simply make the best games on the planet? Or were they an entertainment franchise (*Halo* games, books, paraphernalia, and a movie were already on the shelves)? Would Halo be the only game they would ever create? No matter their successful past, the focus was on determining the new vision that unfolded Bungie's future. Deciding who you are and what you want to become is critical in developing the Creed.

Once we know where you're from and what you're about, you must identify yourself. *Icons* are the next piece of code: quick concentrations of meaning that signal who you are and what you *mean.* We often think of icons as the company logo, but icons can engage any or all of the senses: sight, sound, taste, touch, and smell. They instantly signal the brand essence. Because these icons *mean* something, our brains tell us whether we should approach or avoid.

Taste is an icon, a concentration of meaning that conjures up places, people, and moments in time. The taste of McDonald's French fries. The taste of KFC fried chicken. The taste of your mother's food. Food companies explore sensations of texture, mouth feel, and the flavors of bitter, sweet, sour, salty, and umami when developing new products.

Sound is iconic. Examples include the ring on your smartphone, honking taxis, and music—"your song."

Product packaging and logos are icons that are self-evident and quickly signal brands. Examples include the Nike swoosh, Mercedes Benz logo, the shape of an iPad, team uniforms, and national flags.

Corporate campuses, such as the headquarters for Google, Apple, and IBM, and destinations such as Central Park, the Taj Mahal, and Red Square are also iconic physical domains that embody the spirit and vision of corporate momentum and civic power.

If icons identify your brand, rituals *are your brand in motion.*

The fourth piece of primal code, rituals are the repeated interactions you have with your consumers and brand community. The vitality of a community comes from the repeated positive engagements between your product and the brand community. Ritual is behavior. Ritual is process. Ritual is habits (both good and bad). Sacred and secular rituals replace chaos with order, and these repeated activities provide emotional reassurance: years, seasons, memories that add meaning and continuity to the rhythms of life.

"Logging on" to the Internet is a ritual, so is "searching" and going to Facebook. Calling on your cellphone is a ritual. The way you travel to work each day is a ritual. Shopping, preparing a meal, dining at a restaurant, checking into a hotel, buying a car, clubbing, and going to school, the doctor or to a soccer game are all rituals that are part of our daily lives.

During the months of October and November, India experiences mass human migrations as people travel long distances to celebrate religious festivals with their families. These festivals are also rituals, and so is the annual journey by car, train, bus, bicycle, and airplane. The gift-giving and other purchases accompanying this travel are also ritual events.

Many marketers today mine for these ritualistic behaviors in online media, in order to determine when and where consumers intersect with their brands—it can even be as specific as when an individual connects to out-of-home billboards with their mobile devices. Ritual behaviors are powerful tangents that enable marketers to judge the depth and velocity of their marketing programs.

Within organizations, rituals are the systems of behavior that determine how we act toward our customers and each other. Meetings, conventions, and teleconferences are rituals that say something about how we work together as a company or a team. They become process or procedure.

Smiling is a ritual.

Belief systems also have a unique *Lexicon.* These are words understood by members of the community, but often unintelligible to others, for example, *iced grande skinny decaf latte* or a *tall no foam macchiato*—phrases we had to master if we wanted to order anything from Starbucks, which has discreet names to describe its thousands of variations of coffee and other drinks.

Even product names as pervasive as Apple's iPhone, iPad, iTunes, iTV and other language become emblematic of the brand—especially, as in Apple's case, when other companies adopt them to create accessories and flanker products.

In social media, when we scrape the web for chatter, we look at the longitude and latitude of the conversations taking place, and fashion word clouds to analyze how people are talking about our brand. We want to know what words are being used to describe our brand, the context, geographic location, and time. Most of all, we want to know what our community and those outside our community are saying about us: Are they enthusiastic, happy, confused, angry, frustrated, or delighted?

MORE ABOUT THE DIGITAL COMMUNITY

"*lol*" is a hugely popular acronym in the English language for the words "laugh out loud." It has long been used as shorthand by people texting on their cell phones. The unique thing about *lol*, however, is that *lol* is also used in China, where the characters do not exist in Mandarin. *lol* is also used in Moscow, where it also does not have an equivalent in the Russian Cyrillic alphabet. Why? The three letters *lol* are language used by the growing global cyber community that has its own reasons for being, its own culture—and its own language. *brb.*

We are back.

All belief systems face *Nonbelievers,* people who believe something else. These "pagans" or heretics are the sixth piece of primal code, familiar to anyone attuned to the tense rivalries between Coke and Pepsi, Mac versus PC, Audi versus Mercedes, and Manchester United versus Bayern Munich.

Understanding our nonbelievers helps us understand *what we are not* and *what we never want to become.*

There is nothing like pitting one group against their rival, to solidify the beliefs of both. Imagine putting Manchester United football fans nose to nose with Bayern Munich fans—calamity. As a famous cigarette advertisement once declared, they would "rather fight than switch."

Social media offers tremendous opportunities to understand the polarity of the discussions taking place, which helps guide us toward a better understanding of category issues and opportunities. For example, an online discussion of commonplace products like Kraft's Macaroni and Cheese and General Mills' Hamburger Helper includes comments that range from "love it," "indulgence," and "nostalgia," to opposite reactions of "unhealthy," "homemade is better," and "awful." Each extreme point of view provides fresh insight and the potential for new opportunities to support and embrace the communities for those brands. Also if you can identify a group of people who do not want sugar, you can create sugar-free.

The final and seventh piece of primal code is the *Leader.* This is the individual who set out against all odds to recreate the world according to their own point of view. At one level, they are leaders like Steve Jobs, Mark Zuckerberg, Ratan Tata, and others. At the micro level, they are the division heads, group managers, supervisors, team leaders, and others responsible for putting together the seven pieces of primal code to create communities and provide vision-driven, successful brands.

Chatterjee shifts in his seat. "Very interesting! But surely some categories lend themselves to *primal branding* more than others?" he asks. No. Because the primal code is intrinsically human, it is category agnostic, resonating wherever there is an opportunity for people to be engaged. And because brands are communities, we rid ourselves of the traditional industry perspectives of business to business, business to consumer, and so forth. As individuals, we belong to many communities: we can be a business person, a father, son, wife, daughter, husband, cousin, cricket player, gambler, mathematician, teacher, student, boss, diabetes sufferer, gourmand, gardener, citizen, and more. You'll discover that each of these roles has a creation story, a creed, icons, and the other pieces of primal code. Small or large, they are communities.

When the seven pieces of the primal construct work together, they create vibrant sticky brands that not only seize attention, but also gain permission to believe and to belong. This leads to preference, which leads to sales.

The structure of belief is written in seven simple lines of code. Just as computer code can balance finances, create music, send an aircraft through space, or create a feature length movie, so can primal code create a belief system and community to surround products and services; create corporate culture (the internal brand); personality brands (the brand within); political and social movements; and actual civic communities (New York City, Beijing, or Mumbai).

Why do some companies mean something to us, while others don't? Because some companies have all seven of these pieces of primal code. And the products or services we don't care about, *don't.*

Understanding the primal code helps you design a resonant, relevant brand community. Better, it helps you manage the intangibles of your brand—how people feel about you.

Chatterjee leans forward. "I see." *Brands* resonate beyond the product's primary functions and benefits—their value proposition. When today so many products have become commoditized—consumers have hundreds of different cars, phones, electronics, and soft drinks to choose from—how people *feel* about you can truly differentiate you and influence preference. And increased preference increases sales.

"Wonderful!

"But can you give me another example? Maybe it's not even a product on the shelves?"

Let's try. Brands are consensual communities driven by a core belief system. This means that nearly any group of people who join together can become—or already are—a "brand," whether it is two people in their kitchen making street enchiladas for sale, or 2 billion people joined as a nation. Brands are consensual, because they give permission to one another to be together. If you are a soccer fan, you consent to be together in the soccer stadium enjoying soccer. There is shared trust, and a tacit understanding that you will observe and participate in what is happening down on the field. You may also be a newcomer and know nothing at all about soccer, which means that you are not yet a member of the community—but as you take your seat in the stadium, you now have access and permission to *join the community* of soccer lovers in that stadium as well as the larger community of soccer fans around the world.

To the bystander not a part of the soccer community, the game is meaningless. But as you learn the history, players, famous plays, teams, the vernacular of the game in motion, and the referee calls, your understanding grows and you become more interested. You begin to know which teams come from which cities, and identify the colors (icons) associated with each team. You learn the technical aspects of soccer and understand the names of the positions and which players play those positions best. Some actions (rituals) cause certain reactions from players, coaches, referees, and fans. You learn the stories behind great teams and star players (creation story) as well as what sucks about some games, some teams, and some players and their coaches.

The game is transformed from an activity that is *meaningless*, to a gradual understanding that every play of the game, every team, every player, is not only understood, but—during intense lean-forward moments, when you're screaming your head off—it actually *means* something to you.

What was once invisible, mysterious, and hidden is slowly illuminated by the torchlight of understanding. The individual is transformed from someone who was ignorant about the game, to becoming a soccer fan.

Chatterjee jumps from his seat and walks quickly around the table. He slaps his hands together. "Of course! This is a wonderful explanation!" he exclaims. "Why else could there be teams who play poorly—and still they have fans?"

Chatterjee stops and turns.

"But do all the pieces of code have to pieced together at the same time?" he asks.

"Do they have to be created in sequence? Tell me."

He sits back down at the table and smiles; his brown eyes pool with dark but twinkling light.

Typically, these pieces have been developed at random. Companies like Nike, Apple, Coke, and others have had great gut instincts. They have hired smart partners (including advertising and public relations companies), and they have had ample funding to carry them through dark periods. Over time, they have been able to assemble the seven pieces of primal code randomly, realizing only that as their business grew, something magnetic was happening that felt innately correct.

As global brand enthusiasts, we gather around a campfire of shared delights and consensual passions. The spiritual essence and luminous power of the "brand" takes shape outside of the product or service's features, benefits, manufacturing, and the people who create them. Brand radiance is a laddered-up, aspirational, higher order consequence of the trust derived from the functional product itself.

It becomes more *Nike* than *shoe.*

For example, the global brand Coke exists in joy bubbles of effervescent fun and happiness that reside in an atmosphere outside of the soft drink experience alone. There is meaning implied in the brand that extends beyond the aura of a sweet, carbonated beverage.

The Tom's Shoes brand is meaningful because it donates a pair of shoes to deserving others. This fact lies outside of the fashion sensibilities of men and women on the streets of Manhattan, London, Paris, and Mumbai. The brand resonates with the like-minded values of its consumers, who deliberately consent to be part of an inspired community based upon shared beliefs.

As marketers, we realize these are not people who simply "Like" you on Facebook and move on. They are the mother lode of your P/L. They are the geeks, fans, and advocates who not only consume what you produce—these people are super engaged and constantly sharing and bringing new people into the community.

The role of powerful brand narratives is to remind us who we are as a people, what we stand for, what matters most to us (what we cannot live without), what we love and hate and fear, what we never want to become, and who leads the way. These messages are revealed to us in new and meaningful ways over and over again in thriving brand communities, so that we feel our senses refreshed and our passion for belonging rekindled. Rather than dulling us with the steady trod (or calamity) of daily life, they enrich the moment, they inspire us, they lift us up. Each new sacrifice to the gods is both a reminder of our frailty and a reminder of what we aspire to become.

Traditional and new social media must be woven together as omni-channel marketing to collectively communicate your brand's legacy, brand assets, values, icons, rituals, the unique vocabulary that surrounds your brand, and the essence of your brand personality. These become the superstructure that guides the daily thread of advertising, public relations, CSR, social media, and other assets that complete your brand communications portfolio. As the author Adam Gopnik writes in the *New York Times* as he describes reasons for the success of J.R.R. Tolkien's *The Lord of the Rings* trilogy, "his fantasies are uniquely 'thought through': every creature has its own origin story, script, or grammar; nothing is gratuitous." So, in the same way, are brand narratives for Coke, Samsung, Mercedes, and other marketers' simple tales told over complex interconnected, cross-channel integrative media.

Everyone talks about being a part of the conversation, but if that conversation is meaningless or is not driven back to the brand in a positive and actionable way, then that conversation is a pointless waste of time, funding, and talent.

Your overarching brand narrative consists of separate panels of bought, earned, and shared media: traditional media, social media, direct marketing, corporate reports, employee training, catalogs, Internet, new product announcements, investor reports and employee communications—and more—in an interwoven storyline that includes the social and spiritual components of building brand community. If you are GE, P&G, Siemens, Samsung, or General Motors, such a media plan can be extensive and complex (Mercedes USA refers to theirs not as a spreadsheet, but as a "bedsheet," because it often seems just as large).

Chatterjee raises his finger in the air. A question: "But tell me," he says. "What about strictly online brands? Do the elements of primal code still work for those brands? Do any pieces of primal code work better in social media?"

It does not matter whether brands are online or offline. Brand communities whose relationships are fostered solely over the Internet (e.g., Facebook, as well as retailers like Amazon.com, zappos.com, Gilt Groupe, Fab, and countless others) have the same opportunity that bricks and mortar enterprise does—to use the seven pieces of primal code to wrap their company's product or service with emotional context and meaning—and foster community.

This conscious narrative approach to brand building is growing. In workshop sessions on content strategy and community building,

Google's YouTube video network cites the Primal Branding construct as one of their recommended best practices. Rachel Lightfoot leads these sessions in programming strategy at YouTube Next Lab, and endorses the elements of Primal Branding because the elements of primal code are present in today's most successful YouTube videos.

While it is relatively easy to communicate the primal elements, *creation story*, *creed*, *rituals*, *lexicon*, *nonbelievers*, and *leader* online, iconic elements like smell, taste, and touch are (so far) sensory areas where online brand experiences fall short. To help meet this challenge, purely online companies like eyewear marketer Warby Parker have taken their online experience to the streets.

"The future of retail is at the intersection of e-commerce and bricks-and-mortars," announces Warby Parker's co-founder Neil Blumenthal in "Why Warby Parker Opened a Retail Store," in Inc. magazine.

Google is another popular example of an online primal brand. The creation story of how founders Larry Page and Sergey Brin started their company as students at Stanford University has been steady inspiration for new start-ups. While the company began as a search engine, today they are a multinational corporation with offices around the world.

Google started as an effort to organize the world's information and to make it accessible online. But today's Google is poised to seize the future. Google chief executive officer Larry Page outlines Google's creed in his 2012 investor update. "Sergey and I founded Google because we believed that building a great search experience would improve people's lives and, hopefully, the world," he writes. "Excellence matters, and technology advances so fast that the potential for improvement is tremendous … I've pushed hard to increase our velocity, improve our execution, and focus on the big bets that will make a difference in the world." Page also stakes a claim for having "a healthy disregard for the impossible," a statement he discovered while at the University of Michigan, which means that sometimes taking on impossible tasks yields better results than trying for short-term incremental gains. When someone at Google was brazen enough to suggest a vainglorious effort to understand the Web, their failed attempt resulted in the technological innovation behind AdSense, which has had an over $30 billion payout.

Another foolhardy attempt—this time to integrate multi-person video into Google+—resulted in the successful Google Hangouts.

While not as succinct as Apple's "Think different" or HP's "Invent," Google customers and employees have a good sense of not only why Google exists on the planet, but why Googlers come to work in the morning. But more on that later.

Google icons include the logo, a home page so unique that it is patented, the Googleplex headquarters in Mountainview, California, leaders Larry and Sergei, and more. The fact that the Google logo and home page are visited tens of billions of times each year makes them some of the most visible icons on the planet.

Google's lexicon is too large to include the entire vocabulary here, but a quick snapshot includes words like "Google," "Google docs," "Gmail," "Google Maps," "Google glasses," "Google it," "Chrome," "Feeling lucky?"; technical phrases like "hot-wording"; as well as the names of its acquisitions like "YouTube," "Double Click," and others.

Nonbelievers include competitors like Yahoo!, Microsoft, and the Chinese search company Baidu.

The leaders, of course, are founders Larry Page and Sergey Brin, as well as chief executive officer Eric Schmidt, and the thousands of project managers, team leaders, division heads, and others who steer Google forward.

And while Google engages all seven elements of primal code to create a terrific online brand community for its *outward*-facing consumer public, it also enjoys an offline community of stalwart staffers within the walls of Google.

This is because the primal code can also be used to create and inspire culture *inside* companies.

The community of advocates *inside* the Googleplex is perhaps the company's biggest asset. Google employees are staunch zealots who do not just have jobs, but also are literally inventing the 21st century.

Google campuses are littered with rituals and iconic spaces that celebrate a work ethic that revels in sleeping at the office and dining at the company's many micro kitchens. Free food and espressos are carried in one hand, and laptops, tablets, and smartphones in the other as employees rush to find cubbyholes in which to work or meet. Gbikes and skateboards roll through the hallways in this post-collegiate utopia.

You cannot help but think, this is what work was meant to look like.

The rituals and icons inside Google are purposeful and have solid outcomes. The point of all the free lattes and nap pods is that staffers stay late, come early, and never seem to leave. Focused Googlers stalk the hallways with thousand-yard stares that reveal killer dedication and commitment that makes all the hoodies, Campers' footwear, and grizzled slouch just insulation absorbing molten high voltage. A row of historic vintage computers lines one wall. Basketball hoops, pingpong tables, foosball tables, Xboxes, and other play tools accessorize key locations to let brains play.

The creation story inside the Googleplex is the same as it is for the millions of consumers who use Google products and services. But the origin mythos and creed become especially important as leaders and recruiting firms try to hire people away from Google competitors Facebook, Samsung, Apple, and elsewhere. New hires yearn to become a part of Google's continuing legacy.

Inside the campus, three words painted over a doorway read, "Don't be evil"—an admonishment originally intended to mean, *Let's not be like Microsoft.* This also plays into the element of nonbelievers as *what we don't want to become* and *who we don't want to be like,* which helps set the tone for what Google *does* want to be.

Words and descriptors also build corporate culture.

While "Googlers" is a word that might describe just about everyone wandering around the Google campus, only an elite few are "the Eng"—short for deep science *eng*ineers who write the millions of lines of code necessary for Google's digital Googliness. The cultural lexicon includes words that are known by those who are part of the Google tribe, but get only a quizzical stare from persons outside the community. Hence, words like "Googliness," "Nooglers," "MKs" (mini-kitchens), "people ops" (human resources), and others make it easy for insiders to spot those who are not a part of the Google tribe.

The leaders, of course, are Larry Page, Sergei Brihn, Eric Schmidt, and other team leaders, segment directors, and others.

These seven elements of primal code create the wireframe that makes "Googliness"—the essence of Google culture—possible.

Let's move on.

Whether your social content is a corporate report detailing your corporate brand, an employee handbook that advises co-workers of the brand's values, video content running on YouTube, television advertising, or an advertising campaign championing a new product launch, each piece is part of the total tapestry that defines your brand's storyline. Woven together, these pieces create a differentiated brand narrative that not only presents products and services, but also the aspirations and ideals of your brand. They explain not only why the company exists and why people buy your products and services, but also why employees can't wait to show up for work each morning.

The role of all brand communications is to create a dramatic and meaningful moment that is transformational, and moves consumer citizens from "*Who* cares?" to "*I* care!"

It is due to the numinous nature of brands that we feel something deep and sacrosanct when we come into contact with them. Brands that resonate (those that have filled all the pieces of primal code) not only fill coffers, but also fulfill genuine pieces of the human psyche. They attach themselves to people in ways that product benefits, solutions, and value propositions cannot answer for.

Can we feel the same way about a political candidate as we do about Coca-Cola? *Yes.* Do the same principles apply? *Yes.* As we have shown, *Primal Branding* reveals how to manage those intangibles.

The primal code gives entrepreneurs—and intrapreneurs inside multinational giants—the tools to launch new products and services and re-engineer existing ones by designing a compelling brand narrative that helps them gain funding, puts product on shelves, and attracts consumers.

It comes down to perspective. The hard rigors of day-to-day sales objectives make the issue of how customers *feel* about us seem soft. But in today's parity world, the soft sciences of human persuasion reveal very concrete business results in terms of preference, increased brand value, improved employee retention, greater job satisfaction, and higher morale.

Consumers or customers may buy the first time from a sense of surprise, novelty, or curiosity. But whether or not they come back to become brand advocates and repeat customers depends on if and when you fill in the information delivered by pieces of *primal code.* Who are you? Where are you from? What are you about?

Who is running the show? Only when you have filled in these blanks will they decide if they want to opt in and become a resonant member of your consumer community.

As human beings, we are hardwired to be communal and to participate in communities. Our brains are also hardwired to profile people, places, and things, to determine whether we should approach, or avoid. These two phenomena also make us hardwired to accept brands. Whether they are cult brands, tribal brands, love brands, brands large or small, they are all driven by a core system of belief. They find each other on Facebook, Pinterest, in clubs, online groups, organizations, associations, shopping clubs, in political parties, societies, towns, and states. If their number is large enough, they become a sect, culture, or nation. The *primal code* helps turn people from passive observers, into the active role of believers. Those who believe, feel they belong. This feeling of belonging is acted out by preference and advocacy, and their enthusiastic engagement sparks others to join.

All of this accrues to the fact that brands are more valuable than products.

Chatterjee closes his eyes and nods his head. "We all want to be a part of something that is bigger than ourselves," he sighs.

Yes.

In the hours it has taken me to write this, I have crossed the planet. The airplane is now descending and my rite of passage is nearly complete. Flight attendants scurry up and down the aisles, as the intercom tells everyone to shut down anything with a battery. I peer outside the airplane window and look down over the salt marshes and sandy beaches of Long Island, New York. The aircraft shudders as the wheels touch tarmac at JFK International Airport. If I ever see Chatterjee again, I will thank him for asking his questions. Maybe I will buy him a Coke.

Understanding brands as belief systems is a new lens that differentiates your brand and creates success in an increasingly competitive marketplace. It can help you sustain sales and market share. For whatever reason, when all seven pieces of a belief system are in place, people not only take notice, they take part. They don't want to be just the consumer of a product, they want to become part of a movement.

The seven pieces of primal code don't just help brands come alive, they make brands part of life.

Chapter 17

Passion Brands: The Extraordinary Power of Brand Belief

Helen Edwards and Derek Day

WHAT IS A BRAND FOR?

The commercial answer to that question is both simple and well-rehearsed. It is to achieve the potential for a higher value in the minds of consumers than the generic, unbranded product, or service. Numerous brands in virtually all categories have demonstrated this power at work. Evian costs more than the commodity that emerges from the tap; Dove persuades us to part with more for its bars than we would for good but unbranded soap; even where the formulations are identical, branded consumer medicines such as Nurofen can sell for many times more than the generics. A brand—the leanest definition of which is "a product or service, plus values and associations"—enjoys a value pull over mere products and services in which values and associations are either absent or weak.

Still, this gets us only so far, since most brands do not compete exclusively with generic products or services. They tend to compete with other brands. Tall trees may enjoy a greater share of natural resources than pygmy trees, but this is not such an overwhelming advantage in a forest of tall trees.

That gives way to a second question. How can any given brand earn advantage over other brands? How can this tree grow a little taller than the other tall trees? Again, the answers are well-rehearsed but they are not so simple, at least, not in practice. Advantage may be pursued by means of a whole range of disciplines and activities:

consumer understanding, innovation, segmentation, new distribution channels, bundling, packaging, design, communications, service initiatives, and pricing.

The problem with this list is not that any one of the tasks is superfluous but that all of them are necessary just to keep up, let alone forge ahead. Branded competitors will be engaging in each and every one of these disciplines and actions, at the same time as you are, in order to gain advantage over you. It is actually worse than that; not only will they be doing much the same things, but the outcomes will also tend, in any single category, to converge on much the same answers. Brands will arrive at similar understanding, devote time and money-chasing similar innovations, and employ similarly brilliant agencies to devise similarly ingenious communication ideas and media strategies.

This point is crucial to anyone seeking to differentiate their brand according to the latest fashionable doctrine. Right now, that doctrine is consumer insights. These are chased with enormous zeal by both brand owners and their agencies, deploying the latest research techniques to prise open new nuggets of revelation. But since those research techniques are available to all, and since consumers are likely to reveal similar glimpses into their souls irrespective of who happens to be asking, it is unlikely that you will end up knowing anything your competitors don't.

Convergence among brands within a category is almost as inevitable as convergence in the average height of the tall trees of the forest. You cannot shrink back from toiling at the list above—since to do so will stunt your brand's ability merely to keep up—nor can you expect it, except in the rarest circumstances, to lead to lasting advantage. What it leads to instead is the mall-like world of "consumer-led brands," in which consumer needs are met in predictable ways by brands whose quirks and rough edges have been erased as though they had been through a wind tunnel, which, in a sense, they have.

UNCONVERGE

Yet there is one element within your brand's DNA that can promote divergence from other brands, one facet that is hard to copy because, often as not, it does not "present" to competitors an easy-to-spot advantage. (In fact, sometimes the very reverse: it can appear, short term at least, to be a disadvantage.) What is this elusive, mercurial, and apparently sacrificial quality?

It is a belief. It is the reason for the existence of the brand in the first place. It is the idealism that moved somebody in the perhaps murky past to start the whole thing going, in spite of all the obstacles that would have needed to be overcome. For Henry Ford, it was a belief in freedom of mobility, with his vision to "open up the highways for all mankind." For Pleasant Rowland, the founder of American Girl, it was a belief that better role-model "narratives" were needed for preteen girls in the ersatz world of Barbie-like dolls. For Luta's Luke Dowdney, it is a conviction that martial arts can give young people the impetus to end gun crime in the favelas (see the panels later).

Now we arrive at a quite different answer to the question posed at the outset: "What is a brand for?"

It is for changing the world. It is for improving the lot of human existence. It is for making a small difference based on big convictions. This is the social answer, one that may lead to the commercial answer, and to advantage, precisely because it does not start there. In this paradigm, a brand is the embodiment of the expression used by the supply-side economist George Gilder in his book *Wealth and Poverty* (Regnery, 2012): "Capitalism begins with giving."

That is how brands came about in the first place. Their genesis dates to a time when people were regularly cheated by shifting and unaccountable traders. Dirty practices included adding water to butter, chalk to flour, and sand to sugar, along with routine cheating at scales.

Then more upright individuals and groups, often driven by a common morality such as that of the Quakers, developed enduring trade names and marks that came to symbolize their commitment to fair dealings.

Many of those early belief-led brands prospered and are still forces for good today: Cadbury, Carlsberg, Clarks Shoes, Hershey, John Lewis, Krupp, Lever (now Unilever), Philips, Price Waterhouse, and The Co-operative. On the other hand, the recent fate of Barclays and Lloyds—both originally Quaker banks—demonstrates what happens when the drive for gain is allowed to take precedence over the founding tenets of, in their case, "simplicity, honesty, and integrity." Had they adhered to those foundational ideals, they would have better served not only their customers and the wider community, but also themselves.

Brand belief is a potent force. It doesn't obviate the necessity for the normal watchful duties of good brand stewardship, but it refracts all the research findings, all the R&D ideas, all the service initiatives, product upgrades, and communications platforms through a powerful lens, one that focuses on a single question: "Is this true to what we believe about the world?" When the answer is "no," the brand doesn't go there, changes things around, remolds its offer to conform to its convictions, even if that means knowingly flying in the face of consumer wants and opinions. Belief is therefore the foundation of those much-sought-after brand qualities: character and authenticity, the hallmarks of what we will call Passion Brands.

Four questions typically ensue from this line of reasoning.

How Does Belief Confer Commercial Advantage?

Belief-led brands enjoy two natural advantages over brands that merely pander to the latest consumer whim. They inspire deeper emotional engagement among customers, and more impassioned commitment among employees.

Why should brand belief have the power to move consumers who, after all, might simply be choosing an aftershave or a canned soup? The answer takes us into the realm of self-identity, and the role that consumption plays within it. Over the past four decades, this has been the subject of intense research by the leading behavioral and psychological academics—a list that includes, but is by no means limited to, Aaker (J), Bauman, Belk, Elliott, Featherstone, Giddens, Ritson, Thompson, and Yi Fu Tuan.

Their body of work shows that people construct a "narrative of self" to help them navigate their lives and the world around them. A range of cultural resources can be used—consumed—by the individual to reinforce and calibrate this sense of self-identity. The available repertoire includes brands, which are a potentially vivid means of self-endorsement: "This is the person I am inside, and this brand helps me feel that." Note that the point is not outward display—not "badge values" signaling status to others—but rather the internal whispering of self to self. The upshot is that all kinds of brands are potentially involved—even those kept out of sight from others in cupboards, handbags, or sports lockers.

The more authentic the brand—so the more it is held integral by a belief and a strength of character that ensues from it—the more potency it has as an artifact of self. People will orient toward these beacons of belief—or steer clear of them—but they are less likely to ignore them.

Strong, clearly articulated belief is also a motivator for employees, a constituency that Oxford University's Richard Pascale likes to describe as "volunteers who decide each day whether or not to contribute the extra ounce of discretionary energy that will differentiate the enterprise from its rivals." According to a study by the global quantitative research agency Millward-Brown, organizations with "a strong ideology" enjoy advantages in their ability to both recruit and retain the most capable people.

There is a caveat to all of the above. The belief must be genuinely held, and must be adhered to even when things get tough. Sometimes, this may imply commercial sacrifice. Such is life.

Is Belief Just for Certain Kinds of Brand?

Is it just for founder-led brands? Or just for brands in naturally "heroic" categories, such as business systems or healthcare? Or just for one-off "cult" brands, such as Harley or Apple?

The answers are no, no, and no. While founder zeal can be a great inspiration, it is not the only ideological source from which to draw. Category should be no barrier: even humdrum consumer sectors—cleaning fluids, insurance, pet foods—have their own heroism if you get beneath the surface, as Unilever has shown with its belief-led reinvigoration of Omo, Rinso, and Breeze. As for cult brands, too much has been written about Harley and Apple, such that their stories blind us to those whose paths have been subtler. It is time we hear more about brands like KY, with its belief in the importance of intimacy, or the UK beautycare brand The Sanctuary, with its belief that beauty and pleasure are mutually reinforcing—a trenchant counterpoint to the prevailing science-and-Botox trends.

Belief is for any brand where the imagination, courage, and sensitivity exist to see it through, along with the wisdom to recognize that commercial goals, can be more harmoniously achieved by prioritizing social ones.

Is a Passion Brand Simply a Brand with Belief?

It is not quite that simple, and it's not hard to see why. Even so potent a force as belief would not do much for a brand whose other qualities were myopia, stubbornness, and introspection. It follows from this that while belief is a necessary component of a Passion Brand, it is not, alone, sufficient. Belief must accompany a deep understanding of people, and must be fused with the capability, confidence, and exuberance to make it relevant to their lives.

Passivity is not part of the Passion Brand make-up. The objective is not for belief to sit there as inert ballast at the center of the strategic brand diagram. Instead, it is an active force that exerts influence over everything the brand does and is. A Passion Brand's constantly renewed feel for people, markets, and the deep, swirling themes of contemporary life is the feedback mechanism through which it ensures that its belief stays relevant in a protean world. The belief is steadfast and unchanging; the way it is manifested is dynamic and free.

Can a Passion Brand Be Created from the Basis of an Existing Brand?

Let us take this question to the extreme. Imagine a brand in a humdrum category, neither market leader nor fashionably small, with a choppy history, no living founder to galvanize the workforce, a so-so record of innovation, and a me-too current positioning. Can such a brand make the transition to become a Passion Brand, with an identity based on belief, a view about how to make a difference in the world, the exuberance to make it meaningful to consumers, and the willpower to make it happen?

The short answer is "yes." The long answer takes the form of the Passion Brand strategic methodology which we will now go on to describe—a process that is rigorous, proven, potentially thrilling, but not for the fainthearted.

DEFINITIONS

Brand
A product or service plus values and associations.

Consumer-led Brand
A brand that habitually uses the findings of consumer research for direction, not illumination.

Brand Belief
The brand's take on the world, a view on what would make the world a little better, and how the brand can work toward making it happen

Passion Brand
A brand with a clear belief, a deep understanding of people, and the capability, confidence, and exuberance to connect the two.

AMERICAN GIRL: A BELIEF IN LEARNING THROUGH PLAY

American Girl was founded in 1986 by Pleasant Rowland, a former elementary school teacher then in her mid-40s. The idea was born of two separate moments of revelation that had struck her over the previous year. In the first, accompanying her husband on a business convention in Colonial Williamsburg, she sat on a bench and reflected how badly children were taught history at school.

The second was shopping for dolls to give her nieces for Christmas, and finding herself horrified by the choice between Barbie and Cabbage Patch Kids. As she recounts, "Here I was, in a generation of women at the forefront of redefining women's roles, and yet our daughters were playing with dolls that celebrated being a teen queen or a mummy."

Rowland believed that preteen girls would become interested in history by identifying with dolls based on historic periods. She wanted to celebrate the active roles that women had played, so that today's girls would not be persuaded to merely accept the roles society creates: "If we can [make] girls excited about history, we can inspire them to create history."

Success was achieved through a combination of books that focused on life in a specific historical period—perhaps the colonial or depression years—and dolls with historically accurate clothes and accessories, with which girls could play out the stories.

The brand has always aimed to provide meaningful experiences for mums and girls—"story over stuff." Average time spent inside an American Girl store—often a planned outing involving three generations—is over two hours.

Rowland eventually sold the business to Mattel in 1998. The irony of placing her vision in the hands of the company that made Barbie was not lost on her, so she sought reassurances that her brand would maintain its characteristic blend of imagination, history, and values: As Rowland puts it, "chocolate cake with vitamins."

LUTA: THE FIGHT-WARE BRAND FROM THE FAVELAS

When Luke Dowdney, a British anthropology graduate living in Brazil, took a cab across Rio to meet a girl, he didn't realize she lived in the heart of the city's notorious favelas. After getting out of the taxi and turning a corner, he was confronted by a 13-year-old brandishing an M16 rifle.

His immediate reaction was not one of fear—that came later—but one of sorrow for wasted life. He wondered: "What can I do about this?"

As a former British universities' boxing champion, Dowdney understood the disciplinary power of combat sport. He speaks of it as the "cornerstone" of his youth, giving him focus and a goal to work toward.

Having volunteered in Rio previously, Dowdney was no stranger to seeing kids lose their lives to gang violence. But instead of trying to stop them fighting, he wanted to get them doing it even more—this time in the ring, rather than on the streets.

In 2000, Dowdney opened a small boxing club called "Luta Pela Paz" ("Fight for Peace") in a neighborhood where war-grade weaponry was part of the everyday scenery. The idea was for boxing to replicate the macho sense of inclusion that lured so many kids into gang culture, and to be a way of introducing youth work.

By 2011, almost 7,000 youths had gone through an expanded Fight for Peace scheme. Dowdney did not want to rely on pleading for donations; however, he envisaged a new, completely sustainable social model—one where "you ultimately can't tell if it's a business or something making a difference to society." Enter Luta: a new kind of sportswear brand, created by Dowdney with technical help from London art college students and creative input from favela-dwelling kids, an enterprise that ploughs 50 percent of its profits back into Fight for Peace.

Luta—which translates somewhere between "to fight," "to struggle," and "to never give up"—was founded on the belief of "real strength." This belief didn't come from a team of marketers or a brainstorm meeting. It came from the young people Luke worked with on the "Fight for Peace" program, from watching what they had to endure to get to school or training, or even just to make it through the day.

Luta sportswear is designed for both pro fighters and regular gym-goers keen to "be part of something." And it seems there's no shortage of people wanting to tap into the idea of "real strength," with stockists secured around Europe, and thriving online sales. In 2012, the brand was launched in the United States, where it hopes to continue its success.

THE PASSION BRAND STRATEGIC METHODOLOGY

Objective

The objective is to create a Passion Brand from the basis of an existing brand. What will be set down at the end of the process is a completed Passion Brand strategic codification, but of course, that is more of a beginning than an end, since what really counts is the integrity, commitment, and zeal with which that brief document is translated into action.

And the document will, indeed, be brief—governing the bare headings necessary to capture the essentials of what a Passion Brand is, with belief at the fore. The power of what falls under those headings will reflect the rigor and imagination that the team puts into the process.

Methodology Overview

The process splits into two distinct stages, each governed by the framework shown in Figure 17.1. The tasks involved in stage 1—the more analytical phase—are usually best undertaken by a multidisciplinary team. The tasks in stage 2—a more dynamic phase in which tough decisions will often need to be made—are usually best handled by a tight, senior team with at least one creative person on board.

Stage 1

The first phase of the process is the rigorous analysis of the subject matter covered by the key words at each of the four corners of the framework. The two corners on the left are internal factors, relating to the brand or company itself. The two corners on the right are external factors, relating to the world beyond the brand. The general aim of stage 1 is to provide the raw materials from which the Passion Brand identity will be forged in stage 2, and to highlight any barriers that might need to be overcome. The more honest, open, and rigorous this analysis, the better the eventual results of stage 2 will be.

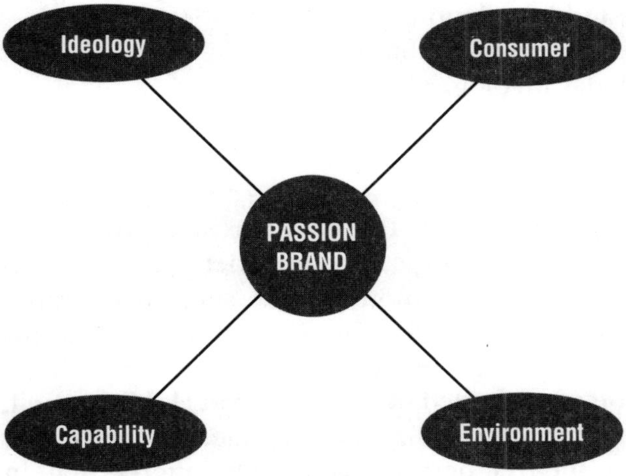

Through a process of rigor and imagination the Passion Brand codification emerges at the intersection of the two internal forces (left) and the two external ones (right). Analytical rigor ensures that brand belief is arrived at in full recognition of all the influences and constraints that might impinge upon it; it is never simply something "dreamt up" by a team or individual insulated from reality.

Figure 17.1 The Four-Corner Framework That Guides the Passion Brand Methodology

SOURCE: Author.

We will now take the four corners in turn, outlining, for each, why the analysis matters, what needs to be captured, and how to go about it, including a few tips and tools to help.

Corner 1: ideology

Why

The aim is not to crystallize belief—that is for stage 2—but to throw light on the current and historical ideals, values, and behavioral mores from which an inspiring belief statement might eventually be crafted.

What

An ideological audit of the brand and the organization of which it is a part, is governed by three headings:

- Brand history and foundations
- Current stated values and ambitions
- Current day-to-day ideological reality

How

Original Purpose: How and why was the brand created? Was it just something opportunistic at the time, or were there deeper roots and reasons? Often it is a case of both, so the subject will repay some exploration. You're looking for the foundational vision, for the thinking that was big enough to create success out of nothing.

For example, Avon was founded in 1886 by David H. McConnell, a traveling book salesman, after realizing his female customers were far more interested in the free perfume samples he offered than in his books. McConnell also noticed something deeper: that many women were isolated at home while their husbands went off to work. So he purposely recruited female sales representatives from this untapped labor pool, believing they had a natural ability to market to other women. At a time of limited employment options for women, the Avon earnings opportunity was a revolutionary concept.

The ideal of "female empowerment" is still what guides this $10 billion global business today, which styles itself, simply, "The company for women."

"Living Archives:" Talk to people who have been in the company forever—the longest serving employee, people who knew the founders, people who worked at the place or on the brand when it was in its prime. Or talk to industry journalists or venerable commentators with long memories. See what it was that made the brand famous, great, and special in any way.

For example, in 2012, Smith & Nephew, a global healthcare business, was looking to relaunch its longest established and biggest selling wound care brand, Allevyn. Many innovations had been added in to the original, 27-year-old technology, but the team wanted to ensure that the new positioning reflected the truth at the brand's core. So they traced the sales rep who had sold the first-ever box of Allevyn for his perspective and experience. This, and other similar interviews, strongly influenced the resulting "People First" brand strategy.

Obvious Sources: These include statements of values, current mission or vision statements, leadership interviews, annual reports, PR releases, CSR programs, and digital exchanges, anything that might include or hint at an ideological expression of today's brand.

Behavioral Reality: An audit worthy of the name should record practice, not just theory, and often there is considerable variance between the two. Try to get a feel for the behavioral and ethical norms in all markets. You should also probe the extent to which values are respected all the way through the supply chain.

For example, Apple's stated ideal of "deep collaboration" does not appear to extend to the workforce in some of its Chinese supplier factories, who have had a hard time being heard about "inhuman" working conditions.

Being There: It can be revealing—walking the place, taking your meals in the canteen, talking with people who work in the company every day, and getting a feel for the unwritten codes that pervade the organization.

For example, when David Bates took over as the new CEO of Krug, the thing he did for the first three months was nothing. No executive decisions, no reorganizations, no rousing speeches. Instead, as Professor Mark Ritson tells it, he "hung out at the house of Krug, with the ancestors, with the family, at the site of production and he learned about the nature, the style, the ways in which it was done. The guy imbibed the culture the way you'd imbibe the champagne."

Corner 2: capability

Why

The aim is to provide raw material for decisions you will make in stage 2 of the methodology. At that stage you may be looking for ways to improve your end product, or to harmonize capabilities more effectively. Since Passion Brands are about activating belief, since they refuse to become—in Naomi Klein's memorable phrase—"all strut and no stuff," you will certainly need to ensure that belief and capability can be aligned.

What

A summary of the capabilities and resources, both tangible and intangible, of the organization behind the brand. These will be broken down into subsections as follows.

1. Tangible
   a. Operational
   b. Financial
   c. Assets
2. Intangible
   a. Culture
   b. Knowledge and relationships
   c. Reputation

How

Stakeholder Interviews: Plan for one-hour interviews with the heads of Operations, Finance, R&D, and HR, plus other specialist leaders according to sector, for example, medical director, in healthcare brands.

Baseline Probing: In stage 2 of the methodology it is not uncommon for improvement in capability to become part of the discussion, so you will want to understand what "elasticity" might exist now, or what constraints might need to be overcome, for each of the key capability disciplines.

Open Questions: The aim here is twofold: to draw out ideas from leaders of the capability disciplines that no-one might have previously imagined, and to seed the notion that things might need to be done differently down the line, at the end of the process.

- What could we do better?
- If we were creating this business from scratch, in what ways might it (and your function) be different?

- If your budget had to be cut by 50 percent, how would you achieve it? If your budget could be doubled, how would you spend it?
- Looking at your discipline strictly from the customer's point of view, what is the first thing you would change?
- If this brand didn't exist, what would people miss? (Potentially a very revealing question, often answered after a long silence.)

Reputation and "Soft Assets:" Your audit should seek to honestly appraise the reputation of the brand, and the company behind it, with customers, partners, suppliers, trade commentators, competitors, bank, local community, and, if appropriate, higher levels such as government or civil service.

Social Media Monitoring and Sentiment Analysis: A way to assess current reputation among all important audiences. Volume of data is an issue, but there are specialists who can help with sifting and analysis.

Corporate Culture: Capability isn't just about what the organization can do, but what its culture inclines it to do. Is it entrepreneurial? Conservative? Far-sighted? Does it favor self-starters or team players? Does it cherish innovation? Is it "can-do" or "get-permission-first"? Goal or process? Formal or touchy-feely? Understanding these, and other, cultural traits and biases, is another step toward knowing what the brand might be capable of in the future, which developments would be supportable, and which might imply a challenge to cultural norms.

Corner 3: consumer

Why

A Passion Brand necessarily caries its belief to consumers with exuberance and skill, making it manifest in everything the brand does. This cannot be achieved without a close understanding of the people the brand serves, and the way they live their lives. The aim is illumination, not direction. Relevance is the prize that we seek, which means this consumer understanding must go way beyond the normal category-centric findings of focus groups.

What

The objective is *rich description* of the people who buy and use the brand, or who might do so in the future. Rich description starts with the basics—who your customers are, and how they relate to the brand—and then progresses to more finely grained detail of behavior, desired self-identity, and the cultural, social, and psychological factors that influence contemporary lives.

How

Research Mix: The most important single piece of advice is to use a mix of research methodologies—what academics call triangulation—to identify and corroborate significant underlying themes. Where possible, embrace both qualitative and quantitative techniques. Here are some to consider.

Ethnography: This anthropological methodology explores what people are actually doing, as opposed to what they merely report. It typically implies three to six weeks of observation, in the appropriate real-life context, with video running much of the time. What it produces are rich, actionable discoveries that might not have been uncovered by standard techniques alone.

Ethnography Lite: This is to be considered when time, cost, or practicality rule out a full ethnographic study. Audio diaries, video diaries, and accompanied shopping trips all make use of established ethnographic concepts, and capture the sights, sounds, and spontaneous feelings of people in real-time, real-life contexts.

Cooperative Inquiry: This is an interesting technique from the social sciences, only recently pioneered for commercial use. The idea is to erase the line between researcher and respondent, observer and observed; instead the technique produces "active subjects," fully aware of the research objectives, and fully participating in the generation of findings.

Employee Insights on Customers: Potentially illuminating, especially in service industries, a favorite technique of Apple and Emirates.

Social Listening: Get a feel for the prevailing themes in your customers' lives through the analysis of relevant conversations and content in social media: blogs, social networks, and forums.

Conjoint Analysis: This quant methodology is still the most useful tool for determining the relative importance people put on product or category features, including price. By forcing respondents to repeatedly trade off pairs of values, and assigning weightings to each as it goes along, it can capture the optimum combination with a high degree of confidence.

Idealized-Self Mapping: The Idealized Self is the most interesting thing you can know about your customers. It is part of the Theory of Possible Selves from the seminal 1986 paper by the U.S. psychologists Markus and Nurius.

Figure 17.2 gives you a simple way to imagine it, a bit like a metro map. The Actual Self is everyday reality. Nobody wants to make the journey backward, toward Worry-state Self; everyone makes the mental journey across to Fantasy Self, but in only daydreams, not in reality. The journey that people are powerfully motivated to make is the short one from Actual Self to Idealized Self: the person they are at their best.

Corner 4: environment

Why

Brand ambitions can be helped or held in check by factors in the wider competitive environment, so here we look at everything from

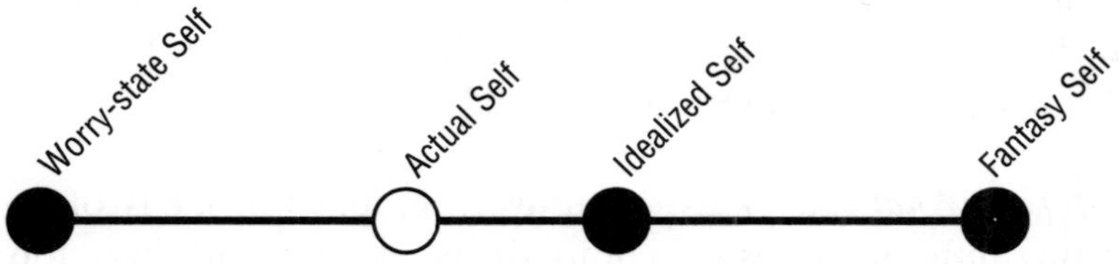

People Are Powerfully Cognitively Motivated to Make the Journey from Actual to Idealized Self.

Figure 17.2 The Spectrum of Self, Based on the Work of Marcus and Nurius

SOURCE: Author.

competitor activity to upcoming legislation. Since the competitive environment is in constant flux, and since you will need to project forward in the second phase of the methodology, some sense of prevailing trends, as well the documentation of current facts, is required.

What

A summary or presentation governed by the following headings:

1. Micro

    a. The category and its assumptions
    b. The immediate competitive set
    c. Category hotspots and warning signs

2. Macro

    a. The Big Five factors
    b. Macro hot-spots and warning signs

How

Category Basics: How do you define the category in which your brand operates? What are the main strategic divisions within it?

Category Assumptions: Note all the generally accepted success factors without which it is tacitly agreed that no brand in the category can prosper. Then—much harder, but tremendously useful for the second stage of the methodology—probe which of these might be open to question, or challenged by a brand determined to gain leadership by doing things differently. (The Value Curve, from Insead's Kim and Mauborgne, is a useful tool here.)

Who–What–How Analysis: This deceptively simple format is often the most revealing way to assess competitive strength and direction of travel. Simply capture, for each relevant competitor, *who* they are targeting, with *what* products or services, and *how* they deliver their offer to customers.

The Big Five Factors: The five macro factors are demographics, economics, socio-politics, legislation, and technology. Anyone who's done a PEST analysis (Politics, Economics, Social, Technology) will have confronted something similar, but while that stalwart of MBA programs is designed for overall corporate strategic planning, our five factors would be captured as they relate specifically to the brand and its future.

Talk to Trade Gurus, Journos, and Bloggers: Sometimes business teams can be so caught up in their own brand world that they fail to perceive important category hot spots and warning signs. Often trade gurus, journalists, and bloggers, with their finely spun networks and frequent contacts, can be the most informed and up-to-the-minute sources of valuable information: what is coming round the corner and why, which initiatives are making an impression and which are drawing flak. Court them; they love to share.

Stage 2

Stage 2 opens with a debrief and discussion of the four corners of analysis. It will close with the team capturing the essentials of their Passion Brand strategic codification—belief, role, forever values, idealized self, and connecting idea.

Between those two points is a structured process created deliberately to tease out from the four-corner debrief not just themes, but also, and much more importantly, tensions. And there will be tensions—most typically between what the brand espouses in its current values set and what it actually has to do to make money. It is the heat generated by tensions, and the creativity and soul-searching needed to resolve them, that propels the team to decide what really matters, what sacrifices might need to be made, and what must be done differently in the future.

> *Example:* A global brand audit for the NGO Fairtrade, which lobbies for a better deal for developing-world farmers, showed "youth" to be a common theme. Every market reported that the brand needed to do more to be relevant to a new generation. The tension was clear, though: older consumers accounted for over 80 percent of all Fairtrade purchasing, so alienating them would be a serious financial issue. This tension helped the team focus on a positioning concept centered on personal empowerment—The Power of You—that could unite and inspire both audiences.

The passion questions

This is the process by which tensions are thrown into sharp relief, and rounded on by the team. Each passion question is designed to pit two different corners of the analysis against each other, to probe for incompatibilities or contradictions between them. Since the permutations of two from four is six, that is the number of passion questions to resolve.

Question 1: What Are We Good at That Is Good for People?

This question is designed to push the team deep into the "capability" and "consumer" corners. Probe your capability hard and describe with guts and flair the real significance it assumes in people's lives. What is your company's deep purpose? How does your brand improve lives? Why does it have a right to exist? You are taking the first tentative steps toward revealing your brand belief.

> *Example:* Johnson & Johnson's personal lubricant product, KY, had always been sold as a "problem-solution" functional aid. In 2003, the team explored the deeper emotional significance that the brand fostered, the enhancement of "healthy intimacy," and all the human benefits that ensue from that. The brand was successfully relaunched based on a belief that centered on the importance of passionate intimacy in people's lives.

Question 2: Which Values Will We Still Hold When the World Moves on?

This question connects the "ideology" and "environment" corners. It is quite normal for the ideological audit to have thrown up a fairly long list of values at the levels of both the brand and the organization behind it. By projecting forward, and imagining how the future competitive environment might look, in perhaps five or ten years time, it forces the team to consider which values are for all time, and which are merely serving a convenient purpose for now.

> *Example:* See the panel on Camper. Note how the shoe brand's values are bound up within a deeper concept—respect for the peasant way of life—and how this links seamlessly with the brand's overall belief. These are "forever values," from which the brand will not shift no matter how fast and crazy our world becomes. They are grounding, in every sense.

Question 3: What Should We Stop Doing Now in Order to Stay True to Our Values?

This question links "ideology" and "capability." It forces the team to examine its most cherished values in the light of commercial reality—all the things the company does to survive, thrive, and meet those shareholder demands. Principles-versus-profit is therefore one inevitable turn for the debate to take. Values integrity is the outcome that must be sought.

> *Example:* Starbucks has always been proud to display its tenets of good global citizenship in its stores. Yet it came under fire from activists for alleged exploitation of third-world farmers. Starbucks responded by completely reviewing its supply chain, clarifying the environmental and social criteria it would now demand, and dropping suppliers who wouldn't meet them or demand them in turn of those further back in the chain. In so doing, it improved its value integrity.

Question 4: How Is Our Industry Currently Letting People Down?

This question links "consumer" and "environment" and is by no means as simple as it might seem. It is not confined to inquiring what consumer "unmet needs" might be. The question has a deeper purpose: to look at how your industry quietly, unthinkingly, perhaps even cynically, mis-serves people in ways of which they are not yet aware.

> *Example:* For 20 years, Staples was the leading office supplies retailer in the United States. When growth slowed in the late 1990s, it did a simple thing: just followed shoppers round the store and observed. The team was struck by how an industry norm made things harder for customers: the things they bought most regularly—printer ink and paper—were placed at the back of the store, to entice impulse purchases. Staples decided to break that norm, moving the items to the front of the store, as part of a whole range of initiatives to make things easier for customers. "Easy" became the brand's one-word customer promise; renewed brand leadership was the reward.

Question 5: How Might Our Historical Ethos Be Reinterpreted for People Today?

This question links "ideology" and "consumer." It looks your brand's values, roots, and ethos, and plots them against today's life, as lived by today's consumers. The aim isn't to allow consumers to dictate what your ethos and values should be, but to ensure that their expression—in everything the brand does—is framed with relevance for modern life.

Example: See the panel on Ford.

Question 6: What Is Our Future Credible Capability?

This question actually links all four of the corners of analysis. "Capability" is obviously involved, since the aim is to imagine how the organization might be able to develop its capability in the coming years. The word "credible" hints at the wider task: to explore future capability in light of imagined future consumer needs, the projected future shape of the market, and deeply held organizational values. All four corners are therefore necessarily involved.

FORD: REINTERPRETING FOUNDATIONAL BELIEF

In 1903, Henry Ford founded his eponymous brand with an uncompromising vision: "To open up the highways for all mankind." It was always a democratizing mantra: a belief that the ordinary man had a right to extend his horizons—physically, and therefore commercially—and achieve more from life.

Henry Ford

Ford grew to become the world's No. 2 automaker, close on the heels of GM. There were troughs, though, too—often felt by insiders to be those times when the brand "moved away from its true self."

The financial crisis brought an all-time low, with the business teetering on bankruptcy. Alongside the macro problems were some that had been self-imposed: a loss of focus through the acquisitions of Volvo, Jaguar, Land Rover, and Aston Martin, and intercine rivalry between Ford divisions and geographical units.

In 2008, the new CEO Alan Mulally instigated a strategy of simplification under the banner "One Ford." He divested the brand of its acquired

Go Further

marques, and challenged his team to reframe Ford's statement of "deep purpose." Headed by Executive Vice President, Global Marketing, Sales and Service, Jim Farley, a small team of leaders from global markets, along with communications agency Team Detroit, began to probe for the "soul of the organization."

The team kept returning to Henry Ford's original vision. Though its literal meaning was outdated for modern life, they noted a deeper meaning that lay in those original words. For ordinary people, Ford had also opened up "new highways of possibility." That deeper meaning still held. The brand's natural blue-collar franchise—people looking to the future and striving to move forward—was well served by Ford's range of modestly priced vehicles, including workhorse trucks and vans, as well as cars.

The ensuing brand belief focused on the significance of "helping people go further in their lives." It was captured pithily with a two-word connecting idea: "Go further." Significantly, the business capitalized on this as an internal mantra, too, galvanizing its own people to go further in their quest to serve customers better.

CRYSTALLIZING THE PASSION BRAND STRATEGIC CODIFICATION

The passion questions should have helped you close the gap between analysis and its ultimate distillation. They should have helped you glimpse your brand belief, reduce and refine your values, sharpen your view on the market, and reveal what is special about your core.

Now is the time to allow imagination and courage to come to the fore and to set down, as crisply and memorably as possible, the codification by which the brand is prepared to live and develop long into the future.

There are five headings that will capture that future brand.

Belief

This is the brand's take on the world, a view on what would make the world a little better. Aim to inspire: a statement of belief should be at once connected to, and yet bigger than, the category in which the brand exists.

Role

This is a statement of what the brand actually does to bring about the furtherance of its belief. These first two statements taken together amount to the brand's deep purpose in the world.

Forever Values

The list should be potent yet spare: three or four values, simply stated, strongly felt; values that will be held even when the world moves on. Do not be afraid to use words outside the accepted business lexicon.

Idealized Self

This is about your customers. It is a brief description not of who they are, but of who they want to be: the self they imagine and aspire to in moments of reflection, the better version of themselves that transcends day-to-day reality. Both practically and symbolically, your brand should help them on their journey from actual to idealized self.

Connecting Idea

The simple phrase that connects your brand belief with consumers. Pithy, motivating, and brief, and therefore a natural contender for a slogan, it should unite all aspects of the brand's outward expression, from behavior to communications.

Lorenzo Fluxá

Camper was founded in 1985 by the fourth-generation shoemaker Lorenzo Fluxá in his native Majorca. It is now a global brand, with a dedicated following, trading from over 100 of its own stores, with sales of $300 million. Fluxá has always promulgated a belief in slowness: he feels we are all too obsessed with speed in our modern lives, and counsels us to slow down and take in the beautiful world around us. The brand's iconography is deliberately earthy—the word "camper" means "peasant" in Catalan, and the brand's stated values are those of the peasant way of life. The full strategic codification below was extrapolated from an interview with Lorenzo Fluxá conducted by Dr Helen Edwards in 2004.

Belief
On life's journey, slow is more rewarding than fast

Role
To provide the safest and cheapest vehicles possible—comfortable shoes

Forever Values
Austerity, simplicity, discretion

Idealized Self
Creative but grounded

Connecting Idea
The Walking Society

A New Brand Future

The crystallization of a Passion Brand identity is the end of a process but the beginning of a new future for the brand. It is one that will demand total integrity—such that everyone in the organization intuitively "feels" the brand—and the kind of imagination that can keep the belief relevant in an ever-changing world. The reward for this endeavor is the renewed enthusiasm of employees, suppliers, and partners, and deeper emotional engagement with consumers, as they welcome this belief-led entity inside their membrane of self. The feelings are not so bad for leadership, either—to be part of a brand that counts for something in the world, socially as well as commercially, in that forest of tall trees, standing taller for all the right reasons.

Chapter 18

Lovemarks in the Age of Now

Kevin Roberts

INTRODUCTION

When a great brand is withdrawn, people usually find a replacement. But what if Coca-Cola canceled its original formula (as it tried to in 1985)? Apple discontinued the iPhone? Harley-Davidson shut shop? Toyota withdrew its hybrid Prius? In sports, could the New York Yankees baseball team, the Manchester City football team, or the New Zealand All Blacks rugby team, cherished icons for many, be ended? Blood would boil. Headlines would turn into protest lines. Social upheaval may follow.

Some brands reach the threshold of being all but irreplaceable and then go a giant step further. They become irresistible.

Take away a part of someone, you've got a fight back on your hands, and some tangible things do become a part of us. These deep connectors give us a sizzling feeling about who we are, about what we can be—and this feeling can't be beaten. We don't just "like" or "respect" these deep bonds, nor just "admire" or "appreciate" them. We *love* them, and *love* goes to the core. So we stay with them through bad times as well as good, rave about them to others, and pay a premium for them again and again.

This is Loyalty Beyond Reason, the "mark" of love, and its creation is the road to victory in business. The biggest and best way to make money in business is to create a Lovemark.

While brands are owned by companies, stock holders, and brand managers—the makers and marketers of products—Lovemarks are owned by people—the choosers and users. Lovemarks win because their purchase is motivated by emotionality, not by attribute. So long as an entity continues to inspire love, it remains invulnerable to attacks by price, quality, feature, tech, range, and the entire brand arsenal.

It is the job of every CEO, of anyone in any contest anywhere, to create Lovemarks if they want to win. ESPN Coach of the Century Vince Lombardi said: "Winning isn't everything, but wanting to win is." Lombardi lays down our objective:

> Running a football team is no different than running any other kind of organization—an army, a political party or a business. The principles are the same. The object is to win—to beat the other guy. Maybe that sounds hard or cruel. I don't think it is.

This chapter describes how to "beat the other guy" with Lovemarks. It shows how to:

- Create new perceptions about your product, category, or company
- Grow your sales volumes, share, and margins
- Turn people into unstoppable advocates for your enterprise
- Transform your brand in new ways that reach new audiences
- Build the reputational capital of your company, your brands, and yourself.

PART 1: JOURNEY TO LOVEMARKS

Part 1 describes how brands have given way to Lovemarks, and how marketing—an interruptive model for brand building—gave way to an interactive model that inspires what people love.

Dead End for Brands

The journey from products to trademarks and trademarks to brands was one of the great stories of the 20th century. What started as simple swaps of benefits progressed into the protection of commercial territory and then stepped up to multitrillion dollar declarations of superior attributes built off hard core research and innovation.

Brands were invented to create premium margins and profits for owners. Engineering these high-performance machines was all about process, reason, and demonstrating rational benefits to captive audiences. Dynastic companies commanded and controlled the world around them to power up. Brands spread out around the globe, pumping the global economy, defining and growing marketing by boosting its complexity and scale.

In the 1970s and 1980s—the heyday of brands—brand managers were kings reveling in their power. The almighty brand commanded respect, reverence, and revenue. I was in the thick of it with Gillette, PepsiCo, and Procter & Gamble, the inventor of brand management.

Power constantly departs, and inevitably it shifted away from brands. We saw the rise of retailers, power players like Walmart, Tesco, and Carrefour, fulfilling a key position in the supply chain. At the same time, everything was becoming a brand, leaching out all the premiums. A prolific replication of business through product lines, processes, innovations, and geographies meant that everything was taking on the respect attributes of a brand: quality, performance, and service. Markets looked like bad wallpaper. Points of difference were now shades, unable to support premiums or maintain loyalty.

When I became CEO at Saatchi & Saatchi, in 1997, I could see the Consumer Republic coming. My gut told me that the era of brands was ending.

Marketing brand benefits with "–ER" words like "newer," "brighter," "stronger," and "faster" was on its last legs. This comparative mania was the *modus operandi* brands were sold around for 50 years by fist-pumping marketing teams. Clobber people with rational claims, pipe on some emotional icing, high five, and go again.

As the 21st century turned, not only were brands commoditized, and the "–ER" claims shouting louder, but technology was also making consumers smarter. People seized power in the market, and now marketers were talking to themselves. Not a great way to sell stuff.

Power in the Age of Now

Today brands are indistinct, effectively extinct. The Internet has revved up, channels have fragmented, and power is surging around consumers. The world is accelerating and connecting on a family of screens around a global consuming class.

People in this rapid frame have instant information, choice, convenience, price knowledge, and word of mouth (the ultimate advertiser), all at a touch or swipe or gesture, and this speed and light show is just getting started.

"New" as a value construct is being compressed by "Now." There is no event horizon, because we live in the blur of a volatile, uncertain, complex, and ambiguous (VUCA) world. In fast and furious times, people live and decide based on what's in front of them, not thinking behind or ahead. Protected from the past's regrets and the future's unknowns, there is evidence indicating that living in the moment is where people are happiest (Killingsworth and Gilbert, 2010; TED Talks/TEDx). And when we are happiest, we are most open to influence.

Consumer purchase in a hi-tech moment world is intelligent, social, fast, and spontaneous, and it has to be inspired not persuaded. Getting noticed was always a core function of advertising, but the Mad Men era of "selling by yelling" is over. People are too switched-on, too instantly aware, and too immediately connected. They want to participate, control the relationship, and interact directly with the makers.

Brands were victims of an "Attention Economy," where everything competes for attention to the point of cacophony. In a "Participation Economy," the job is to create a movement, build it through interaction not by distraction, and then inspire more people to join you.

From Information to Inspiration

The CEO's challenge is to inspire the creative people (the pirates, the free thinkers) who love the enterprise, both internal and external people, and let their passions scale the company.

Most companies don't do this. They try to inch their way to glory. At key moments, the rationality vampires and accountancy goblins suppress risk-taking, kill ideas, squeeze out efficiency, and bury consumers under avalanches of near-useless information.

There is no competitive advantage left in having information. Information has been commoditized. With knowledge just a click away, competitive advantage is in inspiration—and at its best inspiration is about love. We are most inspired by the people, places, and products that we fall in love with.

Inspiration is about being "in spirit." People these days want to be part of an idea, a trend, a wave, a movement of light shared at warp speed. This is reflected in *Loveworks: How the World's Top Marketers Make Emotional Connections to Win in the Marketplace,* a book of 20 case stories by Syracuse University Associate Professor Brian Sheehan.[1]

Guinness, much loved in Africa, is a classic case of loading inspiration to win. Several powerful thoughts, as executed in Guinness' marketing programs, have driven the brand's success in Africa for well over a decade. The first idea is that there is "greatness" inherent in Africa, in general, and within African men, in particular. The greatness and quality of black men parallels the greatness and quality of the world's most famous black beer. The second idea, still more inspirational, is that for Africa and its men to succeed, they need to "believe" in their greatness. Looking at sales, Nigeria—which has the largest population in Africa (over 160 million people)—is now one of the top three Guinness markets in the world.

The level of love, respect, and trust African consumers share with the Guinness brand is astounding. Guinness VIP, a mobile phone community, has become one of Africa's premier social networking platforms. Over 8,000 people are on it at any given time and over 1.2 million people every week. It is the continent of Africa's largest mobile phone community. In Nigeria, more people are talking to Guinness, and to each other through Guinness, than Facebook has users in Kenya (Sheehan, 2013a).

[1] Associate Professor of Advertising at the S.I. Newhouse School of Public Communications, Syracuse University. Previously, Sheehan was with Saatchi & Saatchi for 25 years, with CEO roles at Team One Advertising in Los Angeles and at Saatchi & Saatchi Australia and Japan.

The finance guys will always want traditional ROI measures but, in Lovemarks lexicon, the core measure of success is Return on Involvement. How involved are consumers with your ideas? Do they want to lead your R&D? Are they expanding your digital presence? Do they bust blocks to get into your events?

Deepening involvement is about inspiring people at the right moment with content they can't wait to share. An example comes from T-Mobile (a division of Deutsche Telecom). In 2008, T-Mobile focused its marketing strategy on "sharing," and this was captured in the advertising line "Life's for Sharing." What happened in the depths of a recession turned strategic into ballistic.

In 2009, with "Dance," T-Mobile exploded the concept of a "flash mob" (sudden brief assemblies of people to do something interesting or unusual) by making it participatory, inspiring rather than just attention-grabbing. In the dreary post-Christmas depths of a recession, the main waiting hall of London's Liverpool Street station came alive for three minutes with hundreds of dancers, dressed as everyday commuters, moving in synch to a series of music pieces.

Other people joined in, and before long stories, videos and imagery from both T-Mobile and the wide-eyed public were all over the media. *The Sun* newspaper said: "Dance" created an "Epidemic of Joy." Within 36 hours, video and photos had been turned into a fully integrated advertising campaign online and on-air.

By 2010, "Dance" was in the top 10 in viewership for all viral videos. The event was shared and generated free publicity in a major way. It was measured to have delivered £15 million of incremental sales. "Dance"—which had no storyboards or scripts—was about risk-taking, courage, massive awareness, and achieving salience—enabling a conversation with the audience about the products.

T-Mobile extended the "Life's for Sharing" campaign with other real world, share-crazy and join-in ideas, not least "Royal Wedding," a rocking tongue-in-cheek take on the 2011 British Royal Wedding using look-alikes. By combining, at high risk, the popularity on YouTube of surprise wedding marches with a major royal event, the film became the second-most-viewed video of 2011. T-Mobile estimates that "Royal Wedding" delivered £6 economic return for every £1 spent on it (Sheehan, 2013b).

PART 2: STARTING UP LOVEMARKS

Part 2 explains the emotional and relational foundations for Lovemarks, and provides data in support of Lovemarks.

Emotion Leads to Action

Winning in the Age of Now starts with understanding your audience and the force that drives them. Humans are emotionally powered beings, no matter how logical we say we are. It shows best in the big decisions. How do we choose a car, a house, a husband, a wife, a dog or cat? We spend ages rationalizing the decision, and then do the opposite!

The primacy of emotion over reason is best summed up by the neurologist Donald Calne (2000): "The essential difference between emotion and reason is that emotion leads to action while reason leads to conclusions." More emotion equals more action. That's what the "motion" part of emotion is all about.

If you want to win, you usually want others to act in some way, which makes engaging people emotionally the winning play. Traditional marketing never got this, being fixated on value as interpreted by price and product benefit. The same goes for management and its meeting mania which is obsolete in the Age of Now.

I've always felt that emotional factors, not rational ones, factors were the key to the next world. As quality and performance become embedded in everything from toothpaste to tablets, and innovation becomes incremental, it is the depth of emotional experience that will set you apart.

There are different trajectories for achieving this, from the sensuality of Apple to the streamlining of Amazon, which determines what customers need, and works backward. The customer obsession at Amazon has been reflected in the role of specific employees as "Customer Experience Bar Raisers."

Getting to What Matters

Once you understand the issue or opportunity space you are in, the first step of Lovemarks is getting to the heart of what people want, with an understanding that people often don't know themselves. This means getting very close to the audience. It's complex because mass communication is dead, because every consumer is different, and because information and knowledge are table stakes.

Today's freshly minted MBAs head out fully equipped with information and are super smart about how to use it. This is not enough to win. These table stakes must be used quickly, and then it takes empathetic insight into consumer motivation and the creative foresight to act on that before the competition.

Today, instinct and speed blow strategy and management away. In Figure 18.1, the left-hand column describes most businesses today: strategically driven, by the book, MBA-obsessed, ponderous. The second column shows where companies operating in the Age of Now need to be: fast, instinctive, focused on action, not assessment. These businesses will fail a few times, but if they fix fast, they won't lose momentum.

Data and analytics help to unlock human patterns and preferences. They do not generate insight and foresight, nor do focus groups. As the advertising maestro David Ogilvy apparently said: "The trouble with market research is that people don't think how they feel, they don't say what they think, and they don't do what they say."

Most insights are not insightful. For proof, check the latest management consultancy bulletin or communication agency update. Usually it's repackaged information, with a twist of lemon. Who cares? A true insight is an astonishing disclosure of truth about people, a revelation uncovered through instinct and intuition.

One of the best ways to discover what matters to people is to go exploring and observe people in their real everyday lives, physical

	Era of New	Age of Now
Assess	**50%** *Interrogating, checking, assessing.*	**20%** *People have the same information; what's to interrogate?*
Decide	**30%** *Discussion and consensus.*	**10%** *Follow your gut. Decide.*
Execute	**20%** *Pass the overcooked potato!*	**70%** *Go with the flow, course-correct, drive it home relentlessly.*

Figure 18.1 Age of Now Table

to virtual. This is about going inside lives without prepared notions or questions, and bringing the authentic, the immediate, and the emotional into sharp focus.[2] If you want to understand how a tiger hunts, don't got to the zoo, go to the jungle.

This approach helped create—out of an advertising agency pitch process in early 2011—the idea for the first global campaign for a Chinese brand, Lenovo. Lenovo needed an idea that would ultimately be advertised in over 32 countries.

Lenovo is a company about doing, not just saying. And a consistent message that came through the exploring trips was that Millennials cared a lot more about what their computer could do than how pretty it looked.

The poster case of the audience mood was a young DJ from a Tokyo nightclub who was using five Lenovos to mix his music. He said: "Computers are not a badge; they are tool." The idea that emerged was *Lenovo: For Those Who Do.* This hits on a product truth and a consumer truth, and positioned Lenovo as the "Anti-Mac." Importantly the idea was loved internally, and it was simple and powerful enough to work across borders. Nothing differentiates or advertises better than truth.

Some results. From July 2011 to January 2012, unaided consideration for the brand among consumers 18–34 years old increased in the United States from 11.1 percent to 17.3 percent. In Japan, it increased from 8.2 percent to 12.3 percent. In Mexico, it increased from 20.8 percent to 25.3 percent. Increases were seen in every key market. Increases were also seen across the board for the core 18–24 age group, which Lenovo calls the "Net Generation." The campaign has been part of a global marketing, merchandising, and distribution push that has seen Lenovo move from the fourth largest toward the top of the world's biggest PC maker rankings (Sheehan, 2013c).

From Transactions to Relationships

The idea that people love brands has met a lot of resistance. When I cut the L-word loose in boardrooms a decade ago, it was like a hand

[2] Saatchi & Saatchi calls this approach Xploring, the trademarked name for a special type of qualitative research it has pioneered.

grenade going off in a luxury spa. Buttoned-up stiff-jaws were diving for cover under the table everywhere.

Susan Fournier, a brand-relationship pioneer, took on left-brain brand robotics back in 1998 by showing the complexity of brand relationships through a typology of 15 consumer–brand relationships (Fournier, 1998).

These run positive through negative, ranging from "brand marriages," best friends, casual friends, and childhood friendships through to flings, dependencies, and enslavements. In an interactive global consumer culture, it's hard to refute that people form relationships with brands. Once we understand that people do, a world of possibilities opens in how we connect with them.

Lovemarks is an idea underpinned by the highest human emotion of all. Love defines who we are. With love we are at our best, and its complexity can formulate many types of love relationship—not just for family, pets, team, or country, but also for music players, shoes, cars, beer, soap, spreads, jeans, diapers, movie stars, and sports teams—even for chainsaws and stepladders!

Primal emotions such as joy, anger, sorrow, fear, surprise, and disgust lack the relational quality of "secondary" emotions such as guilt, shame, pride, envy, and *love*. Lovemarks combine head and heart in super-positive mixes of emotion, drawing strongly from inspiration, identity, belonging, friendship, revelation, euphoria, and beauty.

The power of love has made understanding the mixology of positive emotion that leads to love an ongoing project. We know anything can be a Lovemark. We know what love looks like in a relationship matrix (e.g., committed partner or best friend versus flings or casual friendship). We are advancing the methodology that turns the range of drivers into love.

Begin with the Love/Respect axis (Figure 18.2), the complex made simple. Everything of value can be intuitively positioned on here. It is the single most powerful way to show why Lovemarks matter and why Lovemarks status is the only goal to aspire to.

Fail to form a relationship with your audience, and you're just a transaction, off the human grid, unable to inspire winning loyalty, and going nowhere fast.

In the old days, volume and margin wrote the rules: Low Volume/High Margin = Luxury and High Volume/Low Margin = Mass—dry

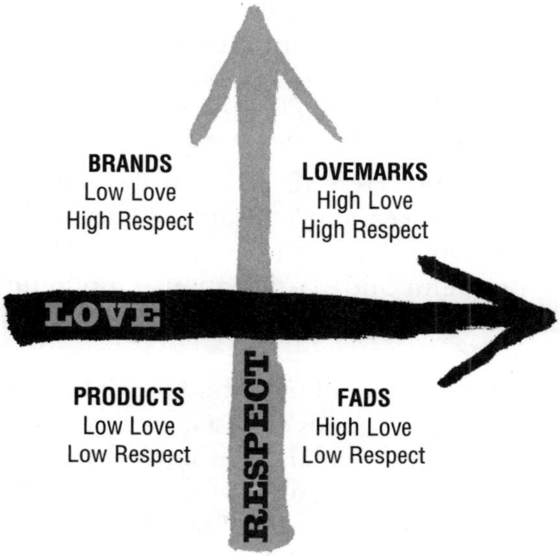

Figure 18.2 Love/Respect Axis

SOURCE: Saatchi & Saatchi.

formulas with no connection to the emotional reality of a connecting marketplace. Love and Respect are what define the space.

Low respect, low love. Raw materials to raw deals. Consumers are ruthless, putting most products here as low-value transactions. They range from commodities and utilities to corruption and pollution. There is zero brand heat here to inspire love in people. Some of the major airlines of the United States have fallen into this zone.

High love, low respect. This is the zone of fads, trends, and infatuations. Hairstyles, pop stars, and reality shows. Crocs shoes through to the Atkins Diet. It's a trial zone of high-intensity gambles and quick profit cycles. A few fads, like text messaging, break out, and go north. Most fads have too little respect to juice a long-term relationship, however profitable in the short term.

High respect, low love. Here is where brands sit. Highly respected and fixed on "e-r" words like cleaner, shinier, better, and bigger. The pressures of commoditization have eroded the value of respect on its own. You've got to have it, but it's not enough. Competition, fast-cycling innovation, rapid imitation, rising standards, and high-maintenance "smart" customers have seen to that.

High love, high respect. Lovemarks. Here there is a truly symbiotic relationship between producer and consumer. This is premium territory for margin, share, and preference. This is where returns are premium and participation is optimum. This is where value takes on priceless meaning (Figure 18.3).

Lovemarks is a response to the mind-numbing brand formulas institutionalized by fast-moving consumer goods (FMCG) companies for more than 50 years. Like love itself, Lovemarks is nonprescriptive. It is a series of intuitive emotional paths, not an advertising formula.

The usual direction to Lovemarks on the Love/Respect axis is from product to brand to Lovemark. Gather respect and then inspire your way right to high love. The trick is to stay there because love can be won and love can be lost. It's certainly something that you have to earn every day and you can't take it for granted.

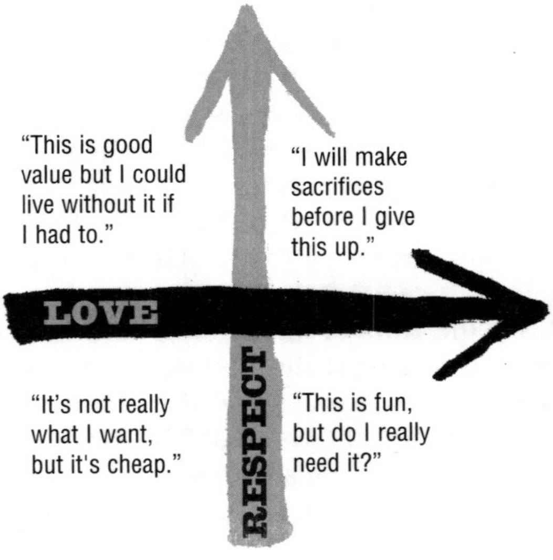

Figure 18.3 Love/Respect Axis through the Eyes of Consumers

SOURCE: Saatchi & Saatchi.

Take Nike, which sang the anthem of a generation "Just Do It." Nike started life classically as a product, out of the University of Oregon. In the 1970s, Phil Knight and Bill Bowerman moved Nike top-left on the Love/Respect axis. With a new name, the swoosh, a "waffle soled" innovation (thanks to Bowerman's wife's waffle iron), Steve Prefontaine, and good advertising, Nike became a great brand.

It was Michael Jordan who shot Nike deep into the Lovemarks zone, from irreplaceable to irresistible. This is because Jordan gave Nike soaring aspiration; he gave it emotional connectivity. If you wore Nikes, you could be like Mike. This inspired love for the brand and powered the premiums that went with Air Jordan.

Jordan retired and there was the "sweatshop" crisis. Nike lost love and a lot of respect. It's hard to love a company or a brand that is seen to be exploiting. So Nike went back to its roots. It went more and more local into grassroots, sponsoring local college teams, local soccer teams, and local athletes. It tackled the ethics issue. Today Nike understands the Participation Economy, and is on the edge of Love. They've continued sponsoring heroes, though some have fallen, pressing Nike down the vertical axis.

Proof of Love

When you wait for the data to catch up with an exciting idea, you miss the best part of the trip. As Albert Einstein said, "Any man who can drive safely while kissing a pretty girl is simply not giving the kiss the attention it deserves."

Since I took love to town on business, solid proof has swung in behind Lovemarks. We expect more ahead as the right brain plays catch-up with the left. Here's some data:

2005: QiQ International Ltd finds strong evidence that the relationships that consumers have with brands are much more heavily influenced by emotional rather than rational factors (Figure 18.4).

2005: QiQ International data suggests that Lovemarks are between 4 (cereals) and 7 times (cars) more likely to be bought than products. And between 1.6 (cereals) and 2.3 times (cars) more likely to be bought than brands. This effectively means that moving a brand from being highly respected to a Lovemarks position, where it is both loved and highly respected, can double volume (Figure 18.5).

QiQ International also previously showed (for cereals) that the average consumer uses their respected brands 26 days per year on average. For Lovemarks, it is 119 days (Figure 18.6).

2007: The Firms of Endearment study for a 2007 book researched hundreds of companies people love to arrive at 28 Firms of Endearment (FoEs): companies "truly loved by all who come in contact with them." The public FoEs returned

	Cars	Cereals	Magazines
Emotional Processes	**63%**	**75%**	**85%**
Rational Processes	**37%**	**25%**	**15%**

Figure 18.4 The Influence of Emotional and Functional Factors on Consumer–Brand Relationships

SOURCE: John Pawle and Peter Cooper, "Measuring Emotion—Lovemarks, The Future Beyond Brands," *Journal of Advertising Research*, Vol. 46, No. 1, March 2006, p. 46.

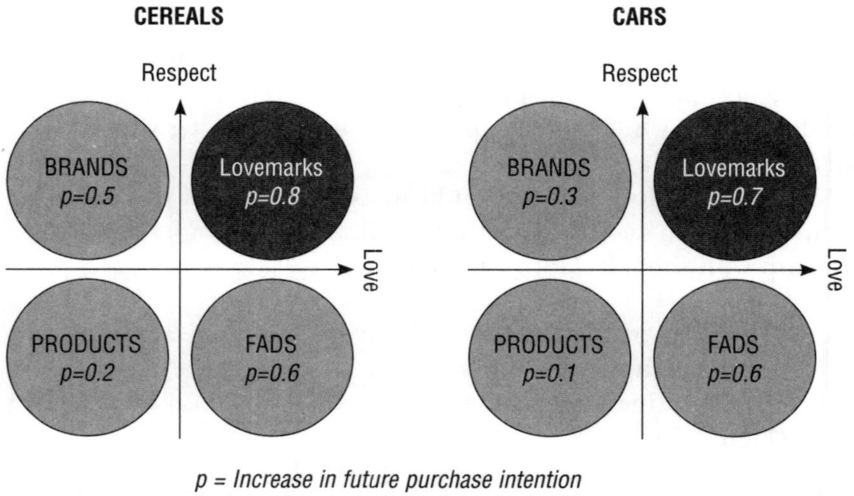

Figure 18.5 Future Purchase Intention Probabilities

SOURCE: John Pawle and Peter Cooper, "Measuring Emotion - Lovemarks, The Future Beyond Brands," *Journal of Advertising Research*, Vol. 46, No. 1, March 2006, p. 47.

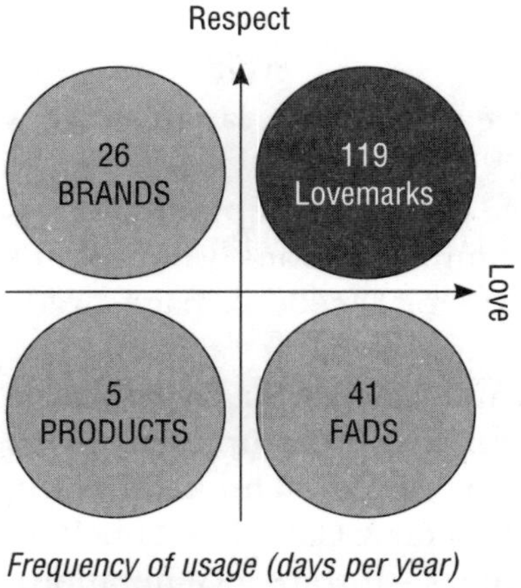

Figure 18.6 Frequency of Using a Lovemark (Cereals)

SOURCE: QualiQuant (QiQ) International Ltd Research.

1025 percent to investors over a decade. The S&P 500 returned 122 percent for the same period, and the companies profiled in Jim Collins book *Good to Great* returned 316 percent (Sisodia et al., 2007).

2012: In a *Journal of Marketing* paper, researchers identify seven components of brand love. They found that when consumers feel a sense of love for a brand, they have a higher sense of brand loyalty, spread positive word of mouth, and resist negative information about that brand (Batra et al., 2012).

2012: Research showed that men who feel "love" for their beer of choice would buy nearly 40 percent more than the average consumer, and women who feel "bonding" with their laundry detergent purchase 60 percent more than average (Rossiter and Bellman, 2012).

PART 3: WINNING WITH LOVEMARKS

Part 3 covers the "how to" of Lovemarks. It describes the inspirational purpose, the creative approach, and the magic ingredients for inspiring love, and it provides a "Lovemarks Profiler" to get started with.

Revolution Begins with Language

To grow a company or a country, a career, or a cause, language goes to the heart of it.

Language drives purpose. Language directs perception and sets expectations. Language frames all communications whether it's an organization's position, YouTube video, Facebook page, trade advertisement, expo display, or conference speech.

If you get the language right, you can frame a winning conversation and head into the High Love zone. Some examples are: U.S. President Barack Obama—Yes We Can; Apple—Think different; BMW—the Ultimate Driving Machine; Procter & Gamble—Touching lives, improving life; The London Olympics—Inspire a Generation.

At its most potent, language captivates with a dream. Dreams are about reaching for the stars not counting them. They are greater than missions, involving employees, partners, and customers in something bigger than themselves. Martin Luther King did not say: "I have a mission statement." He said: "I have a dream ...." Dreams are purpose-inspired, the generator of a feeling beyond respect.

In an Age of Now, functional elements sit behind inspirational impact. The big question that consumers have isn't about price or quality or service, because nowadays they expect all these things to be running in their favor. There will always be price shoppers, but if a race to the bottom is your only play, you'll soon go out of business.

Before "pumping markets" gave way to "creating movements," it was all about your product. People's big question today is: "How will you improve my life?" How can you make *me* the hero, not *your* product?

In China, Safeguard is a case in point. It is more than soap; it is about better health. It is very much a movement led by Chinese mothers. Procter & Gamble likens it to a family's everyday insurance policy. Today, Safeguard's share of the bar soap market in China stands at over 50 percent. Safeguard commands a premium price in a category where commodity pricing is the norm (Sheehan, 2013d).

Starbucks is a classic purpose pioneer. People found a home away from home, with over-the-counter friends. Such irresistible feelings transform a price-focused experience into a priceless experience, and "priceless" opens the portal to Lovemarks.

Creative Leadership

In business, reengineering and restructuring and re-everything have exhausted people and only added incremental growth. Exponential growth lies in an idea.

The tracks into the High Love quadrant are driven off creativity, because creativity has unreasonable power. Creativity is the fuel, the emotional surge of a Lovemark.

Ideas are today's currency, not strategy, and the power of an idea is intense. It's a time for creative leadership, and for creative leaders to reframe downside to upside. Their "VUCA" world is not volatile, uncertain, complex, or ambiguous. It is vibrant, unreal, crazy, and astounding. In this outlook, CEO becomes "Chief Excitement Officer," CIO means "Chief Ideas Officer," and CMO is "Chief Magic Officer."

Creative leadership is about driving business results from creative commitment—commitment to building creative environments, and to unlocking and unleashing creativity through radical thinking and relentless execution.

Virgin Group founder Sir Richard Branson's creative leadership has disrupted industries where consumers have been getting a rough deal. Virgin Atlantic made flying at 35,000 feet fun and entertaining. Renzo Rosso, the man behind Diesel, is another creative leader. Diesel is a disco, a science-fiction movie, art museum, block party, and protest all wrapped into one unforgettable experience (Roberts, 2008).

Creativity is not some mysterious outcome of deep contemplation. It is a noisy, involving, and fast-moving dynamic that draws from art, culture, sports, media, entertainment, politics, and commerce. To win, you need an environment where the unreasonable power of creativity thrives. This means giving talented people four things that lift companies into the sky: responsibility, learning, recognition, and joy. Give people permission to walk on water, and many will. At The Ritz-Carlton, all staff—without approval from their general manager—can spend up to $2,000 on a guest if they consider it necessary to improve service or solve a problem (Sheehan, 2013e).

The key is to have lots of small ideas, fast, because it's the Age of Now. Big ideas are scarce, strung out over time, and investment hungry. The big idea is usually stumbled on, found one degree away from where you are now, or your audience makes it for you.

A great idea understands what the audience cares about and, through an emotional truth, delivers an outcome that changes the customers' world. It is important that:

1. The idea is original. An idea is only an idea once! Great ideas are surprisingly obvious. Nike advertising has applied the classic symptoms of addiction to running. Great ideas also reframe—as when Bob Dylan went from acoustic to electric at the Newport Folk Festival in 1965, and music changed forever.
2. The idea is relevant for the space, right for the moment, on time, and able to work across multiple screens, executions, and formats.
3. The idea is participatory, and it plugs into a conversation. The Age of Now audience only has three questions that call all ideas to account: (1) Do I want to see it again? (2) Do I want to share it? (3) Do I want to recreate it?

Unlocking the Three Secrets

In Part 2 we saw that High Respect, Low Love—the commoditized zone of brands—is not a winning zone. When everything is a brand, the brand hallmarks of performance, trust, and reputation are simply table stakes to compete.

Inspired by purpose, the winning difference of High Love lies in creative infusions of mystery, sensuality, and intimacy. We all know the power of this trio in our own lives: getting to know people, learning their stories, joining their celebrations, sharing meals and secrets—falling in love.

These three Lovemarks qualities, above all, lead people to *act.* They are certainly not confined to our personal life, but try finding them on MBA courses or in corporate boardrooms.

There are many paths to love, and each Lovemark is infused with its own blend of mystery, sensuality, and intimacy. Figure 18.7 shows the ingredients of winning.

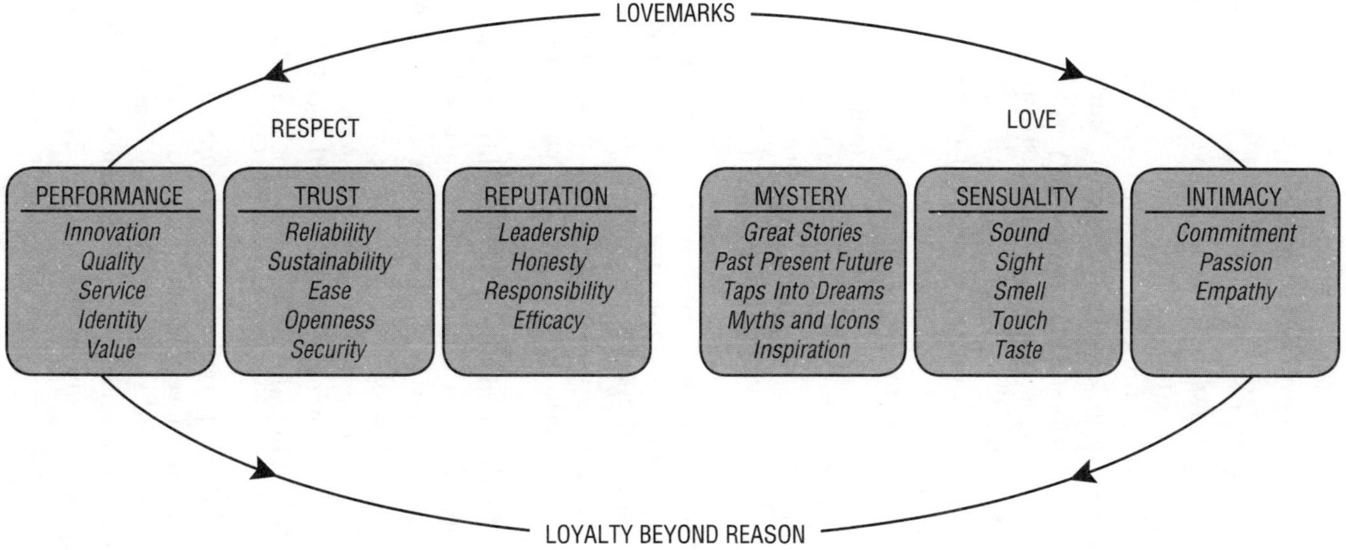

Figure 18.7 Ingredients of Lovemarks

SOURCE: Saatchi & Saatchi.

Mystery

When we know it all, there is nothing left to surprise, excite, and delight us. Mystery draws together what gives a relationship its complexity, layers, and texture to keep it alive. The unexpected, the unanticipated, and the unbelievable are invaluable.

Last century, Rolf Jensen, a Futurist, said: "the highest-paid person in the first half of the next century will be the 'storyteller'" (Jensen, 1996). Great stories touch us, outstripping our reason and logic with their compelling truth. They bring people together in a Participation Economy, introducing great characters who we want to spend time with.

Stories provide the meaning thread, the single equity that runs through and connects across a multichannel media world. The more platforms we invent, the more stories we are going to need, to transport people to better places. Most brands assault people with information, when success is about a shared journey with a clear trail to follow.

Stories are contagious. An online forum called "The Camry Effect"—where quietly competitive Toyota Camry owners could share their stories—helped generate about 100,000 stories. Among campaign results, for this U.S. campaign, new leads jumped by 19 percent, and real-world interest in the car jumped 800 percent (Sheehan, 2013f).

Myths and icons, and how a brand calibrates past, present, and future together are critical to unlocking favorable emotional states. Disney, with the iconic mouse, is expert on both. A cool case is Reebok's "Taikan" line of athletic clothing, which improves posture. It reached a broad audience through a historical icon in Japan. The super-popular morning exercise TV show "Rajio Taiso"—on radio in the 1920s before it became a TV show—got an update in a YouTube version.

Instead of three people in gym clothes, three gymnastic contortionists went from regular routines to near-impossible acts of balance, flexibility, and strength. The only branding was at the performance's end, a zoom in on the Taikan logo on a performer's leg, with a website address under the video on YouTube. This is mystery at work. Reebok's Rajio Taiso 4 was the second-most-viewed online video in Japan in 2010 (Sheehan, 2013g).

Mystery is also inspiration, a hallmark of the Olympics, and mystery is tapping into dreams, like the open road of Harley-Davidson.

Sensuality

Sensuality is how human beings experience the world. Our senses are portals to the emotions. Hitting the sensory buttons can pump fast results, often in the High Love fad zone where getting respect is an issue. Snacks, music, movies, and clothing are drawn in here. Spain's Inditex, parent of Zara, became the No. 1 fashion retailer in the world through fast and fresh *now* turnarounds.

When all five senses are stimulated together, the results are unforgettable.

Apple knew this when they advertised their brightly colored Apple Macs—strawberry and grape and blueberry—with one compelling word: YUM!

Vision is critical as a way to interpret, think, and connect. Get your ideas up on the wall, because when we can see what we are thinking or talking about, patterns emerge. The Love/Respect axis was born on a napkin at the airport. Vision is a way to the truth. The campaign line "Life flows better with Visa" is strongly visual.

People are instinctively drawn to beauty, and to me great design is form following emotion. It's love at first sight. The psychologist John Bargh (2008) has indicated that everything is evaluated as good or bad within a quarter of a second.

How many brands have an instantly recognizable sound? Music creates mood like nothing else. Music is a shortcut to the heart. How about musical food? BGH, Argentina's top home appliance brand, changed out the painful "beep," "beep," "beep" of a microwave with programming your favorite song. The product was launched with a limited edition of 1,000 microwaves, and stock sold out in a week. The campaign engaged a younger audience on the web, and the product redesign went viral (Sheehan, 2013h).

Smell is hugely powerful. While humans have four genes for vision, there are over 1,000 allocated to smell. Scent is a direct conduit for memory; no wonder businesses—notably retailers—have been putting it to work as a heavy lifter for selling. A brand with a great scent can help customers to fall in love.

And so can the perfect touch. A Lovemark understands that the way something feels shapes how we feel about it. Being physical not just virtual, getting real people, points of presence and tactile touches into the experience offered, this is a game breaker.

Intimacy

Intimacy is the fastest way into the High Love zone. It's the toughest to get right, a perfect pitch where thinking and feeling come together most closely. Today consumers own the media, so there are no hiding places or excuses for cold corporate shoulders. The journey from zero to hero, and back, is in a gesture.

Google was not the first search engine, but when they arrived they showed such obvious empathy for the needs of people in their search for information that they became (and remain) the overwhelming choice. Empathy is the art of knowing the right thing to do. It is intuitive user experience, stunning service, attentive follow-up, and genuine caring. It is the guy at your favorite store giving you a tissue to wipe your child's hands before you even thought to ask. And empathy is humor, the shortcut to the heart.

The essence of Lovemarks is the brand in the consumer's context not the other way round. The secret is to put yourself in the audience's heart, not the audience at your heart. The Ritz-Carlton changed "Please stay with us" to "Let us stay with you." Among results, it reestablished itself as "1st Choice Preference" in the luxury hotel category, according to the brand's tracking study (Sheehan, 2013i).

U2 on their 360° tour positioned the stage in the middle of a packed audience. Bono said to the audience: "We built this spaceship to *get closer to you.*" The huge concert stage had no defined front or back and was surrounded on all sides by the audience. The stage design also included a cylindrical video screen and—most importantly for the numbers guys—increased the venues' seating capacities by about 15–20 percent. "The band is just sitting in the palm of the audience's hand," said Designer Willie Williams.

Long-term commitment is part of intimacy too. It will be tested, and certainly can falter, but love has extraordinary reserves that get a relationship through the hard times.

And what is more intimate than the intensity and spark of passion? Passion is what makes people want to get up close and personal.

Passion is how to get people involved in the cause. Never give an audience what they want; give them what they never dreamed possible. The questions in Figure 18.8 provide a basis for creating love.

RESPECT

1. Does the brand consistently outperform competitors?
2. Does the brand always do the right thing?
3. Is the brand's heritage cared about?
4. Does the brand offer the best possible value?
5. Does the brand get consistent positive feedback?
6. Is there a put-it-right plan when things go wrong?
7. Does the brand welcome challenges to business-as-usual?
8. Does the brand attract recommendations?
9. Does the brand consistently deliver more than it promises?
10. Is the brand a leader in its field?
11. Does the brand keep its promises, even if it might hurt the bottom line?

LOVE

1. Is great design a standout feature of the brand?
2. Is the brand associated with a strong icon, logo, symbol, or character?
3. Is the brand connected with dreams and aspirations?
4. Is there a sound, scent, or taste associated with the brand?
5. Is there a physical sensation or special touch not felt in anything else?
6. If the brand withdrew its offering, would there be a protest?
7. Is the brand felt to be inspirational?
8. Is it great at listening, empathizing, and responding?
9. Does the brand share, collect, generate great stories?
10. Is there a strong visible thread connecting past, present, and future?
11. Does the brand compel commitment no matter what?
12. Is there passion for the brand?

Figure 18.8 Lovemarks Profiler

SOURCE: Saatchi & Saatchi.

LAST WORD

The desire to win is an irrepressible human characteristic, and Lovemarks comes forth as a radically optimist pathway in a competitive dynamic. Business is the engine of progress, and I believe its role is to make the world a better place for everyone. What better framework than the ingredients of love to fulfill this role?

A core tenet of Lovemarks is this: No Respect, No Love. Respect is irreplaceable. The job ahead is to be irresistible. On top of performance, trust, and reputation, create what matters most to people. Bring mystery, sensuality, and intimacy into the commercial equation. The dimension missing in business is L-O-V-E.

REFERENCES

Bargh, J.A. (2008). "Free Will Is Un-natural," in *Are We Free? Psychology and Free Will*, J. Baer, J.C. Kaufman, and R.F. Baumeister (eds) (p. 137). New York: Oxford University Press.

Batra, R., A. Ahuvia, and R.P. Bagozzi (2012). "Brand Love," *Journal of Marketing* 76(2): 1–16.

Calne, D. (2000). *Within Reason: Rationality and Human Behavior*. New York: Vintage Books.

Fournier, S. (1998). "Consumers and Their Brands: Developing Relationship Theory in Consumer Research," *Journal of Consumer Research* 24(4): 343–373.

Jensen, R. (1996). "The Dream Society," *The Futurist* 30(3[May–June]).

Killingsworth, M.A. and D.T. Gilbert (2010). "A Wandering Mind Is an Unhappy Mind," *Science* 330(6006): 932.

Roberts, K. (2008). *Diesel: XXX Years of Diesel Communication*. New York: Rizzoli.

Rossiter, J. and S. Bellman (2012). "Emotional Branding Pays Off: How Brands Meet Share of Requirements through Bonding, Companionship and Love," *Journal of Advertising Research* 52(3): 291–296.

Sheehan, B. (2013a). "Case Story on Guinness," in *Loveworks: How the World's Top Marketers Make Emotional Connections to Win in the Marketplace* (pp. 28–37). Brooklyn, New York: powerHouse Books.

———. (2013b). "Case Story on T-Mobile," in *Loveworks: How the World's Top Marketers Make Emotional Connections to Win in the Marketplace* (pp. 74–83). Brooklyn, New York: powerHouse Books.

———. (2013c). "Case Story on Lenovo," in *Loveworks: How the World's Top Marketers Make Emotional Connections to Win in the Marketplace* (pp. 92–101). Brooklyn, New York: powerHouse Books.

Sheehan, B. (2013d). "Case Story on Safeguard," in *Loveworks: How the World's Top Marketers Make Emotional Connections to Win in the Marketplace* (pp. 108–115). Brooklyn, New York: powerHouse Books.

———. (2013e). "Case Story on the Ritz-Carlton," in *Loveworks: How the World's Top Marketers Make Emotional Connections to Win in the Marketplace* (pp. 116–121). Brooklyn, New York: powerHouse Books.

———. (2013f). "Case Story on Toyota Camry," in *Loveworks: How the World's Top Marketers Make Emotional Connections to Win in the Marketplace* (pp. 44–51). Brooklyn, New York: powerHouse Books.

———. (2013g). "Case Story on Reebok," in *Loveworks: How the World's Top Marketers Make Emotional Connections to Win in the Marketplace* (pp. 84–87). Brooklyn, New York: powerHouse Books.

———. (2013h). "Case Story on BGH," in *Loveworks: How the World's Top Marketers Make Emotional Connections to Win in the Marketplace* (pp. 164–167). Brooklyn, New York: powerHouse Books.

———. (2013i). "Case Story on The Ritz-Carlton," in *Loveworks: How the World's Top Marketers Make Emotional Connections to Win in the Marketplace* (pp. 116–121). Brooklyn, New York: powerHouse Books.

Sisodia, R.S., D.B. Wolfe, and J.N. Sheth (2007). *Firms of Endearment: How World-Class Companies Profit from Passion and Purpose.* Upper Saddle River, New Jersey: Wharton School Publishing and Pearson Education, http://www.firmsofendearment.com, accessed November 2012.

TED Talks/TEDx. "Matt Killingsworth: Want to be happier? Stay in the moment," November 2011, video, http://www.ted.com/talks/matt_killingsworth_want_to_be_happier_stay_in_the_moment.html, accessed November 2012.

About the Editor and Contributors

EDITOR

Kartikeya Kompella is the founder of Purposeful Brands. He is the author of *Building Brands, Building Meaning*, and *Applying the Branding Iron.* He has written for many websites on branding and run a column on Interbrand's web portal brandchannel.com for five years. He is a regular contributor of papers to WARC.

Kompella has been associated with brands in various ways from an advertising planner, brand consultant, DM & CRM professional to marketer. He has worked in different roles from a brand consultant in India's first brand consultancy to President of Lowe & Partner's DM division. His various roles have helped him look at branding from a somewhat "unique" perspective.

Kompella has spoken at several international conferences on various topics from Cause-related Branding to Market Research to CRM. He is especially passionate about Cause-related Branding. In 2001, Kompella was nominated for the John & Mary Goodyear Award for Excellence in International Market Research. He has conceived and worked on thought leadership initiatives across disciplines. He was responsible for the first ever study on consumer attitudes toward CSR in India.

Kompella is married and lives in Bangalore with his wife Vinitha and daughter Mithya. He is an avid Pink Floyd fan and is passionate about reading and cricket.

CONTRIBUTORS

Douglas Atkin is chief community officer and E-staff member at Airbnb. He is the co-founder of Peers.org, a global movement for the sharing economy; founder of theglueproject, a blog and venture to create social glue through community; co-founder of Purpose, an organization that mobilizes millions for social change; board member of AllOut.org, the world's largest LGBT movement; and meetup fellow and former partner and chief community officer at Meetup, the world's largest network of communities.

He authored *The Culting of Brands: How to Turn Customers into True Believers*, a book about how to build cult-like community around almost anything. He is former brand strategist and partner at leading New York and London Advertising Agencies and is Chairman of the U.S. Account Planning Group.

Atkin lives in San Francisco with his Partner Matthew and two beagles.

Mark Batey is a brand consultant who has over 25 years experience with major international advertising agencies, handling the brands of companies such as Coca-Cola, Unilever, Nestlé and Mondeléz International. A language graduate of Oxford University, he has worked in England, Central Europe, Latin America and the United States. His book *Brand Meaning* explores how people find and create meaning in brands. The book has been translated into Spanish, Portuguese and Chinese, and was recently released in India. His articles have appeared in leading marketing journals and newspapers.

Batey helps companies to develop more compelling and iconic brands using his proprietary IconBuilder® program. He divides his time between consultancy, brand workshops, keynote and guest speaker assignments and teaching. He was recently visiting professor at ESCP business school in Paris, whose Master in Management was then ranked No.1 worldwide by the *Financial Times*. Besides English, Mark is fluent in Spanish, and speaks Portuguese, French, and German.

Michael B. Beverland is the professor of Brand Management in the School of Management, University of Bath. He is also an adjunct professor in the School of Economics, Finance and Marketing at RMIT University in Melbourne. Beverland's research interests include consumer culture and brand management, design thinking and innovation, the craft of management and consumer practice, and authenticity. His research has been published in a wide range of journals including (among many others) *Design Management Review, European Journal of Marketing, Journal of the Academy of Marketing Science, Journal of Advertising, Journal of Business Research, Journal of Consumer Research, Journal of Management Studies, Journal of Marketing Management,* and *Journal of Product Innovation Management.* His current book *Building Brand Authenticity: 7 Habits of Iconic Brands* provides a detailed exploration of managing for brand authenticity and is based on a decade of research into the drivers of long-run brand success.

Tom Blackett is a brand advisor. He worked for Interbrand for 25 years, retiring in 2008 as deputy chairman. During his time at Interbrand, he helped the company grow into an international business, with 32 offices in over 20 countries. Blackett carried out assignments for clients throughout the world, spoke at international conferences, and contributed to many books and articles published by Interbrand on brands and branding. He wrote and/or edited *Trademarks* (1999), *Co-Branding* (2001), and *Brand Medicine* (2002).

Toward the end of his time at Interbrand, Blackett became increasingly involved as an expert witness in legal disputes between brand owners. This is something he continues to do, together with more general consultancy on the development and management of brands. Blackett is married and has two sons, both of whom are involved professionally in brand marketing. He is a very keen oarsman, and each week rows the University Boat Race course, between Putney and Mortlake, with like-minded friends. (And, unlike the students, they row their boat back again!)

Blackett's earlier career was spent in market research, with companies such as Research International. It was there that he acquired his interest in brands, which led to him joining Interbrand in 1983, undoubtedly the best—and luckiest—move that anyone could have made.

Derek Day is a founding partner of Passionbrand, and the co-author of *Creating Passion Brands: How to Build Emotional Brand Connection with Customers* (2005). He was previously Global Creative Director, Unilever, JWT. With over 30 years' experience working with brands, he has created global brand ideas for Unilever, Emirates,

Mercedes-Benz, Smith & Nephew, and The BBC, winning creative and effectiveness awards on both sides of the Atlantic. He has contributed articles for *Marketing* and *Market Leader* on brand-related subjects.

Helen Edwards is a founding partner of Passionbrand, and the co-author of *Creating Passion Brands: How to Build Emotional Brand Connection with Customers* (2005). She has a PhD in marketing and an MBA from London Business School, where she now guest-lectures on the MBA brand management elective. She is an award-winning columnist for *Marketing* magazine, where her no-nonsense "on branding" column is a must-read for the U.K. marketing industry. She has over 20 years' experience working with brands.

Clare Fuller is executive director, Promise Communispace, United Kingdom. She has spent the last 30 years working with some of the leading practitioners in the brand, marketing and communications field and is co-author of *Brand Together*—how co-creation generates innovation and re-energizes brands (2012). Her passion is developing new products and services that positively change people's experiences of big businesses. She enjoys helping organizations grow and co-founded Promise (now Promise Communispace) in 2004 to do just that—for clients and for herself. She has a Maths degree and an MBA from the London Business School. In her spare time, she enjoys travel, gardening, collecting tribal rugs and being with people: be they friends, family, colleagues, or strangers!

Patrick Hanlon is recognized as one leading branding practitioners in the world. He is CEO and founder of THINKTOPIA®, a global brand and strategic innovation practice for Fortune 100 clients including American Express, Levis, Kraft Foods, Wrigley, PricewaterhouseCoopers, PayPal, the United Nations, and others. His book *Primal Branding: Create Zealots for Your Brand, Your Company and Your Future* is in many languages and is listed as one of the top 10 books in marketing and branding.

Primal Branding is a primer on looking at brands as belief systems—and in 2006 anticipated creating social communities around brands, whether products and services, personality brands, political or civic movements, or actual civic communities. Since 2013, *Primal*

Branding has been actively endorsed and taught by YouTube Next Lab as their recommended construct for designing brand narratives. They have determined that the most-viewed videos on YouTube contain the "primal code" outlined in the book.

Hanlon has been a keynote or guest speaker at IDEO, HP Innovation Series, New York University, American Marketing Association, American Advertising Federation, Syracuse University, Urban Land Institute, and elsewhere. He has also been a featured speaker in emerging geographies around the world including China, India, and South America.

Hanlon has been featured, quoted, or interviewed in Fast Company, Entrepreneur, Inc., Advertising Age, National Public Radio, as well as frequent overseas publications. He is listed as one of the top 50 people to follow on Twitter, and is also an online contributor of *Forbes* magazine.

Nicholas Ind is an associate professor at Oslo School of Management and a partner in Equilibrium Consulting. He is the author of 11 books, including *The Corporate Image, Terence Conran: The Authorised Biography, The Corporate Brand, Living the Brand,* and *Brand Together.*

Ind is a member of the advisory board of Corporate Reputation Review and the editorial board of the *Journal of Brand Management.* He is a visiting professor at ESADE, Barcelona, and Edinburgh Napier University. Ind has received his PhD from the European Graduate School in Switzerland.

Jean-Noël Kapferer is an expert in brand management. His reputation is worldwide. PhD from Northwestern University, teaching at HEC Paris, he has brought to the field many innovations such as the concept of brand identity, the brand identity prism, the notion of brand architecture, and the notion of managing by the brand. Author of *The New Strategic Brand management, Reinventing the Brand, Rumors,* and *The Luxury Strategy,* he consults extensively all around the world. He is advisor to the president of Inseec Business School.

Arunima Kapoor is associate director at Flamingo since July 2013, United Kingdom. Previously she spent six years at Promise Communispace, and has been involved in branding for the past seven years, with a special interest in co-creating with big groups to achieve growth and create impact in businesses. She has also worked as a journalist, has a masters in English literature, and an MSc in Media and Gender from the London School of Economics. Kapoor was born in India and is fluent in three languages. She loves music, the theater, and art, coupled with a passion for ice cream and dogs.

Jan Lindemann is an international expert on the value creation of intangible assets, in particular, customer franchises and brands. He is founder of Richmond Capital Management Ltd and portfolio manager of the JL Best Global Brands Fund. The fund generates superior long-term returns by investing in companies that own strong global brand and customer franchises that are already or have the potential of generating attractive returns in the global markets. Previously, Lindemann was Global Managing Director at Interbrand Group where he built the firm's global brand valuation and analytics practice. He was also a mergers & acquisitions advisor for The Chase Manhattan Bank. He holds an MA in International Economics and International Politics from The School of Advanced International Studies (SAIS) of The Johns Hopkins University, Washington, DC.

Lindemann is the author of several publications on the value creation of brands and customer franchises. His book *The Economy of Brands* was published in June 2010. Lindemann has created and managed the ranking of the Best Global Brands league table that was published annually in the *BusinessWeek* magazine. He also contributed several chapters including "The Financial Value of Brands" (*Brands and Branding*, 2009) and "Creating Economic Value Trough Co-Branding" (*Co-Branding*, 1999). He was featured in a variety of media on business and marketing issues including BBC, CNN, CNBC, ZDF, *BusinessWeek, FT, Advertising Age, The Economist, Forbes, Marketing, Marketing Week, The Times, CFO Magazine* and *Bloomberg*.

Adam Morgan is the highly respected author of *Eating the Big Fish: How Challenger Brands Can Compete against Brand Leaders*, a seminal work in the world of branding.

It not only coined the phrase Challenger Brand, but also outlined a process for doing more with less, the principles of which have been widely praised and much imitated around the world. In 1997, Morgan founded eatbigfish and established the Challenger Project, a research project into how challenger brands succeed across a variety of different categories. It is no exaggeration to say that his consultancy has created entirely new ways of thinking about both the development of distinctive brands and the cultural conditions necessary to support them, reshaping how many large corporations have thought about structuring their businesses for success. His ideas will challenge your habits and the formulas of the past, and provide new ways to think about insight, sources of growth, and sources of meaning for modern businesses and the people who run them.

Richard Mosley is widely recognized as one of the leading world authorities on employer brand development and management. His first book *The Employer Brand*, co-authored with Simon Barrow, has become a global best seller. His thinking draws on over 20 years' experience in both brand management and HR consulting. As Senior Vice President of the global employer brand consultancy, People in Business, and the recruitment advertising agency, TMP Worldwide, Mosley has led major employer brand development projects for companies including Bacardi, BP, Coca-Cola, GSK, HSBC, Lafarge, LEGO, JTI, Met Life, Nokia-Siemens, PepsiCo, Tesco, Unilever, and Verizon.

Al Ries is the author or co-author of 11 books on advertising, including *Positioning: The Battle for Your Mind*, a book that has sold more than 1.4 million copies worldwide. In 2009, the readers of *Advertising Age*, the leading U.S. marketing publication, ranked *Positioning* as the "best book they've ever read on marketing." Ries started his career in the advertising department of General Electric, and then went to work for two advertising agencies in New York City. In 1961, he founded his own advertising agency, Ries Cappiello Colwell, which eventually became Trout & Ries. In 1994, he started a marketing consulting firm (Ries & Ries) with his daughter and partner, Laura Ries. Together with affiliates in other countries, Ries & Ries works with a large number of high-profile global companies.

Kevin Roberts is CEO Worldwide of Saatchi & Saatchi, part of Publicis Groupe, the world's third largest communications group. Saatchi & Saatchi works with over half of the top 50 global advertisers. Roberts' career was built in sales, marketing, and leadership roles at Mary Quant, Gillette, Procter & Gamble, PepsiCo, and Lion Nathan. He has authored several books and is best known for his creation of Lovemarks, an idea that transforms conventions in marketing. His book *Lovemarks: The Future Beyond Brands* has been published in 18 languages. Roberts was the first non-Latin American to be inducted into the FIAP (Festival Iberoamericano de Publicidad) Hall of Fame. His academic appointments include Honorary Professor of Creative Leadership at Lancaster University, England, and Honorary Professor of Innovation and Creativity at the University of Auckland Business School. Roberts is a Companion of the New Zealand Order of Merit.

John Simmons is a writer primarily in the world of brands and business, with a particular focus on language. He was a director of identity consultancy Newell and Sorrell, and then of Interbrand in London where he established the discipline of verbal identity before pursuing his independent consultancy in 2003. His books have helped to make words a central issue of branding, from *We, Me, Them & It* through to *26 Ways of Looking at a Blackberry to Room 121.* He was series editor of Great Brand Stories and wrote books about Starbucks, Innocent, and the Arsenal in that series. He also writes fiction (*The Angel of the Stories*) and brings creative writing techniques to his training work as part of the Dark Angels program. He is a founder director of 26, the writers' collective, and an honorary fellow of University College Falmouth. He blogs regularly at www.26fruits.co.uk/blog.

Daryl Travis is CEO and founder of Brandtrust. As an advisor to many of the largest and best brands in the world, including Coca-Cola, Harley-Davidson, GE, Kraft, General Mills, Nestlé, Intel, among others, Travis helps many leading companies nurture and grow their brands.

His groundbreaking book *Emotional Branding: How Successful Brands Gain the Irrational Edge* explores the new realities of growing brands. Travis advocates the critical need to change the way we think about how people think. "Most customer research discloses what happens," he says. "However, it often fails to reveal why it happens or the underlying emotional drivers that are critical for creating a competitive advantage." He passionately encourages marketers to shift their focus from the "voice of the customer" to the "mind of the customer."

Travis leverages breakthroughs in the social sciences to improve the customer research process, tapping into the deeper underlying emotions and subconscious motivations to reveal deep insights. He could be described as a professor, detective, journalist, anthropologist, and writer all rolled into one.

Travis and his wife are active members of Chicago's philanthropic community, volunteering time and resources to support education and literacy programs for underprivileged children throughout the city.

Sicco van Gelder is one of the world's leading brand strategists. He is chief marketing officer at PharmAccess Group, an organization dedicated to realizing access to quality healthcare for the Base of the Pyramid in Africa. He is the author of books on Global Brand Strategy and City Branding, and he has contributed numerous chapters and articles to books and journals on branding.

van Gelder is the founder of Placebrands, an international consultancy dedicated to helping cities, regions, and countries develop and implement their brand strategies.

Index